FAMILY LAW

AUSTRALIA
LBC Information Services Ltd
Sydney

CANADA and USA
Carswell
Toronto

NEW ZEALAND
Brooker's
Auckland

SINGAPORE and MALAYSIA
Thomson Information (S.E. Asia)
Singapore

FAMILY LAW

Sweet & Maxwell's Textbook Series

By Stephen M. Cretney, D.C.L., F.B.A.

One of Her Majesty's Counsel honoris causa, Solicitor, Fellow of All Souls College, Oxford

Third Edition

LONDON
SWEET & MAXWELL
1997

First Edition ⎫ as *Elements of Family Law* 1987
Second Edition ⎬ 1992

Published in 1997 by
Sweet & Maxwell Limited of
100 Avenue Road, London NW3 3PF
(http://www.smlawpub.co.uk)
Typeset by LBJ Enterprises Ltd,
Aldermaston and Chilcompton
Printed in England by
Clays Ltd, St. Ives plc

No natural forests were destroyed to make this product;
only farmed timber was used and replanted

A C.I.P. catalogue record for this book is available from the British Library

ISBN 0–421–587 202

For
ALC
MCAC
EAFC

PREFACE

My aim in writing this book remains to serve the needs of students — whether lawyers or not — who need a clear and concise guide to the basic principles of English family law and who are prepared to accept that such a guide can only be produced at the cost of some sacrifice in range and depth of coverage. I have tried to put these principles into historical and social context.

I believe the law to be a rigorous intellectual discipline in its own right; and it may be necessary to emphasise that this is a book about the law (and not a book about child development or psychology, for instance). Of course, the family lawyer needs to understand the language, skills and approaches of others professionally concerned with the law; but the lawyer's distinctive contribution to the family justice system is to understand (and thereby be able to explain and apply) the normative rules laid down by Parliament and the courts. In addition, the lawyer should understand the issues of legal policy which have had to be resolved in determining those rules; and I have tried to highlight relevant concerns — for example, about the circumstances in which the state and others should be entitled to bring issues about a child's upbringing before the courts. The revelations made in the Cleveland and other enquiries suggest that misunderstanding of the law has been widespread even amongst some of those who have to administer it; and I hope that this book will be of some use to all those who seek an understanding of how the legal system operates. To that end I have made extensive use of the rich body of decided case law. Reported cases may by definition be untypical, but they provide a wealth of detailed information about the issues with which the legal system has to deal.

I have tried to make the law comprehensible; and I hope that the charts setting out the main steps in the divorce process and in obtaining occupation and non-molestation orders under Part IV of the Family Law Act 1996 will help to clarify the legal structure and thereby justify my decision not to explore in great detail the legislative complexities in which some may think the legislation over-indulges.

The first two parts of this book (dealing with marriage and the legal position of married and unmarried couples) draw on the relevant chapters of *Principles of Family Law* (6th ed., 1997); but the sections of that book dealing with children and the law have, since publication of its 5th edition in 1990, been entirely the work of its co-editor, Professor Judith Masson. Accordingly, the sections of this book dealing with children and the law (almost half its total length) have been written by me entirely from my own perspective.

The typescript of this book was delivered to the publishers in January 1997, but it has been possible to incorporate to a greater or lesser extent important developments (both statutory and otherwise) down to today, June 11, 1997.

S. M. CRETNEY
The Feast of St Barnabas the Apostle

TABLE OF CONTENTS

Part 2: FAMILIES: MARRIED AND UNMARRIED

TABLE OF ABBREVIATIONS

The following abbreviations are used in the text:

CA	Children Act
CSA	Child Support Act
FLA	Family Law Act
HF&EA	Human Fertilisation and Embryology Act
LPA	Law of Property Act
MCA	Matrimonial Causes Act
TLATA	Trusts of Land and Appointment of Trustees Act

TABLE OF CASES

TABLE OF STATUTES

TABLE OF STATUTORY INSTRUMENTS

Introduction: The Family and the Law

A. CHANGING PERSPECTIVES

The family as a social institution

The legal systems of western democracies generally reflect a favourable view of the family as an institution. For example, the European Convention on Human Rights expressly requires governments to respect family life, and the home and the right to found a family; whilst Article 41 of the 1937 Constitution of the Republic of Ireland went even further and proclaimed that the family was the "natural primary and fundamental" unit group of society, possessing "inalienable and imprescriptible rights", that it was the "necessary basis of social order" and was "indispensable to the welfare of the Nation and the State".

Transmitting values and providing support

Provisions such as these reflect the traditional view of the family as the basis for a life of domestic peace and tranquility within which emotions and sexual needs can be fulfilled and from which the concerns of the outside world can be excluded. In this traditional view the family is also seen as a powerful means for promoting the well-being of the state's citizens, and as an institution within which the citizens of the future can be born and reared — whether to defend the state on the battlefield or to provide economically for elderly parents. It is only recently that over-population rather than under-population has been seen as a problem in Western societies, and even now there is concern that changing patterns of mortality and fertility will result in there being insufficient young people to provide the financial support that their elders need. Families provide support — emotional, social and financial — for their members; and they also instil values in those members. In particular, they act as an instrument of the social control necessary in a civilised community: Lady Thatcher has said that the breakdown of families has been the starting point for a wide range of social ills; and that it is only by strengthening the "traditional family" that problems such as the increasing crime rate can be successfully tackled (M. Thatcher, *The Downing Street Years* (1995) p. 629).

So the family has its uses as an instrument of state policy; but at the same time it has traditionally been seen as a protection against the claims of the state to control decisions which ought to be personal. The state may need more fit recruits for its armies or to manage its overseas possessions (constant preoccupations in countries such as France and Britain in the first half of the twentieth century) and social policies could be and were deliberately formulated to encourage an increase in the population of fit young people. But there could be no direct government intrusion into decisions whether or not to bear a child. Again, the trained social worker or the official of the Department of Health might in fact know far better what is good for children than do the child's parents, but the officials are only to be allowed to interfere with the private citizen's own decisions in exceptional circumstances. This thinking underlies decisions by the United States Supreme Court asserting the right of married couples to take their own decisions on such matters as the use of contraception: see *Griswold v. Connecticut* (1965) 381 U.S. 479; but it also underlies the provision of the Irish

1

Constitution that the family is the "primary and natural educator of children", and that it is the "inalienable right and duty of parents" to provide for the education — religious and moral, physical and social, as well as intellectual — of their children. Reflections of this view can be found in English case law: see for example *Re K(D) (a minor) (ward: termination of access)* [1988] A.C. 812, *per* Lord Templeman ("The best person to bring up a child is the natural parent. It matters not whether the parent is wise or foolish, rich or poor, educated or illiterate. Public authorities cannot improve on nature."

A contrasting view: the family as an instrument of oppression

This favourable view of family life is not universally held. Indeed, in 1967, Sir Edmund Leach (Provost of King's College Cambridge and a distinguished anthropologist) told listeners to the *Reith Lectures* that the family, "far from being the basis of the good society" was "with its narrow privacy and tawdry secrets . . . the source of all our discontents": *The Listener,* November 30, 1967; whilst many writers — often, but by no means always, taking a distinctively feminist view — have depicted the traditional family as a means whereby the economically or physically powerful (usually men) dominate and often abuse the weak and vulnerable (usually women and children). The criminal statistics demonstrate the reality that home and family are aften associated with violence and indeed with violent death: for example, no less than 32 per cent of all recorded homicides are committed by a member of the victim's family whilst the phenomenon of domestic violence perpetrated against women in the home has become a major concern. Even the view that the family will invariably be an effective means of protecting children from harm is difficult to reconcile with the evidence. Karl Marx claimed children needed more protection against economic exploitation by their own parents rather than by their employers; whilst in recent years a succession of enquiries has demonstrated that there are families within which children are repeatedly and sometimes systematically abused — by their being raped, buggered, or violently assaulted — by the very adults who are supposed to offer protection.

The family and the law: a blinkered vision

It is clear that the student of the family must today confront many difficult and controversial issues. What is for one person the transmission of desirable social values will be the perpetuation of an oppressive social structure for another; one person's necessary child protection measure will be another's unwarranted social workers' interference. But for many years these difficulties were almost concealed from the law student by reason of the very narrow perspectives of the common law and the almost simplistic approach embodied in the English law of persons. The legal family was founded on marriage — the voluntary union for life of one man to one woman to the exclusion of all others: *Hyde v. Hyde* (1866) L.R. 1 P. & D. 130, 133. Marriage created a legal status — that is to say, the law conferred rights (for example, about the ownership of property) and imposed duties (for example, a husband had a duty at common law to maintain his wife); and it was not open to the parties to vary the legal consequences of marriage by any private contract they might choose to make. The law did, of course, define some of those legal consequences (such as those regulating entitlement to property); but it was content to accept that within the family the husband had power to impose his will about matters such as the children's upbringing and to take decisions about where the family should live, and about its lifestyle. The notion that the law of England allowed a man to beat his wife (provided he did it with a stick no thicker than his finger) lingered on, and the criminal law offered little real protection. The role of the law in relation to the family was thus extremely narrow.

Breakdown of adults' relationships

It is, of course, true that marriages sometimes broke down; but, although the common law allowed a husband to sue his wife's lover for damages for adultery, no court could dissolve the marriage. An ill-treated wife could ask the Ecclesiastical Court to relieve her of the duty to live under the same roof as the man who had abused her; but it was only in 1857 that Parliament empowered the court to dissolve a valid marriage, and thereby to allow the parties to remarry. This decision marked the emergence of family law (then described as the law of matrimonial causes) but for many years the subject was effectively confined to a study of the law governing the legal consequences of marriage and its breakdown. The ground upon which divorce should be allowed has remained a subject of strong feeling and sometimes bitter controversy; and it remains the policy officially articulated by Parliament that the institution of marriage should be supported (see Family Law Act 1996, s.1(a)). But the divorce rate has escalated over the years — from less than a thousand applications a year before World War I, to 10,000 a year in World War II, and peaking in the 1990s at more than 180,000; and there is a substantial body of evidence that the breakdown of parental relationships may damage children. Questions have to be asked about how far changes in divorce law and procedure (often described as "making divorce easier") have increased the incidence of breakdown and its damaging consequences.

Children's rights?

Conflict in families is not, of course, confined to disagreement between parents. The common law notion that a parent has "authority" over a child almost inevitably entails the possibility that the exercise of that authority may be questioned; but perhaps surprisingly it is only in comparatively recent years that the law has begun to consider the principles governing the resolution of such conflicts — indeed whether a child should in an extreme case be allowed to "divorce" his or her parents. The failure of Mrs Victoria Gillick's attempt to have it declared illegal for young teenagers to be prescribed contraceptives without parental agreement marked the beginning of a move towards greater recognition of children's rights — rights to be heard and to do what the child considers best rather than what well-intentioned outsiders consider to be in the child's best interests. Needless to say, this is a controversial subject on which the broad generalisations to be found in documents such as the United Nations Convention on the Rights of the Child (1989) do not provide ready answers.

The parental duty to support children

The family may traditionally have been seen as a bulwark against state interference, but the state could never wholly close its eyes to situations of family breakdown and crisis. The Poor Law in particular could not ignore the fact that children were born outside marriage, and the problem of how best to prevent the burden of supporting those once described as "bastards" from falling on the taxpayer was a major concern. To this day there is little disagreement about the general principle that parents should provide for the cost of maintaining their children, and it is tempting to think that the Poor Law officials would have been impressed by the advantages of a system under which the maintenance liability in respect of children in one-parent families is calculated according to clear mathematical formulae (as the Child Support Act 1991 attempts to do). But it seems improbable that until recently anyone would have contemplated a society in which more than one-third of all children were born outside marriage; and the policy (consistently pursued over recent years) of seeking to remove any stigma from the fact that a child's parents are unmarried may perhaps be questioned.

Defining the limits of state intervention

For many years the state's interest in children was effectively confined to the attempts by the Poor Law to enforce a parental maintenance liability to maintain them. But towards the end of the nineteenth century child neglect was widely publicised; and the state increasingly responded with measures of regulation, inspection, and (increasingly) assistance. The Education Act 1870 introduced the principle of compulsory education, and has thus some claim to be the most radical legislative intervention in the right for the family to transmit its own values to succeeding generations; but other legislation (again originating in the Poor Law) increasingly had to grapple with the problem of how far the state should be empowered to take compulsory measures to override the once sacrosanct parental right to control children's upbringing. Measures to protect children from economic exploitation began to be taken in the nineteenth century; but there was also increasing concern about child neglect. Eventually, the Children Act 1948, one of the keystones of the post-Word War II welfare state, cast on the state extensive responsibilities to care for children in need; and since then there has been what a judge aptly described as a "cascade of legislation" dealing with these matters. The powers and duties of the state in relation to children and their families are now so extensive that much of a typical family law syllabus could fairly be described as a branch of public rather than private law. Almost everyone would accept the principle that families should have the right to make their own decisions; and equally almost everyone would accept that there must be some limit on this freedom and that in certain situations the state can and should intervene. Quite where the balance should be struck between these conflicting principles is a matter on which different communities may take different decisions. The law student cannot ignore the fact that there may often be a conflict between the wishes of parents about the upbringing of their children and the views of social workers and other professionals about what should be done so as to best promote a child's welfare.

The impact of a multi-cultural society

These problems are difficult enough in a socially homogenous society with a wide measure of agreement on its basic values. But they become much more difficult in pluralist societies. Should we accept that parents have a right to bring up their children with the aid of disciplinary measures, such as severe corporal punishment, which are accepted as normal and desirable in the parents' country of origin and indeed in their own neighbourhood here but which are no longer regarded as acceptable by informed opinion in this country? There are even more difficult problems in relation to sexual matters. In *Alhaji Mohammed v. Knott* [1969] 1 Q.B. 1 a court held that a 13 year-old Nigerian Muslim girl living with the man to whom she was validly (and apparently happily) married was by virtue of that fact "exposed to moral danger" and thereby liable to be taken into care by the local authority. "A continuance of such an association would (notwithstanding the marriage) be repugnant to any decent-minded English man or woman" said the court. However, the Appeal Court thought this view ignored the way of life in which the couple had been brought up, and quashed the lower court's decision. But how should the law view an arranged marriage in which a young woman has participated solely out of a sense of obligation to family or religious convention? Again, the traditional view of marriage in this country is firmly monogamous: the union of *one* man to *one* woman, as we have seen. How far, then, should a relationship in which a man has more than one wife at the same time be recognised as a marriage? Finally, the traditional view of marriage in this country is that it is a relationship between a man and a woman. But the question of how far the law should provide facilities for the creation of a marriage-like relationship between a couple of the same sex is becoming increasingly discussed, while the approach which English law takes on the legal consequences of gender-reassignment techniques (in which a transsexual is by surgery and other treatment given some of the physical attributes of the sex to which the patient feels he really belongs) has already led to a number of applications, so far unsuccessful, to the European Human Rights Court.

Who is a parent?

Medical techniques, conveniently if inelegantly described as Human Assisted Reproduction, have been developed which effectively separate procreation from sexual activity between parents, and indeed mean that a child may be born to and reared by "parents" neither of whom has contributed to any part of the child's genetic inheritance. The Human Fertilisation and Embryology Act 1990 seeks to provide answers to the most pressing questions (such as who is to be regarded as the "parent" of such a child) but in some ways this merely opens up the whole question of the nature of authority and responsibility within the family and the role of the law in dealing with these matters. For example, should a woman who has brought a child into the world have a greater right to preserve a legally recognised link with the child than the woman who has perhaps cared for the child for many years? Should a man who marries a mother have any authority over, or responsibility towards, the children she has had with other partners?

Who is to decide: the role of the courts

The question of how far the legal system should involve itself with the consequences of family breakdown, or indeed with decisions taken within the ongoing family, is thus one of considerable difficulty. But even when it has been decided that issues should be the subject of legal procedures there is a separate question about the nature of the legal procedures which should be invoked. For example, is the system of adversarial justice traditional in the common law courts — in which each party puts his or her opposing view points to a judge who is confined to choosing between the solutions they put forward — appropriate to resolving issues about the arrangements to be made for the children of parents who no longer wish to live together? Are such procedures appropriate to resolve disputes between adults about what should happen to their finances after the breakdown of a relationship, or do they serve to increase the bitterness and distress often inevitable in such circumstances? How far should the law encourage (or even allow) those concerned to make their own arrangements, perhaps providing assistance by expert mediators or conciliators? The Report of the *Finer Committee* (1974) Cmnd. 5629 drew attention to the case for a distinctive "family court"; whilst the notion that many family disputes could best be resolved by mediation or conciliation has strongly influenced the reforms of divorce law and procedures to be effected under the Family Law Act 1996. Court structures have been extensively modified, but there remain many difficult questions about the role of lawyers and others in balancing often conflicting interests.

B. DEMOGRAPHIC FACTORS

It may now be helpful to summarise some of the more notable demographic facts about the modern English family to help the reader understand the background against which the law has to operate and to evaluate its role and effectiveness as an instrument of policy.

An ageing population, and its impact

The expectation of life of a boy born in 1901 was 45; the life expectancy of a boy born in 1993 is 74.5 and a new born girl can expect to live to age 79. Couples who remain together until they are parted by death will thus spend much longer in that relationship than their forbears would have expected to do, and it is possible that this fact has some impact on divorce rates. But notwithstanding the enormous increase in divorce, it has been estimated that nearly 50 per cent of all married couples will celebrate their silver wedding: J. Haskey, "The Proportion of Married Couples who divorce" (1996) 83 *Population Trends* 25. The dramatic improvement in mortality rates has other consequences. First, parents are far more likely to survive throughout all their children's infancy than was once the case; secondly, children will often have comparatively young grandparents who may well feel excluded from contact with their grandchildren if the parents' relationship breaks down; and thirdly, the ever increasing burden of providing physical care for ageing relatives (it is estimated that by 2034 the number of persons aged 75 and over will increase from 4 milion in 1994 to 6.8 million [Social Trends 27 (1997) page 17.]) is far more likely to fall on women than on men, thus often affecting the respective economic opportunities of husband and wife.

Marriage supplanted by cohabitation?

In the late sixties, marriage had become an almost universal experience. But this is no longer the case: the marriage rate has fallen dramatically in the past fifteen years, and in 1993 the number of marriages, for the first time in fifty years fell below 300,000: Mariage and Divorce Statistics 1993, p. xiii. In part these figures may indicate that many people are opting for a single life — one third of men aged from 16 to 59 have never married (J. Haskey, "The proportion of married couples who divorce: past patterns and current prospects" (1996) 83 *Population Trends* 25) whilst the number of never-married people living alone in owner-occupied property has risen dramatically in recent years, from 370,000 in 1977–78 to one million in 1995–96: *Survey of English Housing 3rd Report* (Office for National Statistics, 1997). But there is now irrefutable evidence that a large number of people are cohabiting with "partners" to whom they are not married: *Social Trends* 27 (1997) p. 45.

For some time, the conventional view was that in many such cases marriage was simply deferred whilst the couple assessed their compatibility, and statistics provided support for this view: it is estimated that over a quarter of all women aged 20 to 24 are cohabiting, more than a fifth of couples who do marry give the same address, and the median age for marriage has risen sharply (to 25 for women and 28 for men). But the evidence suggests that in addition to such "trial marriages" there has been a substantial increase in long-term cohabitation by couples who have no intention of marrying and never do so. Demographic projections suggest that only 70 per cent of the population will ever marry; and whilst some of the "never-married" will no doubt, as throughout history, abstain from any long term heterosexual relationship, for many a long term family relationship will be formed outside marriage and thus ignored by the formal registration machinery of the state.

Increase in numbers of children born outside marriage

The proportion of births outside marriage has risen from around 6 per cent of all births in the post-Word War II period to more than one-third. But four-fifths of all such non-marital births are registered jointly by both parents, and of those parents four-fifths living at the same address; and it may be that in social (as distinct from legal) terms the life-experience of many of these children is completely unaffected by the fact that their parents are unmarried. At one time the illegitimate child was likely to be the child of an unmarried mother living on her own; but this is no longer true.

Increase in number of single-parent families

The problems of the single-parent family, whether created by parental death or divorce or by birth to a single woman, were sympathetically analysed in the Report of the *Finer Committee* (1974) Cmnd. 5629; but more recently the image of the single parent as a feckless teenager deliberately becoming pregnant in order to establish a claim to an independence buttressed by the allocation of social housing has been allowed to become part of the conventional rhetoric of political debate. Nevertheless, although it remains true that the majority of children are brought up by their own married parents, the percentage of all dependent children living in lone-parent families has more than doubled since 1972 to reach 17 per cent by 1991. The great majority of the parents concerned are lone mothers rather than lone fathers. Questions inevitably arise about the provision of adequate economic and other support for such children.

Increase in divorce and remarriage

Reference has already been made to the high divorce rate: there are some 150,000 divorces, and more than 13 out of every thousand married people in this country divorce each year: one of the highest rates in Europe. The growing number of divorces is particularly remarkable given the fall in the number of marriages referred to above, but perhaps even more remarkable is the number of cases in which divorced people remarry: in 1990, there were more than 80,000 marriages in which one or both parties had been divorced; and 69.9 divorce persons per 1,000 divorced persons aged 16 and over remarried in that year: *Population Trends No. 70* (1992) Table 22. By 1994 more than a third of all marriages were remarriages: Social Trends 27 (1997) p. 46. Regrettably, these remarriages are significantly more likely to end in another divorce than are marriages between those who have never previously married: see J. Haskey, "The proportion of married couples who divorce: past patterns and current prospects" (1996) 83 *Population Trends* 25.

Changing family structures

Although about one-third of divorcing couples have no children, more than 88,000 couples who divorced in 1994 had one or more children under 16 and in that year there were 165,000 children under 16 whose parents divorced. In 1991 there were around one million children living in families which included one or more step-children: *Social Trends* 27 (1997) p. 44. It has been estimated that half of all the children of divorcing parents are cared for by their mother and the man she subsequently marries; and the mother may often have further children in the new relationship — each year there are more than 40,000 births within marriage to remarried women. There are more than three times as many stepfathers as step-mothers. The kinship links in such families may be complex, and difficult social relationships may be experienced, sometimes exacerbated by hostility between the adults concerned and their former spouses.

C. MARRIED AND UNMARRIED COUPLES

We have seen that marriage is demographically of much less significance than was once the case, and that a significant proportion of family groups are not founded on marriage. Nevertheless, marriage remains a subject of great legal importance for two reasons. First, as a matter of *fact,* there are still far more married than unmarried couples and the majority of children live in households formed by their two married parents. Secondly, as a mater of *law,* marriage remains important because it creates a *status* in the sense in which that word was explained by Lord Simon of Glaisdale (see *The Ampthill Peerage* [1977] A.C. 547, 577): "the condition of belonging to a class in society to which the law ascribes peculiar rights and duties, capacities and incapacities."

The significance of status. If a couple are married they automatically have certain rights and duties; and, in principle, the nature and quality of their relationship is irrelevant; for example, a wife who (as in *Re Rowlands, dec'd* [1984] FLR 813) has not lived with her husband for more than 40 years is nonetheless still in principle entitled to succeed to her husband's property on his intestacy. This principle is even more dramatically illustrated by the case of *Re Collins (dec'd)* [1990] 2 FLR 72:

Mrs Collins left her husband — a man with a record of violent crime — shortly after their marriage in 1978. She was given the leave which (as the law then stood) she needed to bring divorce proceedings within the first three years of the marriage on the ground that the case was one of exeptional hardship or depravity. A decree nisi was granted but the decree had not been made absolute at the date when Mrs Collins died. Accordingly, she was in law still married; and her husband became entitled on her intestacy to the whole of her estate.

In contrast, neither of the partners in a relationship outside marriage is automatically entitled to the legal rights stemming from the status of marriage. It is irrelevant that they have been living together happily for many years, and that they have for long been regarded as a married couple by all their friends and neighbours. The case of *Burns v. Burns* [1984] FLR 216 furnishes a dramatic example of the consequences of being one of an "unmarried couple" (to adopt the terminology used in the Social Security legislation):

Mr and Mrs Burns lived together for 19 years. Mrs Burns (as she was known) give up her job to look after Mr Burns and their two children. Although she put her earnings into the housekeeping, and bought domestic appliances and other household goods, she was held to have no claim to the house or any of the assets and see *Windeler v. Whitehall* [1990] 2 FLR 505, pp. 113–114 below.

It is true that legislation now sometimes gives rights to those who have lived together as husband and wife, but an understanding of marriage and its legal consequences must have priority in any understanding of English family law — not least because so many important legal consequences flow from the dissolution of marriage by divorce. The first Part of this book deals with the legal consequences of marriage; and the remainder of the book deals with the legal consequences of family relationships whether the family is founded on marriage or not.

PART ONE

MARRIAGE AND ITS LEGAL CONSEQUENCES

Chapter 1

FORMATION OF MARRIAGE

Introduction

If marriage is regarded in social rather than legal terms it is (as the historian L. Stone has pointed out) a complex and often lengthy process; but in legal terms marriage comes into existence in a moment and is independent of the parties' social relationship. This is not to say that the law has not had to resolve difficult social and moral issues some of which have already been mentioned. Is marriage to be (as it is in English legal theory) the voluntary union for life of a woman and a man to the exclusion of all others, or is a person to be allowed to have several spouses at the same time, and if so, how many? And what do we mean by a "man" and a "woman"? Can a transsexual marry? Can a 15-year-old marry? What formalities have to be completed to create a marriage?

Not surprisingly, although virtually all legal systems do have ground rules governing such matters, the content of those rules differs greatly from country to country, and from time to time. For example, until the enactment of Lord Hardwicke's Marriage Act in 1753 English law required no formal procedures at all for the creation of a marriage. If a couple agreed between themselves that they were married, that sufficed to create what is correctly called a "common law marriage", *i.e.* a marriage as valid as if it had been celebrated by the Archbishop of Canterbury in Westminster Abbey in the presence of a large congregation (in sharp contrast to the situation of an unmarried cohabitant — or, as a former President of the Divorce Division put it, a "mistress, lover, concubine, doxy or live-in girl-friend" — who is *not* recognised in law as a spouse even though for some purposes she may be treated as such.)

The common law marriage continued to be available in Scotland (a fact which originally accounted for the popularity of Gretna Green as a place for runaway marriages) until as recently as 1940, and it still exists in some parts of the world. But English law now prescribes quite elaborate formalities with which those who wish to be legally married must comply:

In *Rignell v. Andrews* [1991] 1 FLR 332 a man had lived with a woman for 11 years and she had changed her surname to his. He claimed that she was accordingly his "common law wife" and that he was entitled to the higher rate of personal allowance for income tax purposes then available to a man whose "wife" was living with him. The claim was unsuccessful. The judge held that the term "wife" meant a woman who had entered into a legally recognised marriage with a man, and did not extend to the case of a woman merely cohabiting with a man, however permanent or close the relationship.

Again, there have been remarkable changes in the English rules about who can validly marry whom. It was only in 1929 that Parliament decided that English law should not allow a 15-year-old child to marry, and the rules about marriages between relatives have been changed as recently as 1986 by the Marriage (Prohibited Degrees of Relationship) Act which (as we shall see at pp. 23–24, below) even allows a person in certain circumstances to marry his mother-in-law or her father-in-law. Again, modest steps have been taken towards privatising the marriage ceremony: the Marriage Act 1994 allows marriages to be celebrated in a wide range of venues, ranging from the Ritz Hotel, through the Newcastle United football stadium, to the First Class departure lounge at Ashford International Railway Station.

The basic rule

The basic rule of English law is that a marriage can be created between any two people who have the necessary legal capacity and comply with the stipulated formal requirements. The text deals first (in this Chapter) with formalities. Chapter 2 then deals with the rules about capacity.

THE MARRIAGE CEREMONY

One thing which can be said with certainty about the English law is that it is complex, so much so that the Law Commission said that it was "not understood by members of the public or even by all those who have to administer it" (Law Com. No. 53, Annex. paragraph 6). It would serve no useful purpose to try to explain in an elementary textbook the details of the law as contained in the Marriage Acts 1949 to 1994. All that can be done is to highlight some of the main characteristics of the law. Much of the complexity is caused by the fact that English law gives intending spouses a very wide choice of marriage ceremony: they can marry according to the rites of the Church of England; they can marry according to the rites of other religions; or they can marry in a secular procedure, either in a Register Office or in premises approved under the Marriage Act 1994.

(i) Parental consent sometimes required

If either party to an intended marriage is under 18 the consent of that person's parents or guardians is normally required. If the child is in local authority care under a care order, the local authority's consent is required in addition; and if the court has made a residence order under the provisions of the Children Act the consent of the person with whom the child is to live under the terms of that order is required in substitution for that of the parents and guardians. The court can override a refusal to give the necessary consent.

A marriage solemnised without the requisite consent will be valid; but the parties may be liable to prosecution for making a false statement.

These rules are of much less importance than was once the case because of the trend towards marriage later in life: in 1971 nearly one-third of all brides were teenagers, but today the median age for marriage is 25. The "problem" of the teenage marriage seems to have been supplanted by that of the teenage pregnancy: in 1995 there were some 42,000 live births to teenagers (and some 20,000 teenage pregnancies were terminated by abortion).

(ii) Requirements for banns, licence or certificate

The law stipulates that certain preliminaries must take place before a marriage can be solemnised. The objective is to give an opportunity for people to point to what the Book of Common Prayer describes as a "just cause or impediment" to the marriage. The formalities required depend on whether the marriage is to take place according to the rites of the Church of England or not.

(a) *Anglican marriages.*
   If there is to be an Anglican ceremony, banns will usually be called. But alternatively the parties may obtain a common licence from the Church Authorities or a special licence issued on behalf of the Archbishop of Canterbury. Banns are the cheapest preliminary (the fee currently being £13) but involve the longest delay. A special licence is at the other extreme: it can authorise a marriage at any time and in any place. At one time the cost was such as to make it available only to the affluent, but the fee (now £90) has not kept pace with changes in the value of money, and more than 3,000 marriages by special licence now take place each year.

(b) *Preliminaries to other forms of marriage.*
   If there is to be a civil ceremony, or a non-Anglican religious ceremony, the parties may obtain a Superintendent Registrar's certificate, which can be regarded as an equivalent to banns in so far as it is the cheapest procedure but requires the longest waiting time. A Superintendent Registrar's certificate and licence, often (incorrectly) called a "special licence", costs rather more (the total cost of a register office marriage on licence will be £89, as compared with £44 for a register office marriage on notice) but permits marriage after the expiration of one whole day from the giving of the notice.
   In either case, prescribed information has to be given and recorded in a marriage notice book which is by statute open to public inspection. And there are special preliminaries to facilitate the marriage of the terminally ill, the housebound, prisoners, and people in mental hospitals.

(iii) The marriage ceremony

The legislation permits four types of ceremony. First, marriage according to the rites of the Church of England; secondly, the secular ceremony in a register office or on approved premises; thirdly, marriages according to the rites of the religion concerned in a registered place of religious worship; and finally Quaker and Jewish marriages. The only feature which is common to all types of ceremony is that the parties must at some stage express their consent to the marriage in a prescribed form of words.

(a) *The Church of England.*

The marriage must be celebrated by "a clerk in Holy Orders in the Church of England", *i.e.* by a priest or deacon. The minister will use the rite laid down in the Book of Common Prayer or an authorised alternative form of service. In fact, two-thirds of all marriages with a religious ceremony are performed in Anglican churches; and the proportion might be even higher if it were more widely known that the clergy are obliged by law to celebrate marriages whatever the intending parties' religion or lack of it (although the clergy cannot be required to marry the divorced so long as the other party to the marriage is still alive).

(b) *Register Office weddings; and weddings on approved premises.*

The Register Office ceremony is simple in the extreme, and must be entirely secular. Under rules laid down in the Marriage Act 1949 as amended by the Marriage Ceremony (Prescribed Words) Act 1996 the parties must declare that they are free lawfully to marry (or that they know of no legal reason, or lawful impediment, to the marriage); and they either "call upon these persons here present to witness that I, A.B., do take thee, C.D., to be my lawful wedded wife (or husband)" or say "I, A.B., take you (or thee), C.D., to be my wedded wife (or husband)".

A Register Office ceremony takes place in the office, "with open doors" and two or more witnesses must be present. People may of course (like the Oasis pop star Liam Gallagher: see *The Times*, April 8, 1997) by careful timing or otherwise take steps to ensure that they have what the Superintendent Registrar at the Westminster Register Office described as a "very private and very personal" ceremony; but it is a fundamental principle of English law that a marriage ceremony be a public event.

Responsibility for the provision of Register Offices falls on local authorities; and as a result of changes made by the Marriage Act 1994 the parties may choose a Register Office outside their own registration district. It was hoped that the change in the law would encourage local authorities to provide more attractive amenities and would introduce an element of competition between different authorities.

In a further attempt to give people choice, the Marriage Act 1994 allows *civil* marriages to be solemnised on *approved premises, i.e.* premises approved by the local authority. The Authority must satisfy itself that the premises provide "a seemly and dignified venue", that they have no recent or continuing connection with any religion, and that the marriage room is identifiable and separated from any other activity on the premises at the time of the ceremony. There are also restrictions on the sale and consumption of food and alcoholic beverages in the hour preceding the ceremony.

(c) *Marriages in a registered place of religious worship.*

These provisions were originally intended to allow Roman Catholic churches and non-conformist churches and chapels to be used for marriages, but it is possible for any building which is a place of meeting for religious worship to be registered for this purpose. The question of what "religious worship" means can present difficulties. The courts have held that the expression does not extend to the practices of scientologists: *ex parte Segerdal* [1970] 2 Q.B. 697. However, there can be no doubt that Sikh and Hindu temples, and mosques, are entitled to be registered (although it seems that only comparatively few are in fact registered).

The building is registered by the Registrar General, but the form of the ceremony (which will usually be conducted by a minister of the religion concerned) is a matter for the parties and the body controlling the building, subject to one vital qualification.

This is that at some stage in the proceedings the parties must make the statements set out above in either English or Welsh. (There is no requirement that they understand the language used.)

(d) *Jewish and Quaker weddings.*

The celebration of Jewish and Quaker marriages has, ever since Lord Hardwicke's Act, been entirely a matter for the religions concerned. There is no requirement that such marriages take place in public in a registered building, or that they be performed by an authorised person, and the state's role is limited to requiring that an appropriate preliminary should have taken place, and that any such marriage be registered.

(iv) Registration

All marriages celebrated in this country must be registered. Registration provides proof that the ceremony took place, and also facilitates the collection of demographic information.

Chapter 2

CAPACITY TO MARRY: ANNULMENT

Introduction: void and voidable marriages

Who can marry whom? What is to happen if someone knowingly or unknowingly goes through a marriage ceremony although the rules prohibit the marriage? The simple answer would be to say that the marriage ceremony has no legal effect. But this could be unjust: should a woman who was tricked into a bigamous "marriage" be debarred from seeking any support from the "husband" with whom she may have lived for fifteen years, say? In response to pressures such as these the law has been adapted over the years, but only at the price of some complication.

Void and voidable: the distinction and its consequences.   One important complication, which has little to do with achieving justice in the modern world but more to do with the historical development of the law and the relationship between the common law courts and the ecclesiastical courts in the seventeenth century, is that English law treats marriages affected by certain types of irregularity as being *voidable* whilst others are held to be *void*. The main differences between the two categories are as follows:

(a) A decree of nullity can be pronounced in relation to a *void* marriage at any time, even after the death of the parties. A decree can only be granted annulling a *voidable* marriage during the lifetime of both parties.
(b) If the marriage is *void*, no valid marriage ever existed. But if the marriage is *voidable*, it is valid unless and until annulled.
(c) If the marriage is *void*, any "interested person" may take proceedings to have it declared so, whereas only the parties to a *voidable* marriage can take proceedings to have it annulled.

But even void marriages may have legal consequences.   This basic distinction between the voidable marriage (which is perfectly valid unless and until it is annulled) and the void marriage, (which does not exist and requires no decree to bring it to an end) is comprehensible enough. However, the distinction has in recent years become blurred. To avoid hardship, many of the legal consequences of a valid marriage have been attached even to void marriages provided that a decree of nullity is obtained. Hence, although it is never *necessary* to obtain a decree annulling a void marriage, it may be very much in a petitioner's interest to do so.

This can be illustrated by considering the case of a woman who has entered into a bigamous marriage. That "marriage" is void. Any children will, in principle, be

19

illegitimate. Neither of the parties to the "marriage" will have any legal right to succeed to property on the intestacy of the other. Neither of the parties will have any statutory or other rights to be provided with housing by the other partner. Neither will be entitled to bring legal proceedings to compel the other to provide financial support. If one of them becomes dependent on Income Support, the Department of Social Security will have no right to claim reimbursement of the amounts of benefit paid (as it would if the one were a "liable relative" of the other).

Examples of such "marriages" are not uncommon in the Law Reports. For example:

> In *Re Spence (dec'd)* [1990] 2 FLR 278, C.A., Addie Elizabeth married Frederick William Love in 1895, and Mr Love survived until 1953. The marriage appears not to have been happy: Mrs Love left her husband, set up home with Thomas Spence, had two sons by him, and in 1934 "married" him. Since Mr Love was still alive at that time the purported "marriage" to Mr Spence was void; and Nourse L.J. said that such a "marriage, both as a matter of language and by definition . . . is a nullity. It is only an idle ceremony. It achieves no change in the status of the participants. It achieves nothing of substance." Accordingly, the sons were illegitimate and as the law then stood not regarded as legally related to one another for succession purposes.

So far, this may seem logical, if harsh. But suppose that Addie Elizabeth's relationship with Thomas Spence had also been unhappy. Since the "marriage" was in fact void, she could have petitioned for a decree of nullity and the court would have had power to make orders for financial relief for her and for the children in the same way as it could have done on dissolving a valid marriage by divorce (although that is not to say that the court's discretion would be exercised in precisely the same way). Bringing proceedings to establish that there is *no* marriage thus, paradoxically, seems to create legal consequences similar to those that would flow from the dissolution of a valid marriage.

Must be "something like a marriage"?

One question remains unresolved. Can the court refuse to pronounce a decree of nullity on the ground that there is "nothing like a marriage" in respect of which it can exercise its jurisdiction?

> In *Gereis v. Yagoub* [1997] 1 FLR 854 (H.H.J. Aglionby) a couple went through a marriage ceremony conducted by a Coptic Orthodox priest in a Coptic Orthodox church in Kensington. However, the church was not licensed for marriages under the provisions of the Marriage Act 1949: see p. 16 above; and in due course the "wife" petitioned for a decree of nullity on the ground that, the ceremony not having complied with the formalities laid down in the Marriage Act, the marriage was void: see MCA 1973, s.11(a)(iii). The husband riposted with the defence that there was nothing which could be described as a marriage at all; but this defence was unsuccessful. The ceremony bore all the appearance of and had the hallmarks of an ordinary Christian marriage, and had the church been licensed there would have been no doubt at all about the validity of the marriage.

However, the possibility that a decree of nullity might be refused (perhaps in a case where the couple were, and knew themselves to be, both men; or where the ceremony takes place as part of a theatrical performance) seems to remain open. Moreover, as already pointed out, the fact that the court has power on or after granting a decree of nullity to make financial provision and property adjustment orders does not mean that in the exercise of its discretion it will necessarily do so: see further the discussion of *J v. S-T (formerly J) (Transsexual: Ancillary Relief)* [1997] 1 FLR 402. C.A. below.

The Significance of Nullity

At one time the law of nullity was important as a technique for dealing with the legal consequences of the breakdown of a matrimonial relationship. This was because until 1857 there was no judicial divorce, and nullity was the only way (short of an Act of Parliament) of getting legal release from an unhappy relationship. Moreover, until the coming into force of the Divorce Reform Act 1969 the "guilty" party to a marriage could not divorce the "innocent" partner, so that in some cases a man wishing to remarry might petition to annul the marriage with his "innocent" partner. The introduction of divorce on the ground of irretrievable breakdown under the Divorce Reform Act 1969 greatly reduced the significance of nullity in this context: if a marriage had irretrievably broken down, one party would sooner or later be able to get a divorce. In 1995 there were only 516 nullity decrees, compared with 153,317 divorces. But nullity cannot be ignored. Apart from the possibility that the complications and delays which seem likely to be involved in obtaining a divorce under the provisions of the Family Law Act 1996 may lead to a small increase in nullity petitions on the part of elderly persons who wish to remarry nullity is of fundamental conceptual importance because it is the law of nullity which effectively determines who may marry whom. A brief account of the modern law therefore follows.

The Modern Law of Nullity

Law now statutory
The law governing nullity — for long derived from the practice of the ecclesiastical courts — was comprehensively reformed by the Nullity of Marriage Act 1971, and the legislation is now consolidated in the Matrimonial Causes Act 1973. The conceptual framework derived from the canon law is still apparent, and the doctrines of the ecclesiastical courts may thus still be relevant in deciding, for example, what is meant by "consummation" of a marriage; but statute now constitutes an exhaustive codification of the law. The law is discussed under three heads: (a) the grounds on which a nullity petition may be presented; (b) the bars to the making of nullity decrees; (c) the effects of a nullity decree.

THE STATUTORY GROUNDS

Void marriages

The modern law preserves the distinction, resulting from the historical development of the law, between void and voidable marriages.

The grounds on which a marriage is void are (MCA 1973, s.11):

   (i) parties within prohibited degrees;
  (ii) either party under 16;
 (iii) non-compliance with formalities;
 (iv) marriage bigamous;
  (v) parties not male and female.

Voidable marriages

The grounds on which a marriage is voidable are (MCA 1973 s.12):

   (i) incapacity to consummate;
  (ii) wilful refusal to consummate;
 (iii) lack of consent;
 (iv) venereal disease, pregnancy by third party, and mental illness.

A. VOID MARRIAGES

1. Prohibited Degrees: consanguinity and affinity

In order to understand the law and the policy to which it gives effect, we must first clarify the distinction between rules dealing with relationships of consanguinity (that is to say, marriage between blood relations, such as parent and child or brother and sister) and those based on affinity. Relationship by affinity is a relationship created by marriage. Relatives by affinity are called "affines", and consist of the spouse (or former spouse) of one's own relatives, and relatives of one's spouse (or former spouse). The term thus extends to in-laws and to step-relations.

The Prohibitions. English law prohibits marriage with a parent, child, grandparent, brother or sister, uncle or aunt, nephew or niece. Unlike some other western systems of law it has no restriction on marriage between cousins.

There are sound genetic reasons for forbidding marriage between close blood relations, since there is a higher chance of mutant genes being present in common in two persons with a close common ancestor. But even this issue is not altogether clear-cut, because the characteristics which appear in the offspring of a union between blood relatives may be either favourable or unfavourable. This is, after all, the secret of breeding racehorses.

Genetic objections of this kind cannot apply to prohibitions on marriage between affines. Historically, these prohibitions originate in the canon law doctrine whereby marriage makes man and woman one flesh. Thus, if it is wrong to marry my sister it must be equally wrong to marry my wife's sister. Since my sister is within the prohibited degrees of consanguinity, my sister-in-law (that is to say, my wife's sister) was for the church within the (correspondingly prohibited) degrees of affinity.

More recently, justification for prohibiting marriages between affines has been based on broader considerations of social policy, and in particular on the argument that disturbing sexual relationships should be excluded from the home circle. Yet many of these considerations are difficult to apply consistently without causing hardship.

Should a man be allowed to marry his step-daughter, for example? At first glance, the answer might seem very clear: surely the law should protect girls from the danger of sexual exploitation by those in authority over them, and not allow a man to look on a young girl as a potential bride when his true role has been that of a father? But suppose that the facts are that a man married a widow whose daughter was an adult living away from home, and suppose that he first met and fell in love with the daughter only after her mother's death? Is there any justification for not allowing this couple to marry?

Over the years, the law has been progressively relaxed. The increase in divorce and remarriage since the end of World War II greatly increased the risk that a couple who have never in fact been members of the same family unit would be debarred from marriage by reason of a legal relationship created by a relative's marriage, and this was one of the factors which led to the liberalisation of the law by the Marriage (Prohibited Degrees of Relationship) Act 1986.

The 1986 Reforms.   The basic principle of the 1986 legislation is that marriage with relatives by affinity is now permitted, but in two cases marriage to an affine is permitted only subject to conditions. The rules can best be understood by taking two examples.

(i) *Marriage to a step-child.*

Marriage to a step-child is only permitted if two conditions are satisfied. First, at the time of the marriage both parties must be 21 or over. Secondly, the step-child must not have been a child of the step-parent's family at any time whilst the step-child was under 18. (For present purposes it is sufficient to say that a child of the family is somebody who has been "treated" as a child of a particular marriage. In effect, the policy of the law is that marriage should not be permitted where one of the parties has effectively acted as the other's father or mother during the step-child's childhood.

(ii) *Marriage to a son- or daughter-in-law.*

A man may only marry his daughter-in-law (or a woman her son-in-law) if both parties are 21 or over, and the child's spouse (through whom the "in-law" relationship arises) and that spouse's mother (or father) are dead.

In this case, it appears that the policy is to prevent marriages if it could be thought that the man's sexual overtures had been responsible for the breakdown of the daughter-in-law's marriage to his son. But the drafting of the legislation is complex, and the legislation does not seem always to give effect to any coherent policy. As the Scottish Law Commission commented:

> "Suppose that a man aged 40 married a woman aged 25 who has never known her father. The wife is killed in a road accident and, some time later, the man and his former wife's mother, who is closer to his own age, want to get married. Why should it matter whether the former wife's father, who might not even know that she ever existed, is alive or dead? What is the point of this restriction on a marriage between two people who are both unmarried and unrelated by blood?" (and see the further comments and examples in *Principles of Family Law* (6th ed. 1997, page 46–48).

Whether or not the policy is tenable, there seems little doubt that its complexity makes it difficult to understand.

> In *Smith v. Clerical Medical and General Life Assurance Society and Others* [1993] 1 FLR 47, C.A., a man married the mother of a 13-year-old girl and they all lived together in the same household. Six years later the man left with the girl, and they set up house together, apparently intending to marry. In fact, such a marriage would have been void before the enactment of the 1986 Act, and it would not have been validated by that Act since the girl had (before attaining 18) lived in the same household with her intended husband and he had treated her as a child of the family.

Adoption.   There are two rules which have a special bearing in cases where a child has been adopted and thereby ceased to be the child of the original birth parents and become legally the child of adoptive parents. First, the child remains within the same prohibited degrees in relation to the natural parents and other relatives as if there had been no adoption. Hence, a marriage between a couple who are in fact brother and sister will be void even though neither of them knows about the relationship. There are now special provisions in the legislation entitling a person to have access to the recorded facts about the birth, so that the risk that a marriage will be celebrated in ignorance of the biological relationship has been to some extent reduced.

The second rule relevant to cases where a child has been adopted is that an adoptive parent and the adopted child are deemed to be within the prohibited degrees, and they continue to be so notwithstanding that the child is subsequently adopted by someone else. This clearly reflects the policy that the law should discourage sexual relationships within the home circle.

There are no other express prohibitions arising by reason of adoption, and it is thus possible, for example, for an adopted child validly to marry his adoptive sister.

Prohibited Degrees and the Crime of Incest.   Since 1908 it has been a criminal offence for a man knowingly to have sexual intercourse with his daughter or certain other relations. However the class of relations is more narrowly defined than for the purpose of the prohibited degrees of marriage: a man may, without committing the crime of incest, have intercourse with his aunt, niece, or step-daughter, for example, notwithstanding the fact that they are within the prohibited degrees.

2. Minimum Age

No marriage under 16.   A marriage is void if either party is under 16. This rule (which applies whether or not either knew the facts) should be distinguished from the rule which requires parental consent where a person intending to marry is under 18. Failure to comply with the parental consent rule has no effect on the validity of the marriage, so that, for example, if a 17-year-old girl gets married without her parents' consent the marriage will be perfectly valid. But in contrast, a marriage between a boy of 17 and a girl whom everyone believes to be 16 is void if it is subsequently, perhaps many years later, established that she was in fact one day short of her sixteenth birthday: and it makes no difference that both sets of parents consented to the marriage.

This rule seems capable of creating hardship. It is true that the "teenage" marriage is now something of the past for most people in this country but this is not necessarily true for some ethnic minorities. If a couple marry, genuinely but mistakenly believing that they are both of marriageable age, it seems harsh to hold the marriage void. Moreover, if a couple have lived together for many years believing their marriage to be valid, it would seem to be quite wrong to let a third party challenge it — perhaps to gain financial benefit under the succession laws. These criticisms have particular force in cases where the wife was born outside this country, there is no formal record of her birth, and no one realised that she had in fact been under the age of 16 at the time of the marriage.

3. Defective Formalities

In general only deliberate disregard of the marriage formalities will invalidate a marriage. The Marriage Act 1949 provides that if the parties "knowingly and wilfully" disregard certain requirements, then the marriage shall be void: see *e.g. Gereis v. Yagoub* [1997] 1 FLR 854 (H.H.J. Aglionby) where the parties had been told that it was necessary for them to go through a Register Office ceremony and the judge accordingly held that they had "knowingly and wilfully" intermarried in defiance of the statutory provisions. In contrast the Act stipulates that evidence of certain irregularities (for example, failure to obtain parental consent) is not to be given in proceedings touching the validity of the marriage, and it follows that such defects cannot invalidate the marriage. But the Act is silent as to the consequences of some irregularities, for example, the requirement that the marriage be celebrated with open doors, and that certain prescribed words be used. It seems probable that such irregularities would not affect the validity of the marriage.

4. Bigamy

A purported marriage is void if it is proved that at the time of the ceremony either party was already lawfully married to a third party ("X"). The fact that the parties on reasonable grounds believed X to be dead makes no difference: if it is subsequently established that X was in fact alive at the time of the ceremony the "marriage" will be void.

In practice, difficulties quite often arise because there is no evidence as to whether X was alive at the date of the ceremony or not, but these cases can often be resolved by applying a presumption that a person is dead if there is no evidence that he was alive throughout a continuous period of seven years: see *Principles of Family Law*, (6th ed. 1997), page 392.

The question whether a marriage is void for bigamy is answered once and for all by reference to the facts as they existed at the date of the ceremony which is under consideration. A marriage which was void because at that time one of the parties was married remains void even if the lawful spouse dies the day after the bigamous ceremony.

5. Parties of Same Sex

General Principle. The Act provides (s.11(c)) that a marriage is void if the parties are not respectively male and female. English law does not accept that homosexual or gay relationships can constitute legal marriages: "single sex unions remain proscribed as fundamentally abhorrent to" the classical understanding of marriage as the voluntary union for life of one man and one woman, to the exclusion of all others: see *J v. S-T (formerly J) (Transsexual: Ancillary Relief)* [1997] 1 FLR 402, 439, C.A. below, *per* Ward L.J. But this provision has been most frequently invoked in respect of relationships involving transsexuals. The medical term for this condition is "gender identity dysphoria" and as the European Court on Human Rights has put it (in *The Rees Case* [1987] 2 FLR 111) transsexuals are generally people who:

> "whilst belonging physically to one sex, feel convinced that they belong to the other; they often seek to achieve a more integrated, unambiguous identity by undergoing medical treatment and surgical operations to adapt their physical characteristics to their psychological nature."

In short, a transsexual comes to think that he is a female imprisoned in a male body (or vice versa): *Corbett v. Corbett* [1971] P. 83, 91. In this country, treatment — which may involve hormone treatment, and (in the case of a male to female transsexual) the surgical removal of the male genitalia and the construction of an artificial vagina or (in the case of a female to male transsexual) mastectomy, hysterectomy and phalloplasty — is available at specialist clinics sometimes under the National Health Service; and a person who has successfully undergone such treatment will be treated as having effectively changed sex for many official purposes. National insurance records will be amended, and a passport will be issued in a female name, for example (but the Registrar General regards a birth certificate as a document which records historical facts, rather than the current situation, and he will not normally alter the entry stating the sex recorded at birth: see *Re P and G (Transsexuals)* [1996] 2 FLR 90, Q.B.D.).

But what is the position about transsexuals' marriage? The orthodox view for the past 25 years has been that for the purposes of the marriage laws a person's sex is fixed for all time at birth, and that the only relevant tests of sexual identity are biological. In this view a person born with male genitalia and a male chromosomal structure remains a "man" for the purpose of the marriage laws, notwithstanding the fact that the patient has, after the reassignment therapy, lived and been accepted as a woman, possessed the external attributes of a woman and in most ways had become philosophically, psychologically and socially a woman. From this orthodox viewpoint successful gender reassignment therapy is irrelevant, and a person correctly classified as a male at birth (applying biological tests) will never be able to marry as a woman. The leading case on the subject remains *Corbett v. Corbett* [1971] P. 83:

> April Ashley had undergone what was then described as a sex change operation, had lived as a woman, and indeed worked successfully as a female model; she had also been recognised as a woman for national insurance and passport purposes. It was held, applying the principles stated above, that she remained a man and that her marriage to the petitioner was accordingly void.

The decision in the April Ashley case was based on the state of medical knowledge at the time; and there have been many advances in medical understanding in the intervening quarter of a century. Moreover, the case was decided under the common law which regarded the question as being whether the parties were properly described as a "man" and a "woman". In contrast, the 1973 Matrimonial Causes Act uses the words "male" and "female", and it would seem possible to argue that these terms refer to a person's gender (that is to say, the sex to which he or she psychically belongs) and that accordingly the question whether a person is "male" or "female" is not to be resolved solely by reference to tests of biological sexuality.

Such arguments have not in the past been influential in reported cases (see, e.g. *R v. Tan and Greaves* [1983] Q.B. 1053, C.A.; and note that in *J v. S-T (formerly J) (Transsexual: Ancillary Relief)* [1997] 1 FLR 402, 422, C.A., below, Ward L.J. refused to express a view on the point); but in the most recent English cases in which transsexualism has been discussed the Court of Appeal was prepared to accept "as a possibility . . . (that) the *Corbett* criteria used on their own have become . . . out of date: see *Re P and G (Transsexuals)* [1996] 2 FLR 90, 97, *per* Kennedy L.J.; and in *J v. S-T (formerly J) (Transsexual: Ancillary Relief)* [1997] 1 FLR 402, 419, C.A., Ward L.J. expressed the view that the *Corbett* decision would "bear re-examination at some appropriate time." But there is still no reported case in which an English court has accepted the validity of a purported marriage between two persons who were at birth of the same sex. Indeed, decrees of nullity have been granted in cases in which at least partial gender reassignment therapy has taken place:

In *J v. S-T (formerly J) (Transsexual: Ancillary Relief)* [1997] 1 FLR 402, C.A., a wealthy nineteen-year-old sexually inexperienced and unhappy female theology student went through a ceremony of marriage to a partner eleven years older than herself who had been brought up as a girl. Before meeting the wife he had undergone hormone treatment (as a result of which he had developed secondary male characteristics including the growth of a beard) and had had both breasts surgically removed; but the surgery had been so difficult for him that he never underwent the surgical construction of a penis recommended in such cases and he retained the genital formation of a woman. Notwithstanding this, the couple lived as husband and wife for seventeen years, having sex using a false penis made of plaster of paris. The wife did not know the husband's true gender; and she bore two children by AID having told the clinic that her husband had had a vasectomy. The relationship broke down, and eventually the husband presented a nullity petition which was undefended. (The substantive issue before the Courts of Appeal was whether he could claim financial relief against her).

Transsexuals feel that English law prevents their forming any legally recognised marital relationship: they are treated as men for the purpose of determining whether a union with a man can constitute a valid marriage; and the treatment which they have undergone may make it legally impossible for them to contract a marriage with a woman, because they will be unable to consummate such a marriage. Perhaps not surprisingly, therefore, transsexuals have invoked the provisions of the European Convention on Human Rights, and specifically Article 12 which protects the right to marry, and Article 8 which protects the right to respect for private and family life (see most recently *X, Y and Z v. The United Kingdom, The Times*, April 23, 1997, Registrar-General's refusal to allow female to male transsexual to be entered as "father" of children born to female partner following artificial insemination not inconsistent with Article 8 although it appears that the European Commission on Human Rights may take a different view: see *Horsham v. The United Kingdom* (1997) Application No. 23390/94). In both *The Rees Case* [1987] 2 FLR 111; and *Cossey v. United Kingdom* [1991] 2 FLR 492, the European Court on Human Rights accepted that the right to marry protected by the Convention is a right to contract a traditional marriage between persons of opposite biological sex. But it is noteworthy that the evidence before the Court indicated a general move towards greater legal recognition of gender reassignment, that the Court's judgment stressed the need for States which adhered to the Convention to keep their law under review, and that it appears that medical opinion may be moving away from acceptance of the views accepted in the *Corbett* case. There also appears to be some parliamentary support for a change in the law:

> In 1995 Mr Alex Carlile (supported by Mrs Edwina Currie and Glenda Jackson, amongst others) introduced a Gender Identity (Registration and Civil Status) Bill which would have empowered the court to grant transsexuals born in this country a "recognition certificate" in cases in which sex reassignment treatment had been carried out in the United Kingdom in accordance with the Act's provisions. This certificate could be registered by the Registrar General, and a new birth certificate issued.

6. Polygamous Marriages

MCA 1973, s.11(d) (as amended) provides that an actually polygamous marriage entered into after July 31, 1971 is void if either party to the marriage was at the time domiciled in England and Wales. The question of how far English law will recognise polygamous marriages contracted by those domiciled abroad is outside the scope of this book: see J.D. McClean, *Morris: The Conflict of Laws* (4th ed. 1993, page 168).

B. VOIDABLE MARRIAGES

1. Incapacity to Consummate

MCA 1973, s.13(1) provides that a marriage shall be voidable if it has not been consummated owing to the incapacity of either party to consummate it. This is a statutory codification of a basic principle of the canon law: although marriage was formed simply by consent, it was an implied term of the contract that the parties had the capacity to consummate it. Physical capacity was thus as much a basic requirement of marriage as the intellectual capacity to consent. The law is still influenced by its origins in the canon law.

Salient features of the law.   The main principles of the law can be summarised thus:

(i) *Meaning of "consummation".*
   Consummation means sexual intercourse which is "ordinary and complete": there must be both erection and penetration for a reasonable length of time. It is not necessary for either party to have an orgasm nor is infertility relevant.

(ii) *May be psychological.*
   Although some cases of incapacity are based on physical abnormality, many derive from psychological causes. This question of causation is irrelevant in deciding the issue of capacity. It follows that it is immaterial that the impotence is only *quoad hunc* or

hanc, *i.e.* that the respondent is capable of having intercourse with other partners. It also follows that a spouse who suffers from what is traditionally called "invincible repugnance" to the act of intercourse with the other will, for this purpose, be regarded as incapable of consummating the marriage. But it would seem that some element of psychiatric or sexual aversion is necessary, and that a rational decision not to permit intercourse is insufficient:

> In *Singh v. Singh* [1971] P. 226, the petitioner was a 17-year-old Sikh girl who reluctantly went through a marriage ceremony arranged by her parents with a man she had never previously met. Karminski L.J. said that she "never submitted to the physical embraces of the husband, because . . . it does not appear that she saw him again." Since she did not want to be married to him it was "understandable that she did not want to have sexual intercourse with him" but (the judge said) this was "a very long way from an invincible repugnance."

(iii) *Pre-marital intercourse irrelevant.*

The fact the parties have had intercourse prior to the marriage ceremony is irrelevant to the issue of whether the marriage has been consummated.

(iv) *The incapacity must be permanent and incurable.*

Incapacity will be deemed to be incurable if any remedial operation is dangerous, or if the respondent refuses to undergo an operation.

(v) *Evidence required.*

It is for the petitioner to prove that the incapacity exists. The court has power to order a medical examination, and may draw adverse inferences against a party who refuses to be examined.

(vi) *Either party can petition.*

Before the enactment of the Nullity of Marriage Act 1971 (subsequently consolidated in MCA 1973) a spouse who relied on his or her own incapacity would fail if, at the time of the marriage, the petitioner knew of the incapacity, or if it would in all the circumstances have been unjust to allow the petition to succeed. But there is nothing in the modern law to suggest that this rule survives, and it seems that a petitioner who knows of his or her incapacity will be entitled to a decree unless the respondent can establish the statutory bar of approbation as laid down in the Matrimonial Causes Act 1973.

(vii) *Must have existed at time of marriage?*

It was a basic requirement of the canon law that the incapacity exist at the date of the marriage. This rule reflected the great theoretical difference between recognising that incapacity could be said to have prevented a marriage coming into existence at all and dissolving a valid marriage because of some supervening cause.

Has this basic principle been changed by the modern legislation, which does not in terms require that the incapacity should have existed "at the time of the celebration of the marriage?" Could a wife whose husband is made impotent as a result of a car accident on the way from the church to the honeymoon now petition successfully for nullity? It seems clear that the statutory codification of the law was not intended to effect any change, and the courts might well interpret the provision in the light of the classical distinction between nullity and divorce, and refuse a decree in such a case.

2. Wilful Refusal to Consummate

MCA 1973, s.12(b) provides that a marriage is voidable if it has not been consummated owing to the wilful refusal of the respondent to consummate it. Conceptually, wilful refusal (which is something which occurs *after* marriage) should not be a ground for nullity, but in 1937 Parliament altered the law to allow a nullity decree to be granted on this ground.

The main features of the law are:

(i) *Must be refusal.*

A decree will only be granted if an examination of the whole history of the marriage reveals "a settled and definite decision" on the part of the respondent, "come to without just excuse." A husband (it has been held) must use appropriate tact, persuasion and encouragement and his wife will not be guilty of wilful refusal if he has failed to do so. Moreover:

> In *Potter v. Potter* (1975) 5 Fam. Law. 161, C.A., a wife was refused a decree because the husband's failure to consummate resulted from natural "loss of ardour" after a prolonged history of sexual difficulties.

(ii) *Without excuse.*

If the respondent can show a "just excuse" for the refusal to consummate there is no wilful refusal:

> In *Ford v. Ford* [1987] Fam. Law. 232 the marriage had taken place whilst H was serving a sentence of five years' imprisonment. H and W were left alone on visits for periods of up to two hours and W had heard from other visitors that it was not unusual in such circumstances for intercourse to take place. The judge held that H's refusal to have intercourse in prison (in breach of the Prison Rules) would not by itself have justified a finding that H had wilfully refused to consummate the marriage, but a decree was granted on the basis of evidence of other incidents.

The question of whether there is a just excuse for refusal to consummate a marriage has become of some importance since in the Sikh and some other ethnic minority traditions it is the practice for the parties to go through a civil marriage ceremony, and thereafter for a religious ceremony — essential by Sikh religion and practice to the recognition of the marriage — to take place, and it has been held that a husband's failure to organise the religious ceremony is not merely a just excuse for the wife's refusing to consummate the marriage, but itself amounts to a wilful refusal on his part to consummate. Thus:

> In *Kaur v. Singh* [1972] 1 W.L.R. 105 a marriage was arranged between two Sikhs. A civil ceremony took place, but the husband (notwithstanding the fact that he knew it to be his duty) refused to make arrangements for the religious ceremony. It was held that the wife was entitled to a decree on the grounds of his wilful refusal to consummate the marriage.

(iii) *Meaning of "consummation".*

The meaning of consummation has already been discussed; but the case law did not help to decide whether a marriage could be annulled if one party insisted on using a condom (as a means of birth control) or if the other refused to allow intercourse without the use of a condom. In 1947, the House of Lords (on the basis that the word "consummation" must be interpreted as understood in common parlance and in the light of social circumstances known to exist when the legislation was passed) held that a wife's refusal to allow intercourse unless her husband used a condom was not a refusal on her part to consummate the marriage: *Baxter v. Baxter* [1948] A.C. 274, H.L.

3. Lack of Consent: Duress, Mistake, Insanity, etc.

No marriage without consent.   For the Canon Law, marriage was created by the consent of the parties, and without true consent there could be no marriage. As a result of a somewhat controversial amendment made by the Nullity of Marriage Act 1971, a marriage celebrated after July 31, 1971 to which either party did not validly consent (whether in consequence of duress, mistake, unsoundness of mind or otherwise) is no longer void, but is voidable: MCA 1973, s.12(c).

The mental element in marriage: the dilemma.   Cases of lack of consent usually involve situations in which there has in fact been an *expression* of consent: for example the husband may admit that he spoke the words of consent but say that he only did so because his bride's father was standing behind him with a shotgun. In such cases it can be argued that the apparent consent is not real, and that there should in principle be no marriage; but it would obviously give rise to uncertainty if an apparently valid marriage could be avoided by subsequently claiming the existence of a state of mind or belief which was not evident at the time of the ceremony.

The solution.   English law seeks to resolve this juristic dilemma by, on the one hand refusing to allow private reservations or motives to vitiate an ostensibly valid marriage, whilst on the other hand accepting that there may be cases in which there has been no consent at all. The law is complex, and the cases can best be considered under the three heads specifically referred to in the legislation: (a) insanity; (b) duress and fear; (c) mistake and fraud.

(a) Insanity.   Marriage (according to a 19th century judge) is a very simple contract, which it does not require a high degree of intelligence to understand: Sir James Hannen P. in *Durham v. Durham* (1885) 10 P.D. 80, 81. Mental illness or incapacity will only affect the validity of consent if either spouse was, at the time of the ceremony incapable of understanding the nature of marriage and the duties and responsibilities it creates.

Such incapacity is hard to establish, and it is difficult to believe that petitions will now be brought on this ground. A husband or wife who wants to terminate the marriage because of the other's mental condition will usually be able to rely on the alternative "mental illness" ground introduced by legislation precisely because it was so difficult to establish lack of consent.

In the past relatives whose succession rights had been adversely affected by the marriage might claim, after the death of one of the parties, that the marriage had been invalid, but since the Nullity of Marriage Act 1971 a marriage affected by lack of consent is voidable only and no claim can be brought by a third party or after the death of either spouse.

(b) Duress and fear.   Unlike some parts of the law of nullity, this is a matter of practical importance — particularly in the context of marriages arranged in accordance with ethnic minority customs and marriages contracted in order to acquire citizenship or immigration rights.

The question for the court is whether there has been a real consent. Hence (it has been said) "where a formal consent is brought about by force, menace or duress" a yielding of the lips, not of the mind, it is of no legal effect: see *Szechter v. Szechter* [1971] P. 286. The main conditions seem to be as follows:

(i) *Must be overriding fear.*

This principle is most clearly illustrated by an American "shotgun" marriage case: the marriage was void because (said the judge) "if there had not been a wedding, there would have been a funeral": *Lee v. Lee* (1928) 3 S.W. 2d 672.

In contrast, if the marriage is deliberately contracted, (albeit only out of a sense of obligation to family or religious tradition) it cannot be annulled on this ground:

> In *Singh v. Singh* [1971] P. 226, the bride had never seen her husband before the marriage, and only went through the ceremony out of a "proper respect" for her parents and Sikh traditions. The court refused to annul the marriage because there was no evidence of fear.

(ii) *Test subjective.*

At one time, case law supported the view that only a threat of immediate danger to life, limb or liberty could suffice to justify the granting of a decree of nullity on this ground. But the reality is that a weak-minded person's will may be overcome by threats which would have had no impact on a stronger character. Accordingly, the view adopted by the Court of Appeal in *Hirani v. Hirani* (1982) 4 FLR 232 — a case in which a 19-year-old Hindu girl was told by her parents to break off a relationship with a Muslim boy-friend and that she "had better marry someone we want you to, otherwise pick up your bags and go" — that the test is simply whether the threats or pressure are such as to destroy the reality of the consent and to overbear the will of the individual is much to be welcomed, leading as it did to a decree in that case. Again, in the Irish decision of *W(C) v. W* [1989] I.R. 696:

> A pregnant woman was pressurised by her parents to get married. She was told by her employer that she would lose her job if she remained unmarried. She was granted a decree of nullity.

(iii) *Fear must arise from external circumstances, but not necessarily from acts of the other party.*

This may be a factor in cases in which the decision to marry was influenced by the wish to acquire the other party's immigration or nationality status. For example:

In *Szechter v. Szechter* [1971] P. 286 threats to life and liberty arising from the policies of a totalitarian regime were held to suffice: the parties married so that they would be allowed to leave the country and thus avoid imprisonment.

The *Szechter* case demonstrates the fine distinctions drawn in the application of the law. On one view, although the parties were no doubt frightened, their decision to marry was a conscious and a rational one: they wanted to be married so that they could enjoy the legal consequences of matrimony. Had that view been taken by the court the application for a nullity decree would have had to be dismissed (although today a divorce order, permitting the parties to remarry, would readily have been made).

(iv) *Does it make any difference if the threats are justly imposed?*

Suppose that (as in *Buckland v. Buckland* [1968] P. 296) a man is told he will be prosecuted for unlawful sexual intercourse unless he marries the girl with whom he is alleged to have had intercourse. On one view such a petition will fail if the petitioner is guilty: a decree may be obtained only if the accusation is false, or if the petitioner was threatened with a more severe penalty than the courts impose (as in an American case where the man was told that having sexual intercourse with a minor was "a hanging matter"). But it is submitted that this view of the law is illogical and contrary to principle. The justice of the threat has nothing to do with the subjective question of consent.

(c) **Mistake and fraud.**   Generally neither mistake nor fraud avoids a marriage. The maxim "caveat emptor" ("let the buyer beware") applies, it has been said, just as much to marriage as it does to other contracts. Even fraud is not a vitiating factor if it induces consent, but only if it procures the appearance without the reality of consent. Hence, a marriage into which a woman tricked a man by concealing the fact that she was pregnant by a third party was valid at common law. (Since 1937 it has been possible, subject to certain conditions, to have a marriage annulled on the ground that the respondent was pregnant by a third party). Hence, mistake can only be relevant if it destroys the apparent consent. The cases fall into three groups:

(i) *Mistake as to the person as distinct from his attributes.*

If I marry A under the belief that she is B this is sufficient to invalidate the marriage; but if I marry A erroneously believing her to be a rich heiress the marriage will be unimpeachable.

(ii) *Mistake as to the nature of the ceremony.*

False beliefs that the petitioner was appearing in a police court, or that the ceremony was a betrothal or religious conversion ceremony (*Mehta v. Mehta* [1945] 2 All E.R. 690) have been held sufficient to invalidate the marriage. The fact that one of the parties was so drunk (or under the influence of drugs) as not to know what was happening is also sufficient: *Sullivan v. Sullivan* (1812) 2 Hag. Con. 238, 246.

(iii) *But mistake about legal consequences of marriage insufficient.*

This principle is exemplified by *Messina v. Smith* [1971] P. 322:

W went through a marriage ceremony, knowing that it was such a ceremony, and that the purpose of it was to enable her to obtain British nationality and a British passport and thereby protect herself against the risk of deportation for offences incidental to her trade of prostitution. A petition to annul the marriage failed. The parties did intend to acquire the status of married persons, and it was immaterial that one or both of them may have been mistaken about, or unaware of, some of the incidents of that status.

There may be thought to be public policy factors pointing in favour of denying legal remedies to those who have contracted marriages in such circumstances, but the rule that mistake as to the legal consequences of the relationship will not found a nullity petition caused hardship in a number of cases at the end of World War II in which men discovered that the Soviet authorities would not allow wives to join their spouses in the West: see for example *Way v. Way* [1950] P. 71. Today, once again, the solution would be found in divorce but at the time divorce was only available on proof of a matrimonial offence.

4. Venereal Disease, Pregnancy by Another and Mental Illness

The remaining grounds on which a marriage may be annulled were primarily intended to deal with problems caused by the absence of any matrimonial relief for fraudulent or wilful concealment of material facts: for example, a man who discovered that his wife was carrying another man's child had no ground for matrimonial relief; deceit was not a ground for annulment, and the pregnancy did not establish that the wife had, since the marriage, committed adultery. New grounds were accordingly created in 1937; and they are now:

(i) that at the time of the marriage the respondent was suffering from *venereal disease* in a communicable form. (It is unclear whether AIDS is a venereal disease for this purpose: it was felt necessary to amend the National Health Service (Venereal Disease) Regulations 1968 No. 1624 to include all sexually transmitted diseases, and not merely those commonly known as Venereal Disease: see *X v. Y and others* [1988] 2 All E.R. 648);

(ii) that at the time of the marriage the respondent was *pregnant by some person other than the petitioner*;

(iii) that at the time of the marriage either party, though capable of giving a valid consent, was suffering (whether continuously or intermittently) from *mental disorder* within the meaning of the Mental Health Act 1983, of such a kind or to such an extent as to be unfitted for marriage. A petitioner may rely on his or her own mental disorder for the purpose of a petition on this ground. This provision is intended to cover the case where, although the afflicted party is capable of giving a valid consent to the marriage, the mental disorder makes him or her incapable of carrying on a normal married life.

C. bars to the grant of a nullity decree

If one of the grounds set out above is established, the petitioner will usually be entitled to a decree. However, if the marriage is voidable (there are no longer any bars to the granting of a decree where the "marriage" is void) the petition may still fail if one of three bars contained in MCA 1973 s.13 is established. The three bars are:

1. Time

In the case of proceedings on the ground of (a) lack of consent, (b) venereal disease, or (c) pregnancy by a third party it is an absolute bar that proceedings were not instituted within three years of the marriage.

2. Knowledge of Defect

A petition founded on (a) venereal disease or (b) pregnancy by a third party will fail unless the petitioner can satisfy the court that, at the time of the marriage, the petitioner was ignorant of the facts alleged. It is not sufficient that the husband knew that the wife was pregnant, he must also have known that she was pregnant by another man.

3. "Approbation"

MCA 1973, s.13(1) provides that the court shall not grant a decree of nullity on the ground that a marriage is voidable if the respondent satisfies the court:

> "(a) that the petitioner, with knowledge that it was open to him to have the marriage avoided, so conducted himself in relation to the respondent as to lead the respondent reasonably to believe that he would not seek to do so; and
> (b) that it would be unjust to the respondent to grant the decree."

This bar replaces the complex and uncertain bar of approbation inherited from the ecclesiastical courts. Three separate matters must be proved:

(i) *conduct* by the petitioner in relation to the respondent which resulted in the respondent reasonably believing that the petitioner would not seek to have the marriage annulled;

(ii) *knowledge* on the petitioner's part at the time of the conduct relied on that the marriage could be annulled; and

(iii) *injustice* to the respondent if a decree were to be granted.

These bars have been relevant in one not uncommon fact situation: *the case of companionship marriages*. Suppose, for example, that an elderly widower marries a spinster on the understanding that they are not to have sexual relations and that their marriage is to be "for companionship only." After living together for some years, the husband changes his mind and seeks to have sexual relations. The wife (who had at the husband's request given up a job carrying pension rights) refuses. Will she be able successfully to defend a nullity petition alleging wilful refusal?

It would seem that if the wife could prove that the husband knew that nullity was available in cases of non-consummation she might do so, since in this case the loss of pension rights could probably constitute injustice to her.

But it is important to note that there is *no general public interest bar* to the grant of nullity decrees (although as seen at p. 35, above it is possible that public interest factors have had some influence on the interpretation of the grounds on which a decree may be granted). The law is now only concerned with the conduct of the parties towards each other and with injustice to the respondent. It is not concerned with representations which have been made to third parties, or with considerations of public policy. For example,

> In *D v. D (Nullity: Statutory Bar)* [1979] Fam. 70 the fact that a couple adopted a child (and thus represented to the court considering the adoption application that they were husband and wife) did not debar one of them from subsequently petitioning for nullity on the ground of wilful refusal. The fact that it might be thought contrary to public policy to allow either party subsequently to assert that the marriage was a nullity was not relevant.

D. EFFECTS OF A DECREE

Historical evolution

At one time a void marriage had no legal consequences. Hence, for example, any children born to the parties would necessarily be illegitimate; neither party to the relationship would be entitled to acquire the other's British citizenship or to inherit on the other's intestacy, and a man could not be required to maintain a woman who had been living with him in the belief that they were married. In the eyes of the law they were not, and never had been, more than a man and mistress.

The same consequences followed even if the marriage was only voidable. This was because, although the marriage was valid until annulled, the decree, when made operated retrospectively: the marriage became void *ab initio, i.e.* from the outset.

Modern law

Over the years the law has been reformed in attempts to meet hardship sometimes caused by the common law rules:

(a) Voidable marriages: decrees not retroactive. Under the law as it stood before 1971 the parties to a voidable marriage were validly married until annulment, but once a decree absolute had been pronounced they were deemed never to have been married. Thus:

> In *Re Rodwell* [1970] Ch. 726 the deceased's daughter could only qualify as a "dependant" for the purposes of making a claim under the Inheritance (Family Provision) Act 1938 if she had "not been married." The daughter's voidable marriage had in fact been annulled; and Pennycuick J. held that because of the retrospective effect of the decree she qualified as a person who had not been married. (It will be noted that in this case the rule worked to the daughter's advantage.)

This rule was abolished in 1971 on the basis that it was anomalous, inconvenient and uncertain, and a voidable marriage which is annulled is now treated as if it had existed up to the date of the decree.

Unfortunately, it has become apparent that in some cases the new rule may have unfortunate consequences:

In *Ward v. Secretary of State for Social Services* [1990] 1 FLR 119 the widow of an army officer went through a ceremony of marriage. The husband — as the petitioner discovered for the first time after the ceremony — was a manic depressive and behaved in an aggressive way towards her. Within less than a week the marriage had effectively come to an end. In due course a decree of nullity was granted on the ground that the marriage had not been consummated. It was held that, since the "marriage" had come into existence, the petitioner had thereupon ceased to be the army officer's widow, and was thus no longer entitled to a widow's pension.

(b) Legitimacy of children. Children of voidable marriages are legitimate because the marriage is treated as valid. Even the child of a void marriage will be "treated as" the legitimate child of the mother and father provided that at the time of the act of intercourse resulting in the birth (or at the time of the celebration of the marriage if later) both or either of the parties reasonably believed that the marriage was valid. It is immaterial that the belief in the validity of the marriage was based on a mistake of law: see Legitimacy Act 1976, s.1(3) as amended by the Family Law Reform Act 1987, s.28. However, a child will only be treated as legitimate under these provisions if the birth occurred *after* the void marriage: see *Re Spence (dec'd)* [1990] 2 FLR 278, C.A.

(c) Financial provision for parties. If the marriage is voidable, the parties financial rights are the same before annulment as if the parties had been validly married; and the court has similar financial powers on granting a decree of nullity to those which it has on divorce.

If the marriage is void the parties are not married, and they have no legal rights as husband and wife. But if a decree of nullity is obtained, the court will have the power to order one party to make financial provision for the other in much the same way as it would have on making a divorce order in respect of a valid marriage. Hence, in *Cossey v. The United Kingdom* [1991] 2 FLR 492, 496, a transsexual obtained a decree of nullity precisely because she had been advised that this was the only means open to her of obtaining financial relief. Again a "wife" or "husband" who has obtained a nullity decree is eligible to apply to the court for reasonable provision out of the other's estate after the death. But the fact that the court has power to make financial orders does not mean that it will in fact do so:

In *Whiston v. Whiston* [1995] 2 FLR 268, C.A. Mr Whiston married a woman from the Phillipines who knew that her first husband was still living. Sixteen years later the couple (who had had two children) separated, and the fact that the "marriage" was bigamous came to light. The Court of Appeal held that Mrs Whiston would have had no right to financial orders under the court's discretionary matrimonial jurisdiction had she remained an unmarried cohabitant; and any rights she might have under that jurisdiction therefore flowed from the fact that she had committed the crime of bigamy. The Court of Appeal accordingly held that her claim was defeated by the principle of public policy debarring a criminal from profiting from the criminal act.

Does this mean that anyone who has committed a criminal offence in connection with the "marriage" is debarred from claiming financial relief under the matrimonial code?

In *J v. S-T (formerly J) (Transsexual: Ancillary Relief)* [1997] 1 FLR 402, a female to male transsexual was held to have committed the crime of perjury by making declarations under the Marriage Act 1949 that there was no impediment to a marriage with a wealthy female theology student. The Court of Appeal unanimously held that the transsexual's claim for financial relief should be dismissed; but the majority based their decision on the very wide discretion conferred on the court by the matrimonial finance legislation, and were not prepared to extend the *Whiston* principle beyond the bigamist. It seems that in the view of the majority a claim for financial relief could successfully be made notwithstanding some comparatively unimportant misrepresentation perhaps about the parties' residence.

E. CONCLUSION: DO WE NEED THE LAW OF NULLITY?

The law of nullity has lost much of its practical importance because many of the legal consequences of marriages have now been attached even to a void marriage, while virtually all marriages can sooner or later be dissolved by divorce if either party wishes it. The law has been totally transformed since the days before the Divorce Reform Act 1969 when a divorce could be obtained only if one party could prove that the other had committed a matrimonial offence, and nullity was the only alternative legal way of escape. As Anthony Lincoln J. put it in *A v. J (Nullity Proceedings)* [1989] FLR 110, 111:

> "Nullity proceedings are nowadays rare, though not wholly extinct. It is unfortunate that these had to be fought out . . . there would have been no difficulty in pronouncing mutual decrees nisi, dissolving the marriage, if the necessary consent (to a divorce) had been forthcoming."

In view of the unpleasantness of nullity proceedings (which may involve medical examinations and will normally involve a full court hearing) it is sometimes suggested that the concept of the voidable marriage might be abolished; instead the parties should be left to obtain a divorce based on the breakdown of their marriage. This has been done in Australia, but the Law Commission rejected such a solution for this country. However, the additional complexities introduced into the divorce process by the Family Law Act 1996, and in particular the length of time which may have to pass before the marriage is finally terminated, may mean that in a small number of cases nullity proceedings founded on non-consummation may become the preferred method of obtaining what is sometimes irreverently called a "licence to remarry."

Chapter 3

ENDING MARRIAGE: DIVORCE

A. INTRODUCTION: THE NATURE OF DIVORCE

For the lawyer, marriage creates a legal status from which legally enforceable rights and duties arise. From the same perspective, divorce simply terminates that legal status: thereafter, neither party has the legal rights or owes the legal duties attaching to marriage. Divorce brings to an end a legal relationship, but it has no direct bearing on personal relationships: a couple may have cohabited for only a few days after marriage and thereafter lived apart for many years, consumed with mutual hatred and bitterness. But so far as the law is concerned they remain a married couple entitled to the rights flowing from the legal relationship of man and wife. Conversely, divorce does not necessarily bring the parties' personal relationships to an end; and the fact that there will often be children to be cared for is one of the strongest arguments used in favour of a divorce procedure which will minimise the risk of damaging the ability of the spouses to continue to act as parents.

B. EVOLUTION OF THE LAW

The Family Law Act 1996 will bring about a fundamental change in the legal rules governing the dissolution of marriages; but the law cannot be understood without some knowledge of its historical development.

Before the Matrimonial Causes Act 1857: divorce by Act of Parliament. Until the Reformation, English law followed the canon law of the Catholic Church in not permitting divorce in the sense in which that word is used today. By the 18th century a procedure for divorce by private Act of Parliament had been developed, but this procedure was expensive and was increasingly criticised.

Judicial Divorce: the Matrimonial Offence 1857–1969. In response to this criticism, the Matrimonial Causes Act 1857 created the Court for Divorce and Matrimonial Causes, and gave the court power to dissolve marriages if the petitioner could prove adultery, that he was free of any matrimonial guilt, and that there was no connivance or collusion between the parties. Divorce by judicial process was thus made available, but only to an injured and legally guiltless spouse.

Modifications were made to the law over the years. In 1923, Parliament allowed a wife (who had previously to prove some aggravating feature) to petition for divorce on the same ground as a husband. In 1937 the grounds for divorce were widened to include cruelty, desertion and incurable insanity, but in theory at least it was still not possible to obtain a divorce by consent. More importantly, it was not possible to obtain a divorce against an "innocent" spouse unless he or she was incurably insane. A man might have left his wife 20 or 30 years ago and committed himself to another woman by whom he had children. But he would not be able to marry her so long as his first wife refused to divorce him and (by abstaining from committing any matrimonial offence) did not provide her husband with any grounds for divorce. Such "stable illicit unions" not only caused unhappiness to the two adults but condemned their children to the category of bastard with all the legal disadvantages then flowing from illegitimacy.

Pressures for reform.   The administration of the law founded on the matrimonial offence law also involved much unpleasantness; for example a petitioner who had committed adultery was not guiltless, and could thus only obtain a divorce if the court "exercised its discretion" in the petitioner's favour. This involved the petitioner filing a so-called "discretion statement" containing full details of the petitioner's transgressions. As recently as 1969, the Court of Appeal held that it was not sufficient for a solicitor to make sure the petitioner understood the meaning of "adultery" (unlike the petitioners who had told a judge: "I did not think it was adultery during the daytime"; "I thought it meant drinking with men in public houses"; "it is not adultery if she is over 50": see *Barnacle v. Barnacle* [1948] P. 257.) The solicitor also had to warn the client of the need to disclose adultery committed at any time before the case was actually heard: *Pearson v. Pearson* [1971] P. 16. Not surprisingly, therefore, there was strong pressure for change not only from those who wished to be able to remarry but also from within the legal profession.

Bills designed to allow divorce on proof of seven years' separation attracted considerable support, but the crucial breakthrough came with the publication in 1966 of *Putting Asunder*, the report of a Committee set up by the Archbishop of Canterbury. This report favoured, as the lesser of two evils, the substitution of the doctrine of breakdown for that of the matrimonial offence and was essentially the catalyst for the divorce reforms effected by the Divorce Reform Act 1969. But the Archbishop's Committee thought that in order to answer the question whether the marriage had indeed broken down the court should carry out a detailed inquest into "the alleged fact and causes of the 'death' of a marriage relationship." The Committee also proposed that the court should be obliged to refuse a decree (notwithstanding proof of breakdown) if to grant it would be contrary to the public interest in justice and in protecting the institution of marriage.

The Field of Choice.   The Lord Chancellor immediately referred *Putting Asunder* to the newly established Law Commission. The Commission took as its starting point that a good divorce law should seek "(i) To buttress, rather than to undermine, the stability of marriage; and (ii) when, regrettably, a marriage has irretrievably broken down, to enable the empty legal shell to be destroyed with the maximum fairness, and the minimum bitterness, distress and humiliation." The Commission rejected the view that a divorce law, which is directed essentially towards dissolving the marriage bond, could do nothing towards upholding the status of marriage. The Commission considered that the law could "and should ensure that divorce is not so easy that the parties are under no inducement to make a success of their marriage and, in particular, to overcome temporary difficulties. It can also ensure that every encouragement is afforded to a reconciliation and that the procedure is not such as to inhibit or discourage approaches to that end." But the Commission rejected, on the ground that it would be humiliating and distressing to the parties, and would necessitate a vast increase in expenditure of money and human resources, the Archbishop's Committee's proposal that an inquiry be held in every case into the breakdown.

Eventually, the Commission and the Archbishop's Group reached agreement on the principles ultimately embodied in the Divorce Reform Act 1969. This principle is that breakdown should be the sole ground for divorce, but breakdown was not to be the subject of a detailed inquest by the court; instead it was to be inferred, either from the occurrence of certain facts akin to the old matrimonial offences of adultery, cruelty (renamed "behaviour") and desertion or from the fact that the parties had lived apart for two years (if the parties agreed on divorce) or for five years (if they were not agreed).

The divorce process under the Divorce Reform Act 1969. The Divorce Reform Act 1969 (which came into force in 1971) certainly achieved its objective of allowing the "empty legal shells" or many marriages which had irretrievably broken down to be crushed: in 1971 nearly 30,000 petitions (more than a quarter of the total) were based on the five year "living apart" fact. But the Act seems to have been much less successful in its other declared objectives:

(i) *Buttressing Marriage?*
Notwithstanding the view that once the initial "bulge" of those who had been denied divorce had been dealt with, the divorce rate would stabilise, in fact until very recently it continued to increase. In 1971 (the first year of the operation of the new law) there had been 110,017 petitions, and by 1993 the number of petitions had increased to 184,171. The divorce rate (13.5 divorces per thousand married couples) was one of the highest in Western Europe. As many as 150,000 children each year were exposed to the experience of parental divorce, and the legislation seemed to have been ineffective in encouraging couples to have recourse to reconciliation procedures. Nothwithstanding the fact that the number of divorce petitions fell somewhat in 1994 and 1995 (when 173,966 petitions were filed) it seems beyond argument that there has been much more divorce since the 1969 reforms.

(ii) *Minimising bitterness, distress and humiliation?*
Proponents of the 1969 reforms assumed that breakdown would usually be inferred from the fact that the parties had lived apart for two years and were agreed on divorce, but this belief was soon falsified. Three-quarters of all divorce petitions were based on adultery or "behaviour", and in 1988 the Law Commission concluded that the necessity of making allegations in the petition "drew the battle-lines" at the outset, and that the ensuing hostility made the divorce painful for the parties and the children.

(iii) *Divorce process incomprehensible and incoherent?*
Perhaps the most significant change in the divorce process was not the new substantive law contained in the Divorce Reform Act 1969, but the introduction in 1973 of the so-called "special procedure" intended to achieve simplicity, speed and

economy (Latey J., *R v. Nottinghamshire County Court, ex parte Byers* [1985] FLR 695). Under the "special procedure" a petitioner completes a standard form of petition, which is lodged (together with an affidavit verifying the truth of the answers to a standard form of questionnaire) at the court office and considered by a District Judge in private. If the District Judge is satisfied that the petitioner has sufficiently proved the contents of the petition and is entitled to a decree — and there are occasions when District Judges reject petitions, perhaps (for example) if the allegation of "behaviour" is simply "that the Respondent often went to see football matches at Aston Villa": see District Judge A. Armon-Jones, (1997) 147 New L.J. 434 — he will make and file a certificate to that effect. There is no machinery for investigating the truth of the allegations unless there are circumstances which give rise to suspicion: see e.g. *Callaghan v. Hanson-Fox and Another* [1991] 2 FLR 519 (where a respondent to a petition founded on living apart subsequently claimed that at all material times he had been living with the petitioner and continued to do so until her death); and *Moynihan v. Moynihan (Nos. 1 and 2)* [1997] 1 FLR 59 (where a petitioner obtained a decree based on his wife's alleged adultery without her having any knowledge of the proceedings at all). Once the District Judge has given the certificate the divorce decree can then be pronounced in open court, often by using the formula "I pronounce decree nisi in cases 1 to 50". Neither party need attend.

The "special procedure" is only available in undefended cases — and occasionally petitions are defended, and the defence sometimes succeeds:

> In *Butterworth v. Butterworth* (1997) February 7, unreported, C.A. the wife's divorce petition alleged that the husband was an alcoholic, violent, possessive, jealous and sexually demanding. He denied these allegations and denied that the marriage had broken down irretrievably. At first instance the judge held that the wife had failed to prove any of the allegations; but he nonetheless pronounced a decree because he was satisfied that the marriage had broken down irretrievably. The Court of Appeal held that he had been wrong to do so. The judge had been wrong not to require proof of facts constituting "behaviour", and to have given the impression that it was unreasonable for husbands to object to divorce and that evidence in support of a petition was little more than a formality.

But such cases are rare. The reality is that almost all divorce petitions are undefended. There are a number of reasons for this. First, if either party wants a divorce he or she will today in practice sooner or later be able to obtain one, and a solicitor is therefore likely to advise a client not to oppose the grant of the decree but perhaps rather to bargain for satisfactory financial and other arrangements as the price for not putting the petitioner to the trouble and expense of dealing with a defended case. Secondly, the cost of litigation usually makes it "unrealistic, if not impossible" for most couples to pursue their suits to a fully contested hearing, and if it is clear that the marriage has irretrievably broken down legal aid is not usually available to a respondent to enable him or her to defend a divorce petition. Finally, as the *Report of the Matrimonial Causes Procedure Committee* (Chairman, Mrs Justice Booth DBE) put it in 1985, the court itself "discourages defended divorce not only because of the futility of trying a contention by one party that the marriage has not broken down despite the other party's conviction that it has, but also because of the emotional and financial demands that it makes upon the parties themselves and the possible harmful consequences for the children of the family."

There is evidence that the special procedure made the divorce law incoherent and confusing for those involved. The incidents relied on in the petition may be exaggerated, one-sided or even untrue (as the Law Commission put it in its report *The Ground for Divorce*, Law Com. No. 192, 1990, paragraph 2.17), and those who believed themselves denied any realistic possibility of putting the record straight might well suffer a burning sense of injustice. The resultant bitterness may then find some expression in proceedings relating to the financial and child-upbringing consequences of divorce, which (if contested) continue to be dealt with in a traditional court hearing.

The move for further reform: background to the Family Law Act 1996. Dissatisfaction with the law and practice led the Law Commission to re-examine the divorce process, and a Report with draft legislation, *The Ground for Divorce*, was published in 1990. The Commission accepted most of the criticisms set out above, and thought the law defective in that it failed to give the parties an "opportunity to come to terms with what was happening in their lives, to reflect in as calm and sensible way as possible upon the future, and to re-negotiate their relationship." The Commission thought that the law should concentrate rather on bringing parties to an understanding of the practical reality of divorce — what it would be like "to live apart, to break up the common home, to finance two households where before there was only one, and to have or to lose day to day responsibility for the children . . ." (paragraph 2). The Commission considered that, above all, the law failed to reflect the reality of divorce as a *process*: divorce was not a final product but part of "a massive transition" for the parties and their children; and it was crucial in the interests of the children as well as the parties that the transition be as smooth as possible in order to make the quality of the parents' post-divorce relationship with the children as good as possible.

What then should replace the defective law? The Commission rejected a number of possible options for reform: return to a wholly fault-based system, divorce after a full enquiry into whether the relationship had indeed irretrievably broken down, divorce by unilateral notice, divorce by mutual consent, divorce based on living apart for a period of time; and thought the law should treat divorce not as a separate event but as part of a process of facing up to and resolving its practical, social and emotional consequences over a period of time. The Commission concluded that there was still "overwhelming support" for the view that irretrievable breakdown should remain the "fundamental basis" for divorce; and the complaint, it seemed, was not of the breakdown principle itself but rather of the legal rules and procedures by which breakdown was established.

The Government, after an extensive further consultation process, accepted the main thrust of the Law Commission's proposals for "divorce after a period for the consideration of future arrangements and for reflection"; and the Conservative Government introduced the Family Law Bill in November 1995. However, the Bill — the first Government sponsored Bill on the ground for divorce this century — did not have an easy passage through Parliament. No fewer than one hundred and twelve Conservative MPs (including the Home Secretary and four other ministers) voted against the Government in a free vote in the House of Commons on whether a fault-based ground for divorce should be retained; and many concessions had to be made to groups whose ideology was very different from that which had influenced the drafting of the Bill. The result is legislation which is in some respects internally inconsistent.

C. the divorce process under the family law act 1996

The 1996 Act seeks to promote a remarkable relationship between the legal process necessary to end the legal status of marriage and various measures (perhaps most accurately classified as measures of applied social work), which seek, first, to identify marriages which can be saved, and secondly, to minimise the damage done to children by marital breakdown and its consequences. Section 1 of the Act itself embodies a statement of the general principles underlying the legislation which constitute an assertion of the framework within which the legislation is intended to operate:

> "The court and any person, in exercising functions under or in consequence of Parts II and III" of the Act (*i.e.* those provisions relating to Divorce and Separation and to Legal Aid for Mediation in Family Matters) "shall have regard to the following general principles:
>
> (a)   that the institution of marriage is to be supported;
>
> (b)   that the parties to a marriage which may have broken down are to be encouraged to take all practicable steps, whether by marriage counselling or otherwise, to save the marriage;
>
> (c)   that a marriage which has irretrievably broken down and is being brought to an end should be brought to an end:
>
>> (i)   with minimum distress to the parties and to the children affected;
>>
>> (ii)   with questions dealt with in a manner designed to promote as good a continuing relationship between the parties and any children affected as is possible in the circumstances; and
>>
>> (iii)   without costs being unreasonably incurred in connection with the procedures to be followed in bringing it to an end; and
>
> (d)   that any risk to one of the parties to a marriage, and to any children, of violence from the other party should, so far as reasonably practicable, be removed or diminished."

The Act makes a potentially significant breakthrough in two respects. First, it contains provisions intended to strengthen marriage support and thereby to diminish the force of the criticism that the law has given inadequate weight to the need to buttress marriage. Secondly, it contains provisions designed to encourage those whose marriages have broken down and who wish to have them dissolved to come to their own agreements (rather than submitting to adjudication by a court) on the consequences of the divorce by providing the assistance of a third party facilitator or mediator.

The text summarises, first, the provisions dealing with marriage support, secondly, the framework for facilitating recourse to mediation rather than litigation, and thirdly, the details of the procedures whereby a court may make a divorce order dissolving the parties' marriage.

1. Marriage Support

Public financial support for marriage counselling was first provided following a recommendation made by a Committee under the chairmanship of Mr Justice Denning (formerly a judge of the Divorce division of the High Court) as long ago as

1947. But such support has always seemed to have been given on a severely restricted basis. The Family Law Act (s. 22(1)) seeks to put this funding on a more secure basis by giving the Lord Chancellor, who has taken over responsibility for marriage support from the Home Office, power to make grants in connection with (a) the provision of marriage support services; (b) research into the causes of marital breakdown; and (c) research into ways of preventing marital breakdown.

In 1995 the Lord Chancellor launched a "Marriage Taskforce", and a number of pilot projects intended to reduce the incidence of marriage breakdown — ranging from a media campaign to change the culture of marriage, through marriage preparation for couples not marrying in church, to various telephone helplines — were launched in April 1997. The Family Law Act 1996, reflecting the general belief that prospects of reconciliation are sharply reduced with the passage of time, provides that the Lord Chancellor is to have regard, in particular, to the desirability of marriage support services being available when first needed: s.22(3).

Information about the availability of counselling is to be given at the information meeting which everyone contemplating divorce must attend before starting proceedings: s.8(9)(a). Legal representatives are to be required to inform clients about the availability of marriage support services and to supply names and addresses of people qualified to help effect a reconciliation (s. 12(2)) and it seems that a person seeking a divorce order will be required to state the steps taken to explore the possibility of reconciliation: see *Official Report* (H.L.) February 29, 1996, cols. 1689–1692.

There are also provisions enabling a couple who feel that they need additional time to attempt a reconciliation to stop the running of the period for reflection and consideration. (The period starts again if *either* party gives notice that the attempted reconciliation has been unsuccessful (s.7(8)(b)).

These provisions are undoubtedly well-motivated, and the Lord Chancellor's Department has launched a research programme to investigate the causes of marriage breakdown and ways of preventing it (s.22(1)(b), (c)). But quite how effective they will be in practice remains to be seen: there was some suggestion in the parliamentary debates that funding for marriage support services would be conditional on the organisation concerned proving that its attempts had led to marriages being "saved", and there are obvious difficulties in assessing "effectiveness" in such a context.

2. Mediation to be preferred to adjudication

Marriage support is intended to save marriages: the parties will not go through with the divorce they had contemplated. Mediation has a different objective: it is concerned to help divorcing couples negotiate their own arrangements for the consequences of the breakdown — particularly in relation to the arrangements to be made about children's upbringing and about financial matters. The Government's White Paper *Looking to the Future* (1995, Cm 2799, paragraphs 5.4–5.6) defined the process in these words:

> Family mediation is a process in which an impartial third person, the mediator, assists couples considering separation or divorce to meet together to deal with the arrangements which need to be made for the future. Because the parties discuss these matters face to face, family mediation is much better able to identify marriages which might be capable of being saved than is the legal process . . . [It] has as its primary objectives: to help separating and divorcing

couples to reach their own agreed joint decisions about future arrangements; to improve communications between them; and to help couples work together on the practical consequences of divorce with particular emphasis on their joint responsibilities to co-operate as parents in bringing up their children.

This enthusiasm for mediation was surprising for those who had noted the mixed messages derived from research and the scepticism displayed by previous official enquiries (not to mention the consistent refusal by Government to provide any assurance of funding for the various mediation services established by voluntary initiatives); but the 1996 Act is based on an unequivocal acceptance that mediation has "enormous potential" to minimise the adverse consequences of marital breakdown. Thus, the Act contains provisions to ensure that the parties are aware of the benefits offered by mediation, are given the opportunity to take advantage of mediation services, and (if they are eligible for legal aid) have the cost of mediation met from public funds. These provisions are explained at the appropriate stages in the text below.

3. The legal procedures for obtaining a divorce order

The legal process for obtaining a divorce order is complex, involving the following steps:

(a) Attendance at an information meeting;
(b) Filing a statement of marital breakdown;
(c) The passage of a period of time for "reflection and consideration";
(d) Settling the parties' arrangements for the future;
(e) Obtaining the divorce order.

Some readers may find it helpful to refer to the schematic table on p. 62.

(a) The information meeting
Although it is the making of a statement of marital breakdown ("a statement") which starts the legal process leading to the making of a divorce order, the Family Law Act 1996 provides that a spouse must have attended an information meeting not less than three months before filing the statement. Details of the information meeting are to be left to delegated legislation, but the Act provides (section 8(9)) that Regulations *must* make provision with respect to the giving of information about (a) marriage counselling and other marriage support services; (b) the importance to be attached to the welfare, wishes and feelings of children; (c) how the parties may acquire a better understanding of the ways in which children can be helped to cope with the breakdown of a marriage; (d) the nature of the financial question that may arise on divorce or separation, and services which are available to help the parties; (e) protection against violence, and how to obtain support and assistance; (f) mediation; (g) the availability to each of the parties of independent legal advice and representation; (h) the principles of legal aid and where the parties can get advice about obtaining legal aid; (i) the divorce and separation process. The meeting is also to be used to give the parties an opportunity (which they are to be encouraged to take) of having a meeting with a marriage counsellor (section 8(6) (b)).

Pilot schemes have been set up and are being monitored prior to implementation of the Act, but many questions remain to be answered. It seems clear, for example, that the meetings are intended to be individual (rather than group) encounters, but little is known about who is to provide them, where they are to be provided, or about such important matters as confidentiality and privacy. The Government at one stage (see the *1995 Divorce White Paper*, paragraph 7.9.) insisted that the purpose of the meetings was to be strictly limited to the provision of *information* and that legal *advice* (in the sense of an explanation of how the law would apply to the facts of a particular case) was not to be given; and it will be interesting to see how far those attending an information meeting will be adequately informed about the provision which might best suit their own particular circumstances and values. Suggestions have been made that the choice of those selected to participate in the pilot projects reflects an excessive reliance on organisations connected with the provision of mediation, and that the "information" given may be overinfluenced by belief in the advantages of mediation: see S. M. Cretney, "Lawyers under the Family Law Act 1996 . . ." [1997] Fam. Law 405. There may well be some people who find the obligation to attend what they may see as a patronising and humiliating lecture about, for example, their continuing parental responsibility both embarrassing and stigmatic. It is certainly not easy to see the utility of requiring people such as the eight-times married Elizabeth Taylor to have the implications of marital breakdown explained.

(b) Filing the statement of marital breakdown
The making of a statement of marital breakdown in the prescribed form — declaring the maker's belief that the marriage has broken down and that he or she is aware of the purpose of the period for reflection and consideration — is the key event in the process for the legal termination of marriage established by the Family Law Act 1996. As a matter of law, the court cannot make a divorce order unless a statement in the prescribed form has been made by one or both spouses; and the receipt by the court of a statement is to be treated as the commencement of proceedings. The parties' "uncoupling" process thus moves from the possible ambiguities of the information meeting (and any counselling following from it) into the world of legal procedures.

The Family Law Act perpetuates the rule that divorce proceedings are not to be started within the first year of marriage: a statement made before the first anniversary of the marriage to which it relates is ineffective for the purposes of any application for a divorce order (a separation order — see p. 61, below — may be obtained, however).

The making of a statement has four significant legal consequences:

(i) It starts the period of reflection and consideration running.
(ii) Thereafter, the court will have power to make financial and other orders.
(iii) Once a statement has been made, the court has power to make directions requiring the parties to attend meetings at which the facilities available for mediation will be explained to them.
(iv) A statement once made can only be withdrawn with the agreement of both parties. If one spouse makes a statement the other may apply for a divorce order at the end of the period for reflection and consideration notwithstanding a change of mind (or heart) on the part of the maker.

(c) The passing of the period for reflection and consideration
The Family Law Act provides that a marriage is to be taken to have broken down irretrievably if (but only if) a period "for the parties to reflect on whether the marriage can be saved and to have an opportunity to effect a reconciliation, and to consider

what arrangements should be made for the future" has passed before any application for a divorce order may be made.

In the Bill as first presented to Parliament the period stipulated was twelve months; but various amendments were made, and the outcome is now somewhat complex:

(1) *The beginning of the period.* The period starts on the fourteenth day after the statement of marital breakdown is received by the court. (This is intended to allow the court time to serve the statement on others concerned);

(2) *The length of the period.* It is provided that the period for reflection and consideration is nine months from that date. However, the period is extended by a further period of six months (*i.e.* to fifteen months in all) if *either*;

   (a) one party applies for a divorce order but the other seeks time for further reflection, *or*

   (b) there is a child of the family under the age of sixteen at the time when application is made (*i.e.* after the end of the period) for a divorce order, *unless* either;

      (i) at the time when application is made for a divorce order, an occupation or non-molestation order under Part IV of the Act ("Family Homes and Domestic Violence") is in force against the other party; or

      (ii) the court is satisfied that delaying the making of a divorce order would be significantly detrimental to the welfare of any child of the family.

The minimum time element stipulated for the divorce process is thus:

(a) Three months from attending an information meeting to making a statement; *plus*

(b) Nine months, in any case — this period cannot be abridged in any circumstances even if both parties for good reason so wish; *plus*

(c) A further six months if one party opposes the divorce and in cases involving a child (unless the case is one in which there have been "domestic violence" proceedings, or one in which the court considers the child's welfare would be affected by delay).

In briefest summary therefore the minimum period which is to elapse between the start of the divorce process and the application for a divorce order is twelve months from attending the information meeting, but if one party objects to the divorce or there is a child the period will often be 18 months.

(3) *Interrupting the period: "stopping the clock" to allow additional time for reconciliation*

It may be thought that the calculation of the period for reflection and consideration as explained above is complex enough, but the Act — in an attempt further to encourage attempts at reconciliation — allows the period for reflection and consideration to be interrupted by the parties giving joint notice to the court that they are attempting a reconciliation but require additional time. When such a notice is received by the court, the period stops, but either party may unilaterally start it running again by serving a notice that the attempted reconciliation has been unsuccessful. Moreover, consistently with the policy that divorce proceedings should not be allowed to hang over the family's heads indefinitely it is provided that if the period for reflection and consideration is interrupted in this way for a continuous period of more than 18 months, any application for a divorce order by either party will have to be by reference to a new statement received by the court after the end of that 18 month period: in effect the original statement is spent, and the court process must be started again.

(4) *The maximum period allowed for reflection and consideration in the divorce process.*

Consistently with this policy, the Act effectively prescribes a maximum period within which the question whether the marriage is to be ended must be resolved: no application may be made for a divorce order if more than a year has elapsed since the end of the period for reflection and consideration; in effect, at the end of that time the statement lapses. However, this lapse period, like the period for reflection and consideration, may be extended for up to 18 months if the parties jointly give notice to the court that they need further time for attempts at reconciliation.

(d) Settling arrangements for the future: using the period for reflection and consideration constructively
The intention, according to the Government's 1995 Divorce White Paper, paragraph 4.16, is that couples should spend the period reflecting on whether their marriage can be saved and if not to face up to the consequences of their actions and make arrangements to meet their responsibilities. The Act contains provisions intended to promote constructive use of the time available:

(i) *Attendance at a mediation meeting.*
    The court may give a direction requiring each party to attend a meeting arranged for the purpose (a) of enabling an explanation to be given of the facilities available to the parties for mediation in relation to disputes between them; and (b) of providing an opportunity for each party to agree to take advantage of those facilities. It should be noted that the direction is not a direction to *participate* in mediation, and the parties will have the right to decline to take advantage of any facilities offered. In particular, it seems likely that the courts will use the powers to draw the attention of the parties not only to facilities provided by private sector mediators but to the facilities for long provided by the Court Welfare Service in respect of difficulties relating to child upbringing and also to court based facilities for Financial Dispute Resolution currently being developed.

(ii) *Legal Aid for mediation.*
    It has already been noted that the Government considered that in many cases parties would do well to settle their arrangements about financial and child upbringing matters through mediation rather than by negotiation (perhaps culminating in a contested court hearing) between lawyers acting separately for the two spouses. This view is reflected in provisions in the Act which empower the Legal Aid Board to fund mediation in disputes relating to family matters: Family Law Act 1996, Part III. The Legal Aid Board will have important

responsibilities in respect of the quality of the services which it funds in this way; and the Legal Air Board has launched pilot projects in 13 pilot areas. The selected service providers include solicitors' practices offering a comprehensive mediation service, specialist mediation services (such as the long established Bristol Family Mediation Service) and (it seems) a number of private mediators: see *Franchising Family Mediation Services* (Legal Aid Board, 1997) and [1997] Fam. Law 308.

At one time it was the Government's intention to require the Legal Board to consider recourse to mediation as more appropriate than taking proceedings, thereby in effect directing those dependent on legal aid to mediation rather than the legal representation traditionally preferred by those able to pay for it. But, in response to criticism, this preference was modified. It is true that under the provisions made by the Family Law Act 1996, a person seeking legal aid must attend a meeting with a mediator to determine whether mediation appears suitable to the dispute and the parties and all the circumstances, and in particular, whether mediation could take place without either party being influenced by fear of violence or other harm, and if mediation does appear to be suitable "to help the person applying for representation to decide whether instead to apply for mediation". But if an applicant persists in preferring legal representation, the Legal Aid Board is merely required to have regard, in the light of the mediator's report, to whether and to what extent recourse to mediation would be a suitable alternative to undertaking the proceedings.

(iii) *The requirement to make arrangements for the future.*

The divorce law was for a long time structured on the basis that the question whether or not the marriage should be dissolved was of overriding importance; and hence, for example, it was only if a divorce decree had been made that the court could make financial orders (other than interim orders). This became increasingly out of touch with reality, and in particular, the reality after the introduction of the "special procedure" was usually that the marriage would be rapidly dissolved without any direct involvement of the parties in court proceedings, and only afterwards did issues relating to money and other matters come to be settled. Perhaps not surprisingly it seemed that people deprived of any opportunity to put forward their feelings of anger and hostility in proceedings leading to a "quicky" divorce were encouraged to transfer those feelings to the legal proceedings still available (and often funded by legal aid) to deal with the financial and other consequences of the breakdown.

The Family Law Act 1996 seeks to transform the position. The parties are to be required to spend a significant period considering the arrangements for the future, and their marriage is not to be dissolved unless and until they have met the requirements imposed by the legislation about the arrangements for the future. The Lord Chancellor considered that this would do "far more to reinforce and underline the institution of marriage and its inherent obligations and responsibilities than the present system which allows quick divorce following allegations of fault".

Procedures for making the necessary arrangements. The arrangements which will usually have to be made following the breakdown of a relationship relate to the upbringing of the children and to financial matters.

The hope is that these matters will be settled in many cases by agreement, perhaps following mediation or perhaps following negotiation between lawyers. So far as *arrangements for children* are concerned, the parties will have to file a statement detailing the arrangements proposed, and the court's powers and duties in relation to such a statement are explained below. If there is no agreement, an application will be made under the Children Act 1989 for example, seeking an order settling the arrangements to be made as to the person with whom the child is to live (a "residence order") and requiring the person with whom the child is to live to allow the child to visit or stay with the other parent or other persons (a "contact order"). The way in which the court will deal with these matters is explained in Chapter 12 below.

In contrast, the Family Law Act 1996 imposes no obligation on the parties to disclose the terms of any agreement they have made about financial matters (although, as explained in Chapter 4 below in many cases the parties will wish to have the terms of any agreement embodied in a so-called *consent order*, while evidence that matters have been resolved will have to be produced to the court when application for a divorce order is made and it is possible that the Rules (unlike the Act) will require the parties to provide the divorce court with some information about their financial affairs. A pilot scheme requiring greater advance disclosure, and envisaging the possibility of the court seeking to assist the parties to reach a negotiated settlement has already been introduced in some parts of the country: see the Family Proceedings (Amendment No. 2) Rules 1997, S.I. 1997 No. 1056). In the absence of an agreement the court will resolve any application for financial orders under the provisions of sections 23–24 of the Matrimonial Causes Act 1973; and the way in which the court exercises its wide discretion under those provisions is dealt with in Chapter 4 below.

Satisfying the Court that arrangements for the future have been made

(1) *Children.*

In respect of *arrangements for the children's upbringing* the Act builds on provisions dating back to 1958 requiring the court to consider any arrangements proposed for the upbringing and welfare of any child of the family who has not reached the age of sixteen — the court may direct that the provisions should also apply to older children — and decide whether it should exercise its powers under the Children Act 1989 with respect to any of them (Family Law Act 1996, s.11(1)(a)).

The practice under the Children Act 1989.

Since the coming into force of the Children Act 1989, this exercise has usually been conducted by a District Judge on the basis of a written statement submitted by the parties. The Rules provide that the District Judge may require the parties to file further evidence or to attend a hearing, and the District Judge has power to direct the making of welfare reports in order to help decide whether the court needs to exercise its Children Act powers. The court may also, if it appears that it may be appropriate for a care or supervision order to be made, direct a local authority investigation (Children Act 1989, s.37).

In the light of its consideration of the statement of arrangements, the court may in exceptional circumstances direct that the divorce is not to be granted until the court orders otherwise, but in practice it seems to be rare for the court to go behind what the parties choose to say.

Provisions of the 1996 Act.

The Family Law Act 1996 builds on this structure. Section 11 of the Act requires the court, in deciding whether it needs to exercise its powers under the Children Act (*i.e.* to direct reports or even to make orders notwithstanding the fact that neither party has asked it to do so) to treat the welfare of the child as paramount (section 11(3)), and "to have particular regard, on the evidence before it, to:

(a) the wishes and feelings of the child considered in the light of his age and understanding and the circumstances in which those wishes were expressed;

(b) the conduct of the parties in relation to the upbringing of the child;

(c) the general principle that, in the absence of evidence to the contrary, the welfare of the child will be best served by:

  (i) his having regular contact with those who have parental responsibility for him and with other members of his family, and

  (ii) the maintenance of as good a continuing relationship with his parents as is possible; and

(d) any risk to the child attributable to —

  (i) where the person with whom the child will reside is living or proposes to live,

  (ii) any person with whom that person is living or with whom he proposes to live, or

  (iii) any other arrangements for his care and upbringing.

The court's duty thus remains comparatively restricted: it is first to consider whether the court should exercise its powers under the Children Act 1989, and secondly, if the court is not in a position to do so without further consideration, to decide whether there are exceptional circumstances such as would make it desirable to hold up the dissolution of the marriage. Unless the court considers that circumstances are sufficiently "exceptional" that it is "desirable in the interests of the child" to direct that a divorce order is not to be made until the court orders otherwise the court will be bound to grant a divorce order to an applicant satisfying the other legislative requirements. As the Lord Chancellor put it (*Official Report* (H.L.) June 27, 1996, column 1074):

> "Essentially, . . . the function of the court under this procedure remains the same as under the current law; namely, consideration of whether there are children of the family to whom the section should apply and, where there are any such children, whether it should exercise any of its powers under the Children Act 1989. The court has no jurisdiction . . . to make a residence or contact order under this provision. Such orders, if they are to be made, must continue to be made under the Children Act itself. In exercising jurisdiction under that Act, the court will apply the welfare criteria set out in Section 1(3) of that Act"

It is not easy to believe that the limited scope of this provision (which allows a divorce order to be made even if the parties are still quarrelling about residence, contact and other matters) can have been appreciated by those who urged that all arrangements would "have to be decided before divorce": although no doubt in the majority of cases the court will have disposed of any issue about the making of a residence or contact order before the end of the period of 18 months which will have elapsed between the start of the divorce process prescribed by the Act and the application for a divorce order. The truth is that the provisions of the Children Act in general are based on a philosophy of non-intervention which does not sit easily with the more interventionist philosophy of the 1996 Act.

(2) *Financial arrangements.*

In respect of the parties financial arrangements the Act requires certain evidence that arrangements have been made to be produced on the application to the court for a divorce order. The requisite evidence is one of the following:

(a) a court order dealing with their financial arrangements; or
(b) a negotiated agreement as to their financial arrangements; or
(c) a declaration by both parties that they have made their financial arrangements; or
(d) a declaration by one of the parties (to which no objection has been notified to the court by the other party) that —
    (i) he has no significant assets and does not intend to make an application for financial provision;
    (ii) he believes that the other party has no significant assets and does not intend to make an application for financial provision; and
    (iii) there are therefore no financial arrangements to be made.

The significance of these requirements will become clearer after the reader has read the explanation in Chapter 4 of the court's powers to make financial orders; but it will be apparent at the outset that there seems very little recognition of the law's traditional concern (emphasised by the *1995 Divorce White Paper*) to ensure that "weaker or vulnerable parties and their children are sufficiently protected and that the potential for litigation is minimised". In particular, the statute contains no obvious protection against one party succumbing to pressure to make a declaration that the couple have made their financial arrangements; nor is there any provision aimed at deterring a dishonest spouse from making a false declaration that there are no significant assets. However, it should be borne in mind that some protection against these risks may be incorporated in the secondary legislation upon which the 1996 Act is so heavily dependent; and also that the provisions set out above relate to what has to be done *to obtain a divorce order*, and compliance with them will not necessarily prevent the court from subsequently re-opening the financial arrangements under the procedures set out in Chapter 4.

Court's power to make divorce order even though requirements relating to financial arrangements not satisfied. The 1995 Divorce White Paper recognised that there could be circumstances ("for example, where it would be in the best interests of the children that an order be made notwithstanding that arrangements had not been settled") and the Act provides four exemptions from the requirements set out above. If an applicant satisfies the court that the case falls within one of those four categories the court has an apparently unfettered discretion to make a divorce order. The four categories are:

(i) *The first exemption: application to court for financial relief frustrated.*

This exemption requires proof that the applicant has, during the period for reflection and consideration, taken such steps as are reasonably practicable to try to reach agreement about the parties' financial arrangements; and that the applicant has made an application to the court for financial relief and complied with all the requirements of the court in relation to those proceedings. However, (i) the other party has delayed in complying with the requirements of the court or has otherwise been obstructive; or (ii) for reasons which are beyond the control of the applicant, or the other party, the court has been prevented from obtaining the information which it requires to determine the financial position of the parties.

(ii) *The second exemption: no agreement made or likely to be made because of illness, etc.; delay in granting divorce detrimental to child or prejudicial to applicant.*
This exemption requires proof of three separate matters:

(a) **Applicant's efforts to reach agreement**. The applicant must, during the period for reflection and consideration, have taken such steps as are reasonably practicable to try to reach agreement about the parties' financial arrangements.

(b) **Those efforts frustrated because of illness, etc**. It must be shown that the applicant has, by reason of the ill health or disability of the applicant, the other party or a child of the family (whether physical or mental) been unable to reach agreement with the other party about those arrangements and it is unlikely that he will be able to do so in the foreseeable future.

(c) **Delay prejudicial to applicant or detrimental to child's welfare**. The applicant must establish that delay in making the divorce order would be significantly detrimental to the welfare of any child of the family, or would be seriously prejudicial to the applicant.

(iii) *The third exemption: no agreement because other party cannot be contacted.*
This exemption is comparatively simple. Proof is required that the applicant has found it impossible to contact the other party, and that as a result, it has been impossible for the applicant to reach agreement with the other party about their financial arrangements.

(iv) *The fourth exemption: applicant with occupation order or non-molestation order; no agreement made or likely to be made; delay in granting divorce detrimental to child or prejudicial to applicant.*
This exemption was added at a late stage in the Bill's progress through Parliament and seems to have been influenced by an appreciation on the Government's part of the strength of pressure further to protect the victims of domestic violence. The applicant must show that there is in force in his favour an occupation order or a non-molestation order, and in addition he must show that he has taken "such steps as are reasonably practicable" to try to reach agreement but that he has been unable to do so and is unlikely to be able to do so in the foreseeable future, and that a delay in making the divorce order would be significantly detrimental to the welfare of any child of the family, or would be seriously prejudicial to the applicant.

It may have been necessary to include exemptions such as these in the Act, but it is not easy to see how their existence is consistent with the policy of minimising hostile litigation. In particular, it seems unlikely that the temptation to make an application on the ground that the other party has been "obstructive" or to defend on the ground that the applicant has made no serious attempt to negotiate an application made by someone who has already obtained possession of the family home by reason of an occupation order will always be resisted.

(e) Obtaining the divorce order

The court is required to make a divorce order on the application of either party to the marriage, provided that (i) the requirements set out above are satisfied; (ii) the application is accompanied by a declaration that having reflected on the breakdown, and having considered the requirements of the Act as to the parties' arrangements for the future, he or she believes that the marriage cannot be saved (i.e. for the first time the applicant must assert that the marriage has *irretrievably* broken down).

Orders preventing divorce.   However, the court *cannot* make a divorce order if an *order preventing divorce* is in force. The Divorce Reform Act 1969 included a provision, much more restrictively drafted than the agreement between the Law Commission and the Archbishop's groups would have suggested, giving the court a discretion to dismiss a divorce petition founded solely on the basis of five years' living apart if the dissolution of the marriage would result in grave financial hardship to the respondent and if it would in all the circumstances be wrong to dissolve the marriage (Matrimonial Causes Act 1973, s.5). In practice, this provision was rarely successfully invoked in reported cases. The main reason for this was that the hardship in question had to result *from the divorce* (*i.e.* from the ending of the legal status of marriage between the parties) rather than from the *breakdown of the marriage*. In reality it was usually the breakdown, and the financial consequences in terms of the need to support two households where formerly there had been one (not to mention the emotional trauma associated with the collapse of the couple's relationship) which caused hardship. The Act required that what had to be contrasted was the position of those concerned as divorced spouses as against their position as separated spouses and since the courts had extensive powers to make financial orders on divorce it was rarely possible to show any significant financial hardship stemming from the dissolution of the parties' legal relationship, whilst the courts tended to look sceptically on claims that the divorce had caused other hardship. It therefore came as a surprise to some when the Government, in proposing to retain this bar but applying it to all divorce cases rather than only to those based on five years' living apart, claimed that the bar "in its present form provided significant protection" from the hardship which could arise as a result of divorce, even where that hardship is not financial (*1995 Divorce White Paper*, paragraph 4.46). In response to pressure, the Government introduced amendments which seem to have significantly extended the scope of the bar beyond what was originally proposed: (see *Official Report* (H.L.) March 4, 1996, column 27).

The Family Law Act 1996, s.10, now provides that, if an application for a divorce order has been made (which, as pointed out above at page 53 can only be done after the expiration of the period for reflection and consideration, and after the applicant has stated the basis on which he proposes to satisfy the court about the arrangements for the parties' future) the court may, on the application of the other party, order that the marriage is not to be dissolved. The court must be satisfied:

(a) that dissolution of the marriage would result in substantial financial or other hardship to the other party or to a child of the family; and

(b) that it would be wrong, in all the circumstances (including the conduct of the parties and the interests of any child of the family), for the marriage to be dissolved.

Requirements for order preventing divorce. To establish this bar, the applicant must prove (i) that hardship of the specified type and degree would result from the dissolution of the marriage (rather than from the breakdown); (ii) that such hardship is "substantial"; (iii) that the hardship would be caused to the applicant or to a child of the family; and (iv) that it would be wrong for the marriage to be dissolved.

Hardship must be caused by dissolution of marriage (not separation). The requirement that the hardship flow from the *dissolution* of the marriage remains as under the old law, explained above. Many of the cases in which the 1969 hardship bar applied related to cases in which divorce would affect a wife's pension expectations:

> In *K v. K (Financial Relief: Widow's Pension)* [1997] 1 FLR 35, H.H.J. Collins, the parties' only substantial asset consisted of rights under the husband's occupational scheme, and divorce would deprive the wife of a widow's pension of nearly £8,000 per annum. It was held — notwithstanding some improvements made by the Pension Act 1995 and case law in relation to pension rights on divorce — that the court could not make orders which would prevent her suffering grave financial hardship. The judge indicated that he would withhold the decree (although it appears that in fact the husband eventually put forward satisfactory proposals to protect her position).

Hardship other than financial hardship. Much of the reported case law on the 1969 hardship bar was based on the applicant's religious susceptibilities. The courts held that it was not sufficient to show that divorce was contrary to the applicant's religion and would cause unhappiness and a sense of shame. But in contrast the fact that the applicant lived in a community in which she would be ostracised following the divorce was capable of constituting the "grave hardship" then required.

> In *Banik v Banik* [1973] 1 W.L.R. 860 a Hindu wife's pleadings that she would be ostracised were held to establish a prima facie case of grave hardship; but on examination of the evidence it was held that her pleading was not substantiated and a decree was granted: *Banik v. Banik (No. 2)* (1973) 117 S.J. 874.

It is not easy to make any rational prediction as to how the courts are likely to approach pleas that divorce would cause "substantial" hardship by reason of the offence divorce causes to religious feelings, but it is to be noted that the House of Commons defeated on a division an amendment providing that "hardship" included hardship attributable to the fact that the person concerned had a deeply held religious belief that marriage is indissoluble (*Official Report* (H.C.) June 17, 1996, column 630; and see the debate at columns 561–581). In the circumstances, it may still prove difficult to make out such a plea.

Substantial (rather than grave) hardship. It seems incontestable that the substitution of the word "substantial" for the word "grave" (which appeared in the 1973 Act) is intended to make the relevant test less demanding, and the Lord Chancellor stated that the effect of the change would be to reduce the statutory criterion to "as low a standard as it can go" consistently with the principle that the law does not in any case take account of insubstantial considerations (see *Official Report* (H.L.) March 4, 1996, columns 25–33).

Hardship caused by divorce to children sufficient.   The extension of the bar so as to encompass hardship caused by the divorce to children as well as the parties to the marriage was apparently intended to apply to cases where objective hardship of some kind (such as the need to sell a house specially adapted to meet the needs of a disabled child: see *Lee v. Lee* (1973) 117 S.J. 616) could be demonstrated. A child's feelings of hurt and distress were not to suffice (see *Official Report* (H.L.) March 4, 1996, column 30–31).

Even if "substantial hardship" established, divorce only to be withheld if "wrong".   It is to be left to the courts (having regard specifically to the parties' conduct and the interests of children and also applying the general principles laid down by section 1 of the Act), to decide whether a divorce order should be made notwithstanding the hardship divorce would cause. It seems probable that guidance from the appeal courts will be required as to the approach which the court should adopt in striking a balance between what may well appear to some to be the conflicting principles of supporting the institution of marriage on the one hand and bringing a marriage which has irretrievably broken down to an end with minimum distress to the parties and to the children affected (*c.f.* Family Law Act 1996, s.1(a) and s.1(c) (i)) on the other. These would not appear to be easily justiciable issues, but it is to be noted that in the course of the parliamentary debates on the Bill for the Family Law Act the Chancellor of the Duchy of Lancaster gave an assurance on behalf of the Lord Chancellor that the new provision would be "transmitted to judges in such a way that they will realise that when people involved in divorces say that they do not wish to be divorced against their will, their feelings will be taken into account" (*Official Report* (H.C.) March 25, 1996, column 749). The debates made it clear that there is a body of opinion which would wish the hardship bar to be applied much more often than was the case under the 1969 legislation.

Cancellation of order preventing divorce.   The Family Law Act 1996 s.10(3) provides that the court must cancel an order preventing divorce on the application of either or both parties, unless the court is still satisfied that dissolution of the marriage would result in substantial financial or other hardship to the other party or to a child of the family, and that it would be wrong in all the circumstances for the marriage to be dissolved. The court is given power to impose conditions on the making of an order preventing divorce, and it seems that conditions may well be imposed relating to financial matters (for example, that the husband should give information about financial matters or undertakings to effect transactions which the court lacks the power to order, such as to make pension provision).

D. IMPLEMENTATION OF THE DIVORCE PROVISIONS OF THE FAMILY LAW ACT 1996

The provisions of the 1996 Act asserting the general principles to be kept in mind by those carrying out functions under the new divorce law, making provision for marriage support and governing the legal aid funding for mediation were brought into force on March 21, 1997: The Family Law Act 1996 (Commencement No. 1) Order 1997, S.I. 1997 No. 1077. But the need for the Government to ensure adequate provision for the information meetings (which must be available to those contemplating divorce) and for the Legal Aid Board to put itself in a position to discharge its responsibilities for funding mediation meant that the main provisions of the 1996 divorce legislation could not be brought into force immediately. The Lord Chancellor's Department have stated that the substantive changes in the divorce law are expected to be in force "early in 1999" although it appears that the Legal Aid Board does not expect to have finalised the ongoing arrangements for funding mediation until the year 2000. It is possible that the Lord Chancellor's Department underestimates the logistical and other problems in securing the nationwide provision of information meetings; and it remains to be seen how great is the demand for mediation services and whether adequate provision to meet that need can be met: see S. M. Cretney, "Lawyers under the Family Law Act 1996 . . ." [1997] Fam. Law 405. It should also be noted that the Labour opposition was critical to the failure of the Conservative government to give any realistic costing of the changes to the divorces process; and the possibility that the Labour government will decide to give a higher priority to other calls on public expenditure cannot be excluded. But for the purposes of a students' book, however, it has seemed sensible to assume that the Act is fully in force; and the text is written on that basis.

E. the effect of the family law act 1996 on the divorce process

Will the Family Law Act 1996 improve the divorce process?

The Government spokesman introducing the Bill into the House of Commons said that its purpose was:

> "to strengthen the institution of marriage by encouraging the process of reflection and consideration and by giving couples every opportunity to effect a reconciliation before divorce is granted. It will better protect the interests of the children of a marriage by reducing unnecessary acrimony . . ."

These are ambitious objectives, but there are good reasons for believing that the Act will improve many aspects of the divorce process. In particular, the fact that it will no longer be necessary to make allegations of fault (with all the consequences sometimes resulting in terms of bitterness and hostility); the fact that support services are to be available, and that (by information meetings and other means) those whose marriages are in difficulty are to be apprised of the available options before making any irreversible decision; the expectation that mediation will do something to improve communications between the parties and thereby minimise damage to the parties and the children (coupled with provisions seeking to give greater emphasis to the interests of children) all suggest that important and positive changes are in issue.

But there are also legitimate grounds for concern and anxiety about the likely impact of the legislation. It is difficult to deny that divorce is now to be available on the unilateral demand of one party, and there are those who believe that the message conveyed by the change in the basis of the law will inevitably be that divorce is to be viewed less seriously, and that (in particular) the removal of any requirement to demonstrate fault on the respondent's part is likely to have seriously adverse consequences. In the words of Baroness Young (*Official Report* (H.L.) November 30, 1995, column 733):

> "The removal of fault undermines individual responsibility. By removing it, the state is actively discouraging any concept of lifelong commitment in marriage, to standards of behaviour, to self-sacrifice, to duty, to any thought for members of the family. It declares that neither party has any responsibility for the breakdown of marriage. Furthermore, it undermines the legal basis of marriage by making the contract meaningless; and it weakens the distinction between marriage and cohabitation . . . Now, marriage can be ended just on the say-so of one or other, or both, partners. It flies in the face of experience."

At a different, more detailed, level there must remain grounds for scepticism about the likelihood that the process of divorce to be introduced under the 1996 Act will in practice have the beneficial effects that its promoters claim; and it is to these concerns that we now turn.

1. Fuelling the appetite for hostile litigation. An important objective of the legislation is to reduce unnecessary acrimony and the conflict incidental to adversarial litigation. Yet the Act as passed into law seems to furnish many additional opportunities for such litigation. Of these, the most important is that those who do not wish to be divorced (or, perhaps more to the point, those who believe they can obtain better financial terms by threatening to resist the divorce which the other party wants) will apply for *orders preventing divorce*, and it is not easy to see how the court could adjudicate on such an application without considering a wide range of potentially wounding matters. There would also seem to be considerable scope for litigation (or the threat of litigation) arising from the following provisions of the Act:

(a) A person resisting divorce has a *right to seek "time for further reflection"* — notwithstanding the fact that at least twelve months will have passed since the divorce process was started and all requirements about the parties' arrangements for the future will already have been satisfied. Conversely, a party anxious for a speedy divorce has the right to seek an abridgement of the period for reflection and consideration on the basis that delay in making the divorce order would be significantly detrimental to the welfare of any child of the family.

(b) *Arrangements for the future*. The provisions of the Act requiring the parties to have made arrangements for the future seem almost designed to provide opportunities for litigation. Thus, for example, a person wishing to end a marriage may be tempted to allege that the other party has been obstructive in making financial arrangements and to claim that the divorce order should be made notwithstanding the fact that financial matters remain unresolved; whilst the other spouse will be advised that he or she has a considerable bargaining "chip" inasmuch as the divorce process will lapse twelve months from the end of the period for reflection and consideration. The temptation to drag matters out, irrespective of any improvements in court procedures which have been made to minimise delay, might be almost irresistible to some.

(c) *Reformulation of court's financial powers.* The legislation governing the court's powers to make financial orders has been substantially reformulated, and although it was not intended to make major changes of principle, experience suggests that problems on the construction of the legislation will arise.

(d) *Encouragement to raise issues of conduct.* One of the most difficult dilemmas confronting the Conservative Government was apparently how to reconcile the need to minimise acrimony with the demands (often made by its own supporters) that conduct should play an appropriate role in determining the arrangements in relation to financial matters and the children's upbringing. Under this pressure, the Government agreed a number of amendments — notably relating to the role of conduct in relation to the children's upbringing and financial matters (dealt with in Chapter 4) which put conduct more clearly into the text of the legislation.

2. Excessive reliance on benefits of mediation.   The Government, as has already been made clear, place substantial reliance on mediation as a means of reducing the bitterness sometimes encountered in divorce proceedings. But although mediation (as Lady Young put it) "sounds so soothing" it is difficult not to feel some unease about the extent to which the Government's expectations are capable of being fulfilled.

At one level there is simply the question of resources: the Government consistently refused to make substantial funding available to the voluntary schemes already established, and in many parts of the country there are currently few if any trained mediators. To fill the gap with appropriately trained people is a task the scale of which the Government may not have fully appreciated, all the more so since (outside the Legal Aid Scheme) they have not undertaken any obligation to provide support of any kind but preferred to rely on private sector initiatives. At a different level there remain real concerns about some aspects of the mediation process, and particularly about the extent to which mediation is likely to lead to the exploitation of the vulnerable. The Government's failure to provide any control over the professional competence and ethics of those providing mediation outside the Legal Aid framework seems remarkable; and disquiet on this score is only partially allayed by initiatives such as the creation of the U.K. College of Family Mediators, committed to establishing and maintaining standards, for example by prescribing codes of conduct and competence. The difficulty is that there seem to be no powers to require the unwilling to comply with such requirements, and a high price may have to be paid for the Conservative government's distrust of the concept of professional organisation.

3. Unrealistic assumptions about human behaviour.   The third, and perhaps the most worrying, concern about the divorce process under the Family Law Act 1996 is that it is based on unrealistic and sometimes patronising assumptions about how human beings involved in the turmoil of marital breakdown are likely to react. The Act requires couples to spend a substantial period of time reflecting on whether their marriage can be saved and, if not, considering the arrangements which should be made for the future; and they are to be required to sign papers indicating that they have discharged this obligation. But how realistic is this? As Baroness Elles put it (*Official Report* (H.L) January 11, 1996, column 334):

"I wonder if anyone in this House really knows how people live in their homes. Can one believe that for one year they are going to sit at the kitchen table with a cup of tea wondering how they are going to reflect and consider their future at the end of one year of marriage? It is totally unrealistic. I simply do not see how people living in the real world can go through this appalling performance . . ."

Again, it is not easy to see how the "requirement" to reflect and consider is to be translated into reality. It has been asked:

"May not some of those concerned prefer to spend their time in the far more pleasurable activity of conceiving — necessarily illegitimate — babies? May not some spend the time seeking means of exploiting their emotional or financial advantage, or brooding on grievances and perhaps using the available legal procedures as a way of seeking satisfaction for the wrongs they have suffered? . . . We would all *hope* that the parties will indeed give anxious consideration to whether their marriage has broken down irretrievably and to the consequential arrangements. We must all hope that mediation and counselling will be successful in this respect. But the evidence for believing that these expectations will be fulfilled is not overwhelmingly convincing" (S. M. Cretney, in MDA Freeman (ed.) *Divorce, Where Next?* (1996)).

The fear that the reformed divorce law will in practice perpetuate and even aggravate the incoherence and confusion experienced under the existing divorce law is not reduced by many of the changes introduced into the Family Law Act during its passage through Parliament which have greatly complicated matters — to such an extent that there must be serious doubt as to how far any information meeting can adequately explain even the central features of the scheme (such as the length of time which must elapse before the marriage is ended). Notwithstanding the admirable intentions of those who constructed the reform proposals and the positive aspects of the legislation to which attention has been drawn at the beginning of this section it still seems by no means improbable that the new law will ensnare countless uncomprehending people in a costly legal, social work and counselling nightmare. There may even be a risk that the Family Law Act will turn out to have reinforced the trend, noted elsewhere in this book, to prefer living together as husband and wife without going through any binding marriage ceremony. Regrettably the "message" effectively conveyed by the publicity given to divorce in the light of the Family Law Act may turn out to be that marriage involves a substantial risk of becoming embroiled in costly legalism. The difficulty, as Mr Paul Boateng put it, is that rhetoric and reality seldom meet in family law reforms; and there seems to be a real danger, as prophesied in the last edition of this book (1992, paragraph 5.13), that the cure offered by the 1996 legislation will be worse than the disease manifestly infecting the existing law.

F. AN ALTERNATIVE: SEPARATION ORDERS

The Family Law Act 1996 empowers the court to make a separation order on the application of either party to the marriage. Such an order allows financial and other arrangements to be made but does not permit the parties to remarry. The procedure is dealt with at p. 94 below.

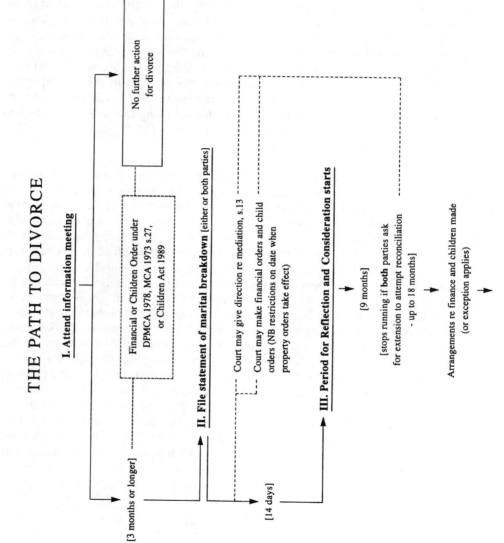

THE PATH TO DIVORCE

I. Attend information meeting

[3 months or longer]

No further action
for divorce

Financial or Children Order under
DPMCA 1978, MCA 1973 s.27,
or Children Act 1989

II. File statement of marital breakdown [either or both parties]

[14 days]

Court may give direction re mediation, s.13

Court may make financial orders and child
orders (NB restrictions on date when
property orders take effect)

III. Period for Reflection and Consideration starts

[9 months]

[stops running if both parties ask
for extension to attempt reconciliation
- up to 18 months]

Arrangements re finance and children made
(or exception applies)

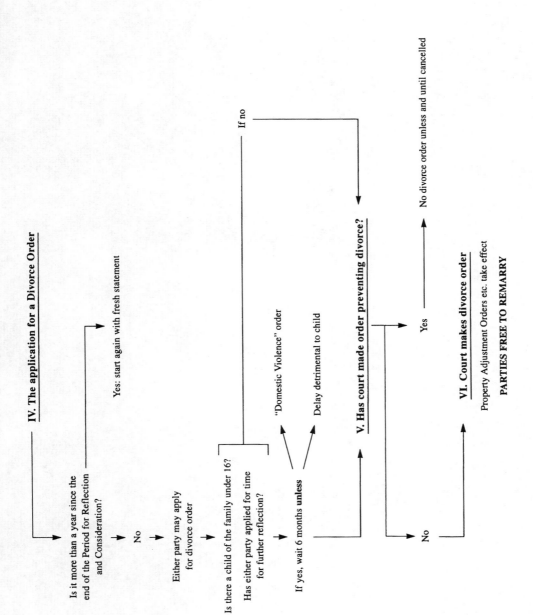

IV. The application for a Divorce Order

Is it more than a year since the end of the Period for Reflection and Consideration?

Yes: start again with fresh statement

No

Either party may apply for divorce order

Is there a child of the family under 16?

Has either party applied for time for further reflection?

If yes, wait 6 months **unless**

"Domestic Violence" order

Delay detrimental to child

If no

V. Has court made order preventing divorce?

No

Yes

No divorce order unless and until cancelled

VI. Court makes divorce order

Property Adjustment Orders etc. take effect

PARTIES FREE TO REMARRY

Chapter 4

THE FINANCIAL CONSEQUENCES OF DIVORCE

Nowadays, divorce has two particularly important legal consequences. First, it allows husband and wife to remarry. Secondly, the divorce court has extensive powers to make financial orders: in one recent case (*Dart v. Dart* [1996] 2 FLR 286, C.A.) the court ordered the husband to pay the wife nine million pounds. The House of Lords rejected an application made by the wife for leave to appeal against the inadequacy of this sum, which she thought should be nearer one hundred million pounds.

For many years, as already noted, the question of the financial arrangements to be made on divorce has been the crucial factor engendering a great deal of sometimes strongly and bitterly contested, litigation. The fact that the divorce process under the Family Law Act 1996 requires the parties to settle their financial arrangements before they can get a divorce order (the "licence to remarry") is likely to increase the importance of these matters.

The Family Law Act 1996 contains many amendments to the law, but most of these are intended (see FLA 1996, s.15) simply to allow the court to make financial orders before the divorce or separation order. (For what it is worth, the 1996 Act retains the old principle that financial orders in nullity are only to be made on or after the grant of a decree.) But the Act does make a perhaps significant change in the weight to be given to the parties' conduct in determining the financial arrangements; whilst amendments were made to the law by the Pensions Act 1995 in a (not wholly successful) attempt to enable Occupational Pension funds to be reallocated on divorce. The result is that the law has become immensely complex, and in a textbook of this kind only an outline analysis of the law as it will be when the Family Law Act 1996 is in force can be attempted.

This Chapter first summarises the extent of the court's powers, then it seeks to outline the principles upon which those powers are exercised, and finally it considers the extent to which the parties can — as the Family Law Act 1996 clearly intends — make their own out of court legally binding financial arrangements.

A. ORDERS THE COURT CAN MAKE

English law is now remarkable for the extent of the powers which the court has in divorce proceedings. For many years, the court could only order income payments, but in 1970 — prompted in part by the need to ensure adequate provision for wives unwillingly divorced under the Divorce Reform Act 1969 by economically dominant husbands, but in part reflecting what Thorpe L.J. (in *Dart v. Dart* [1996] 2 FLR 286, 294, C.A.) has described as "profound social change and . . . compelling social need" — the Matrimonial Proceedings and Property Act greatly extended the court's powers so as to encompass virtually all the parties' economically valuable assets, and in effect to introduce a "remedy of equitable distribution".

The orders the court can make are divided into financial provision and property adjustment orders — the former being primarily concerned with income, the latter with capital (although, rather oddly, an order to pay a lump sum — which may be many millions of pounds — is classified as a financial provision order). This Chapter deals with these orders so far as they relate to the parties to the marriage. The court also has powers to make orders in favour of children of the family; but because of the enactment of the Child Support Act (see p. 146) these will rarely be relevant today, and they are not discussed further in this Chapter. It should also be mentioned that the court has the full range of financial powers if the parties prefer a separation order to divorce.

Financial Provision Orders.   The traditional way of providing support after divorce is by an order for *periodical payments, i.e.* regular income payments (for example, £100 weekly, £500 monthly, £8,000 annually). The court now (Maintenance Enforcement Act, 1991) has power to order payment by standing order or direct debit, and it may make an attachment of earnings order requiring an employer to deduct specified sums from an employee's pay and to pay them over to the court.

The court also has power to make a *secured periodical payments order*, which requires a fund of capital (usually stocks and shares) to be set aside. If there is default in making the stipulated payments, recourse can be had to the fund to make good the default. A secured periodical payments order can therefore be effectively enforced even if the debtor disappears, disposes of other property, or ceases to earn; whilst the legislation also allows a secured order to continue throughout the lifetime of the applicant (unlike an ordinary periodical payments order which must terminate on the payer's death).

Periodical payments orders (secured or unsecured) may also be made for a specified term (for example, three years) perhaps in order to give a spouse who has not been in employment time to find a new job or to make alternative arrangements for child care. All periodical payment orders come to an end if the payee remarries (but not if he or she merely cohabits, in which case the court has a discretionary power to reduce or extinguish the order which it will exercise if the new partner is able to provide financially for the couple: see *Atkinson v. Atkinson* [1988] Fam. 93).

The court's power to order payment of a *lump sum* extends to ordering payment by instalments; and the court may order pension fund trustees to pay over any lump sum payable on the employee's death (MCA 1973, s.25C).

Property Adjustment Orders.   There are three main types of property adjustment order:

(i) *A Transfer of property order: MCA 1973 s.21(2)(a).*

This power enables the court to order that specified property (such as the matrimonial home, or investments) be transferred to the other spouse (or to or for the benefit of a child of the family).

(ii) *A Settlement of property order: MCA 1973 s.21(2)(b).*

The court may direct that property to which a party to the marriage is entitled be settled for the benefit of the other spouse and/or the children of the family. This power is now often used to make arrangements in connection with the former matrimonial home in an attempt to ensure that it is available for occupation as a home for dependent children whilst preserving both spouses' financial interest in it.

(iii) *Variation of marriage settlement order: MCA 1973 s.21(2)(c).*

The court may make an order varying for the benefit of the parties and/or the children of the family, any "ante-nuptial or post-nuptial" settlement made on the parties to the marriage. This power can, of course, be used to make appropriate variations in those (now comparatively rare) cases in which the parties have interests under a traditional marriage settlement; but the term "settlement" has been widely interpreted, and in *Brooks v. Brooks* [1996] 1 A.C. 375 the House of Lords held that in certain circumstances a spouse's occupational pension scheme can be regarded as a marriage settlement, the terms of which may accordingly be varied:

In *Brooks* the husband was in his sixties and had been a successful builder. However, in 1989 after twelve years of marriage he met an entertainer thirty years younger than himself at a holiday camp, became entranced with her, left his wife, stopped trading, and bought a house in which he went to live with his new partner. The husband offered the wife no more than half the value of the former matrimonial home; and asserted that he was now penniless and dependent on income support. But in 1980 the husband's company had established a non-contributory pension scheme funded by policies with a life company; and under the rules he could on retirement elect to give up a portion of his pension for his spouse or any other person dependent on him; while if he died before pension age a substantial lump sum would be divisible at the life company's discretion amongst a class including his wife. The House of Lords unanimously upheld the decisions below that, on the facts, since the husband had entered into the scheme with the intention of providing for the retirement of himself and his wife by the "highly tax efficient means afforded by" the scheme it fell within the definition of a nuptial settlement. Accordingly, it would be appropriate to vary the terms of the pension scheme by directing that pensions be provided for the wife in priority to (and if need be in diminution of) the pension payable to the husband.

The scope of this decision should not be exaggerated (although it has been found of use in other reported cases dealing with pensions: see, *e.g. W v. W (Periodical Payments: Pensions)* [1996] 2 FLR 480, Connell J.); and it certainly does not provide a solution to the overall problem of dealing with pensions on divorce.

In addition to the power to vary settlements, the court also has power (MCA 1973, s.21(2)(d)) to extinguish or reduce the interests of either spouse, and this power could it seems be used to benefit persons other than the spouses or children.

Power to Order Sale.   The court has now (MCA 1973, s.24A) an express power, on making an order for financial relief (other than an order for unsecured periodical payments) to order a sale. In effect, the power is ancillary to the making of the other orders already considered. This power can be exercised even if a third party also has a beneficial interest in the property (although any such person must be given an opportunity to make representations to the court (s.24A(6)). For example:

In *Harwood v. Harwood* [1991] 2 FLR 274, C.A. a firm in which the husband was a partner had an unquantified interest in the matrimonial home. The court ordered that the home be sold and the proceeds paid into court to await ascertainment of the amount to which the husband's partner was entitled.

When orders can be made: when they take effect

Interim orders. The court can make *interim* lump sum or financial provision orders at any time after a statement of marital breakdown has been filed, and an interim order can take effect immediately: MCA 1973 s.22B(1). (There is no power to make divorce-related financial orders before a statement is filed; and if one spouse needs a court order against the other in the three months between the information meeting and filing a statement he or she must make a separate application for a periodical payment or lump sum order — either to the magistrates' court under the provisions of the Domestic Proceedings and Magistrates' Courts Act 1978 or to the High Court or county court under the provisions of the Matrimonial Causes Act 1973 s.27 — on the ground of the other's failure to provide reasonable maintenance: see p. 93 below. Once again, an effect of the new divorce law seems likely to be to increase the number of separate proceedings, with consequent increases in legal costs.)

Orders other than interim orders can also be made at any time after a statement has been filed (see the complex provisions of section 22A) but they cannot *take effect* before the court makes the divorce (or separation) order unless the court is satisfied that the circumstances of the case are exceptional and that it would be just and reasonable for the order to take effect at some earlier date: section 22B(1).

This provision reflects an attempt at compromise between two policies: on the one hand, the philosophy of the Act requires the parties to have settled their financial arrangements before they are freed to remarry; but, on the other (so it was thought) to allow them to have everything re-organised before the end of the period for reflection and consideration could well jeopardise any prospects of reconciliation. It is not easy to predict what is likely to happen in practice:

> Harry and Winifred live in a three-bedroom house with their teenage son and teenage daughter. The best solution would seem to be for Winifred and the children to remain in the house and for Harry to have part of the capital value so that he can rehouse himself with his new partner. Under the pre-Family Law Act rules, this could easily be dealt with by court order made quite soon after the breakdown, but under the new regime the court will only be able to make the necessary property adjustment and other orders effective before the divorce order if the circumstances are "exceptional" (whereas in reality they are depressingly routine).
>
> Are the parties then to be compelled to remain under the same roof for the eighteen months for which Parliament has stipulated they should reflect and consider? Of course, it may be possible for them to agree on appropriate interim arrangements, but otherwise — unless the court is prepared to take a liberal view of what is "exceptional" — it seems probable that Winifred would be advised to seek an occupation order under Part IV of the 1996 Act excluding Harry from the house. This seems unlikely to achieve the Act's stated principle of bringing the marriage to an end with minimum distress (or even without costs being unnecessarily incurred): *c.f.* FLA 1996, s.1(b).

Extent of the Court's powers: wide but not unlimited

Although the Court's powers are very wide, they are (as the House of Lords emphasised in *Jenkins v. Livesey (formerly Jenkins* [1985] A.C. 424) not limitless and the court may only act in accordance with the provisions of the legislation. A number of limitations are particularly important in practice:

(i) *No power to order payment to third parties.*

For this reason the court has no power to order one party to pay insurance premiums on the former matrimonial home direct to the insurers; whilst in *Milne v. Milne* (1981) 2 FLR 286 the Court of Appeal held that, since the statute did not permit the court to order payments to be made save to the other party to the marriage or for the children of the family, the court could not order the husband in effect to execute and pay for a life insurance policy and to assign the benefit of the policy to the wife. In practice, provisions dealing with insurance, repairs, and payment of mortgage interest and other outgoings are often dealt with by the parties giving undertakings which are then annexed to the court's order in a schedule.

(ii) *No power to make order in respect of property not owned by spouse.*

The court has no power to make orders relating to assets which, by their nature, are not "owned" by either spouse. For this reason, the court cannot make orders requiring a company — even a company in which one of the spouses is a majority shareholder — to deal with its assets. The court can of course order a spouse to transfer or settle the shareholding (see *Crittenden v. Crittenden* [1990] 2 FLR 361, C.A., but compare *Nicholas v. Nicholas* [1984] FLR 285) and it will on occasions be prepared to frame the orders it makes in such a way as to "afford judicious encouragement to third parties to provide the maintaining spouse with the means to comply with the court's view of the justice of the case": see *per* Waite L.J., in *Thomas v. Thomas* [1995] 2 FLR 668, where —

> the husband was joint managing director of a family business which adopted a conservative policy in respect of dividends and directors' pay. It was held that the judge had been right to draw the inference that the husband could procure changes in the company's policy to meet any shortfall in income which he would suffer as a result of the orders the court considered necessary to meet the needs of his family.

and —

> In *Browne v. Browne* [1989] 1 FLR 291, C.A., the court made a £175,000 order against a wife on the basis that she had in reality access to substantial funds held in Swiss and Jersey trusts.

(iii) *No power to vary beneficial interest under settlements (other than marriage settlements).*

If a settlor creates a settlement which is unrelated to any actual or projected marriage — to save inheritance tax, for example — the settlement would not fall within the definition of a marriage settlement, and accordingly the court could not vary its terms, even though the settlement might be used to provide substantial assets to meet the family's post divorce needs.

(iv) *No prejudice to third party rights.*

For example, if the matrimonial home is subject to a mortgage a transfer of it to the wife cannot affect the mortgagor husband's contractual liability to pay the mortgage instalments, nor the rights of the mortgagee to take action if the mortgage covenants are broken. In practice mortgage deeds usually contain provisions forbidding the mortgagor from transferring the property without the mortgagee's consent; hence the mortgagee should have notice of the application and be given an opportunity to be heard. There are now statutory provisions empowering the court to order pension trustees to make certain payments to the pensioner's former spouse (see now section 25C, MCA 1973.) Again, in the *Brooks* case the House of Lords was careful to emphasise that the power to vary (as a marriage settlement) the terms of an occupational pension scheme was not to be used in such a way as to prejudice third party rights in the fund.

B. THE EXERCISE OF THE COURT'S DISCRETION

No sex discrimination

The legislation does not discriminate between the sexes. As Scarman L.J. put it in *Calderbank v. Calderbank* ([1976] Fam. 93, 103) "husbands and wives come to the judgment seat . . . upon a basis of complete equality"; and orders — sometimes substantial — have been made against wives. For example:

> In *Browne v. Browne* [1989] 1 FLR 291 C.A., Butler-Sloss L.J. said that an application by a husband (at the time a Member of Parliament) for redistribution of assets was "not in any way an unusual application . . . [and] that it would be a sad reflection if in these times of much vaunted equality of the sexes a husband should be seen to be acting in some way improperly if he exercises the right (to apply for an order) which the law permits and indeed encourages. The wife was ordered to pay the husband £175,000.

However, in practice such orders are the exception; as Lord Nicholls of Birkenhead put it in *Brooks v. Brooks* [1996] 1 A.C. 375, H.L., the major responsibility for family care and home-making still remains with women, and the consequent limitation on their earning power — and sometimes on their opportunity to obtain educational and other qualifications — prevents their building up assets on the scale customary for men of equivalent social and economic standing. Hence, reality often dictates that financial orders be made against the husband in favour of the wife.

The statutory guidelines

The background.   Concern about the impact of divorce on women (and particularly the "innocent" wife divorced against her will) led Parliament to adopt a clear principle: the courts should in principle seek to keep the parties, so far as it was practicable and, having regard to their conduct, just to do so, in the financial position in which they would have been if the marriage had not broken down. But that principle was controversial, and the legislation was amended by the Matrimonial and Family Proceedings Act 1984.

The 1984 Act removed the statutory directive whereby the court was obliged to seek to place the parties in the financial position in which they would have been had the marriage not broken down; and the scheme of the legislation is now, in outline, as follows:

(a) It is the duty of the court in deciding whether to exercise its powers and, if so, in what manner to have regard to all the circumstances of the case, first consideration being given to the welfare while a minor of any child of the family who has not attained the age of 18 (MCA 1973, s.25(1)): see below.

(b) The court is directed "in particular" to have regard to certain specified matters (s.25(2)): see below; and finally,

(c) The court is required to go through a complex decision-taking process designed to facilitate, in appropriate cases, the making of a "clean break" between the parties to the marriage (s.25A): see below.

(a) First consideration to the welfare of children

The Act requires the court, in deciding whether and how to exercise its financial powers to "have regard to all the circumstances of the case, first consideration being given to the welfare while a minor of any child of the family who has not attained the age of eighteen": MCA 1973, s.25(1). This provision arises in the context of the exercise of the court's powers to make orders in relation to the spouses, and is not solely related to the making of orders relating to the children. Thus —

> In *C v. C (Financial Relief: Short Marriage)* [1997] 2 FLR, C.A., the Court of Appeal upheld substantial awards to a wife notwithstanding the fact that the marriage had lasted for only nine and a half months. The statutory obligation to give first consideration to the welfare of the parties' four-year-old invalid child was a material factor in this decision: see *per* Ward L.J.

The court has often regarded it as being a priority to seek to ensure that any children have adequate housing, and to that end the court has made orders transferring the family home to the parent with whom the children are to live. Again, the court may think that the requirement to give first consideration to the welfare of the children requires a mother with care of the children to have periodical payments for her own support at least until the children no longer need her full-time care: see *Waterman v. Waterman* [1989] 1 FLR 380, C.A.; whilst it has been accepted that it is not in the children's interest that their mother be in straitened circumstances: *E v. E (Financial Provision)* [1989] 2 FLR 233.

The statutory directive may also have an indirect effect on the exercise of the court's powers in respect of the parents: for example, in *S v. S* [1987] 1 FLR 71, Waite J., the court favoured a "clean break" between the parents because ending their financial interdependency would remove the only serious source of dispute between them.

There are a number of significant limitations on the scope of the direction to give first consideration to the children's welfare:

(i) *First, but not paramount.*

In deciding issues relating to the upbringing of children the court regards the welfare of the child as the "paramount" consideration even if that means that the just claims of the child's parents or others affected have to be overridden. In considering financial matters, in contrast, the court is not required to go so far, and is required merely to give "first" consideration to the welfare of the child in question. This means that it must simply consider all the circumstances always bearing the children's welfare in mind, and then try to make a financial settlement which is just as between husband and wife:

> In *Suter v. Suter and Another* [1987] 2 FLR 232, C.A. the wife remained in the family home with the two children of the marriage. Her 21-year-old lover (a labourer in the Devonport dockyard earning £7,000 per annum) spent every night in the home with the wife. The judge ordered the husband to transfer his interest in the home to the wife, and to make periodical payments to her of an amount which would cover the whole of the mortgage interest. This was done to protect the children's housing needs; but the Court of Appeal held that the judge had been wrong to elevate the children's interests so as to control the outcome. The wife's lover could be expected to make a contribution to the cost of the housing from which he benefited.

(ii) *Applies only to children of the family.*

The expression "child of the family" is widely defined in the legislation and extends to any child who has been treated by both of the parties to the marriage as a child of their family. But the definition does not encompass all the children who may, actually or prospectively, be affected by the orders made in the matrimonial proceedings in question: the child born to a husband and his cohabitant after the breakdown of the husband's marriage is likely to be outside the definition, for example. The legislation thus seems now to embody the principle that the court is to put the interests of the children of a first marriage before the interests of other children affected, and this same principle seems implicit in the child support legislation.

(iii) *Applies only during infancy of children.*

The court is only required to give first consideration to the welfare "while a minor" of any child of the family who has not attained the age of 18. This has two particular consequences. First, the court is not obliged to give such consideration to the welfare of any child of the family who has at the date of the hearing already attained the age of 18, even if the child is undergoing advanced education or training or is disabled, for example. Secondly, this provision does not require the court to take account of the fact that children in practice often stay in their homes until a later age (whether because they are undergoing education or training or because they are disabled or unemployed or simply because they prefer to do so, particularly during the early stages of their career). This does not of course mean the court will ignore such interests, but simply that they do not have any priority.

(iv) *Must take effect subject to limitations imposed by Child Support legislation.*

As already noted, the Child Support Act 1991 does not make any relevant amendment to the guidelines governing the exercise of the court's discretion in divorce and other proceedings; but in practice it is likely to have a significant impact on the exercise of the court's powers and duties. The Child Support Act will in many cases deprive the court of the power to make any order for periodical payments in respect of a child.

(b) The duty to consider "all the circumstances"

The Act directs the court to consider "all the circumstances of the case" and "in particular" to have regard to an elaborate list of specific matters. It follows that the court must not simply confine its attention to those specifed matters; it must also (as Scarman L.J. put it in *Trippas v. Trippas* [1973] 1 W.L.R. 134, 144) investigate all other circumstances "past, present, and, in so far as one can make a reliable estimate, future" which are relevant to a decision of any particular case. For example:

> In *Jenkins v. Livesey (formerly Jenkins)* [1985] A.C. 424 the wife had remarried at the date when her application for a property adjustment order was made. That fact should have been taken into account; and she should not have been allotted the whole of the parties' only significant capital asset (the former matrimonial home).

Again:

> In *Kokosinski v. Kokosinski* [1980] Fam. 72 the wife had made substantial contributions to building up the family business before the marriage. Although contributions made during the marriage were one of the matters specifically referred to in the legislation, contributions made before marriage were also a relevant consideration.

The specified matters.   The court is now directed "in particular" to have regard to eight matters, and a vast body of case law has developed. The text seeks to highlight points of particular significance.

(a) The income, earning capacity, property and other financial resources which each of the parties to the marriage has or is likely to have in the foreseeable future, including in the case of earning capacity any increase in that capacity which it would in the opinion of the court be reasonable to expect a party to the marriage to take steps to acquire: MCA 1973, s.25(2)(a).
This provision directs the court's attention to the parties' assets, in the broadest possible terms. In many cases, this is a simple matter. The parties have earnings, perhaps a house and a motor car and a few other chattels. But in more complex cases getting at the truth is both difficult and costly; and although the legal system has procedures designed to get at the truth (particularly through the process of "discovery") these enquiries may prove extremely (and sometimes disproportionately) costly —

> In *C v. C (Wasted Costs Order)* [1994] 2 FLR 34, C.A., costs amounting to £130,000 were incurred, but the total assets only justified making an order for a lump sum payment of £20,000.
> In *Dart v. Dart* [1996] 2 FLR 286, C.A. the husband's costs in connection with an application for financial relief amounted to £477,127 and the wife's to £877,025.

— and also give rise to a great deal of acrimony. It is true that costs on the scale reported in *Dart* were said to be "almost unprecedented"; but a great deal of anxiety has been expressed, and new procedures put forward in an attempt to limit pointless dissipation of assets.

Part of the problem is that nothing is excluded from the survey which the court is required to make:

> In *Schuller v. Schuller* [1990] 2 FLR 193, C.A. a divorced wife went to work as a housekeeper. Her employer died before the court had settled the financial arrangements to be made on the divorce and left the wife his flat worth £130,000. The court refused to accept the argument that this acquisition was in no way related to the marriage and that it should accordingly be disregarded. On the contrary, its value was properly taken fully into account in an order dividing all the parties' property equally. It had been right to achieve parity between the parties, and this was done by ensuring that each of them had adequate housing, even if the wife in fact received comparatively little from the assets acquired during the marriage.

The direction to have particular regard to property which each party is likely to have "in the foreseeable future" — whether or not it has any connection with the marriage means that inheritance expectations may be taken into account, for example if a relative is known to be terminally ill: *Morgan v. Morgan* [1977] Fam.122. Again —

> In *MT v. MT (Financial Provision: Lump Sum)* [1992] 1 FLR 362, Bracewell J., the husband had indefeasible rights under German law to inherit a share of his elderly father's estate; and he and his wife had conducted their married life on the basis that large funds would be available to them from that source. The court took the inheritance into account.

— but in practice inheritance expectations are rarely relevant because they are too uncertain: see, for example, *Michael v. Michael* [1986] 2 FLR 389.

The question of *earning capacity* is frequently a source of dispute. The court is concerned with what each spouse could reasonably earn; and the Act — evidently influenced by the belief that the divorced should put the marriage behind them and if need be retrain to fit themselves for employment — now specifically refers to "any increase in earning capacity which it would be reasonable to expect" a spouse to take steps to acquire. This involves two separate issues. The first is a question of fact: has the spouse in fact any earning potential? The second is one of judgment: what would it be "reasonable" to expect?

The case law suggests that English law (in contrast to that in some other jurisdictions such as California and even Scotland) is ready to accept that it will often not be practicable for a wife to create the career to which she might have aspired had she never married:

> In *M v. M (Financial Provision)* [1987] 2 FLR 1, C.A. the wife of a chartered accountant (who himself earned some £60,000 a year) had worked as a secretary prior to her 20-year marriage and done some part-time work during the marriage. When the marriage broke down, she tried "valiantly and persistently" to find some employment, but without success. The judge held on the facts that she was unlikely at her age and with her job experience to achieve more than a "fairly humble job" in the secretarial field and accordingly that her earning potential should not be assessed at more than £6,000 per annum.

Another matter which has given rise to problems is the extent to which a *new partner's earnings and earning capacity* should be taken into account. It is clear that the court has no power to order that a third party, such as the husband's second wife or cohabitant, should provide for the applicant or the children of their family; and it must not make an order which can only be satisfied by dipping into a third party's resources: *B v. B (Periodical Payments: Transitional Provisions)* [1995] 1 FLR 459; but the fact that the third party has means available may be relevant — so that in *Suter v. Suter and Another* [1987] 2 FLR 232, C.A., the man with whom the wife was sharing her life was effectively expected to contribute £600 monthly to her living expenses.

The breakdown of a marriage means that many families — deprived of their main wage-earner — become dependent on *state benefits*; and the courts had to consider how far the availability of such benefits affected the orders they would make. However, in cases where there are children, the Child Support Agency will now seek to compel the "absent parent" to support them in accordance with the formula laid down by the Child Support Act, and this will usually make the question of a court order under the divorce legislation irrelevant. It is however worth noting the two principles which the courts had been accustomed to apply before that Act came into force in such cases. First, a husband was not to be allowed to throw onto the state the cost of supporting his dependants (saying, for example, "there is no point in my paying anything because it will simply reduce my wife's income support"); but, secondly, he would be allowed to keep for himself and his new family at least a subsistence level of income, taking into account expenses on travel to work, housing and so on. Indeed, the courts were ready to give a really significant inducement to what Waite J. in *Ashley v. Blackman* [1988] 2 FLR 278 described as the "genuine struggler".

In that case, the periodical payments which the husband had been ordered to pay since the end of his marriage 16 years previously merely reduced the amount of state benefit to which his former wife would otherwise have been entitled, and did not confer any economic advantage on her. The court held that his obligations should be immediately terminated:

> "no humane society could tolerate — even in the interest of saving its public purse — the prospect of a divorced couple of acutely limited means remaining manacled to each other indefinitely by the necessity to return at regular intervals to court for no other purpose than to thrash out at public expense the precise figure which the one should pay the other — not for any benefit to either of them, but solely for the relief of the tax-paying section of the community to which neither of them has sufficient means to belong."

The question whether this approach is to be preferred to that adopted by the Child Support Act (which makes few allowances for life after breakdown) is one to which the reader may wish to return after considering the details of that legislation.

(b) The financial needs, obligations and responsibilities which each of the parties to the marriage has or is likely to have in the foreseeable future: MCA 1973, s.23(2)(b).

Needs.   When assessing financial orders it is in practice usually the "reasonable needs" of the parties and the children of the family and the "net effect" which the order will have on them, with which the court is primarily concerned. As Butler-Sloss L.J. put it in *Dart v. Dart* [1996] 2 FLR 286, 303, C.A.:

A court "will apply the relevant criteria according to the widely differing facts of each case before it. In the low income cases the assessment of the needs of the parties will lean heavily in favour of the children and the parent with whom they live. If, therefore, the only asset is the house, and the mother is caring for the children, she will get the house and probably outright, even though the effect of that order is to deprive the husband of the whole of the capital accrued during the marriage and directly financed from his resources".

Even in the case of the extremely rich, the courts have come to regard the "needs" (or what in high net worth cases is usually described as the "reasonable requirements") of the parties as the dominant factor. However, these terms are relative and the wife of a wealthy man has been held to be entitled to a high and even luxurious standard of living:

In *Preston v. Preston* [1982] Fam. 17, C.A. the husband had capital assets of £2.3 million, and an annual income of £40,000 (which was subject to only a low rate of income tax in Jersey). The court held that the wife's reasonable requirements included a house costing up to £300,000, and also to have the financial security conferred by the availability of a significant sum of free capital; and a £600,000 lump sum award was upheld (and see also *C v. C (Financial Relief: Short Marriage)* [1997] 2 FLR, C.A.).

In these cases, the courts often make use of a computer programme (the so-called *Duxbury* calculation) to calculate the lump sum needed to produce a certain annual level of spending power over the applicant's lifetime allowing for inflation and making certain assumptions about the yield obtainable from investments and other factors: see *F v. F (Duxbury Calculation: Rate of Return)* [1996] 1 FLR 833, Holman J., *Wells v. Wells* [1997] 1 All E.R. 673, C.A.

It has been argued that it is wrong in very substantial cases to give such attention to the "reasonable requirements" of the parties, and that the wife of an exceedingly rich man should rather be entitled to a fractional share of his assets. (As already mentioned in *Dart* one hundred million pounds was suggested). But the courts have accepted that there is a certain level at which the applicant's "reasonable requirements" level off; and it has been held not to be open to the Court of Appeal to go beyond satisfying such requirements and instead to reorganise proprietary rights within families. The House of Lords has, perhaps surprisingly, refused leave to appeal against that decision.

Contributions. The words of the statute do not give "need" any priority, and although that factor seems to be dominant, it remains true that all the circumstances (including in particular the contributions made by the parties) must be considered: *Smith v. Smith (Smith and others intervening)* [1991] 2 FLR 55, C.A.

Starting points: one-third and one-half? Before the 1970 legislation, the courts tended to work on the basis of fractional allocations (one-third of the joint income for the wife with payments for the children in addition was an approach derived from the practice of the ecclesiastical courts) and some judges are accustomed, at least in "middle of the road" cases to start with what Waite L.J. described as "some convenient and familiar starting point" (such as the one-third proportion when assessing income provision or a 50/50 division when dealing with the interests in a matrimonial home). However, Waite L.J. went on:

"it has been repeatedly emphasised that [such fractions] . . . remain starting points only, and must never be allowed the status of a rule or principle governing (as opposed to initiating) the judicial process involved in exercising the discretion": *Burgess v. Burgess* [1996] 2 FLR 34, 36. (In that case the judge at first instance had said that "where there has been a long partnership marriage, and both have careers of their own, the court should in principle seek to divide their current assets equally and let each go their separate ways". The Court of Appeal held the judge had not misdirected herself).

The need for housing: Mesher and Martin orders.   The needs approach has led the courts to give a great deal of attention to the best way of satisfying the need of the parties for a secure home; and as already mentioned there will be many cases in which it seems best to transfer the house outright to one spouse. But there may be cases in which, although the need to provide secure housing for the wife and children means that the house cannot be sold at the time of the divorce, it seems wrong to deprive the husband for all time of what may be a substantial equity. In such cases, the courts may use their flexible powers to order a settlement, perhaps by a so-called *Martin* order (see *Martin v. Martin* [1978] Fam. 12) under which the wife will have the right to occupy the house until her death or remarriage (or, sometimes, her becoming dependent on another man or living with him as his wife: *Clutton v. Clutton* [1991] 1 FLR 242). Much the same objective may be achieved (as in *Knibb v. Knibb* [1987] 2 FLR 396) by ordering that the house be transferred to the wife on condition that she grant the husband a charge for the appropriate percentage of its value when the charge comes to be redeemed. This reflects the fact that the wife is to be regarded as the true owner of the property — with all the incidental burdens and benefits — whilst the husband's interest is an investment interest in the proceeds of any sale.

Obligations and responsibilities.   How far is one spouse to be allowed to claim that an apparently high income is much lower than it seems because, for example, there are large travelling expenses or heavy mortgage payments on the house in which he or she is living with a new partner? The general answer — as is so often the case in this jurisdiction — is that it depends on what is reasonable:

> In *Slater v. Slater* (1982) 3 FLR 364, C.A. the court thought the husband had been extravagant in deciding to live in a country house with consequent heavy transport and property maintenance expenses, and he was not allowed to deduct those expenses in working out his available income. But if the husband has reasonably decided to buy a new house with a heavy mortgage, leaving his divorced wife and family in the former matrimonial home, the court will not make it impossible for him to service the mortgage: *Stockford v. Stockford* (1981) 3 FLR 58.

Again —

> In *Delaney v. Delaney* [1990] 2 FLR 457, C.A., the Court of Appeal considered it reasonable for a man to contract a substantial mortgage in order to provide him with housing suitable for his children's occupation on access visits, as well as providing a home for his intended spouse and the children they planned to have.

Child care responsibilities.   Child care responsibilities obviously have an impact on a spouse's earning capacity. Again the question is largely one of what is reasonable in the light of the facts, and in *Waterman v. Waterman* [1989] 1 FLR 380 the Court of Appeal did not dissent from the proposition that a ten-year-old child should not require the same degree or intensity of care as would be necessary for a five-year-old. Perhaps the most striking illustration of the court's pragmatic approach to these issues is to be found in the case of *Fisher v. Fisher* [1989] 1 FLR 423, C.A.:

> A wife had a child by a third party some years after the divorce. The husband argued that by allowing the pregnancy to occur she had voluntarily made herself incapable of self-support, but the Court of Appeal accepted that it was impossible to ignore the wife's responsibility to her child.

(c) The standard of living enjoyed by the family before the breakdown of the marriage: MCA 1973, s.25(2)(c)

One spouse is not entitled to keep the same standard of living as had been enjoyed during the marriage, but "adequate recognition" should be given to it in deciding the parties' reasonable requirements:

> In *R v. R (Financial Provision: Reasonable Needs)* [1994] 2 FLR 1044 the matrimonial home was a "superb Queen Anne house" with hard tennis courts and swimming pool standing in 30 acres of grounds. Although the judge held that in one sense it could be said that the wife did not need such a large house, it would be wholly unreasonable to require her to leave the home in which she had lived for seventeen years.

Again —

> In *Leadbeater v. Leadbeater* [1985] FLR 789 the wife had been married for four years to a man worth £250,000, and had in consequence enjoyed a "much enhanced" life-style. That factor was taken into account, but so was the modest lifestyle she had previously enjoyed. Taking all the factors into account a comparatively modest £37,500 lump sum was ordered.

(d) The age of each party to the marriage and the duration of the marriage: C.A. 1973, s.25(2)(d).

It will not often be necessary to consider the parties' ages as a matter distinct from the court's assessment of their needs and resources: if a spouse is young and healthy he or she will be able to work and the need for support will be that much less; an elderly and infirm spouse's needs will be that much greater. But in *C v. C (Financial Relief: Short Marriage)* [1997] 2 FLR, C.A., the fact that the 59-year-old husband was approaching retirement age and that the 40-year-old wife was "in that uncertain period in which it may be said she is not young and so her position in the labour market is obviously less favourable than it was when she was 30" was thought to be a relevant consideration.

But there is likely to be much more concern with the duration of the marriage. Parliament in 1984 repudiated the notion that a wife should be entitled solely by virtue of the status of marriage to be maintained on a scale appropriate to her husband's standard of life. The effect can be seen by comparing a case decided before the 1984 legislation with cases decided afterwards:

In *Brett v. Brett* [1969] 1 W.L.R. 487 the wife — a childless 23-year-old solicitor, whose marriage had lasted for less than six months — was awarded (in 1997 values) yearly periodical payments of some £17,000 and a lump sum of some £200,000.

In contrast:

In *Attar v. Attar* [1985] FLR 649 the court thought a single capital payment of £30,000 was sufficient to enable the wife of an exceedingly wealthy man to retrain after a six-month marriage over a two-year period.

However it does not always follow that a low award will be considered appropriate in short marriage cases:

In what was described as the "highly unusual" case of *C v. C (Financial Relief: Short Marriage)* [1997] 2 FLR, C.A., the parties had met when the husband used the wife's professional services as a high-class call girl. The marriage produced a child, but lasted for only nine and a half months. The Court of Appeal upheld awards to the wife of a £195,000 lump sum, and periodical payments of £19,500. The Court of Appeal agreed with the judge that this marriage had had profound and continuing consequences for the wife's earning capacity not least because of the need to care for the child, but also because of the adverse impact on her health of the break-up of the marriage. Hence, although the awards were generous, they were not outside the generous ambit of the discretion conferred by statute.

(e) Any physical or mental disability of either of the parties to the marriage: MCA 1973, s.25(2)(e).
This provision seems to add little to the matters considered under other heads, and it does not appear to have been considered as a separate matter in decided cases.

(f) The contributions which each of the parties has made or is likely in the foreseeable future to make to the welfare of the family, including any contribution made by looking after the home or caring for the family: MCA 1973, s.25(2)(f).
The law governing property regimes was felt by many not to give adequate recognition to the contributions made, particularly by housewives, towards the acquisition of so-called "family assets", *i.e.* those things which are "acquired . . . with the intention that there should be continuing provision for (the parties) and their children during their joint lives, and used for the benefit of the family as a whole" (as Lord Denning put it in *Wachtel v. Wachtel* [1973] Fam. 72). The *Wachtel* decision made it quite clear that such contributions would be taken fully into account under the post-1969 law, and that where a young couple with little or no starting capital acquired a home with the help of mortgage finance the home would usually be regarded as their joint investment. In practice, of course, in most cases any separate consideration of the parties' contributions will merge into a consideration of their needs. For example, the house will often be transferred to the wife because of the needs of the children and the person with their day-to-day care, and it will not be necessary to consider separately how far the

wife has contributed to the family's welfare. But there will be cases in which contributions do need to be regarded as a distinct matter, particularly if the contributions relate to a business:

> In *Gojkovic v. Gojkovic* [1990] 1 FLR 140, C.A., a Yugoslav couple had come to this country almost penniless, but (in what the trial judge described as "a story of high achievement and . . . glorious success . . . through unrelenting hard work, unlimited self-sacrifice and absolute determination") they built up businesses worth almost four million pounds most of which, in law, belonged to the husband. The Court of Appeal rejected an argument that the wife's claim should be limited to the amount which would satisfy her needs. Equally important was the exceptional financial contribution which the wife had made to the wealth generated during the parties' relationship and marriage.

(g) the conduct of each of the parties *whatever the nature of the conduct and whether it occurred during the marriage or after the separation of the parties or (as the case may be) dissolution or annulment of the marriage*, **if that conduct is such that it would in the opinion of the court be inequitable to disregard it": MCA 1973, s.25(2)(g).**
(The italicised words were inserted by FLA 1996, Schedule 8, paragraph 9(3)(b)).

The extent to which the conduct of the parties should be relevant in determining the financial outcome of divorce has long been controversial. The Matrimonial and Family Proceedings Act 1984 was apparently intended to codify the practice of the courts developed on the basis of the Court of Appeal's decision in *Wachtel v. Wachtel* [1973] Fam. 72. This was based on the belief that the policy of the divorce law was to minimise the bitterness, distress and humiliation of divorce so that in most cases it would be wrong to allow considerations of what was formerly regarded as guilt or blame to affect the financial orders made on divorce. But it was accepted that there would be a "residue of cases, where the conduct of one of the parties had been such that it would be 'inequitable' to disregard it." For example:

> In *Evans v. Evans* [1989] 1 FLR 351, C.A., a wife obtained a divorce from her husband, after a short marriage, in 1951. Over the next 35 years the husband meticulously complied with court orders for maintenance. In 1985 the wife was convicted of inciting others to murder the husband under a contract-killing arrangement and she was sentenced to four years' imprisonment. The husband ceased to make the maintenance payments, and the Court of Appeal held that the wife's conduct had been such as to make it right to discharge the order.

Again:

> In *K v. K (Financial Provision: Conduct)* [1988] 1 FLR 469 the husband suffered from a depressive illness, which made his behaviour unpredictable and suicidal. The wife assisted the husband with suicide attempts not (so the District Judge found) from humanitarian motives but in order that she could set up home with her lover and get as much from the husband's estate as possible. In those circumstances (and also taking into account the wife's wholly deceitful conduct in relation to her association with her lover) it was held that it would be inequitable to disregard the wife's conduct. In the result, the lump sum awarded to the wife was reduced from £14,000 to £5,000.

But in contrast:

> In *Leadbeater v. Leadbeater* [1985] FLR 789 the wife (who had an alcohol problem) had committed adultery with several men whilst on holiday; the husband had insisted on a 15-year-old girl moving into the family home, refused to turn her out, and indeed subsequently had a child by her. The court held that it would "not be inequitable" to disregard the wife's conduct. On the contrary, this was a classic case in which (to use Lord Denning's words in *Wachtel*) "both parties are to blame."

These cases seemed to reflect a principle that marital conduct would only be relevant in exceptional circumstances in which there had been misconduct of some gravity, and notably in cases in which there had been some imbalance of conduct between the parties, such as would lead a right-thinking member of society to say that it would be inequitable to disregard the matters alleged. It seems that solicitors discouraged clients from peristing in making allegations intended to influence the financial outcome; but, however that may be, the debates on the Bill for the Family Law Act 1996 made it clear that many members of Parliament believed the courts never took conduct into account (or that it was only conduct — perhaps a contumacious failure to disclose assets: see *B v. B (Real Property: Assessment of Interests)* [1988] 2 FLR 490 — in relation to the divorce case itself that would be held relevant).

Eventually, as one of the many concessions which the Government was compelled to make in order to secure the passage of the Bill, it was agreed that the italicised words should be inserted into the legislation. The Minister stated that the intention was "to emphasise that conduct of the parties of whatever nature, should it be inequitable to disregard it, has to be taken into account and that it is not only conduct in the course of ancillary relief proceedings that has to be considered" (see *per* Mr Jonathan Evans, Standing Committee E, *Official Report*, May 16, 1996, column 371). But it must be possible to argue that the words "whatever the nature of the conduct" will require the court to consider and take into account precisely those, perhaps trivial, matters which had formerly been excluded from consideration. Certainly solicitors are unlikely to be able convincingly to advise clients aggrieved by the breakdown of their marriage — at least until the new provision has been authoritatively construed by the courts — that it is simply not worthwhile to put conduct in issue.

(h) The value to each of the parties to the marriage of any benefit which by reason of the dissolution or annulment of the marriage, that party will lose the chance of acquiring: MCA 1973, s.25(2)(h) (as amended by the Pensions Act 1995).
The fact that divorce ends the legal status of marriage means that any rights flowing from that status — for example, rights to succeed on a spouse's intestacy — also come to an end. But in recent years it has been the fact that a divorced spouse often loses rights under occupational and other pension schemes which has been the focus of attention. These rights are often very valuable not least because occupational pension schemes enjoy favourable tax treatment: the contributions made by the employer are not treated as the income of the employee, the employee is not charged to income tax on any contributions made out of earnings to the scheme and the fund will be invested by the trustees with virtual immunity from taxation.

The relevant provisions which go some way to enabling pension benefits to be treated in the same way as are other family assets can be briefly summarised:

(1) Focusing on pensions.   The legislation now imposes a specific duty on the court to have particular regard to benefits under pension schemes as financial resources (MCA 1973 s.25(2)(a)) and as benefits likely to be lost (MCA 1973 s.25(2)(h)) and to consider whether to make a financial provision order in respect of these matters. Regulations lay down detailed rules as to the information to be provided: see the Divorce, etc., Pensions Regulations 1996 (S.I. 1996 No. 1676) and the Divorce etc. Pensions (Amendment) Regulations 1997 (S.I. 1997 No. 636).

(2) Taking pension payments into account.

(a) *Compensatory payments.*
    The traditional approach was to compensate the spouse who would lose pension rights in a rough and ready way by allocating an appropriately enlarged share of the parties' other assets. For example:

> In *Richardson v. Richardson* (1978) 9 Fam. Law 96, the court made an enhanced lump sum order in favour of the wife to compensate her for the loss of benefits under her husband's civil service pension scheme.

(b) *Variation of pension scheme as "marriage settlement".*
    As a result of the decision of the House of Lords in *Brooks v. Brooks* [1996] 1 A.C. 375 (p. 67 above) the court may in some cases be able to vary the terms of an occupational pension scheme for the benefit of the pensioner's spouse and children: see, e.g. *W v. W (Periodical Payments: Pensions)* [1996] 2 FLR 480, Connell J. But the variation will only be possible if it meets requirements imposed by the Inland Revenue and does not prejudice the rights of third parties; and accordingly the *Brooks* decision will in many cases not provide a solution.

(c) *"Earmarking" part of the pension benefit.*
    An "earmarking" order requires the pension fund manager or trustee to divert payments from the pensioner to the other spouse. For example, the court could order that half the pensioner's retirement pension be paid over in this way — but the payments would cease as and when the pensioner ceased to be entitled (for example, on his death).

(d) *Dealing with death benefits: exercising powers of nomination, etc.*
    The court may now in effect order that all or part of sums due on a pensioner's death be paid to the other spouse, and the pensioner may be required to "nominate" the other spouse as the person entitled to receive such sums.

(e) *"Splitting" the pension.*
    In many cases, the most equitable method of dealing with a substantial pension fund would be to "split" the pension fund, perhaps by directing a payment of part or all the transfer value — in effect, the amount which the scheme member could

require to be transferred to a new employer's scheme — to another pension scheme under which the other spouse would be the principal beneficiary, or perhaps by giving the other spouse defined benefits under the existing scheme. The Family Law Act contains provisions intended to allow this to be done, but they are technically defective and it is unlikely that they will ever be brought into force. However, the Conservative Government committed itself to introducing fresh legislation to give the courts the requisite powers; and a White Paper, *Pension Rights on Divorce* (1997) Cm. 3564, para. 5.10 states that pension splitting powers should be available to the courts in respect of proceedings started after April 2000.

State pensions.   The National Insurance scheme provides retirement pensions and widow's pensions to those who satisfy contribution requirements. In effect, the law allows one divorced spouse to take over the other's contribution record for the period the marriage was in existence.

(c) The "Clean Break"

In *Minton v. Minton* [1979] A.C. 593, 608, Lord Scarman stated that the "clean break" principle informed the modern legislation, and that:

> "the law now encourages spouses to avoid bitterness after family breakdown and to settle their money and property problems. An object of the modern law is to encourage each to put the past behind them and to begin a new life which is not overshadowed by the relationship which has broken down."

The legislation contains four provisions designed to facilitate the attainment of this objective, and thereby to attain what Thorpe J. has described as "financial as well as emotional independence": *Richardson v. Richardson (No. 2)* [1994] 2 FLR 1051, 1054; and those provisions merit separate treatment (notwithstanding the fact that they are one aspect of the exercise of the court's discretion). But the reader should bear in mind that the expression "clean break" is ambiguous, and above all that it is not the court's function to strive for a so-called clean break regardless of all other considerations: see *Clutton v. Clutton* [1991] 1 FLR 242, 245. Rather, the correct approach is to follow strictly the complex and interlocking statutory provisions:

(i) The duty to consider the termination of financial obligations: MCA 1973 s.25A(1). If the court decides to exercise its financial powers in favour of a party to the marriage, it must consider "whether it would be appropriate so to exercise those powers that the financial obligations of each party towards the other will be terminated as soon after the grant of the decree as the court considers just and reasonable." This duty arises whenever the court decides to exercise its property adjustment or financial provision powers in favour of a party to the marriage. (It has no application to orders for children.) The duty is a duty to *consider* whether it would be "appropriate" to exercise those powers to terminate the reciprocal financial obligations as soon as the court considers would be "just and reasonable." The duty imposed by this provision is entirely general, and there are three other provisions of the Act which are relevant to its discharge: see (ii) to (iv) below.

(ii) Court to consider potential increase in earning capacity: MCA 1973, s.25(2)(a).

As noted at p. 74, above, the matters to which the court's attention is particularly directed now include a reference to any increase in earning capacity which it would in the opinion of the court be reasonable to expect a party to the marriage to take steps to acquire. This factor may be particularly relevant to the duty imposed on the court to consider whether any periodical payments order should be made only for a specified term: see below.

(iii) The duty to consider specifying a term for any periodical payments order: MCA 1973, s.25A(2).

The simplest form of "clean break" involves the court ordering capital transfers between the parties, and dismissing all claims for periodical payments. But there will be many cases in which such a once-for-all settlement is not possible and the court feels it appropriate to make an order for periodical payments. If it does decide to make such an order in favour of a party to the marriage, section 25A(2) of the Act then imposes on it a mandatory duty "in particular" to "consider whether it would be appropriate to require those payments to be made or secured only for such term as would in the opinion of the court be sufficient to enable the party in whose favour the order is made to adjust without undue hardship to the termination of his or her financial dependence on the other party." It follows that in each case in which the court decides to make a periodical payments order it must then consider whether the order should be for a specified term, such as six months or five years; and in making that decision the court is required to consider whether such a period would be sufficient for the applicant to adjust "without undue hardship" to the changed circumstances. Can and should the applicant find a way of adjusting his or her life so as to attain financial independence from the other spouse? Is it possible to predict the time by which such an adjustment will have occurred; for example, because child care responsibilities are likely to have ceased? These are matters about which the court must be satisfied by evidence; it must not rely on wishful thinking: see *Flavell v. Flavell* [1997] 1 FLR 353, C.A.; *G v. G (Periodical Payments: Jurisdiction)* [1997] 1 FLR 368, C.A.; p. 87, below. Thus —

> In *Waterman v. Waterman* [1989] 1 FLR 380, C.A. the marriage of a 38-year-old secretary broke down after some three years' cohabitation (of which only 17 months were within marriage). The wife had the care of the five-year-old child; and had moved to live in her mother and sister's "very overcrowded home" in a remote Lincolnshire village. The judge made an order for periodical payments for the wife; and on the basis that she had an earning capacity, that it was in her interests "to get her life on its feet, to obtain an occupation and some source of income for herself" and that by the time the child was ten the mother ought reasonably to be able to obtain employment, made an order that the periodical payments should terminate in five years' time. The Court of Appeal held that such an order was not plainly wrong and that it should accordingly be allowed to stand.

In contrast:

In *M v. M (Financial Provision)* [1987] 2 FLR 1, Heilbron J., the court concluded that it would not be appropriate to terminate periodical payments in favour of the 47-year-old wife of a £60,000 a year accountant at the end of any fixed period nor would it be just and reasonable so to do. The court considered that it would be unrealistic to suppose that the wife could become self-sufficient; and that termination would cause undue hardship to a woman who, after 20 years of marriage, was entitled to a "reasonably decent" standard of living.

In some cases, the courts have even been prepared to accept that commitments to children over 18 but still in education can make it inappropriate to terminate the mother's financial dependence on her former husband:

In *Richardson v. Richardson (No. 2)* [1996] 2 FLR 617, C.A. Thorpe J. had held that the decisive factor in continuing a periodical payments order was not that the children of the family were no longer minors, but that they were still dependent. "What liberates the mother's deployment of capital is not their eighteenth birthday but their independence achieved through education." The Court of Appeal found no error of principle in the judge's approach.

(iv) Power to direct that no application be made to extend the specified term: MCA 1973, s.28(1A)

The court will have jurisdiction to vary a specified term order by extending any term specified in an order at any time during its existence — although the application (and perhaps even the order) must be made before the specified term has come to an end: *G v. G (Periodical Payments: Jurisdiction)* [1997] 1 FLR 368, C.A. — unless the court has exercised the power conferred by section 28(1A) of the Act to direct that no such application be entertained. It has been said (see *Whiting v. Whiting* [1988] 2 FLR 189, C.A.) that such a direction is "draconian" and that it is inappropriate in cases in which there is real uncertainty about the future — particularly when young children are also involved. However, unless such a direction is made the paying spouse is left at risk:

In *Richardson v. Richardson (No. 2)* [1994] 2 FLR 1051, Thorpe J., husband and wife agreed on what all concerned believed would be a "clean break" under which the husband was to pay £8,000 per annum to the wife for three years; but the order did not include a section 28 (1A) direction. It was held that in the absence of such a direction the court had jurisdiction to entertain an application made by the wife before the end of the term to increase the payments and extend the term for which they were payable. (There was no appeal on this point: see [1996] 2 FLR 617).

(v) The power to dismiss a claim for periodical payments: MCA 1973 s.25A(3).

If complete finality is to be achieved, the court must exercise the power now specifically conferred upon it by statute to dismiss all claims for periodical payments and to direct that the applicant be debarred from making any further application for a periodical payments order. The court will also direct that no application be permitted by a spouse for provision out of the other's estate under the provisions of the Inheritance (Provision for Family and Dependants) Act 1975.

Significance of nominal order.   The reason why the court needs this power is that in principle any periodical payments order — even a nominal order for periodical payments of say 5p per annum — may be varied at any time during the currency of the order; and that accordingly a liable spouse will remain constantly at risk of an application to vary the order being made. In effect, a nominal order gives one party a "last backstop", *i.e.* some protection against unforeseen changes of circumstances such as ill-health or unemployment, but only at the cost of leaving the other party at risk. On one view, therefore, to make a nominal order is to negate the notion of a clean break; but the courts have refused (see *Hepburn v. Hepburn* [1989] 1 FLR 373, 376, *per* Butler-Sloss L.J.; and *Whiting v. Whiting* [1988] 2 FLR 189) to hold that such orders are undesirable in principle; and —

> In *Suter v. Suter and Another* [1987] 2 FLR 232, C.A. (where the wife was cohabiting, but her future was not easy to foresee) a nominal order, unrestricted as to time, was made specifically so that the order could be varied if her financial position were to deteriorate.

The exercise of the discretion to impose a clean break.   What options are, in practice open to the court in carrying out these duties and exercising its powers, and how is it likely that the discretion will be exercised?

(a) The options available.   It may be helpful first to summarise the various types of order which may be made:

(i) *Immediate clean break.*

The court may consider that it would be appropriate to terminate the parties' financial obligations immediately. In that case it may make a property adjustment order; but it will dismiss any claim for periodical payments, and it will direct that neither party be entitled to make any further application for such an order. It will also order that neither party be entitled to apply for provision under the Inheritance (Provision for Family and Dependants) Act 1975. This would be an example of the "clean break" in its simplest form. But the fact that one party may still have entitlements which will only mature in the future — for example, to receive a share of the proceeds of sale of the family home — is not inconsistent with the clean break policy:

> In *Clutton v. Clutton* [1991] 1 FLR 242, C.A. the judge considered that it would be appropriate to effect a clean break, and ordered a transfer to the wife of the family home which was the only significant family asset. The Court of Appeal accepted that to deprive the husband of any share in the sole capital asset of the marriage would be manifestly unfair; and that an order under which the house was transferred to the wife subject to the husband's right to be paid one-third of its value on her death, remarriage or cohabiting — a so-called *Martin* order: see p. 77 above — should be substituted. Such an order did settle matters once and for all, even though it would be fully carried into execution only at a future date.

(ii) *Periodical payment order: nominal or specified term?*

If the court considers that it would not be appropriate to terminate the mutual financial obligations of the parties, it will wish to make a periodical payments order (although this may only be for a nominal amount, with the consequences mentioned above). The court must then consider whether it would be appropriate to order the periodical payments for only a specified term.

(iii) *Deferred clean break.*

If the court decides that it would be appropriate to make a specified term order it must decide whether to direct that the applicant be debarred from applying for any extension of the term. Such an order may be called a "deferred clean break." In the absence of such a direction the applicant will be entitled to apply to have the term extended.

(b) The discretion in practice.   It is clear that where there is substantial capital available (and particularly where the wife is young) periodical payments have become largely obsolescent, and a clean break will be the preferred solution; but there is scope for a wider difference of view in other cases:

> In *Whiting v. Whiting* [1988] 2 FLR 189, C.A. the wife had retrained as a teacher; and was in full-time employment earning in excess of £10,000 per annum, with pension entitlements. The husband had been made redundant, and earned some £4,000 per annum as a freelance management consultant. The husband applied to discharge the nominal order which had been made against him; but the judge refused to do so on the ground that the wife should have the "last backstop" of a nominal order. The Court of Appeal, by a majority, held that the decision was not "plainly wrong" and that accordingly — on the principle that the court will not interfere with a proper application of a judicial discretion — refused to interfere. But it is perhaps significant that all three Lords Justice indicated that they would, if trying the case at first instance, have reached a different conclusion.

It is certainly important to remember that a spouse's claim for financial support can only be terminated if the court is satisfied that he or she can adjust "without undue hardship" to the termination of maintenance payments —

> In *Flavell v. Flavell* [1997] 1 FLR 353, 358–359, C.A., the Court of Appeal adopted the view that the termination of periodical payments in favour of a woman in her mid-50s was usually only justified if she had substantial capital and/ or a consistent and significant earning capacity; and Ward L.J. noted a tendency for limited term orders "to be made more in hope than in serious expectation. Especially in judging the case of ladies in their middle years, the judicial looking into a crystal ball very rarely finds enough of substance to justify a finding that adjustment can be made without undue hardship. All too often these orders are made without evidence to support them".

— and it seems that the facts of *G v. G (Periodical Payments: Jurisdiction)* [1997] 1 FLR 368, C.A., provide an example of such wishful thinking:

> The wife, aged 43, had sacrificed her career as a speech therapist, and when her twenty year marriage broke down was working as a receptionist. She could not, on her earnings, maintain herself to a standard appropriate to that which she had enjoyed during the marriage. There were two teenage children who would continue to make many demands on her time. Although she wished to assert her independence, was more than willing to be financially as well as emotionally free of her husband, and had high hope and dogged determination to succeed, events

established that she was not able to become financially self-sufficient. The Court of Appeal doubted whether an order restricting her right to maintenance to a five year period should ever have been made: "no one . . . looking into the crystal ball of [the wife's] life would confidently have predicted any certainty of achievement of those laudable aspirations".

Notwithstanding this cautious approach in the appellate courts many clean break orders are made, and it seems clear that a significant proportion of the divorcing population prefer to avoid any ongoing maintenance obligation: see *The Consequences of Divorce*, OPCS, 1990, Table 8.14.

C. PRIVATE ORDERING AND ITS LIMITS

The contents of this chapter may have given the reader the impression that the financial consequences of divorce are usually resolved by the courts in adversarial litigation. But in fact a large number of orders — 52,297 in 1995 — are made by consent; and it has for some years been the policy of the divorce law to encourage the parties to resolve matters for themselves. This trend has been reinforced by the Family Law Act 1996 which is based on the assumption that in many cases couples will settle the arrangements which have to be made by agreement rather than troubling the courts. But the law has also long taken the view that the community as a whole has an interest in the financial arrangements made by a couple on divorce: a spouse's rights are not to be bargained away by private agreement, and it is for this reason that statute provides that any provision in a maintenance agreement restricting the parties' right to apply to the court is void: MCA 1973, s.34(1).

The consent order.   A compromise between these two conflicting principles has been found in permitting the parties to seek an order by consent from the court, which will then be decisive — even if it provides for a "clean break" with no right to apply for any subsequent variation. The justification for this is that the order will derive its legal effect from the decision of the court rather than from the agreement of the parties which led up to it: *De Lasala v. De Lasala* [1980] A.C. 546; and in making a consent order the court is not a rubber stamp but will have investigated the arrangements embodied in the order.

The duty to provide information.   In order to facilitate this process, statute provides that the court may make a consent order on the basis of specified information laid down by Rules of Court: MCA 1973, s.33A. The information required deals with such matters as the duration of the marriage, the age of the parties, the parties' capital resources, the arrangements proposed for the parties' accommodation; similar information about the children; confirmation as to whether either party has remarried or has any present plans to marry or cohabit; and "any other especially significant matters": Family Proceedings Rules 1991, rule 2.61.
    Failure to disclose any matter relevant to the exercise of the court's discretion makes the order liable to be set aside:

In *Jenkins v. Livesey (formerly Jenkins)* [1985] A.C. 424, H.L., a wife did not disclose the fact that she intended to remarry. That fact would materially have affected the terms of the divorce settlement under which the husband was relieved from paying periodical maintenance but gave up his entire interest in the family home. Since any periodical payments would have come to an end on the wife's remarriage it is most unlikely that he would have agreed to these terms had be known the facts. The order was set aside.

Again —

In *T v. T (Consent Order: Procedure to Set Aside)* [1996] 2 FLR 640, R. Anelay Q.C., the husband led his wife to believe that there was no free market in his corporate hospitality company and a consent order was made on that basis. He did not reveal that negotiations for a takeover by a public limited company were taking place; and shortly after the making of the order he received £1.6 million for his holding. The consent order was set aside for non-disclosure.

Carrying out the investigation. The court has a statutory duty to consider "all the circumstances" (including those particularised in section 25 of the Matrimonial Causes Act 1973 and discussed at pp. 70–83, above). But in reality the court's scrutiny is restricted to a "broad appraisal of the parties' financial circumstances as disclosed to it in the statutory form, without descent into the valley of detail" (*Pounds v. Pounds* [1994] 1 FLR 775, 780, *per* Waite L.J.); and it may be that in many cases the information available would not be sufficient to allow the court to assess the sufficiency or propriety of the proposed order: see *B v. Miller & Co* [1996] 2 FLR 22. Thus:

In *Harris v. Manahan* [1997] 1 FLR 205, C.A. a district judge made a consent order after a pre-trial review. The effect of the order was that the 51-year-old wife (who had no earnings and no prospects of any) was not to be entitled to any periodical payments, but was to have her claims for support settled for all time by being given a share of the sale proceeds of the family home. Unfortunately, the house did not sell for the price the parties had anticipated, and eventually the mortgagees took possession. The wife (who was left with no capital assets and no income other than income support) applied to the court to set aside the consent order on the ground that it had been vitiated by the inadequate legal advice her solicitors had given. The court held that her application had been rightly dismissed: there had to be finality in litigation, and to that end the wife might (as Ward L.J. put it) have to be the victim sacrificed on the "high altar of policy". No doubt in due course she would have redress in an action for negligence against her advisers.

Agreements not embodied in court order. An agreement not embodied in a court order may be liable to variation as a "maintenance agreement" under the provisions of the Matrimonial Causes Act 1973, s.35; and in any event cannot effectively exclude the court's jurisdiction to make orders in the exercise of its divorce jurisdiction. But the courts do lean in favour of upholding agreements. It has been said that the court must start from the position that a solemn and freely negotiated bargain by which a party with competent legal advice defines his own requirements ought to be adhered to unless some clear and compelling reason is shown to the contrary. The leading case is *Edgar v. Edgar* [1980] 1 W.L.R. 1410, C.A.:

> The wife of a multi-millionaire entered into an agreement whereby she accepted property worth some £100,000 from her husband, and agreed not to seek any further capital or property provision from him whether by way of ancillary relief in divorce proceedings or otherwise. Three years later she petitioned for divorce, claimed a substantial capital sum, and at first instance was awarded a lump sum of £760,000. The Court of Appeal held that the wife had shown insufficient grounds to justify going behind the original agreement. It was immaterial that there may have been a disparity of bargaining power between the husband and the wife, since on the facts he had not exploited the disparity in a way unfair to the wife (who had had the benefit of proper professional advice and had deliberately chosen to ignore it).

This doctrine has been criticised (notably in *Pounds v. Pounds* [1994] 2 FLR 775, 791, *per* Hoffmann L.J.); and it is likely that the encouragement apparently offered by the Family Law Act 1996 to the making of informally negotiated agreements will lead to more litigation. It seems that the fact that the parties' out-of-court arrangements have served as the basis upon which the court can make a divorce order will not prevent the parties from subsequently seeking to escape from those arrangements under the principles set out above.

Effect of unforeseen change of circumstances.   What is to happen if there is a change of circumstances after the making of an order — whether by consent or otherwise — which was unforeseen by either party? For example:

> In *Barder v. Caluori* [1988] A.C. 20, H.L., the court by consent made a "clean break" order under which H was to transfer the matrimonial home to W within 28 days. Four weeks later, W killed her children and committed suicide. All her property would go under her will to her mother. The House of Lords held that the husband should be given leave to appeal out of time; and, on the appeal, that the order should be set aside.

When should such leave be given? The House of Lords held that where there had been an unforeseen change of circumstances leave should be given if four conditions are fulfilled:

  (i) the basis or fundamental assumption underlying the order had been falsified by a change of circumstances;
 (ii) such change had occurred within a relatively short time of the making of the original order — usually no more than one year;
(iii) the application for leave was made reasonably promptly; and
 (iv) that the granting of leave would not prejudice unfairly third parties who had acquired interests for value in the property affected.

There has been a considerable body of reported case law on the jurisdiction to set aside orders; and it seems that the principles to be applied are not dissimilar to those applied in deciding whether a contract is to be set aside by reason of mutual mistake or frustration. Thus, the courts have not been prepared to set aside orders merely because assets have appreciated dramatically in value (see *Cornick v. Cornick* [1994] 2 FLR 530, Hale J., where the husband's shares rose in value by nearly 600 per cent in 18 months) provided that the valuation before the court at the time of the order was correct (see *Thompson v. Thompson* [1991] 2 FLR 530, C.A., where a small business was sold for more than twice the valuation before the court two weeks before; and the court set aside the consent order). But they have been prepared to set aside orders where the parties' needs have changed dramatically — as in *Barder* itself, and in *Smith v. Smith (Smith intervening)* [1991] 2 FLR 432 (where an order had been made to meet the wife's housing needs, but she committed suicide within five months). If the court does give leave to appeal out of time against the order, it will substitute whatever order would have been appropriate on the basis of all the facts as they are known to be. Thus —

In *Smith v. Smith (Smith intervening)* (above) the court held that it was wrong simply to say that at the date of the appeal the wife had no housing needs, so that no order should be made in her favour. Rather, the court should ask what order it would have made had it known that the wife had only five months to live; and in the circumstances it considered a lump sum award of £25,000 appropriate.

Chapter 5

OTHER LEGAL CONSEQUENCES OF MARRIAGE

Introduction

Some readers may think it unduly cynical to suggest that the main legal consequence of marriage is that it permits the parties subsequently to obtain a divorce and the court orders relating to financial matters discussed above. Others may think it a realistic assessment. But although it would be wrong to deny that marriage still has important legal consequences, it has become increasingly true that these consequences are to be found spelt out in statute. The doctrine of the legal unity of husband and wife, like the notion of consortium and the principle that a man has a common law duty to support his wife seem unlikely to be of great practical relevance (see further Cretney and Masson, *Principles of Family Law* (6th ed. 1997, pp. 77–84)). It is true that some aspects of the *criminal law* — for example, that spouses cannot conspire together are still governed by the common law, but in most cases statute has supplanted common law doctrines (for example, that neither spouse could be convicted of stealing the other's property). Again, the law of *evidence* now makes statutory provision about the competence and compellability of spouses; and *citizenship and immigration* are dealt with by statute and delegated legislation. Spouses may by statute sue one another in *tort* — although there is power to stay actions in some circumstances: Law Reform (Husband and Wife) Act 1962; and by statute a spouse may sue a person who has tortiously caused his partner's death for the economic loss thereby caused even if the marriage was only hours or minutes old. Spouses have full capacity in *contract*; and a woman's liability to bankruptcy and other enforcement procedures is not affected by her marital status. All these matters can be found fully explained in texts dealing with the relevant areas of the law, and there would seem to be little justification for seeking to deal with them in an elementary family law textbook.

But the *economic effects* of marriage are still considerable, and it is right to give a brief account of the relevant legal procedures:

A. COURT ORDERS FOR MAINTENANCE

Three different procedures are available whereby one spouse may seek a court order for maintenance against the other:

(a) Application in the High Court or county court under section 27 of the Matrimonial Causes Act 1973. The Act provides that either party to a marriage may apply to the High Court or to a Divorce county court for an order on the ground that the other party has failed to provide reasonable maintenance for the applicant, or that he has failed to provide or to make a proper contribution towards reasonable maintenance for any child of the family. In deciding whether there has been such a failure, and if so what order to make, the court is to "have regard to all the circumstances of the case" including the matters which are specifically referred to under the divorce legislation.

If the applicant establishes that there has been such a failure the court can make orders for periodical payments (secured or unsecured) and a lump sum; but the court has no power to make the sophisticated property adjustment orders dealing with the family home which are often sought in divorce proceedings.

In practice there have been very few applications to the superior courts under this provision. It is possible that there will be some increase in the number of applications by people intending to divorce but unable to start the necessary proceedings because they have not satisfied the requirement of prior attendance at an information meeting.

(b) Application in the magistrates' court.   Since 1878 magistrates' courts have had power to make financial orders in domestic cases, and their powers are now codified in the Domestic Proceedings and Magistrates' Courts Act 1978 — a reforming Act intended to bring the family jurisdiction of the magistrates' courts into line with the reformed law administered in the divorce court. The Family Law Act 1996 once again reforms the law to reflect the changes in divorce law made by that Act: the ground upon which an order can be made is that the respondent has failed to provide reasonable maintenance for the applicant or a child of the family. If that ground is made out the court may order periodical payments and/or a lump sum (not exceeding £1,000). There is also power to make orders by consent (s.6) but these are now rarely made; and also power to make orders reflecting payments previously made voluntarily (s.7), but this provision is virtually a dead letter.

Registration of divorce court orders.   A maintenance order made by the divorce court may be registered for enforcement in the magistrates' court. One important consequence of registration is that the magistrates may thereafter vary the order as if it had originally been made by them; and for long it was this function which formed the bulk of magistrates' matrimonial work.

Again, the magistrates' clerk traditionally played a crucial role in enforcing registered divorce orders; and the Maintenance Enforcement Act 1991 seeks to modernise this aspect of the court's work.

(c) Separation orders.   Under the Matrimonial Causes Act 1973, a petition for judicial separation could be presented to the court by either party to the marriage on the ground that one of the "facts" from which the court could infer irretrievable breakdown — adultery, behaviour, desertion, or living apart for the requisite period — had been established: Matrimonial Causes Act 1973, s.17(1). The court did not need to be satisfied that the marriage had irretrievably broken down. A judicial separation decree (i) made it no longer "obligatory for the petitioner to cohabit with the respondent": MCA 1973, s.18(1); and (ii) deprived the parties of their mutual rights of intestate succession: s.18(2). But in practice it was the fact that the court had power, on or after the making of a decree of judicial separation, to make financial provision and property adjustment orders which accounted for the significant number of petitions.

The *1995 Divorce White Paper*, paragraph 4.49 reported that there was strong support in responses to the consultation for the retention of judicial separation as an alternative remedy for those who needed to make proper arrangements for living apart, but who had objections to divorce, or no wish to remarry. The 1996 Act accordingly, makes provision for the court to make a *separation order* and the provisions mirror those governing divorce. In particular, the marriage must have broken down irretrievably in the sense in which that concept is used in divorce. The only significant difference between the divorce and separation order procedures now seems to be that a statement of marital breakdown made in the first year of marriage is to be effective for the purposes of obtaining a separation order (whereas it will be ineffective for the purposes of any application for a divorce order). The 1996 Act omits the provision that the parties are no longer obliged to cohabit after the making of the order; but it does retain the rule that a couple separated under a separation order shall not be entitled to take on each other's intestacy. The main significance of the separation order procedure is likely to continue to be to provide a means whereby the court's extensive powers to make financial provision and property adjustment orders can be exercised.

The 1996 Act also provides a convenient procedure whereby (subject to certain restrictions, *e.g.* that it may not do so until the second anniversary of the marriage) the court is bound on the application of either or both parties, to convert a separation order into a divorce order without further formality.

B. SEPARATION AND MAINTENANCE AGREEMENTS

Statute (MCA 1973, s.34(1)) now lays down a general rule that financial arrangements contained in a maintenance agreement are to be binding, but that any provision purporting to restrict any right to apply to the court — for example, on divorce — for an order containing financial arrangements is to be void. Legislation gives the court power to vary the terms of any agreement if there has been a "change of circumstances in the light of which any financial arrangements contained in the agreement were made" with the result that the parties do not have the advantage of knowing where they stand. It seems now to be rare for such agreements to be made, not surprisingly since a separation or divorce order does enable the parties to obtain court orders by consent or otherwise which will effectively regulate their futures.

C. MATRIMONIAL HOME RIGHTS

In 1965, in the case of *National Provincial Bank v. Ainsworth* [1965] A.C. 1175, the House of Lords held that although a married woman had a right to be provided with a roof over her head as part of the husband's common law duty to maintain her that right was a personal right incapable of binding a third party even if the third party had notice of the wife's rights. A man might therefore, without consulting his wife, mortgage the family home; and the wife would — unless she could establish that she was entitled to a beneficial interest which bound the purchaser — have no defence to an action for possession brought by the lender to enforce the security. The Matrimonial Homes Act 1967 was primarily intended to remedy this defect in the law, and it did so by giving spouses in occupation of the matrimonial home rights of occupation (including the right not to be evicted during the marriage unless the court otherwise so ordered) and by providing machinery — registration of a Class F Land Charge — whereby a spouse could make those rights bind third parties. Part IV of the Family Law Act 1994 re-enacts the substance of the Matrimonial Homes Act, and calls these rights "matrimonial homes rights"; and matrimonial homes rights are the foundation on which the court has power to make occupation orders in favour of married people even if they have no beneficial interest in the property. The occupation orders which the court may make in this way are not (in contrast to orders available to cohabitants without beneficial property interests) restricted in time, whilst matrimonial home rights can, as mentioned above, by registration be made to bind third parties. In contrast, there is no machinery for making cohabitants' occupation orders have this effect.

D. OTHER RIGHTS IN PROPERTY

It has since 1882 been a cardinal principle of English law that marriage does not create any distinctive property regime for husband and wife: their proprietary rights are unaffected by marriage. The situation is, however, very different when a married person dies without leaving a will disposing of all his or her property: under the rules of intestate succession, the surviving spouse is entitled — even if the marriage has lasted only a few hours or even minutes to a "statutory legacy" of £125,000 or more and to further interests in the deceased's estate: see further p. 127 below. In contrast, if a cohabitant dies his or her partner is entitled to nothing on intestacy, however long their relationship.

PART TWO

FAMILIES — MARRIED AND UNMARRIED

Chapter 6

PROTECTION: DOMESTIC VIOLENCE AND OCCUPATION OF THE HOME

Introduction

Domestic violence can take many forms. There is, of course, the use or threat of physical force but (as the Law Commission pointed out) the law is properly concerned with other forms of physical, sexual or psychological molestation or harassment such as persistent pestering and intimidation, shouting, denigration, threats or argument, nuisance telephone calls, damaging property, following the applicant about and repeatedly calling at her home or place of work and even filling car locks with superglue. The extent of such conduct is impossible to assess, but there seems little doubt that it is widespread.

Sometimes domestic violence involves the commission of a criminal offence; and it is now well settled that marriage does not constitute a licence to assault a spouse against his or her will. But although perpetrators may be charged with offences ranging from murder and manslaughter to common assault, the criminal law had only limited relevance and provided little real protection to the battered wife or other victim of domestic violence. Apart from the fact that there seem often to be problems in obtaining convincing evidence, prosecution will sometimes do more harm than good and precipitate the final breakdown of the family. Imprisonment of the aggressor may well lead to unemployment and consequent financial hardship for the victim and the children, and may even exacerbate the problem by provoking further violence. The principal function of the criminal law is, after all, the punishment of the offender in the interests of society as a whole; and the interests of family members individually are subordinate.

In contrast, the main aim of the civil law in this context is to regulate and improve matters for the future — in particular by making orders about the future use of property or the future behaviour of the parties — rather than making judgments upon or punishing past behaviour, and over the years a number of techniques were used to provide a measure of protection in respect of the right to occupy the family home, and to give relief to the victims of violence and molestation. Part IV of the Family Law Act 1996 (which it is intended to bring into force on October 1, 1997) seeks to rationalise the law and create a comprehensive and coherent body of statute law, creating a single consistent set of remedies available in the courts having jurisdiction in family matters.

The Protection from Harassment Act 1997 was not primarily directed to "family" situations, but may have considerable relevance. The text first examines the provisions of the Family Law Act and then outlines the provisions of the 1997 Act.

Part IV of the Family Law Act empowers the court — whether the magistrates' court, the county court or the High Court — to make **occupation orders** regulating the occupation of a home; and **non-molestation orders** prohibiting molestation. The text first outlines the scope and intended purpose of the orders and explains who is entitled to seek the orders in question and the principles on which the court is to decide whether or not to make an order; and, secondly the text outlines the sanctions available to ensure that the court's orders are obeyed. The law is complex, and many fine distinctions are drawn. This book ignores the refinements and seeks to give a broad outline of the effect of the legislation. The reader may find it helpful to refer to the table at p. 108 below which seeks to demonstrate the scheme of the legislation.

A. OCCUPATION ORDERS UNDER THE FAMILY LAW ACT 1996

It may be tautologous to say that an occupation order deals with the occupation of a home; but the sophisticated drafting of the Family Law Act makes the precise extent of the court's powers depend on the nature of the applicant's interest (if any) in the property. The Act draws an important distinction between an applicant who is "a person entitled" and persons who are not so entitled. The underlying policy seems to be that the court's powers should be more extensive in the case of a person who can point to some recognised legal, equitable, or statutory right than in the case of a person who has merely had the use of a family home.

Who is a "person entitled"?

There are two main categories of person entitled: first persons with matrimonial homes rights (as explained in Chapter 5) and secondly people who are "entitled to occupy a dwelling house by virtue of a beneficial estate or interest or contract or by virtue of any enactment giving him the right to remain in occupation" — the fee simple owner, the tenant, and so on.

The dwelling house in question must either be, or have at some time been, or at some time been intended to be the home of the person entitled and of another person with whom he or she is "associated". This an expression which is widely defined to include a spouse or former spouse, a cohabitant or former cohabitant, a relative, certain children, and parties to the same family proceedings.

The court has wide powers to make orders declaring the nature of the parties' interests, and to make orders of various kinds about who is to be entitled to occupy the whole (or parts) of the house and on what terms. In particular the court may make what has traditionally been called an "ouster order" excluding a person from the house, and it has power to exclude him or her from "a defined area in which the dwelling house is included" — for example, from the block of flats in which the home is situated or from the surroundings. The period for which an occupation order may be made in favour of an entitled person is at the court's discretion.

Exercise of the discretion to make orders: balance of harm

The Act contains an elaborate provision setting out the matters to be taken into account by the court in deciding whether to make an order, such as the housing needs and housing resources of the family, their financial resources, the likely effect of the court's decision on the family's health, safety or well-being, and the conduct of the parties. But the court must make an order if the so-called balance of harm test is satisfied: is the applicant or any relevant child likely to suffer "significant harm" attributable to the other party's conduct greater than the harm likely to be suffered by the other party or a child if the order is not made? The Law Commission identified the policy underlying the law as follows:

> A respondent threatened with ouster on account of his violence would be able to establish a degree of hardship (perhaps in terms of difficulty in finding or unsuitability of alternative accommodation or problems in getting to work). But he is unlikely to suffer significant harm, whereas his wife and children who are being subjected to his violence or abuse may very easily suffer harm if he remains in the house.

Contrary to the recommendations of the Law Commission it is only harm attributable to the respondent's conduct which is taken into account; and the effect seems to be to preserve the decision of the House of Lords in *Richards v. Richards* [1984] 1 A.C. 174, H.L.

> The wife had filed a divorce petition containing allegations described by the judge and her own counsel respectively as "rubbishy" and "flimsy in the extreme." She left the matrimonial home with the children, but was unable to find suitable accommodation for them; and she then applied for an order excluding the husband from the matrimonial home so that she could return there with the children. The wife said that she could not bear to be in the same household as the husband; but the judge found that she had no reasonable ground for refusing to live under the same roof as her husband, expressed the view that it would be "thoroughly unjust" to turn him out of the house, but granted an ouster order because of the importance that he considered case law required him to give to the interests of the children. The House of Lords held that he had been wrong to make the order.
>
> Under the balance of harm test it would appear that the harm caused to the wife and child by their poor living conditions was not caused by Mr Richards' conduct; and even if it were, he might well suffer greater harm than his wife or child.

Applications by non-entitled persons

The category of "non-entitled persons" who may apply for an occupation order is limited to cohabitants, former cohabitants and former spouses. The Act seeks to draw a clear distinction between the claims of the married (who will usually have "matrimonial homes rights" and thus be "entitled") and formerly married on the one hand and the unmarried on the other. There are some (probably unimportant) distinctions between the factors to be taken into account by the court in exercising its discretion; but it seems that the most significant difference will be in the duration of the orders which can be made. The court can renew orders made in favour of former spouses for *successive* six month periods, but an order in favour of a non-entitled cohabitant or former cohabitant can be extended only once.

Ancillary Provisions

The legislation contains a number of useful ancillary provisions; for example it may grant either party possession or use of the furniture or other contents of the dwelling house in question, whether the order be made in favour of an entitled or non-entitled person, and to impose obligations in respect of matters such as outgoings and repairs.

B. NON-MOLESTATION ORDERS

The Family Law Act 1996 also confers on the courts a wide power to make orders prohibiting one person from "molesting" another; but it does not define the term "molestation". The Law Commission stated that molestation includes but is wider than violence, and that the term:

> "encompasses any form of serious pestering or harassment and applies to any conduct which could properly be regarded as such a degree of harassment as to call for the intervention of the court."

The following illustrations of conduct which has been held to constitute molestation may be helpful:

> In *Vaughan v. Vaughan* [1973] 1 W.L.R. 1159, a husband was held to have molested his wife when he called at her house early in the morning and late at night, called at her place of work, and made "a perfect nuisance of himself to her the whole time".
> In *Horner v. Horner* [1982] Fam. 90 the husband repeatedly telephoned the school at which the wife was a teacher, and made disparaging remarks about her. He also hung scurrilous posters about the wife on the school railings addressed to the parents of the children she taught.

The term "molestation" is so wide that it could almost be said to embrace any conduct of which the court disapproves; and there could be concern from a civil liberties perspective about conferring such extensive powers on the court. The 1996 Act (in sharp contrast in this respect to the Protection from Harassment Act 1997) seeks to meet these concerns by restricting the availability of these orders to those who have had a family relationship, and it is apparent that the powers are intended only to be available to deal with dysfunctional relationships within family groups.

(i) **Applications only by "associated persons".** The court may make a non-molestation order if an application has been made for the order by a person who is associated with the respondent. The definition of "associated person" is therefore of crucial importance and the underlying principle is that people who have or have had a family or domestic relationship should, by virtue of that fact, be entitled to legal protection, and that violence and molestation within family relationships is to be treated as a special case such as to make it unnecessary for an applicant to show more than the need for protection.

The Act provides an extremely complex definition of those entitled to protection in this way — including people who are or have been married to or cohabited with each other, people (such as students sharing a flat) who live or have lived in the same household — but not as an employee, tenant, lodger or boarder; relatives, as extremely widely defined; the engaged or formerly engaged; a child's parents, and parties to the same family proceedings.

The fact that a person falls outside this definition does not necessarily mean that he or she is without legal protection against molestation; but such protection will not be available under the Family Homes and Domestic Proceedings Act.

It was in part because of concern about the restrictions on the availability of legal remedies for molestation and harassment that the law did not afford protection in such cases that Parliament enacted the controversial Protection from Harassment Act 1997.

C. EMERGENCY PROTECTION UNDER PART IV OF THE FAMILY LAW ACT 1996

If the court considers it "just and convenient" to do so it may make an occupation or non-molestation order *ex parte, i.e.* without the respondent having been given any notice of the application. The traditional view is that such orders should be made only in circumstances in which it is really necessary to act immediately (see *Ansah v. Ansah* [1997] Fam. 138) and section 45 of the Act lays down guidelines evidently intended to ensure that this is the case.

D. ENFORCEMENT OF ORDERS UNDER PART IV OF THE FAMILY LAW ACT 1996

It is a contempt of court, punishable by imprisonment, to disobey a court order; and, although at one time the conventional judicial view was that penal orders should be made in family cases very reluctantly and only when every other effort to bring the situation under control has failed or is almost certain to fail, the courts' attitudes may be hardening and there are certainly occasions on which a substantial sentence for the contempt of court constituted by breach of the order, may be appropriate.

But the existence of powers to inflict punishment for breach is much less important than the prevention of breaches. In practice, women for long found difficulty in obtaining speedy and effective redress because enforcement of the court's orders was a civil matter, the police would not take the initiative in making an arrest and enforcement was a matter for the appropriate officers of the court (the tipstaff in the High Court and the bailiffs in the county court). In order to remedy this defect, Part IV of the Family Law Act 1996 empowers the court to attach to certain orders a so-called "power of arrest" authorising the police to arrest without warrant and bring before the court any person reasonably suspected of being in breach of the order, and the Act marks a significant move towards promoting greater reliance on this procedure. Whereas at one time it had been thought appropriate to attach a power of arrest only in cases of persistent contempt, the 1996 Act provides that the court *must* attach a power of arrest to an occupation or non-molestation order made after a full hearing if the respondent has "used or threatened violence" against the applicant or a "relevant child". The court may, however, accept undertakings rather than making orders; and no power of arrest can then be attached — although the person concerned can be dealt with for contempt in exactly the same way as if an order had been made against him.

E. THE PROTECTION FROM HARASSMENT ACT 1997 AND OTHER PROCEEDINGS

The provisions of Part IV of the Family Law Act will provide a considerable measure of legal protection against molestation to parties falling within the definition of "associated persons". But the facts of *Khorosandjian v. Bush* [1993] Q.B. 727 demonstrate that some people with a legitimate claim to legal protection do not come within that definition and thus will not be able to seek a non-molestation order under the 1996 Act:

> A young man could not accept the ending of his relationship (which does not appear to have involved any sexual activity, and certaintly did not involve cohabitation) with an 18-year-old woman whom he had met at a snooker club. He continued to harass and pester her. The parties would not come within the Family Law Act definition of "associated persons" and the woman would not have been entitled to a non-molestation order under the 1996 Act. (In fact, the Court of Appeal held that by telephoning the applicant at her parents' home the defendant had been guilty of the tort of nuisance, and that an injunction against commission of that tort was available accordingly, but in *Hunter v. Canary Wharf Ltd* [1997] 2 All E.R. 426 the House of Lords subsequently held that the tort of nuisance was only available to people who — unlike Miss Khorosandjian — had a proprietary right in property).

Hence it is clear that the Family Law Act will offer no protection for those outside the "associated persons" definition against the unwelcome — even if well intentioned — attentions of the obsessed or infatuated, or even against molestation by a spouse's jealous or vindictive divorced partner; and particular concern was felt about the law's apparent difficulty in providing a remedy against the unwelcome attentions of "stalkers". In an attempt to fill this gap Parliament enacted the Protection from Harassment Act 1997 which (in the words of the then Home Secretary, Mr Michael Howard Q.C.) is intended to provide protection "for the terrified victims of someone else's obsession."

The main provisions of the 1997 Act are as follows:

The prohibited conduct: "harassment"

The Protection from Harassment Act 1997, s.1, provides that a person must not pursue a course of conduct which amounts to harassment of another and which he knows or ought to know amounts to harassment of the other. The expression "course of conduct" requires conduct on at least two occasions, and conduct includes speech: section 7. Although the Act (s.7(1)(a)) provides that harassing a person includes "alarming a person or causing a person distress," it contains no definition of harassment. There can be little doubt that conduct such as making repeat telephone calls (for example, 14 "heavy breather" calls within an hour: *R v. Ireland* [1997] 1 FLR 687, C.A.) or lurking outside a woman's house or following her obsessively will come within the statutory language and that there will accordingly no longer be any need for the criminal courts to consider whether such conduct constitutes an "assault" or whether it has caused the victim bodily harm. It is equally true that the term "harassment" is used in some other statutes — notably the Public Order Act 1986, s.4A — and that in the context of discrimination law the courts have moved towards seeing harassment in terms of *unwanted* conduct, whether physical or not: see *e.g. Wileman v. Minilec Engineering* [1988] I.R.L.R. 144, 148, E.A.T. But there has as yet been no fully reported, detailed and reasoned judicial consideration of the boundaries of "harassment"; and on one view the benefits of introducing sanctions against stalking have been gained at the cost of accepting an excessively broad and vague restriction on the rights of freedom of expression and behaviour.

The concept of "harassment" is thus itself problematic; but it seem that there may also be difficulty in interpreting the requirement (section 1(2)) that the person whose conduct is in question should either know or "ought to know" that the conduct in question amounts to harassment. It is true that the Act provides that a person "ought to know" his conduct amounts to harassment if a "reasonable person in possession of the same information would think the course of conduct amounted to harassment of the other": section 1(2). But reasonable people may have very different scales of values. Suppose, for example, that a person feels very strongly about the dangers of smoking and seeks constantly to warn others of those dangers by repeated telephone calls and letters. Would the hypothetical reasonable persons think that this conduct amounted to harassment? Would it make any difference if the victim were a complete stranger, or the defendant's only daughter, or if a close relative of the defendant (or of the victim) had recently died of lung cancer?

Circumstances in which harassment not prohibited

Whatever the precise meaning of "harassment" as used in the 1997 Act it seems clear that by itself the prohibition might make many common forms of activity which cause annoyance — investigative journalism, debt collecting and the work of enquiry agents, for example — illegal. The Act (s.1(3)) therefore provides that the statutory prohibition of harassment does not apply if the person concerned can show that his or her conduct was "pursued for the purpose of preventing or detecting crime", or under any statute or rule of law or to "comply with any condition or requirement imposed by any person" under any statute, or "that in the particular circumstances the pursuit of the course of conduct was reasonable": section 1(3).

Once again, the precise effect of these provisions is difficult to predict. Clearly a store detective who questions a shop assistant about stock shortages would come within the "prevention or detection of crime" exclusion, and no doubt it would be held reasonable for an investigative journalist to "doorstep" a shady arms dealer. But would a man who employed a private detective to tail his former wife in the hope of discovering that she was cohabiting or a woman who sought to shame her former husband into providing financial support for herself or her children by standing outside his office with a poster reciting his misdeeds, be acting reasonably, for example?

It is for the defendant to show that the course of conduct is within one of these exempting provisions. But, by way of additional defence, the Act (s.12) empowers a Secretary of State to issue a certificate that actions done on behalf of the Crown related to national security, the economic well-being of the United Kingdom or the prevention or detection of serious crime; and such a certificate prevents the Act applying to the conduct specified in the certificate.

Legal remedies under the Protection from Harassment Act 1997

(a) *Criminal Sanctions.*

The Act (s.2) provides that a person who pursues a course of conduct in breach of these provisions is guilty of a criminal offence punishable by up to six months imprisonment; and it also provides (s.4) that a person whose course of conduct causes another to fear, on at least two occasions, that violence will be used against him is — subject to defences similar to but not identical with those set out at p. 105 above — guilty of a more serious criminal offence punishable by up to five years' imprisonment. The court may impose a so-called "restraining order" on a person convicted under these provisions: section 5. A restraining order prohibits the defendant from further conduct (described in the order) amounting to harassment or putting a person in fear of violence. Breach of such an order is itself a criminal offence punishable by up to five years imprisonment.

(b) *Civil remedy.*

The Act in effect creates a new tort of harassment: a person who is or may be the victim of harassment prohibited by section 1 of the Act can bring an action in the High Court or the county court. The court may award damages (including damages for any anxiety or financial loss caused by the harassment: section 3(2)) and it may grant an injunction for the purpose of restraining the defendant from pursuing any conduct which amounts to harassment: section 3(3). If the plaintiff considers that the defendant has done anything prohibited by the injunction the plaintiff may apply for a warrant of arrest; and the Act provides (section 3(6)) that it is an offence, punishable by up to five years' imprisonment, to do anything prohibited by the injunction "without reasonable excuse".

Rationale of the remedies provided by the Protection from Harassment Act 1997

It is unusual for an English statute to provide that the same conduct constitutes both a civil wrong and a criminal offence; and, as Lord Meston put it in the parliamentary debates on the Protection from Harassment Bill (*Official Report*, H.L., January 24, 1997, col. 935), the Act seems to intermingle the civil and criminal law and procedure "in a remarkable way". But the underlying policy is comprehensible: the Government wanted the police to be able to arrest, a person reasonably suspected of harassment, and it is for that reason that the Act makes pursuing a course of conduct prohibited by section 1 an arrestable offence: Police and Criminal Evidence Act 1984, s.24(2)(n) (inserted by Protection from Harassment Act 1997, s.2(3)). The Conservative Government wanted the police to be able to investigate complaints of harassment and take proceedings against culprits; and whereas the police have the right and duty to do so in the case of criminal offences they have no such powers in respect of torts and other civil wrongs. Finally, the Government wanted the victim of harassment to have effective protection against any repetition of the conduct in question; and to that end the Act empowers the criminal courts to make restraining orders and the civil courts to grant injunctions (breach of which will constitute an arrestable offence, thus effectively enabling the police to arrest without warrant a defendant reasonably suspected of being in breach of the restraining order or prohibitory injunction: Police and Criminal Evidence Act 1984, s.24(6)).

A Panic Response?

It was for long a valid criticism that English law governing domestic violence was based on a hotchpotch of enactments of limited scope passed into law to meet specific situations: *Richards v. Richards* [1984] 1 A.C. 174, 206–7. The Family Law Act 1996 seemed at last to provide a coherent (if not always easily comprehensible) codification of the law; and it is in this respect that the 1997 Act seems to have turned the clock back. It is true, as explained above, that the technique which the 1997 Act adopts is defensible in principle and skilful in application; but it can hardly be said that it makes any contribution to a rational and integrated code. The 1997 Act relies heavily on founding police protective powers on the creation of, perhaps very wide, criminal offences; and the failure to build on the elaborate (and well-tried) "power of arrest" provisions in the 1996 Act seems particularly regrettable. The fact that a person has been guilty of harassment will not, for example, trigger the provisions of the divorce legislation intended to give special protection to victims of domestic violence; nor is it possible for a person imprisoned under the 1997 Act to obtain his release by "purging his contempt".

"Stalking" may well have been a serious social problem; but it remains to be seen whether such hurried legislation — the Act was rushed through the House of Commons in two days — will not cause disappointment and even injustice. The most worrying problem is in the lack of definition of the statutory concept of harassment; and some will think it remarkable that a serious criminal offence should have been created upon such an unsure foundation. But Parliament and Ministers were evidently convinced that there was a serious social problem for which the law provided no adequate remedy; and that the need to provide legal redress justified the solution embodied in the Act.

Other legal remedies

Injunctions under the Supreme Court Act
   The courts have an apparently wide power to grant injunctions "in all cases in which it appears . . . to be just and convenient to do so": Supreme Court Act 1981, s.37. But in fact this provision is nothing like as wide in scope as would appear at first sight. In particular, the court can only grant an injunction in support of some recognised legal or equitable right; and it was for this reason that the courts were unable to grant injunctions against harassment as such: see *Patel v. Patel* [1988] 2 FLR 179, but note that in *Hunter v. Canary Wharf Ltd* [1997] 2 All E.R. 426, 452, Lord Hoffmann seemed to accept that an injunction could properly be founded on intentional harassment certainly if this resulted in injury to health; and in *Burris v. Azadani* [1996] 1 FLR 226 the court held that it had power to grant temporary injunctions if the applicant could establish an *arguable case* that his legal rights had been infringed).

Powers of Justices of the Peace to bind over
   Magistrates have a wide power — which, as the Law Commission observed in its Report recommending abolition: Law Com. No. 222, "goes back very deep into our history" — to bind a person over to keep the peace and be of good behaviour. Breach of the bind over could be dealt with by imprisonment. This remedy was widely used in domestic and neighbour disputes, but was legally unsatisfactory. It may also infringe this country's obligations under the European Convention on Human Rights. For these reasons, the Law Commission recommended that the courts' powers to bind over be abolished; but in the debates on the Protection from Harassment Act there were those who thought that this procedure was the basis upon which remedies against harassment could appropriately be structured.

OCCUPATION AND NON-MOLESTATION ORDERS UNDER FAMILY LAW ACT 1996, PART IV

A. OCCUPATION ORDERS

Are you:-

(i) Entitled to occupy

(or entitled to "matrimonial homes rights" [s.30(2)])

- a "dwelling house" [s.63(1)] which is or has been or was intended to be the home of applicant and "associated person" [s.62(3)]

If so, court may [s.33(1)]:-

(a) Declare entitlement etc. [s.33(4)]

and/or

If not, are you

(ii) A former spouse

- whose ex husband/wife is "entitled to occupy" "dwelling house"

- at any time their matrimonial home or intended to be so

If so, court may [s.35(2)]:-

If not, are you

(iii) A cohabitant or former cohabitant [s.62(1)]

- whose partner is "entitled to occupy" "dwelling house"

- at any time their actual or intended joint home

If so, court may [s.36(2)]:-

If not, are you

(iv) A spouse or former spouse

- occupying "dwelling house" which is or was matrimonial home

- but neither entitled to remain in occupation

If so, court may [s.37(2)]:-

If not, are you

(v) A cohabitant or former cohabitant

- occupying "dwelling house" which is or was their joint home

- but neither entitled to remain in occupation

If so, court may [s.38(2)]:-

(b) Make s.33 (3) Order	Make s.35(5) Order *	make s.36(5) Order *	Make s.37(3) Order	Make s.38(3) Order
• Enforce entitlement to remain in occupation: s.33(3)(a)			• Requiring respondent to permit entry: s.37(3)(a)	• Requiring respondent to permit entry: s.38(3)(a)
• Require respondent to permit applicant to enter: s.33(3)(b)				
• Regulate occupation of house by parties: s.33(3)(c)	• Regulate occupation: s.35(5)(a)	• Regulate occupation: s.36(5)(a)	• Regulate occupation: s.37(3)(b)	• Regulate occupation: s.38(3)(b)
• Prohibit, suspend or restrict respondent's right to occupy: s.33(3)(d)	• Prohibit, suspend or restrict respondent's right to occupy: s.35(5)(b)	• Prohibit, suspend or restrict respondent's right to occupy: s.36(5)(b)		
• Require respondent to leave: s.33(3)(f)	• Require respondent to leave: s.35(5)(c)	• Require respondent to leave: s.36(5)(c)	• Require respondent to leave: s.37(3)(c)	• Require respondent to leave: s.38(3)(c)
• Perimeter order: exclude respondent from "defined area in which dwelling house included": s.33(3)(g)	• Perimeter order: s.35(5)(d)	• Perimeter order: s.36(5)(d)	• Perimeter order: s.37(3)(d)	• Perimeter order: s.38(3)(d)
• Consequential orders relating to Matrimonial Home Rights: s.33(3)(e), 33(5)				

* If the applicant is not in occupation, the court making s.35(5) or s.36(5) orders must include provision giving applicant right to enter and requiring other to permit exercise of that right: s.35(4), s.36(4). If applicant is in occupation, order must protect that occupation: s.35(3), s.35(3).

OCCUPATION AND NON-MOLESTATION ORDERS UNDER FAMILY LAW ACT 1996, PART IV continued

Duration of Orders

Specified period until occurrence of specified event or until further order: s.33(10)

Specified period not exceeding six months - may be extended for further specified period(s) not exceeding six months each: s.35(10)

Specified period not exceeding six months - may be extended on one occasion for further six months: s.36(10)

Specified period not exceeding six months - may be extended for further specified period(s) not exceeding six months each: s.37(5)

Specified period not exceeding six months - may be extended on one occasion for further six months: s.38(6)

Exercise of Court's Discretion

Balance of harm test: court *must* make order if applicant or child likely to suffer *significant harm attributable to conduct of respondent*, **unless** respondent or child likely to suffer *as great or greater harm*: s.33(7)

Balance of harm test as under s.33(7): s.33(8)

"All the circumstances" [some specified] s.36(6) and balance of harm relevant but not conclusive: s.37(7)(8)

Balance of harm test as under s.33(7): s.37(4)

"All the circumstances" [some specified] s.38(4) and balance of harm relevant but not determinative s.38(4), (5)

B. NON-MOLESTATION ORDERS

Court may make such an order if

(a) applicant associated with respondent: s.42(2), s.62(3) or

(b) if respondent party to family proceedings, by court of own motion for benefit of any other party or relevant child: s.42(2)(b)

"All circumstances" to be taken into account including need to secure "health, safety and well being" of applicant or child: s.42 (5)

C. ENFORCEMENT

Power of arrest to be attached to occupation and non-molestation orders **if** respondent has "used or threatened violence against applicant or relevant child": s.47(2) unless satisfied applicant or child will be adequately protected

Chapter 7

FAMILY CAPITAL

Introduction

Between the end of World War II and 1990 house prices increased by much more than the rate of inflation. Many people made large sums of money, in part because of the phenomenon of "gearing". As the Nationwide Building Society explain:

> A borrower buying a house worth £40,000 with a 90 per cent mortgage starts off with a loan of £36,000 and an equity stake of £4,000. If prices rise by 10 per cent the property will be worth £44,000 but the borrower's equity will increase to £8,000, so that a 10 per cent increase in prices produces a doubling in the value of the property.

For many years, families would often "trade up", using the inflated equity in one property as a deposit on progressively more expensive houses:

> In *McHardy and Sons (A Firm) v. Warren and Another* [1994] 2 FLR 338, C.A., a couple's first home was bought for £3,691 in 1968. The only cash involved was a £650 deposit provided as a wedding present by the bridegroom's father. By 1982 the spouses were able to buy their third home for £42,000.

It is true that in 1990 house prices began to fall; and many house buyers found that, instead of the expected capital profit, they were faced with so-called negative equity — *i.e.* they owed more than the property was worth — but as this book goes to press in the summer of 1997 it seems that the housing market is (at least in some parts of the country) recovering. Whatever the future may hold, it seems likely that a large number of house owning couples will continue to have substantial capital sums invested in the family home and available to be divided up at the end of a relationship. The many cases which have come before the courts for decision about the principles on which the division should be made remain relevant whenever it is necessary to determine the beneficial ownership.

But is beneficial ownership relevant?

Until 1970 (when the House of Lords held that marriage had no effect on entitlement to property) the cases often involved married couples, since before the enactment of the Matrimonial Proceedings and Property Act 1970 the courts had no discretionary power to reallocate property on divorce. But the statutory code now embodied in the Matrimonial Causes Act 1973 has made the common law and equity governing beneficial entitlement largely irrelevant in dealing with the allocation of assets on divorce. As Waite J. put it in *H v. M (Property: Beneficial Interest)* [1992] 1 FLR 229 (a case in which an unmarried couple had lived together for eleven years, had two children, and enjoyed assets worth nearly half a million pounds):

> "Had they been married, the issue of ownership would scarcely have been relevant, because the law these days, when dealing with the financial consequences of divorce, adopts a forward-looking perspective in which questions of ownership yield to the higher demands of relating the means of both to the needs of each, the first consideration given to the welfare of children . . ."

But if a couple are not married, the court has no discretionary power to redistribute their assets:

> In *Windeler v. Whitehall* [1990] 2 FLR 505, Millett J., the plaintiff went to live with the defendant (a successful West End theatrical agent) and looked after his house. Her claim to a share in the house and in the defendant's business failed because (so the judge held) she could not establish any beneficial interest in those assets under the rules governing the ownership or property; and although the courts exercise a statutory jurisdiction to adjust the property rights of a married person on the dissolution of their marriage, "there must be a marriage to dissolve. The courts possess neither a statutory nor an inherent jurisdiction to disturb existing rights of property on the termination of an extra-marital relationship, however long established . . . and however deserving the claimant." As Millet J. put it: "If this were California, this would be a claim for palimony, but it is England and it is not. English law recognises neither the term nor the obligation to which it gives effect . . ."

Many of the cases involving the determination of entitlement to house and other property are therefore concerned with unmarried couples; and unless such a claim can be established great hardship may be caused:

> In *Burns v. Burns* [1984] FLR 216, C.A., a couple had lived together for 19 years and had two children. The mother had given up her job to look after her partner and the children, and had changed her name to his. It was held that she had no right to any share in the proceeds of sale of the home. (Under Part IV of the Family Law Act 1996 she would no doubt have been able to obtain a short term occupation order, but as a non-entitled former cohabitant the maximum duration of the order would be six months.)

But although the legal principles governing the ownership of property are primarily relevant as concerns the breakdown of a non-marital relationship, there are still some occasions in which they are relevant between husband and wife:

(i) *Third party affected.*

The dispute may not be between two spouses, but between a spouse and a third party; for example, a creditor of the husband. The creditor may be able to enforce his legal rights of recovery against the property of the husband; but he will not generally be entitled to seize property which is beneficially owned by the wife unless she has joined in the transaction or done something else to render herself liable. In fact, the two most recent leading cases in the House of Lords relating to matrimonial property — *Williams & Glyn's Bank v. Boland* [1981] A.C. 487, H.L., and *Lloyds Bank plc v. Rosset* [1990] 2 FLR 155, H.L. — have both been concerned with such situations. It is for this reason that questions of beneficial entitlement to property are particularly important when a spouse is adjudicated bankrupt. All the property to which the bankrupt spouse is beneficially entitled vests by operation of law in the trustee in bankruptcy, and it is the trustee's duty to realise the property for the benefit of the bankrupt's creditors. The other spouse's property, in contrast, does not vest in the trustee; and he or she is, in principle, entitled to keep it. But the issue may arise in other contexts:

> In *Harwood v. Harwood* [1991] 2 FLR 274 a firm in which the husband was a partner contributed to the cost of the matrimonial home. The court could not finally resolve matters until the extent of the partner's interest had been established.

(ii) *Death.*

The majority of marriages are terminated by death, and not by divorce. If one spouse dies leaving all his or her property by will to charity, say, or to a lover, the other spouse now has a right to apply to the court for reasonable provision to be made out of the deceased's estate under the Inheritance (Provision for Family and Dependants) Act 1975: but the court, in deciding such applications, may have to balance the applicant's claims against those of others. In such cases it might be advantageous to the surviving spouse to claim that he or she actually owned the matrimonial home (or other asset) so that it did not pass under the deceased's will at all.

(iii) *Disputes about use of property rather than its ownership.*

Such disputes — for example, as to whether a jointly owned house should be sold — are still sometimes dealt with by reference to property law rather than by invoking the adjustive jurisdiction of the divorce court. This is particularly the case when a third party is involved; for example if a creditor seeks to enforce a judgment against a spouse's share in property, perhaps by obtaining a charging order against the debtor's interest in the family home: the creditor may accept that the wife has an interest in the proceeds of sale, but the creditor will want to be able to have the property sold whilst the spouses may well want it to be retained unsold.

Rules for determining entitlement

Formal requirements. Most of the reported disputes about family property entitlement have been concerned with the family home, and there are three rules stipulating that certain formalities are required in connection with land ownership:

(i) *Deed needed for transfer of legal estate.*

Section 52 of the Law of Property Act 1925 stipulates that a deed is necessary to convey or create any legal estate in land. Hence, if the conveyance of the family home was taken in the name of one partner it follows (in the absence of any subsequent conveyance) that the other can make no claim to be entitled to the legal estate:

> In *Lloyds Bank plc v. Carrick and Carrick* [1996] 2 FLR 600, C.A. a widow's brother-in-law (a builder with a number of vacant properties) suggested that she put her house on the market, pay him the net proceeds and move into a flat he owned "which will become yours". The widow paid him the £19,000 proceeds of the sale of her house and moved in to the flat. No conveyancing or other documents were executed. Accordingly, the legal title to the flat remained vested in the brother-in-law. He subsequently mortgaged the flat to the bank; and it was held that Mrs Carrick had no interest in the property which bound the bank.

(ii) *Writing necessary for other interests in land.*

Section 53 of the Law of Property Act 1925 stipulates that no interest in land can be created or disposed of except by a signed written document. Thus:

> In *Gissing v. Gissing* [1971] A.C. 886, H.L. the matrimonial home had been conveyed into the husband's sole name. When the marriage broke up he told his wife: "Don't worry about the house — it's yours. I will pay the mortgage payments and all other outgoings." The wife had no claim on the basis of that statement: there was no deed which could displace the legal estate, and no written document which could give her any other beneficial interest.

(iii) *Contracts for dispositions of land must be written and signed.*

In some cases — for example, *Lloyds Bank plc v. Carrick and Carrick* (above) — it may be possible for the court to find that a couple have made a contract dealing with their rights in respect of the property; but, as the result of a controversial amendment of the law effected by the Law of Property (Miscellaneous Provisions) Act 1989 such a contract can only be made in writing signed by the parties. It seems unlikely, therefore, that the courts will often be able to find the existence of an oral contract helpful in determining the beneficial ownership of family property.

But an interest may be claimed under the doctrines of implied resulting or constructive trust even if those formalities are not complied with.

Section 53(2) of the Law of Property Act 1925 created an important exception to the requirement of writing, and the Law of Property (Miscellaneous Provisions) Act 1989 s.2(5) contains a corresponding exception in respect of the formal rules relating to contract. This is that the formal requirements imposed by section 53 and by the 1989 Act do not affect the "creation or operation of resulting, implied or constructive trusts". It is thus on these equitable exceptions — based on the underlying principle that it would be unconscionable in the circumstances to allow the legal owner to continue to assert the absolute ownership which appears on the title documents: see *per* Lord Templeman in *Winkworth v. Edward Baron Development Company Ltd.* [1987] 1 FLR 525, 529, H.L. — that spouses or cohabitants routinely rely to establish a claim to the family home or other property, and much of family property law now depends on them. The doctrine of estoppel may also sometimes be invoked; whilst there are a number of statutory provisions which may be relevant.

The text analyses in turn:

(a) claims under implied, resulting or constructive trusts;
(b) claims based on contract;
(c) the doctrine of estoppel;
(d) statutory provisions under which property interests may be claimed;
(e) a number of incidental questions arising in relation to the use and ownership of family property.

A. IMPLIED RESULTING OR CONSTRUCTIVE TRUST

There has, over the years, been considerable difference of judicial opinion about the circumstances in which the court will allow the legal ownership of property to be displaced by the imposition of an implied resulting or constructive trust. At one time it was thought by some that the court could impose a trust whenever it would be "inequitable" for the legal estate owner to keep the property for himself alone (*Heseltine v. Heseltine* [1971] 1 W.L.R. 342, 346), or that the court could impose a trust whenever justice and good conscience required: see *Hussey v. Palmer* [1972] 1 W.L.R. 1286. But as a result of a number of decisions culminating in the House of Lords case *Lloyds Bank plc v. Rosset* [1991] 1 A.C. 107 it is clear that the jurisdiction is much more restricted. In particular, it remains a cardinal principle of the law that the fact that a person expends money or labour on another's property does not of itself entitle him to that property or to an interest in it. As Slade L.J. put it in *Thomas v. Fuller-Brown* [1988] 1 FLR 237, 240, C.A.:

> ". . . under English law the mere fact that A expends money or labour on B's property does not by itself entitle A to an interest in the property. In the absence of an express agreement or a common intention to be inferred from all the circumstances or any question of estoppel, A will normally have no claim whatever on the property in such circumstances. The decision of the House of Lords in *Pettitt v. Pettitt* makes this clear . . ."

What, then, are the — exceptional — circumstances in which someone whose claim is based on contributions to the family and the home is likely to succeed under the doctrines of implied resulting or constructive trust? Unfortunately, notwithstanding the apparent clarification made by the House of Lords in *Lloyds Bank plc v. Rosset* (above) there remains considerable uncertainty in the law; and as Mustill L.J. put it in *Grant v. Edwards* [1987] 1 FLR 87, 101, C.A. the time has not yet "arrived when it is possible to state the law in a way which will deal with all the practical problems which may arise in this difficult field, consistently with everything said in the cases." The following summary of principles should accordingly be treated with reserve.

1. Resulting trust

The traditional starting point is that if one partner provides all or part of the purchase price for the family home conveyed into the name of the other he or she will, in the absence of evidence that some other result was intended, be entitled to a share in the property proportionate to the amount of the contribution. If, therefore, one partner pays £100,000, and the other pays £300,000 of a total purchase price of £400,000, the first will in principle be entitled in equity to a one-quarter interest in the property.

The traditional equitable doctrine was that if certain relationships — husband and wife (but not unmarried cohabitants) or parent and child, for example — existed between the parties, the presumption of resulting trust would be supplanted by the so-called *presumption of advancement, i.e.* that (for example) the husband by handing money to the wife or applying it for her benefit intends to "make an advancement" to her, with the result that he will not have any beneficial interest from that contribution. But today this presumption is rarely applied, not least because there will often be evidence of relevant contrary intention.

The application of the resulting trust principle can be seen in the Court of Appeal's decision in *Springette v. Defoe* [1992] 2 FLR 338:

> Two mature people met in 1979, and lived together as man and wife. Eventually they were given the opportunity under the Conservative government's "right to buy" policy to buy the local authority house which they occupied. It was not disputed that the woman should be treated as having contributed 75% of the purchase price and the man 25%; and the Court of Appeal held that, since there was no evidence that they had agreed between themselves on some other division, their beneficial interests were 75% for the woman and 25% for the man.

In fact, cases in which money is paid outright in house purchase transactions are rare: in *Springette v. Defoe* (above) there was a concession about the effect of the contributions — and the reality seems to be that the doctrine of resulting trust is based on the parties' presumed intention: see *Drake v. Whipp* [1996] 1 FLR 826, C.A. In cases where there is no direct financial contribution in cash, the court will seek evidence of any *actual* or *imputed* intention under the doctrines discussed below.

2. Imputed trusts

If there is admissible evidence that at the time when the property was acquired the parties intended it to be jointly owned, the court will impose a trust to that effect *provided* that the applicant shows that he or she incurred a detriment in reliance on the understanding.

There are two main sources of the requisite evidence:

(a) Discussions leading to agreement or understanding. In *Lloyds Bank v. Rosset* (above) Lord Bridge of Harwich said that the first and fundamental question which must always be resolved is whether at any time prior to the acquisition of the disputed property, or exceptionally at some later date, there have been discussions between the parties leading to any "agreement, arrangement or understanding reached between them that the property is to be shared beneficially".

In some (exceptional) cases, there may be clear evidence that the parties had made an agreement about beneficial entitlement:

> For example, in *Barclays Bank v. Khaira* [1993] 1 FLR 343, a husband and wife signed a Land Registry form in the presence of a witness which purported to transfer their house to the wife. Although the document was stamped, it was

never presented to the Land Registry for registration and was thus ineffective to transfer the legal estate to the wife. However, the trial judge held that the transfer was "the best evidence a court could reasonably expect of an express domestic arrangement as to the sharing of a beneficial interest", and it was thus capable of being effective to give the wife an equitable interest in the property.

But in most of the cases which have come before the courts the matter has been much less clear; the question is essentially whether any sufficient understanding can be *constructed* on the basis of which the parties have relied:

> In *H v. M (Property: Beneficial Interest)* [1992] 2 FLR 229, Waite J., legal title to the Essex bungalow purchased as a home by a second-hand car dealer and the former Bunny Girl with whom he shared his life and zest for "luxury cars rapidly changed, comfortable holidays spent abroad, dining out in restaurants, gaming in casinos and raising and racing greyhounds" was taken in the dealer's name; but the judge was satisfied that the express discussions which had taken place established the existence of mutual expectations of a shared beneficial interest.

(b) Drawing inferences from conduct. In the absence of evidence of such an understanding or arrangement, the court will make an enquiry into all the circumstances which — as Waite J. put it in *H v. M (Property: Beneficial Interest)* [1992] 2 FLR 229 — might throw "evidential light on the question whether, in the absence of express discussion, a presumed intention can be spelt out of the parties' past course of dealing". For example:

Help with the mortgage.
Nowadays, most houses are bought with the aid of a substantial mortgage from a building society or bank. If one of the partners formally assumes liability under the mortgage, or even if he or she makes contributions to the instalments, this fact may provide evidence that the parties intended that each should have a beneficial interest: see, *e.g. Bernard v. Josephs* (1983) 4 FLR 179, 187. But it must be emphasised that neither the fact that a person assumes liability, nor even the fact that a person makes the payments, of itself gives rise to any beneficial entitlement. The question is whether the facts constitute evidence of the parties' intentions at the time of the purchase: *Re Gorman* [1990] 2 FLR 184, 291, *per* Vinelott J.

Non-financial contributions.
In a number of cases, the courts relied on the fact that an applicant had made real and substantial contributions to the property as sufficing to show the necessary intention. But:

> In *Lloyds Bank plc v. Rosset* [1991] A.C. 107, H.L., a wife carried out and supervised renovation works on a property intended as the family home. She had some skill "over and above that acquired by most housewives. She was a skilled painter and decorator who enjoyed wallpapering and decorating . . ." She co-ordinated building work, planned and designed a large breakfast room and small kitchen and papered two bedrooms. Although the judge at first instance thought this was sufficient to justify his drawing the inference that she should have a beneficial interest in the property under a constructive trust, her claim was

decisively rejected by the House of Lords. The work which she had done "could not [asserted Lord Bridge of Harwich] possibly justify" the drawing of such an inference. Indeed Lord Bridge said, "it was common ground that Mrs Rosset was extremely anxious that the new matrimonial home should be ready for occupation before Christmas . . . in those circumstances it would seem the most natural thing in the world for any wife, in the absence of her husband abroad, to spend all the time she could spare and to employ any skills she might have, such as the ability to decorate a room, in doing all she could to accelerate progress of the work quite irrespective of any expectation she might have of enjoying a beneficial interest in the property."

Lord Bridge (with whom the other Law Lords agreed) went on to say that, leaving on one side the cases in which there was evidence of an agreement or understanding, it was "at least extremely doubtful" whether anything short of a direct contribution to the purchase price by the partner who was not the legal owner (whether initially or by payment of mortgage instalments) could justify the drawing of the inference of a common intention to share the property beneficially.

Quantifying the interest.
However, it seems that once a claimant has established *some* beneficial interest (however small) the courts will be able to quantify the size of that interest by reference to broader considerations of the course of dealings between the parties over the whole course of their relationship: see *Midland Bank v. Cooke and Another* [1995] 2 FLR 915, C.A., p. 122, below.

Significance of marriage.
The fact that English law has no special property regime governing matrimonial property has made it easier for the courts to develop principles to govern the property rights of the family outside marriage. The principle, according to Lord Upjohn in *Petitt v. Pettitt* [1970] A.C. 777, 813 is that property disputes between husband and wife are to be decided by ordinary principles "while making full allowance" in view of the relationship between the parties. The question therefore becomes "what allowances have to be made?"; and the answer must depend on the content of the parties' relationship rather than on their legal status. The existence or absence of "paperwork" should make no difference; and two couples who have had a similar relationship should find that they have comparable property rights, irrespective of the fact that one couple married and the other never did so. It is true that in 1982 the Court of Appeal (in *Bernard v. Josephs* [1982] Ch. 391) emphasised that marriage by itself involves a commitment to a permanent relationship whereas cohabitation can involve very diverse attitudes; but there is little evidence in the subsequent case law that this attitude has been decisive in the courts' reasoning.

Detrimental reliance.
As pointed out above, in addition to showing the necessary intention, the court must examine the subsequent course of dealing between the parties for evidence of conduct detrimental to the party without legal title referable to a reliance upon the arrangement in question; and only if such detrimental reliance is established will a claim to a beneficial interest succeed. This is because of the principle that equity will not assist a volunteer:

In *Midland Bank plc v. Dobson and Dobson* [1986] 1 FLR 171, C.A. the court accepted that husband and wife had a common intention to share the beneficial interest in the matrimonial home; but the wife nonetheless failed in her claim because there was no evidence that she had acted to her detriment on the basis of that intention. She had made no direct contribution to the acquisition costs or mortgage instalments, and her contributions in buying domestic equipment and in decorating the house were unrelated to the intention that the ownership of the house be shared.

If it were not for this principle, Mrs Gissing [see p. 116, above] would presumably have been successful in her claim; and it is for this reason that the making of contributions is in practice so important. Such contributions may constitute evidence from which the parties' common intention can be inferred, and they will also usually establish that the claimant has acted to his or her detriment in reliance on that common intention. However, the detriment relied on must be of some real weight and significance:

> In *Lloyds Bank plc v. Rosset* Lord Bridge said that on any view the monetary value of the wife's contribution to the purchase of a comparatively expensive house "must have been so trifling as to be almost *de minimis*." He went on to express "considerable doubt" whether the work she had done could have constituted sufficient detriment "even if her husband's intention to make a gift to her of half or any other share in the equity of the property had been clearly established or if he had clearly represented to her that that was what he intended."

3. The remedial constructive trust

We have seen that the reason why claims to an interest in the family home are usually based on "implied resulting or constructive trust" is that such trusts are exempt from the formal requirements normally governing dealings with land; and for many purposes it is unnecessary to distinguish between the three categories. However, to avoid confusion, the reader should note that in recent years the courts have often used the term "constructive" trust to describe the kind of trust dealt with above under the heading *imputed* trust: see *e.g. Lloyds Bank plc v. Rosset* (above) and (especially) *Midland Bank v. Cooke and Another* [1995] 2 FLR 915, C.A., and *Drake v. Whipp* [1996] 1 FLR 826, C.A. The reason why this book follows the traditional (rather than the currently more favoured) classification is that in the cases which have been considered it is crucial that the court find an *actual* intention by the parties as to the beneficial interests or at least find evidence on the basis of which such an interest can be imputed to them, whereas the so-called remedial constructive trust has been applied in many parts of the common law world to enable the courts to impose what is considered in all the circumstances (sometimes focusing on the issue whether the facts suggest that one party has been unjustly enriched at the expense of the other) to be a just and equitable solution. Acceptance of such a doctrine would certainly remove much of the artificiality and injustice involved in the judicial quest for the fugitive or phantom common intention: see *Pettkus v. Barker* as cited by Waite J. in *H v. M (Property: Beneficial Interest)* [1992] 2 FLR 229, 231, but it can be said with confidence that the doctrine of remedial constructive trust in this sense forms no part of the law of England as now laid down by the House of Lords in *Lloyds Bank plc v. Rosset*. Hence it seems best to avoid using the expression "constructive trust" to describe cases in which the courts *impute* an intention to the parties: a *constructive* trust is imposed irrespective of whether or not the parties can be shown to have had any relevant common intention.

Going behind the title deeds.

The principles of implied resulting and constructive trust were developed at a time when it was common for the legal title to the family home to be conveyed into the name of one person (usually the man); but in recent years it has become increasingly common for the legal title to be conveyed to the two partners. (These practices have been influenced by Building Societies and other lenders who at one time were reluctant to recognise joint ownership of mortgaged property but more recently have increasingly made loans measured in part by the joint incomes of the partners). What determines the extent of the parties' beneficial interests in such cases? There are two situations. First, where there is in the transfer or in a separate document a declaration quantifying the beneficial interests. In such a case, that declaration will be virtually conclusive in the absence of fraud or mistake. For example:

> In *Goodman v. Gallant* [1986] 1 FLR 513, C.A. a house was transferred to a couple "upon trust for themselves as joint tenants." It was held that, in the absence of fraud this declaration was conclusive.

It is obviously desirable, in order to minimise the possibility of dispute, that the legal documents should deal with the question of ownership expressly — the mere fact that property is conveyed to two or more persons does not necessarily indicate that the parties are to be equally entitled — and it has been said that solicitors who fail to advise their clients on this issue may be guilty of professional negligence.

Quantifying the beneficial interest — no conclusive declaration in title documents.

If there is no declaration the court will — whether the legal estate is held by one person or two or more — consider, in accordance with the principles explained above whether there was a contribution in money or money's worth such as would give rise to a resulting trust proportionate to the value of the parties' respective contributions and whether there has been an agreement or understanding as to the extent of their beneficial interests, and in the absence of such an agreement or understanding it looks to the parties' conduct as the basis from which to infer their common intentions.

Sometimes, the question is easily resolved:

> In *Dewar v. Dewar* [1975] 1 W.L.R. 1532 a brother contributed £500 to the purchase of a house in which their two families were to live. Goff J. held that he was thereby entitled to 500/4,250 parts of the beneficial interest, since £4,250 was the amount of cash which went into the purchase.

But in many cases the problem will be much more difficult, not least because in many cases even a direct financial contribution will take the form of assuming an obligation under a mortgage rather than making a financial contribution wholly in a cash lump sum. The decision of the Court of Appeal in *Midland Bank v. Cooke and Another* [1995] 2 FLR 915 may provide a way forward in many such cases:

Title to the matrimonial home had been taken in the husband's sole name. The trial judge held the wife to be entitled to an interest by way of resulting trust by reason of her financial contribution to the purchase price — in fact her half share of a joint wedding present from her in-laws; and he held that her interest was to be quantified at 6.47% of the value of the property, that being the proportion borne by her half of the wedding present to the total cost of the property. But the Court of Appeal allowed her appeal, holding her interest to be one-half of the value of the property. The Court of Appeal held that once it had been established that both parties were entitled to *some* beneficial interest the Court was entitled to draw inferences as to the parties' probable common understanding about the ownership of the property, and in doing so the court would undertake a survey of the whole course of dealing between the parties relevant to their ownership and occupation of the property and their sharing of its burdens and advantages. This scrutiny would not be confined to the limited range of acts of direct contribution of the kind needed to found a beneficial interest in the first place.

It seems therefore that once the court has found that the two partners are entitled to *some* beneficial interest they will paint with a broad brush in determining the size of that interest. This will no doubt enable justice to be done in many cases, and it seems that court will often — notwithstanding warnings against applying the maxim "equality is equity": see, *e.g. per* Waite J. *H v. M (Property: Beneficial Interest)* [1992] 1 FLR 229, 239 — find an intention for equal division. But there is still considerable artificiality. Why should a woman who, as in *Burns v. Burns* [1984] FLR 216, C.A. had given up 19 years of her life to the care of a man and their two children emerge with nothing, whereas another (in identical circumstances save that her partner's parents had paid £100 towards the deposit on the house) be entitled to half or even perhaps more?

Severance of joint tenancy.

One final complication — of great practical importance when a relationship is breaking up — must be mentioned. This is that it is of the nature of a joint tenancy that it can be severed, *i.e.* converted into a tenancy in common. Hence if one partner wants to ensure that his or her half-interest in the family home should on death pass under the will or intestacy (perhaps to children by a previous relationship) rather than to the other party he or she will sever the joint tenancy. There are a number of ways in which severance can be achieved, of which the simplest is by one joint tenant giving written notice to the other under the provisions of section 36 of the Law of Property Act 1925. Simply asking for an order in matrimonial proceedings is not by itself sufficient: *Harris v. Goddard* [1984] FLR 209, C.A. It is impossible to sever a joint tenancy by will.

B. CLAIMS BASED ON CONTRACT

A couple may decide to regulate their affairs by contract, and in appropriate cases the court may be able to infer the existence of a legally enforceable agreement between them.

If a contract is to be made out it must be shown that: (i) There was a genuine meeting of minds between the parties, *i.e.* an offer and an acceptance; (ii) the parties intended to create a legally enforceable relationship; (iii) the terms of the agreement are sufficiently precise; (iv) there is consideration (unless the agreement is contained in a deed or document under a seal); (v) the terms which it is sought to enforce are not illegal or contrary to public policy.

For the most part there will be no difficulty in applying the ordinary rules of contract to the domestic situation. Two decided cases illustrating the working of the law may be contrasted:

> In *Tanner v. Tanner* [1975] 1 W.L.R. 1341 the male partner purchased a house for occupation by the defendant and the twin daughters of their relationship. The defendant moved into the house, but subsequently the parties' relationship broke down, and the plaintiff claimed possession on the basis that the defendant was only a bare licensee under a licence which he had revoked. The Court of Appeal held that there was an implied contractual licence under the terms of which the defendant was to be entitled to occupy the house so long as the children were of school age or until some other circumstance arose which would make it unreasonable for her to retain possession.

On the other hand:

> In *Layton v. Martin* [1986] 2 FLR 277 a woman accepted a man's offer that, if she would live with him, he would give her what emotional security he could plus financial security on his death. She failed in an action against his estate after his death notwithstanding the fact that she had lived with the deceased for five years after that offer had been made and that she had been his mistress for 13 years in all. This was because the court refused to find that there had been any intention to create a legally enforceable contract — a decision which seems somewhat harsh on the facts.

If a contract is established, questions of public policy may affect its enforceability. The law has long been reluctant to allow a married couple to regulate the consequences of the breakdown of their relationship by private contract; and it is still the law that a married couple cannot by contract preclude the court from exercising its jurisdiction to make financial provision and property adjustment orders. The possible relevance of rules in this category must be considered in any case concerning the enforceability of marital contracts. In the case of the unmarried, it equally has to be remembered that there is a general rule that a contract "founded on an immoral consideration" will not be enforced; but it seems inconceivable that this rule would be today considered relevant to cases involving a genuine family relationship (as distinct, perhaps, from a relationship of sexual exploitation involving prostitution, for example).

Of much more importance is the provision of the Law of Property (Miscellaneous Provisions) Act 1989 which, as we have seen, imposes a general requirement that a contract for the disposition of land or any interest in land must be in writing and signed by the parties. This rule replaces the much more flexible rule (formerly contained in section 40, Law of Property Act 1925) which merely required such a contract to be evidenced in writing, and permitted contracts not so evidenced to be enforced if the plaintiff could show an act of part performance such as would render it inequitable for the defendant to rely on the lack of formality.

It would seem that the effect of the 1989 Act will do much to restrict reliance on informal contracts as a source of entitlement to property; but the 1989 Act does not affect the operation of implied resulting and constructive trusts and will therefore have no application where a claim can be made under the principles discussed in section A above. Moreover, there will be cases in which a claimant who might have relied on an informal contract will be able to assert an interest by way of estoppel.

C. ESTOPPEL

The doctrine of estoppel is of particular relevance in cases where one party has moved into property owned by another so that it is difficult to show any contribution to the costs of acquiring the property. The general principle of estoppel is that if one party to a relationship incurs expenditure or does some other act to his or her detriment in the belief, encouraged by the other, that the claimant already owns or would be given some proprietary interest in a specific asset, an equity will arise to have the expectations which have been encouraged made good, so far as may fairly be done between the parties — even, in appropriate cases, by requiring the owner of the legal estate in the property to transfer it to the claimant. This doctrine may therefore enable a court to go some way towards giving effect to the parties' reasonable assumptions if to do otherwise would be unfair or unjust. The scope for the application of the doctrine in the context of a non-marital relationship can be illustrated by reference to the case of *Pascoe v. Turner* [1979] 1 W.L.R. 431:

> The defendant and his former housekeeper had lived as man and wife for many years. He then formed another relationship, and told the defendant that the house and its contents were hers. In reliance on that statement the plaintiff made substantial improvements to the house and bought furnishings for it, using for these purposes a large proportion of her small capital. The statement that the property was to be the defendant's was held to be ineffective because the appropriate formalities had not been observed; but the court held that there was an equitable estoppel by reason of the defendant's encouragement and acquiescence in the actions which the plaintiff had taken in reliance on the defendant's statement, and that this estoppel could only be satisfied by transferring the legal estate in the property to her.

And —

> In *Wayling v. Jones* [1995] 2 FLR 1029, C.A. the deceased had a long standing homosexual relationship with a man 35 years his junior who acted as his companion and chauffeur and helped in his catering hotel and other businesses receiving only nominal payment. The deceased told the applicant that he would make provision for him by leaving the Royal Hotel Barmouth to him in his will. He failed to do so; and the Court of Appeal held that the applicant was entitled by way of estoppel.

In contrast:

> In *Coombes v. Smith* [1987] 1 FLR 352, M assured F that he would always provide for her; but it was held that she was not entitled to an interest by way of estoppel since she had not been under any *misapprehension* about her legal rights.
> — and in *Layton v. Martin* [1986] 2 FLR 277 the plaintiff failed to establish an estoppel interest because the expectations aroused by the deceased's representations did not relate to any *specific item* of property.

Estoppel as a defence.   Even if one party is unable to establish a proprietary interest under the doctrine of equitable estoppel there may nonetheless be circumstances in which he or she could successfully resist an action for possession on the basis that there has been a representation that the defendant would be allowed to stay in the property for a period, and that the representation was intended to be acted upon and was in fact acted on: see *Maharaj v. Chand* [1986] A.C. 898, P.C.

D. STATUTE

Two statutes (the Married Women's Property Act 1964 and the Matrimonial Proceedings and Property Act 1970) may, in certain circumstances, enable a married person to claim a beneficial interest in property, while the Law Reform (Miscellaneous Provisions) Act 1970 confers certain rights in respect of property acquired during an engagement to marry. Of much more importance are the provisions of the Inheritance (Provision for Family and Dependants) Act 1975 which gives the court extensive powers to order financial provision out of a deceased's estate for his or her "dependants", and Part IV of the Family Law Act 1996 (which empowers the court to transfer certain tenancies on the breakdown of a relationship and also confers extensive powers on the court to make orders relating to the occupation of the family home and provides machinery, derived from the Matrimonial Homes Act 1967, whereby a spouse's "matrimonial homes rights" may, by registration, be made to bind third parties such as mortgagees and purchasers).

1. The Married Women's Property Act 1964

This was intended to reverse the common law rule under which the husband was entitled to any savings made by his wife out of a housekeeping allowance. The (unsatisfactorily drafted) Act provides that such savings shall in the absence of contrary agreement be treated as belonging to husband and wife in equal shares. The Law Commission has recommended repeal of the Act, and substitution of a statutory presumption that property bought for the joint use or benefit of spouses should (subject to certain exceptions) be jointly owned by them. It seems that the provisions of the 1964 Act are rarely invoked.

2. The Matrimonial Proceedings and Property Act 1970, s.37

This sought to clarify the law relating to the effect of one spouse's contributions to the improvement of property. Provided that the contribution is substantial and in money or money's worth the contributing spouse is, in the absence of contrary agreement, to be treated as acquiring a share (or an enlarged share) in the property. In the absence of agreement, it is for the court to quantify the shares according to what it considers to be just. It should be emphasised that the section is not concerned with the effect of contributions to the *acquisition* or to the *maintenance* of property; nor does it apply to unmarried cohabitants. In view of the extensive powers of the divorce court it appears that it is rarely found necessary to rely on it.

3. The Law Reform (Miscellaneous Provisions) Act 1970

This Act was primarily concerned to abolish the action for breach of promise of marriage. But it was also decided to enact a special code to deal with some of the proprietary problems which may arise from termination of an engagement. The Act accordingly applies the rules of law relating to the property rights of husbands and wives to the determination of beneficial interests in property acquired during the currency of an engagement. In reality this provision is of limited scope: it would seem, however, that the presumption of advancement might be applied to transfers between engaged people and it is clear that the statutory principle embodied in the Matrimonial Proceedings and Property Act 1970 could, in appropriate circumstances, apply so as to create a beneficial interest in favour of a person who has made contributions to the improvement of property. Moreover, if proceedings are instituted within three years of the termination of the agreement, the Act also gives the parties the right to use the summary procedure available under section 17 of the Married Women's Property Act 1882.

The Act does not give the parties to an engagement any right to seek financial provision or property adjustment orders under the Matrimonial Causes Act 1973 or otherwise, since those powers are only exercisable in divorce and similar proceedings: *Mossop v. Mossop* [1988] 2 FLR 173, C.A.

4. The Inheritance (Provision for Family and Dependants) Act 1975

Most marriages are still ended by death (rather than divorce) and marriage does then have a significant effect on the devolution of property. If a married person dies intestate, the surviving spouse will be entitled to the personal chattels and to a "statutory legacy" amounting, if the deceased left issue (whether legitimate or illegitimate) to £125,000. (If the deceased leaves any of certain specified close relatives, but no issue, the legacy is increased to £200,000.) In addition, the surviving spouse will be entitled to an interest in any balance of the estate — a life interest in one-half if there are issue, or half absolutely if there are close relatives but no issue. In the absence of close relatives the surviving spouse takes the whole estate. An unmarried person has, in contrast — however lengthy the relationship — no rights of intestate succession in the partner's estate; and the Law Commission's Report on *Intestacy* recommended no change in this rule.

Under English law anyone of full age and mental capacity can make a will disposing of all his property, and the parties to a non-marital relationship would be well advised to do so. But although freedom of testation is still the basic principle of English succession law, the Inheritance (Provision for Family and Dependants) Act 1975 permits certain defined categories of "dependant" to apply to the court for reasonable financial provision to be made for the applicant out of the deceased's estate.

Application can only be made by a "dependant".   The main "gate-keeping" provision of the Inheritance Act is that only certain categories of people can apply — spouses, former spouses, children, children of the family, any person "who immediately before the death of the deceased was being maintained . . . by the deceased" and (by an amendment effected in 1995) a former cohabitant. To qualify as a former cohabitant under this last head the applicant must have been living with the deceased in the same household immediately before the date of the death and for at least two years before that date, and throughout that period the applicant must have been living as the husband or wife of the deceased: Inheritance (Provision for Family and Dependants) Act s.3(2A) as inserted by Law Reform (Succession) Act 1995.

Court's wide powers.   If the court considers that the will or intestacy does not make reasonable financial provision for the applicant, it may make orders, for example for periodical income payments, payment of a lump sum, etc.

Applicant will only succeed if lack of reasonable financial provision established.   The central issue which must be resolved in the applicant's favour if the court is to have power to exercise its powers is whether the "disposition of the deceased's estate effected by his will or the law relating to intestacy" is "not such as to make reasonable financial provision" for the applicant. The Act lays down guidelines for determining this question but the underlying principle is that it is not the function of the court to undertake a redistribution of the deceased's estate to achieve a fair distribution; whilst in the case of applicants other than a surviving spouse the court cannot interfere unless it considers that provision is required for the applicant's maintenance.
   Thus —

> In *Re Jennings (dec'd)* [1994] Ch. 286 a 50-year-old had been brought up from the age of four by his mother and step-father. There was no contact between father and son after the divorce and the only thing the father did for his son was to send him ten shillings in a birthday card on his second birthday. The father left his residue of his estate (which amounted to some £300,000 after payment of Inheritance Tax) to charities. The son had been successful in business; and the Court of Appeal held that the fact that the son was in reasonably comfortable financial circumstances and that there was no evidence that he was likely to encounter financial difficulties in the future meant that it was impossible to show the necessary requirement for maintenance.

The task facing a surviving spouse is less difficult: he or she need not show a requirement for "maintenance" whilst the court is specifically directed to consider the provision which the applicant might reasonably have expected to receive if the marriage had been terminated by divorce rather than by death:

> Thus, in *Moody v. Stevenson* [1992] Ch. 486 the deceased's 81-year-old husband continued to live in the former matrimonial home, which the deceased had herself been given by her mother. The deceased's will gave her entire estate to her daughter by a previous marriage, and the deceased stated that she considered her husband had adequate resources of his own. The daughter sought possession of the house; and the husband applied for reasonable provision out of the estate. Bearing in mind the provision which a divorce court would have made for the

husband he should be given the right to occupy the house for so long as he was able and willing to do so. However, as the Court of Appeal subsequently pointed out in *Re Krubert (deceased)* [1997] 1 FLR 42 the court in divorce cases is concerned with two people whereas under the 1975 Act no provision needs to be made for the deceased. Accordingly, the "divorce expectation" is merely one factor to which the court must have regard; and the overriding objective is to make provision which is "reasonable".

There is little empirical evidence about the working of the 1975 Act and it may be that payments are made to those falling within the specified categories to avoid the potential cost of an action.

E. INCIDENTAL QUESTIONS

Property law is complex, and there are many important issues which have to be resolved beyond the questions of the parties' entitlement to beneficial interests in and occupation of family property. The remainder of this chapter summarises the law governing two of the more significant of such issues: first, in what circumstances will the court order a sale of property in which a couple are interested? secondly, to what extent will third parties be bound by beneficial interests and other rights about which they may have known nothing?

Ordering sale. Until the coming into force of the Trusts of Land and Appointment of Trustees Act 1996 on January 1, 1997, the Law of Property Act 1925 would usually impose a *trust for sale* on land beneficially owned by more than one person. However, the same legislation normally gave the trustees — in effect whoever held the legal estate and thus usually the parties or one of them — a *power to postpone sale*; and the courts had to grapple with the problem of how these trusts and powers should be exercised. What was to happen, for example, if one party wanted to continue to live in the property (notwithstanding the fact that another party also had a beneficial interest in the proceeds of sale) whilst the other wanted to realise his or her investment?

The Trusts of Land and Appointment of Trustees Act 1996 has now replaced the artificial trust for sale by a *trust of land*; and under the Act those beneficially interested will usually have a *right to occupy* the property: TLATA 1996, s.12. Anyone who has an interest in property subject to a trust of land may make an application to the court for an order (TLATA 1996, s.14) and the court may make orders regulating the occupation of the property or its disposal. In deciding what is to happen, the court is directed to consider a number of matters (TLATA 1996, s.15) including the purposes for which the property is held, the welfare of children who occupy (or might reasonably be expected to occupy the property as a home) the circumstances and wishes of the adults concerned, and the interests of any secured creditor of any beneficiary.

It may be that these guidelines — and in particular the specific reference to children — will lead to some gradual change of emphasis on how the courts approach applications; but there seems no reason to suppose that there will be any dramatic departure from the principles established by case law governing applications for sale under the 1925 Act. Those cases established a clear distinction between cases in which the issues affected only the family on the one hand and bankruptcy cases on the other hand; and that distinction seems to be reinforced under the 1996 law.

Cases within the family.

Under the Law of Property Act 1925 the court had power to order sale, but it also had power to postpone sale and indeed to give one party the right of exclusive possession pending sale — subject to whatever terms about such matters as repairs and outgoings the court might consider fair and reasonable between the parties: *Parkes v. Legal Aid Board* [1997] 1 FLR 77, 82, *per* Waite L.J. In exercising that discretion the court came to adopt the policy that, if the property had been bought as a family home, sale would not be ordered so long as that purpose remained — so that, for example, a sale would not be ordered (unless suitable alternative accommodation were available) so long as the property was needed as the children's home: see *Re Evers' Trust* [1980] 1 W.L.R. 1327.

In appropriate cases the court will no doubt exercise the power now conferred by statute (TLATA 1996) to impose conditions on the one party about matters such as the payment of outgoings, assuming obligations (for example, the mortgage debt), and to make compensation payments as the price of excluding the other.

Sales in bankruptcy cases.   On bankruptcy, all the debtor's assets vest in a trustee in bankruptcy who has a duty to realize them for the benefit of the creditors. Where the bankrupt had a beneficial interest in property — for example, as joint tenant or tenant in common of the family home — the trustee will usually apply to the bankruptcy court for an order for sale. That court is by statute (Insolvency Act 1986, ss.335A(2), 336(4)) required to have regard to the interests of the bankrupt's creditors, to the conduct of the spouse or former spouse "so far as contributing to the bankruptcy" to the needs and financial resources of the spouse or former spouse, to the needs of any children and to all the circumstances of the case other than the needs of the bankrupt; but after one year from the bankruptcy the court is required (unless the circumstances of the case are "exceptional") to assume that the interests of the bankrupt's creditors outweigh all other considerations: Insolvency Act 1986, ss 335A(3), 336(5). In practice, it will be difficult to show that the circumstances are exceptional:

> In *Re Citro (a Bankrupt) and Another* [1991] 1 FLR 71, 78, C.A. Nourse L.J pointed out that there was only a single reported case in which the welfare of children had been allowed to affect a decision on sale following bankruptcy; and that case was unusual because the creditors were in any event following bankruptcy likely to receive all that was due to them together with interest. In the typical case, it could not be said that hardship to the children was exceptional: "... it is not uncommon for a wife with young children to be faced with eviction in circumstances where the realisation of her beneficial interest will not produce enough to buy a comparable home in the same neighbourhood, or indeed elsewhere; and, if she has to move elsewhere, there may be problems over schooling and so forth. Such circumstances, while engendering a natural sympathy in all who hear of them, cannot be described as exceptional. They are the melancholy consequences of debt and improvidence with which every civilised society has been familiar."

Are third parties bound?   In principle it is of the essence of property rights that they bind third parties: the vendor who purports to sell the family home cannot give a purchaser a greater interest than the vendor owns. But the interest of the vendor's partner will often be an interest under an implied resulting or constructive trust and hence only equitable and in such a case the purchaser is not necessarily bound. The position can be summarised thus:

(a) *If the title is not registered under the Land Registration Act 1925.*

A spouse's equitable interest under a trust for sale will bind the purchaser of a legal estate in land only if the purchaser has actual or constructive notice thereof. The question is usually whether the purchaser has made such enquiry as ought reasonably to have been made (LPA 1925, s.199); and a purchaser will normally be treated as having notice of the rights of a spouse who is in occupation at the time of the transaction —

> In *Kingsnorth Finance Co. Ltd. v. Tizard* [1986] 1 W.L.R. 783 a purchaser was held to be bound by a wife's constructive trust interest notwithstanding the fact that his surveyor had inspected the property and seen no evidence of occupation by her or any other female. This was because the inspection had taken place by prior appointment on a Sunday afternoon and the husband had accordingly been able to conceal any evidence of his wife's existence.

If however the interest which is claimed is registrable under the Land Charges Act 1972 (for example, as a matrimonial homes right under the Family Law Act 1996 Part IV) the interest will not bind a purchaser — even if the purchaser has notice of the interest claimed — unless it is registered under the relevant legislation: *Lloyds Bank plc v. Carrick and Carrick* [1996] 2 FLR 600, C.A.

(b) *If the title to the property is registered under the Land Registration Act.*

A claimant's beneficial interest will bind a purchaser if the he or she was "in actual occupation" at the time of registration unless the purchaser made enquiry of her which failed to reveal her rights: see *Williams and Glyn's Bank v. Boland* [1981] A.C. 487, H.L.:

> Michael Boland obtained a loan from the bank, to whom he charged the family home as security. The business got into financial difficulties; and the bank brought proceedings for possession, but failed. Mrs Boland had (it was conceded) a beneficial interest in the property, notwithstanding the fact that Michael Boland was registered as sole proprietor. She had been "in actual occupation" at the time when the loan was made; and the bank had made no inquiries of any kind of her about her rights. Hence the bank took subject to her interest which constituted an overriding interest: Land Registration Act 1925, s.70(1)(g). The House of Lords emphasised that the words "actual occupation" were ordinary words of plain English, connoting physical presence.

However, even plain English may contain a variety of shades of meaning; and there may well be cases in which it is not easy to say whether a claimant is in actual occupation or not:

> In *Abbey National Building Society v. Cann* [1991] A.C. 56, the point again arose for decision. The House of Lords indicated that some degree of permanence and continuity was required in order to establish "actual occupation" and that "mere fleeting presence" could not suffice. It seems doubtful whether this decision clarifies matters.

Waiver of interest.   Because of the risk that someone other than the purchaser of the legal estate in property might be able to assert an interest by way of implied resulting or constructive trust which in certain circumstances could bind a lender, banks, building societies and other mortgage lenders take precautions. They now normally require spouses and other adults likely to share the occupation of the property to execute a document authorising the owner of the legal estate to enter into the transaction — for example, mortgaging it to raise money for improvements or other purposes — and giving that transaction priority to the partner's equitable interest:

> In *H. v. M (Property: Beneficial Interest)* [1992] 1 FLR 229 the family home was acquired in M's sole name. He wanted to use it as security for a loan from a bank. The bank required F to join in the charge "to the extent of her beneficial interest if any."

Even in the absence of any such express waiver it has been held that the court may infer the beneficiary's agreement to the property being charged and to the postponement of his beneficial interest:

> In *Bristol and West Building Society v. Henning* [1985] 1 W.L.R. 778, C.A. a couple were living together in a house which they wished to improve with the aid of a loan from the Building Society. It was clear on the evidence that Mrs Henning (who had only an equitable interest) knew and approved of the loan: and it was held that accordingly she must have taken to have agreed to postpone her interest to that of the Building Society.
>
> In *Abbey National Building Society v. Cann and Another* [1991] A.C. 56, H.L. Mrs Cann's son bought a house for his mother's occupation using the proceeds of sale of another house in which she had lived and a loan of £25,000 from the Building Society. The son falsely told the Building Soceity that he was buying the property for his sole occupation. The House of Lords held that the mother did not have any beneficial interest which would bind the Building Society. But they also accepted the doctrine of the *Henning* case: on the facts, the mother was well aware that there was insufficient money available to complete the purchase without some outside assistance. Accordingly, it was right to draw the inference that she had permitted her son to raise money on the security of the property without communicating any limitation on his authority to the Building Society. Accordingly, even if she had been held entitled to a beneficial interest in the property, she would not have been entitled to assert it against the Building Society.

In practice therefore, the likelihood of one party to a relationship being able successfully to assert a beneficial interest in property is much reduced, since in many cases the greater part of the funding will have been provided by a lender whose charge will take priority.

Chapter 8

FAMILY MAINTENANCE

Introduction

The family is an institution which provides economic support for its members, although the way in which this support is provided differs widely from society to society. English law now provides a number of legal procedures for enforcing economic obligations arising from marriage, and Chapter 7 above has outlined the rules governing the ownership of family capital. This chapter deals, first, with economic support furnished by the state to families in need; and secondly with the legal procedures — including the ambitious but controversial system created by the Child Support Act 1991 — concerned to ensure that parents support their children.

A. STATE SUPPORT FOR THE FAMILY

Family breakdown involves the risk of destitution, and since the Elizabethan Poor Law the state has assumed some obligation to provide for those who would otherwise starve. But in the nineteenth and twentieth centuries public policy became much more broadly concerned with the welfare of children and families; and today all families derive substantial support from the state — in such diverse areas as public health, treatment of illness, housing and education, for example. The commitment of the state to provide for the welfare of its citizens probably reached a peak in the years immediately after World War II but this commitment became increasingly burdensome in economic terms, while radical right wing philosophies seeking to diminish the role of the state and to reinforce the obligations of individuals and families to be self-supporting became particularly influential in the 1970s.

A book dealing with family law must inevitably concentrate on the aspects of public provision which involve direct state interference with family life or are relevant to family breakdown. The extent to which the state can take compulsory measures relating to the upbringing of children is considered in Chapter 13 below. This part of the book deals primarily with the welfare benefits particularly relevant in situations of family breakdown.

Welfare benefits

In 1948, the Poor Law was repealed and replaced by the Supplementary Benefit system. Every person in Great Britain of or over the age of 16 whose resources (as defined in statute) were insufficient to meet his or her requirements (also defined — at a modest level — in statute) became entitled to receive a supplementary allowance. At that time, it was the policy of the law to eradicate the stigma attached to the Poor Law and to insist that supplementary benefits were (as Finer J. put it in *Reiterbund v. Reiterbund* [1974] 1 W.L.R. 788, 797) "the subject of rights and entitlement and that no shame attached to the receipt of them." Supplementary benefit (later called "income support") came to play a crucial role in family breakdown: not only was financial support provided for families deprived of support by a spouse or parent, but the fact that the benefits extended to payment of mortgage interest greatly facilitated the so-called welfare benefit divorce:

> In *Crozier v. Crozier* [1995] Fam. 114, Booth J., the divorce court ordered the husband to transfer his share in the former matrimonial home to his former wife in full and final settlement of all her financial claims against him; the wife was to be responsible for the mortgage payments, and only a nominal order was made against Mr Crozier to support the children. In this way, Mrs Crozier and the children had secure housing (the state paying the mortgage interest) and a modest but guaranteed income from state benefits. Mr Crozier could make a fresh start largely free from financial obligations to his ex-wife and children. It is true that under the so-called "liable relative" procedure he could be required to reimburse benefits paid in respect of his children, but his liability in this regard was assessed at only £4 weekly.

Changing philosophies

The supplementary benefits system was in some ways the victim of its own success. Not only was the number of single-parent families apparently growing at an unprecedented rate — from eight per cent of all families in 1971 to 21 per cent in 1992 — but the 1.2 million lone mothers and their children seemed to consume a disproportionate share of the social security budget. Three-quarters of a million lone parents had come to depend on income support and it was estimated that benefits paid to lone parents had risen from 1.75 billion pounds in 1981–2 to about ten billion pounds in 1996. Moreover, the government's belief that those able to do so should support themselves by joining the labour force and that it was for parents to support their children seemed to have little impact on events. By 1989, less than a quarter of families on income support were receiving *any* support by way of maintenance payments (whereas in 1981/2 about half such families had done so); while the proportion of lone parents in work seemed to be falling, with only 23 per cent of lone parents in full time (and 17 per cent in part time) employment.

In the light of these matters, the Conservative Government made many changes in family law and in the social security system — some intended to improve the employment prospects of parents, some to improve the system whereby maintenance obligations are enforced; but the most radical development has been the enactment of the Child Support Act 1991. This reflected a determination to create an efficient system requiring absent parents to support their children at a realistic level; and was justified not only by pragmatic considerations of reducing unnecessary public expenditure but also by the ideological determination to challenge the common assumption that the state (or taxpayers) should assume financial responsibility for the family when a marriage or other relationship broke down.

As a result of these, sometimes conflicting, policies there remains in existence a system of *Income Support* (the modern replacement for supplementary benefit); and this still represents the major source of income for many lone parent families. There is also a means tested benefit (*Family Credit*) payable to those in low paid work, and it is intended that this should increasingly be available to encourage lone parents to gain independence by their own efforts. *Housing benefit* assists with the housing costs of those living in rented accommodation; and there are a number of other benefits which may be of particular relevance to the lone parent family; some, such as widow's benefits, being available only where prescribed contributions have been paid over the years, some (such as Child Benefit) being payable irrespective of contribution.

In view of the diminishing importance of state benefits, the text attempts only an outline treatment of those aspects of the law which are of particular relevance to situations of family breakdown. For comprehensive coverage of the law and the underlying policies reference should be made to Ogus, Barendt and Wilkely, *The Law of Social Security* (4th ed. 1995) M. Street, *Money and Family Breakdown* (2nd ed. 1994) and other specialist texts.

Income Support.   The general principle embodied in the Social Security Act 1986 is that a person aged 18 or over who is not engaged in "remunerative work" (but is available for and actively seeking employment) and whose income and capital do not exceed stipulated levels ("the applicable amount") is entitled to Income Support.

Only one member of a family can claim Income Support, and the capital and income of "married and unmarried couples" are aggregated for determining entitlement to Income Support.

"Married couple" means a man and woman who are married to each other and are members of the same household. Accordingly, a separated couple whose marriage has broken down fall outside the definition, and each spouse is eligible to claim Income Support. The expression "unmarried couple" — defined to mean a man and a woman who are not married to each other "but are living together as husband and wife . . ." gives rise to much more difficulty. Whereas the decision whether a couple are or are not "married" involves no investigation of their personal relationship or any value judgment about which of the normal incidents of marriage (such as the use of a common name or the existence of sexual relations) is essential to the concept, the decision whether or not a couple are "living together as husband and wife" does involve precisely such a judgment. The investigations into a couple's private life which are made in order to reach a decision on this issue may seem offensive and cause distress; and a recent decision by a Social Security Commissioner — *Re J (Income Support: Cohabitation* [1995] 1 FLR 660 — may mark an end to the tolerant practice of the seventies and eighties in which claimants were not questioned about their sexual behaviour.

As already mentioned, no Income Support is payable to a person in "full-time work", and the maximum number of hours which may be worked without forfeiting eligibility for Income Support (now 16) has been sharply reduced over the years. It seems to have been thought that substituting an entitlement to claim Family Credit would encourage Income Support claimants to "gain independence by their own efforts", but the Family Credit scheme (unlike Income Support) makes no additional provision to cover the applicant's mortgage payments. However, allowance is now made for a Family Credit claimant's child care costs and it appears that since 1992 over 200,000 lone parents have moved from Income Support into work supported by Family Credit.

Favourable treatment of lone parents.   A person who is a lone parent and responsible for a child in the claimant's household is exempt from the requirements to be available for work and actively seeking work. For many years, a special premium rate of income support was available to lone parents, but in November 1996 the Conservative Government announced its decision to withdraw this.

Assessment of the applicable amount.   The Income Support scheme attributes a so-called applicable amount to each claimant and in principle the claimant is entitled to Income Support to bring the income up to the applicable amount (provided that his or her capital does not exceed a prescribed amount). The applicable amount includes housing costs — effectively the claimant's mortgage interest — but the amounts payable are now restricted.

   The rates of personal allowance used in calculating the applicable amount make considerable allowance for individual circumstances, but in further pursuance of the policy of targeting benefits without it being necessary to make detailed inquiries into personal needs, the Regulations provide for the inclusion of weekly "premiums" in the applicable amounts of claimants who satisfy the prescribed conditions.

The means test: calculation of claimant's income and capital.   Calculations of these resources are central to the operation of the Income Support scheme, since possession of capital may disqualify a claimant from any eligibility for Income Support, whilst in principle every pound of income goes to reduce benefit entitlement. The fact that the scheme allows for "disregards" (and in particular for the disregard of the first £15 of earnings) is important; but every penny of periodical payment maintenance is taken into account and goes to reduce the claimant's benefit — a factor of significance in influencing preference for the so-called "clean break" solution in divorce.

   If the total of a claimant's capital (other than disregarded items) exceeds a specified amount (currently £8,000) the claimant will not be entitled to Income Support. But a dwelling occupied as the home, personal chattels (such as furniture) and the surrender value of life policies (perhaps used as collateral security for a housing loan) are disregarded; and these disregards have had a significant impact on divorce settlements since the value of a claimant's equity in the family home will be disregarded.

Family Credit is a benefit designed to provide some assistance for low-earning families with children, and the scheme has been progressively amended in an attempt to give real incentives to lone parents to take up even low-paid work rather than remaining dependent on Income Support. Apart from reducing public expenditure by an average of £50 weekly for each claimant, the Conservative Government claimed that lone parents moving into work with Family Credit helped the average claimant to be £30 weekly better off. Claims are usually processed entirely by post; and, once a claim has been accepted Family Credit will normally be payable for 26 weeks irrespective of changes in circumstances. It appears that in November 1996 666,000 families (including 296,000 lone parents) received Family Credit weekly, and that the average payment was £54.97 weekly.

Entitlement to family credit.   The most relevant conditions for entitlement to Family Credit are: (i) The claimant or the claimant's partner must be "engaged and normally engaged in remunerative work." This condition is only satisfied if the person concerned works for not less than 16 hours weekly. (ii) The claimant or the claimant's partner must be "responsible for" a child member of the household. There are complex rules to cover situations in which several people could satisfy this requirement. (iii) The income and capital of the claimant (and partner) must not exceed certain levels. The general principle is that if the relevant net income of the family (including maintenance payments, subject to a disregard of £15 weekly) is below an "applicable amount" calculated by reference to the number of children in the family, then "maximum family credits" are payable. If the income exceeds that amount, credit is reduced by 70 per cent of the excess. The policy is thus that there should always be an incentive to earn more: a pound earned only reduces Family Credit entitlement by 70 pence. These calculations are based on "net" income; and a significant reform is that allowance is now made in respect of child care costs up to a maximum of £60 weekly, whilst the first £15 of maintenance payments are also now disregarded. As with Income Support, a claimant who has capital in excess of £8,000 is not entitled.

Housing Benefit. The Housing Finance Act 1972 for the first time gave direct cash assistance in respect of rent and rates payable by those with low incomes. The principle was that income support recipients should be entitled to a full indemnity in respect of their eligible rent, and others were to be entitled to a measure of benefit depending on their means. But in the changed political climate of the nineties the Housing Benefit scheme was seen to be excessively generous, and the Government regarded the increasing cost as unacceptable. A scheme giving full indemnity for tenants' rents meant that tenants had no incentive to choose the more economical of two dwellings or to negotiate over their rent level, while landlords were tempted to increase rents accordingly. The deterrent apparently provided by restricting housing benefit to a "reasonable market level" was ineffective since in many areas the market consisted almost exclusively of housing benefit claimants; and housing benefit was being used to meet weekly rents in excess of £350. A new Housing Benefit scheme was introduced in 1996 and further radical changes were announced by the Conservative Government in the November 1996 budget.

Child Benefit is a non-contributory non-means tested benefit, which was chiefly relevant to family breakdown and lone parents because a special payment called one-parent benefit amounting to £6.30 (in addition to the standard rate of £10.80 for the first child and £8.80 for each additional child) was payable to a person not living with another as husband and wife. However, in the 1996 Budget the Conservative Government announced the phasing out of the one-parent benefit.

The Liable Relative procedure. The legislation has long contained provisions whereby the authorities could recover payments of Income Support from "liable relatives", and in 1990 these provisions were extended in scope.

The Social Security Act 1986 provides that a man is liable, for the purposes of Income Support, to maintain his wife and his children, and a woman to maintain her husband and her children. Although spouses cease to be "liable" for this purpose once their marriage is ended by divorce they remain liable to maintain children (but not, for these public law purposes, step-children or other children of the family).

The obligation is only enforceable if there has been a claim for Income Support in respect of a spouse or child; and the maximum liability cannot exceed the appropriate Income Support scale rates. However, the maximum liability in cases where the claimant and the liable relative were never married or have been divorced has been substantially increased by amendments made to the legislation in 1990: the liability now extends not only to the personal allowance in respect of children, but also to certain "child-related" premiums and (more controversially) to a so-called "personal allowance element" (defined as the amount paid by way of personal allowance under the Act to a claimant who has children by the liable person). In effect, therefore, the liable relative is not obliged to support his ex-wife or partner as such although he is liable to support her as the carer for their children.

It was the practice for the DSS to seek to identify and trace a claimant's liable relatives, and to ensure that the relative paid the amount which would remove the dependant's need for Income Support or as much as the relative could reasonably afford. If the liable relative failed to comply, the DSS could apply to the court to enforce the obligation: Social Security Act 1986, s.24(4), s.24A(1) and Income Support (Liable Relatives) Regulations 1990, reg. 2. In practice, however, these provisions have come to be much less important in the light of the far more extensive and sophisticated procedures introduced by the Child Support Act 1991.

B. ENFORCING ADULTS' OBLIGATIONS TO SUPPORT CHILDREN

1. Private law remedies

The court has power in divorce or other matrimonial proceedings to make financial and property adjustment orders in favour of children of the family; and the court is directed to give first consideration to the welfare of children of the family in exercising its extensive powers to make financial orders. There are also powers to make financial orders for children in proceedings under MCA 1973, s.27 (neglect to provide reasonable maintenance) and in matrimonial proceedings under the Domestic Proceedings and Magistrates' Courts Act 1978; and the Children Act 1989 reformed and assimilated other provisions whereby a child's parents could be ordered to make financial provision for the child. Although the provisions of the Children Act 1989 have been in practice to some extent supplanted by the provisions of the Child Support Act 1991 they remain relevant in certain circumstances. The text therefore first summarises the relevant provisions:

  (i) who is entitled to initiate proceedings under the Children Act 1989 in which financial orders may be made;
 (ii) what orders can the court make in such proceedings; and finally
(iii) what principles will the court apply in exercising its discretion to make such orders.

(i) Who can apply for financial orders under the Children Act 1989?   The following person may apply under Schedule 1 Children Act 1989 for a financial order in respect of a child:

(a) *A parent.*
  This expression extends to adoptive parents and to both parents of an illegitimate child. The ordinary meaning of the word "parent" is extended so as to "include any

party to a marriage (whether or not subsisting) in relation to whom the child . . . is a child of the family." The definition of a "child of the family" extends to any child who has been "treated" as such (irrespective of biological parentage); and the Act thus makes it possible for a child's biological parent to claim support for the child against the child's step-parent, or for the step-parent to seek an order against the biological parent.

(b) *A guardian.*

(c) *Any person in whose favour a residence order is in force with respect to a child.* A residence order settles the arrangements to be made about where a child is to live, and accordingly everyone who has been given the right to care for a child by court order can now seek a financial order for the child's support.

(d) *An adult student or trainee or person who can show special circumstances* may make an application for an order. However, in this case, there are two restrictions on the court's powers. First, no order may be made if the parents are living together in the same household (so that it is still impossible for a child to compel parents who are living in a conventional relationship to provide support). Secondly, the court's powers on such an application are limited to making periodical payment or lump sum orders, and there is no power to make the other capital orders mentioned below.

In addition, there are certain circumstances in which *the court may make financial orders even though no application for such an order has been made.* It is provided that the court may make a financial order whenever it makes, varies, or discharges a residence order; and a residence order may be made (whether or not applied for) in any family proceedings if the court considers that the order should be made.

(ii) The orders which may be made.   The range of orders available to the court is now wide. The court may order a "parent" (defined to include a step-parent etc.) to make periodical payments (secured or unsecured), to pay a lump sum, and to settle or transfer property. In an appropriate case these powers may be exercised to deal with the family home. A local authority tenancy might (for example) be transferred to the wife for the children's benefit; or a home belonging to the parents or either of them might be settled on trusts permitting the children to reside there with one of the parents during the children's minority:

> In *H v. P (Illegitimate Child: Capital Provision)* [1993] Fam. Law 515, H.H. Judge Collins, the court held that the child of a man who had annual earnings in excess of £30,000 was entitled to be brought up in circumstances commensurate with the scale of the father's resources; and the court accordingly ordered the father to settle £30,000 on terms that a home be provided for the child during his minority or until his full time education was completed.

Again:

> In *Pearson v. Franklin (Parental Home: Ouster)* [1994] 1 FLR 246, C.A. the Court of Appeal held that an application under the Children Act jurisdiction was the appropriate procedure for dealing with occupation of the family home in non-matrimonial cases. (This case was decided before the Family Law Act 1996, Part

IV, conferred wide powers on the court to transfer tenancies on the breakdown of non-marital relationships).

Against whom are orders to be made?   The general principle adopted by the Children Act is that financial orders are to be made against "parents". However, as explained above, the definition of "parent" includes step-parents and others.

(iii) Principles to be applied.   The Children Act 1989 lays down guidelines for the exercise of the court's powers which are similar (but not identical) to those governing the comparable divorce powers. The court (see Children Act 1989, Sched. 1, para. 4(1)) is to "have regard to all the circumstances" including matters such as the income, earning capacity, property and other financial resources which the applicant, the parents and the person in whose favour the order would be made has or is likely to have; those persons' financial needs, obligations and responsibilities; the financial needs, income, earning capacity (if any), property and other financial resources of the child; and any physical or mental disability. The court's attention is also directed to "the manner in which the child was being, or was expected to be, educated or trained."

The court must give appropriate weight to all the relevant factors, and the child's needs are not the only factor to be taken into account:

> In *K v. K (Minors: Property Transfer)* [1992] 2 FLR 220, C.A. the judge had ordered that the father's rights as joint tenant of a local authority house be transferred to the mother for the benefit of his children. It was held that, although there was jurisdiction to make such an order, the judge had failed to carry out the balancing exercise required by the statute. In particular, he had failed to consider the father's needs, including the possibility that the father would lose his statutory right to buy the house on advantageous terms. A retrial was ordered.
>
> In *Phillips v. Peace* [1996] 2 FLR 230, Johnson J., the Child Support Agency had jurisdiction to make an assessment in respect of the child's maintenance, but in fact assessed the father's liability as *nil*: see p. 142 below. The court held that although the father had ample capital, it would be wrong to make an order for what would in effect be capitalised maintenance since maintenance was a matter exclusively for the CSA. But it made an order requiring the father to settle capital on the child to provide a suitable home.

The legislation contains provisions similar to those in the divorce legislation dealing with the factors to be taken into account where the "parent" against whom the order is sought is (because of the "child of the family" definition) a step-parent or someone other than the child's mother or father.

2. The Child Support Act 1991

The heavy and increasing dependence of one-parent families on state benefits, and the apparent inability of private law procedures to provide effective support for the victims of family breakdown was long a source of criticism; and in 1990 the government published a White Paper, *Children Come First*, which gave the following diagnosis of the problem:

"The present system of maintenance is unnecessarily fragmented, uncertain in its results, slow and ineffective. It is based largely on discretion . . . The cumulative effect is uncertainty and inconsistent decisions about how much maintenance should be paid. In a great many instances, the maintenance award is not paid or the payments fall into arrears and then take weeks to re-establish . . ."

The Government considered that parents had a clear moral duty to maintain their children until they were old enough to look after themselves; and that although events might change the relationship between the parents they could not change the parents' responsibilities towards their children. The Child Support Act 1991 was enacted — with all-party support — in an attempt to give effect to this philosophy.

The essence of the scheme involved a fundamental change in technique: the court system, dealing on a case-by-case discretionary basis with the assessment of child maintenance, was to be supplanted by an administrative system which would assess all maintenance according to criteria expressed in mathematical formulae, with the aim of achieving higher levels of maintenance.

The legislation proved to be controversial, and many changes were made. Eventually, the Child Support Act 1995 allowed for an element of discretion in the calculation of maintenance obligations. The primary and secondary legislation is exceedingly complex, and only a brief summary of its main principles can be given under the following heads:

(1)   The basis of liability under the Child Support Act;
(2)   Meeting the responsibility for maintaining a child;
(3)   Quantifying Child Support Maintenance: the formulae;
(4)   Departing from the formulae: departure directions;
(5)   The relevance of the child's welfare;
(6)   The role of the courts in relation to child support;
(7)   Collection and enforcement.

(1) The basis of liability under the Child Support Act: Liability only on parents
The underlying principle of the Child Support Act is that each parent of a qualifying child is responsible for maintaining the child. The Act, in contrast to the principle developed in matrimonial law and accepted in the Children Act 1989, does not impose any obligation on a step-parent or other person who has treated the child as a child of the family. The Act is based on the principle that children should look to their natural parents for support.

Liability under Child Support Act only arises if parent is "absent"
The Act states a general principle that each parent of a "qualifying child" is responsible for maintaining the child, but a child will only fall within the definition of a "qualifying child" if one or both of his parents is in relation to him an "absent parent". For this purpose, a parent of any child is an absent parent in relation to him if that parent is not living in the same household with the child and the child has his home with a person who is, in relation to him, a "person with care". The Child Support Act is thus concerned with the situation in which a family relationship has broken down (or has never come into existence); and the Act follows the traditional pattern of English law which is to refuse to define the level of support appropriate to a child living under the same roof with the parents.

(2) Meeting the responsibility for maintaining a child

For the purposes of the Child Support Act, an absent parent is to be taken to have met his responsibility to maintain a qualifying child by making periodical payments of maintenance in accordance with the provisions of the Act; and the Act imposes a duty to make such payments on an absent parent in respect of whom a maintenance assessment has been made.

Parents are in principle free to make their own agreements about child support and to abstain from using the services of the Agency but they cannot by private agreement exclude the right subsequently to apply for a maintenance assessment. Moreover, if Income Support or Family Credit is in payment, the person with care of a qualifying child must (if required to do so) authorise the taking of action to recover child support maintenance from the absent parent. Failure to comply with the requirement to give the authorisation or provide the information required may result in the giving of a "reduced benefit direction" as a result of which the amount of the relevant benefit will be reduced in accordance with the provisions of the Act. No requirement to authorise such action is to be taken if the Secretary of State considers that there are reasonable grounds for believing that there would be a risk to the parent with care, or of any child living with him or her, "suffering harm or undue distress" as a result; and, apparently, "good cause" is accepted in the majority of cases in which it is claimed.

(3) Quantifying Child Support Maintenance: the formulae

Although the details of the formulae whereby maintenance is assessed under the Act are undeniably complex, the basic principle is comparatively straightforward. Income Support figures are used to provide a basis for computing basic levels of support, taking the child's applicable amount and adding a so called "parent as carer" element.

The amount which the absent parent has to pay — the maintenance assessment — requires a calculation to be made of the parents' *assessable income* (essentially the parent's net income after tax and National Insurance contributions *less* what is in effect an allowance for the absent parent's necessary personal expenditure, *i.e.* the *exempt income*).

The starting point in calculating the exempt income is, once again, the income support personal allowance for an adult single claimant and adding to that sum Income Support rates for any of the absent parent's children living with the parent. As already pointed out, the legislation makes no allowance for the living costs of the parent's spouse or partner, nor for the living costs of the parent's step-children: it was that the children should look to their birth parents for support. The application of this principle can produce strange results.

The Act is founded on the principle that *each* parent of a qualifying child is responsible for maintaining the child and accordingly it is necessary to calculate the assessable income of both the absent parent and of the parent with care.

The 1991 Act focused attention exclusively on income, with the bizarre result that in *Phillips v. Peace* [1996] 2 FLR 230, Johnson, J., the liability of a man living in a £2.6 million house and running three expensive cars was assessed at nil because he had no income. (As a result of amendments made by the Child Support Act 1995 it is possible that a departure from the formula could be authorised in such cases: see below).

The assessment: the general rule

The general rule for calculating the maintenance assessment is, in contrast to some of the formulae used in the legislation, simple: the assessable income of both the parent with care and the absent parent is added together, and the resultant figure is halved. If the resultant figure is equal to or less than the maintenance requirement the absent parent must pay half his assessable income until the maintenance requirement has been met, or until half the absent parent's assessable income has been exhausted without reaching the maintenance requirement. The Child Support Agency's *Advisers' Notes* give illustrations:

> Peter is separated from Sally, they have two children who live with Sally who does not work. The maintenance requirement is £75 and Peter's assessable income is £140 a week. He is required to pay 50 per cent of his assessable income in maintenance which is £70. He does not have enough income to meet the full maintenance requirement of £75.

and:

> Len and Eileen are divorced. They have two children, Lisa and Ruth who live with Eileen. The maintenance requirement is £75 a week. Both Len and Eileen work, and his assessable income is £120 a week whilst hers is £20 a week (i.e. in the aggregate £140). Half of this figure is £70 which is less than the £75 maintenance requirement. Len must accordingly pay maintenance of 50 per cent of his assessable income which is £60 a week.

In certain circumstances, the formulae provide for the inclusion of a so-called "additional element", which is intended to ensure that the children of affluent parents share in the parents' prosperity.

The assessment: leaving the absent parent sufficient for living expenses — protected income

The Child Support Act 1991 is, as we have seen, based on computing the absent parent's "assessable income" and the exempt income deduction includes an allowance for necessary living expenses; but this method of computing the obligation of an absent parent takes no account of the possibility that the absent parent may in practice have obligations in respect of step-children who are receiving little or no maintenance from their biological parents. For this reason the Child Support Act contains provisions defining an absent parent's "protected income", and giving effect to the principle that the amount of any maintenance assessment should be adjusted to secure that payment of the amounts assessed under all maintenance assessments should not reduce the absent parent's disposable income below the *protected income level*. Moreover, the Act seeks to ensure that the absent parent is not only left sufficient to provide basic essentials at Income Support levels but also given some incentive to remain in (or obtain) employment and to have a measure of choice about his or her expenditure. These aspects of the scheme were given much greater prominence in 1995 when the formulae were adjusted to allow an absent parent to retain 70 per cent of his or her net income.

(4) Departing from the formulae: departure directions

The Child Support Act 1995 (and regulations made under that Act) seek to give effect to the Government's view that, although the formula provides the best means for establishing maintenance liability in a fair and consistent way, there will always be a "small proportion of exceptional cases which cannot be fairly treated by any universal formula". It is now provided that either parent may apply for a "departure direction" (*i.e.* a variation of the formula) on the ground that the facts fall within one of three "cases" specified in the Act.

These three cases are:

(i) *"Special Expenses"*: Regulations provide that if an applicant's expenses on certain specified matters exceed £15 weekly, the excess is to be taken into account in calculating exempt income. The specified matters are:

    (a) Costs incurred in *travelling to work*.

    (b) Costs incurred in *maintaining contact* with a child. Regulations provide that if a "set pattern has been established as to frequency of contact between an absent parent and a child" or if the parents have agreed on a pattern of contact, the absent parent may be given credit for the travel costs incurred for the purpose of maintaining that contact.

    (c) *Debts incurred* for the benefit of the family before breakdown. Regulations provide relief in respect of repayment of certain debts incurred for the benefit of the family. Gambling debts, fines, unpaid legal costs, and credit card debts are amongst debts excluded from relief under this provision.

    (d) *Pre-1993 financial commitments.* Relief may be given in respect of financial commitments entered into before April 5, 1993 from which it is unreasonable or impossible for the absent parent to withdraw.

    (e) *Costs incurred in supporting step-children*, etc. If an absent parent has, prior to April 5, 1993, incurred costs in supporting a step-child, credit may be given for those expenses in so far as they exceed the liability of the child's parent.

(ii) *"Property or Capital Transfers"*

Provision is now made to take account of transfers of property made by court order or agreement before April 5, 1993 which effectively reduced the amount of the maintenance payable with respect to a child. Regulations provide a formula for calculating the "equivalent weekly value" of the transfer; and the child support maintenance assessment will be reduced in accordance with detailed provisions laid down by Regulations.

(iii) *"Additional cases"*

The legislation envisages that application for a departure direction may be made not only by an absent parent who thinks the assessment is too high but also by a parent with care dissatisfied with the assessment of the absent parent's means. Regulations prescribe "additional cases" in which a departure direction may be made:

    (a) Parent has *assets* capable of producing income or higher income.

    (b) *Diversion of income.* If the Secretary of State is satisfied that the person concerned has the power to control (for example) the amount of income he receives from a private company, and that he has diverted income to other persons, a departure direction may be made to take the amount diverted into account.

    (c) *Lifestyle inconsistent with declared income*. The Secretary of State may make a departure direction if satisfied that the current maintenance assessment is based upon a level of income "substantially lower" than that required to "support the overall lifestyle" of the person concerned.

    (d) *Unreasonably high housing costs*. If the housing costs of the person concerned exceed a prescribed limit, a departure direction may be made if they are thought to be "substantially higher than is necessary taking into account any special circumstances".

    (e) *Partner's contribution to housing costs*. A departure direction may be made if the Secretary of State considers it reasonable for the partner of the person concerned to make a contribution to his or her housing costs.

    (f) Unreasonably high *travel costs*; and disregard of travel costs. Departure directions may be made to disallow travel costs which are considered to be unreasonably high, or if the person concerned has sufficient income to make it inappropriate for allowance to be made for travel costs.

If the case falls within one of the above categories, a departure direction may be made, but there is a discretion whether to do so or not. In deciding whether to exercise that discretion regard is to be had to certain "general principles" (for example that parents should be responsible for maintaining their children whenever they can afford to do so) but the ultimate question is whether it would be "just and equitable" to make a direction. The Regulations go to the lengths of specifying that certain matters — for example, the fact that the conception of a child was not planned by one or both parents — are *not* to be taken into account.

    Only time will tell whether these rules will be effective in reducing the widespread sense of grievance to which the Child Support Agency's activities seem to have given rise, or whether their effect will be to increase the already great complexity of the scheme to such an extent that it becomes unworkable.

(5) Relevance of the child's welfare

(a) The general duty to have regard to children's welfare
The Child Support Act provides that where, in any case which falls to be dealt with under the Act, the Secretary of State or any child support officer is considering the exercise of any discretionary power conferred by the Act, he is to "have regard to the welfare of any child likely to be affected by his decision." It is not easy to state confidently the likely effect of this provision. It seems that the duty only arises in respect of the exercise of *discretions* (and thus does not affect the performance of the mandatory duties imposed by the Act, *e.g.* in connection with the computation of the maintenance assessment). Moreover, in contrast to legislation dealing with children's upbringing (which requires courts and others to treat the child's welfare as the "paramount" consideration) the duty imposed by the Child Support Act is merely to "have regard" to children's welfare, and the Act contains no specific provision whereby decisions can be questioned on appeal. It is possible that the issue might be raised on appeals to Child Support Appeal Tribunals and Commissioners; and probable that a failure to apply the rule could lead to judicial review. On the other hand, the duty to have regard to welfare extends beyond the "qualifying children" in respect of whom a maintenance assessment is likely to be sought, so that (for example) a Child Support officer is obliged to have regard to the effect of relevant decisions on the absent

parent's other children, on an absent parent's step-children, and even (perhaps) on a parent who is a "child".

(b) The duty to avoid risk of harm to parents with care and children

As already noted, the Secretary of State may, in cases in which certain benefits are in payment, require a parent of a qualifying child to authorise the Secretary of State to take action to recover child support maintenance from the absent parent; but the Secretary of State must not require a parent to give such authorisation if he considers that there are reasonable grounds for believing that if the parent were to be required to give that authorisation (or if she were to give it) there would be a risk of her, or of any child living with her, suffering harm or undue distress as a result.

(6) The role of the courts in relation to child support

The general principle governing the role of the courts in relation to child support is intended to be simple. When the Act is fully in force — and at the date of going to press it is only in force in respect of cases arising after April 5, 1993 and cases in which income support or family credit is in payment — it is to be for the Agency to have the responsibility for assessing and reviewing child maintenance claims, and the courts are to lose that responsibility.

However, the courts do retain their powers to make financial orders in respect of children in a number of cases — in particular, the courts have power to make lump sum or property adjustment orders; to make orders in respect of children of the family; to make "top-up" orders, *i.e.* orders for periodical payments (whether secured or unsecured) in cases in which the maximum child maintenance assessment is in force; to make education expenses orders; and to make periodical payment orders in respect of a child who is disabled; and to make orders in the case of 17 and 18-year-olds not in full-time education and "children" over 18. In certain circumstances, the court may also make orders to give effect to a prior written agreement, thereby ousting the jurisdiction of the Child Support Agency until the Act is finally brought fully into force.

(7) Collection and enforcement of maintenance

There was a low level of compliance with court orders for periodical maintenance, and the Government pointed out that the improved system of assessment which it believed the formula system would produce would be "worthless" unless the sums were actually collected and where necessary enforced. The Government believed that the Child Support Act would create an "efficient and effective service" for the public, ensuring that maintenance was paid regularly and on time, so that the "habit of payment" was established early and was not compromised by early arrears. The legislation accordingly confers extensive enforcement powers on the Child Support Agency; for example, power to make a deduction from earnings order whereby an employer is required to pay over part of a person's wage or salary entitlement to the agency. There is also power to apply to the magistrates' court for a liability order if it seems "inappropriate" to make a deduction of earnings order — for example because the person concerned is not in employment, or if such an order has proved ineffective — and this gives the Agency power to seek even more draconian measures (including, ultimately, the right to apply to the court to commit a defaulter to prison). It is far from clear that these procedures have proved effective.

Conclusion on the Child Support scheme

The reader must make a judgment on the choice to be made between a judicial discretion-led system for the assessment and enforcement of family support obligations and the administrative formula-based system exemplified by the Child Support Agency. It is difficult to reach a rational and informed conclusion not least because predictions about the Agency's administrative efficiency — so strongly emphasised in the Government's 1990 *White Paper* — have been completely falsified. As the House of Commons Social Security Committee observed (*The Performance and Operation of the Child Support Agency* 1995–1996, H.C. 50. paragraph 2) "the Child Support Act would have been bound to arouse controversy because of the scope of the social change it brought about, even if the administrative performance of the Agency implementing the Act had been impeccable. In the event, the Agency's performance . . . was dire". This judgment is supported by Reports of the Ombudsman confirming a high incidence of administrative failures — for example, inaccuracy, delays in processing correspondence, failure to return telephone calls, and so on. Whatever the benefits of a formula-led system, the administrative failings of the Agency have been so serious as largely to outweigh them.

PART THREE

CHILDREN, THE FAMILY AND THE LAW

Introduction: Children, The Family and the Law

A new-born child is physically incapable of caring for itself, and mentally incapable of reaching reasoned decisions about its own future. Others must therefore assume the burden of care and of decision-taking for the baby. The growing child may increasingly demand a say in the decisions which have to be taken about such matters as education and leisure activities. The fact that society casts on the family the function of socialising children increases the possibility of conflict, for the child may not want to do what the parents or other carers would wish. Against this background, no one should be surprised that studies of child development and family dynamics often reveal a hotbed of conflict. Yet most of these conflicts are resolved without any reference to the law, much less to the courts; and the traditional view is that it is for parents to discipline their children and to make choices on their behalf. Yet there remain cases which cannot properly be resolved by private ordering, not least where parents cannot agree between themselves; while the traditional view has also come into conflict with beliefs, strongly articulated in recent years, which assert children's rights to autonomy and, in particular, to have a say in decisions which affect their future. Increasingly, therefore, the law does have to provide answers to questions about who is to be entitled to take decisions about a child's upbringing, and to provide procedures whereby those issues may be litigated.

Family and state

A further potential source of conflict arises if the parents or other carers are unable or unwilling to adopt the values and child-rearing practices which society generally has adopted whether because the parents have a different scale of values (a matter of particular significance in a multi-cultural society) or because the parents (through illness, poverty or other factors) are unable to achieve levels of parenting skill which are judged acceptable by contemporary standards. Since the end of the Second World War in 1945 the State has assumed increasing responsibilities to provide a wide range of services to benefit children and families and to care for children whose own families are unable or unwilling to provide "good enough" parenting. In many cases, of course, the relationship between the State (acting through Local Authorities) and the family is an entirely consensual one with no element — or at least no apparent element — of compulsion. But as we have seen it has for long been recognised that the State sometimes needs to intervene against the wishes of a child's family in order to provide protection for a child against abuse or neglect. The circumstances which justify such intervention have, in recent years become a matter of acute controversy, not least because the result of local authority intervention may be that a child is removed from home and parents and, ultimately, transferred by the process of legal adoption (which destroys all legal links between the child and the birth parents) to another family group.

The legal structure for determining issues about children's upbringing: the Children Act 1989.   The legal procedures governing the upbringing of children and defining the circumstances in which the state may take compulsory measures of child care have been revolutionised by the Children Act 1989 and the Regulations made under the Act. The Children Act was accurately described by the then Lord Chancellor as "the most comprehensive and far reaching reform of child law which has come before Parliament in living memory"; and it seeks to provide a comprehensive, clear, and consistent code for the whole of child law. The Act has undoubtedly effected a considerable simplification and rationalisation. However, the law, not surprisingly, in view of the sensitive issues with which it has to deal, remains complex: the Act is a finely constructed legislative structure, but (as the reader will see) the user needs not only to understand the underlying structure of the legislation, but also to be aware of a substantial amount of detail. Moreover, the clear structure introduced by the Act served to highlight a number of important issues — the extent to which the normal rules about evidence and proof should apply, whether the principle that a lawyer is bound by a strict duty to protect client confidences can be overridden if the interests of the child would thereby be advanced, for example — to which the language of the Act provided no clear answer; and there have been a number of important appellate decisions (including decisions of the House of Lords) with which the lawyer needs to be familiar. Nor did the Children Act make any fundamental change to the law governing legal adoption (even though, as already noted, adoption is often the final outcome of a decision to take a child into Local Authority care); and at the time of going to press the prospects for draft legislation produced for consultation in 1995 and intended to modernise adoption law and harmonise its underlying principles with those embodied in the Children Act 1989 are uncertain, not least because some of the assumptions on which it was based have come to be questioned.

Chapter 9

LEGAL PARENTAGE

Introduction: what is a parent?

Words describing family relationships; for example "uncle" and "aunt" are often used in different senses by different people, and, in particular, words connoting a relationship are often used to indicate a social reality, rather than a biological fact. For example, someone brought up from birth by a man and a woman may well refer to them as "mother" and "father", and it is not unusual for a young child to look on the mother's partner as his or her "dad" whether or not the man concerned is biologically the child's parent. For many years, the law rarely had to concern itself with these ambiguities and differences of linguistic usage. Leaving on one side legal adoption (which only became possible in this country in 1926: see Chapter 15, below) the law did not take account of social or psychological parentage. For the common law, parentage concerned genetics (*Re B (Parentage)* [1996] 2 FLR 15, 21, *per* Bracewell J.) and genetics alone determined the identity of a person's parents.

Establishing parentage

The man and woman who provided the genetic material (the egg and sperm, or "gametes") which had resulted in conception and birth were thus the child's parents; but there were no reliable methods available to identify those persons. Motherhood was said to be a biological fact which could be proved demonstrably by parturition (*i.e.* in most cases someone would have seen the mother give birth): see *The Ampthill Peerage* [1977] A.C. 457, 577; but paternity remained for long almost impossible to prove (leading one judge to comment cynically that paternity was a matter of opinion rather than a matter of fact). Yet it was important to be able to decide the question if only in order to try to make the father financially responsible for the child's upkeep; and the law therefore took refuge in *presumptions*.

There is a presumption that the father of any child born to a married woman during the marriage is her husband; and at common law this presumption could only be rebutted if there were evidence — for example, that the husband had been out of the country throughout the time when the child could have been conceived — establishing beyond reasonable doubt (as distinct from the mere balance of probabilities normally applied in resolving issues of fact in civil litigation) that the husband could not have been the father. A husband who could have had intercourse with his wife at the likely time of conception would thus be held to be the father of her child even if there were evidence that the wife had also had intercourse with "one, two or twenty men" (*per* Sir F. Jeune, P., *Gordon v. Gordon* [1903] P.141, 142).

There is also a presumption that the man named on the birth certificate is the child's father, but the fact that restrictions were for long placed on entry of any name other than the husband's limited the value of this presumption. Finally, the Civil Evidence Act 1968 created rebuttable presumptions that findings of paternity in specified legal proceedings are correct.

The impact of scientific developments

In recent years, this comparatively simple state of affairs has been transformed by two distinct scientific developments:

(i) Scientific testing.   Certain characteristics are transmitted from one generation to another in accordance with recognised principles of genetics; and it has been known for well over fifty years that comparison of the characteristics of the child's blood with the blood characteristics of the child's mother and of a particular man could provide conclusive evidence that the man could not be the father of the child. Such a comparison might therefore indirectly prove that a particular man was the child's father. For example, suppose that a married woman has, whilst living with her husband, had intercourse with only one other person, X. The question arises as to whether H or X is the child's father. If tests exclude the possibility that H is the father (and do not exclude X) then it follows that X must be the father.

Over the years, blood testing became increasingly sophisticated; and a comparison of samples would often enable a forensic scientist to state the degree of probability that a particular individual was (or was not) the child's parent. But the development of DNA profiling (genetic finger-printing) means that (as Waite L.J. put it in *Re A (A Minor) (Paternity: Refusal of Blood Test)* [1994] 2 FLR 463, 469) today parenthood has become something that can be established *positively* as a matter of virtual certainty provided that the necessary samples of blood (or other bodily fluid or tissue) are available.

Blood test directions

But will those samples be available? To give the court power to compel people to submit to the taking of samples would have been too serious an interference with personal liberty; and the Family Law Reform Act 1969 introduced a compromise. The court may give a *direction* for the use of tests (section 20); but failure to comply with such a direction is not a contempt of court (as would be a failure to comply with a court *order*) punishable by fine or imprisonment. Indeed, the Act specifically provides that in general a sample shall not be taken without the consent of the person concerned (section 21(1)). However, the court is empowered to draw such inferences from a refusal as it thinks fit; and in *Re A (A Minor) (Paternity: Refusal of Blood Test)* [1994] 2 FLR 463, 473, the Court of Appeal held that if a claim were made against someone who could possibly be the father, and that person chose to exercise his right not to submit to be tested, the inference that he was the father would be "virtually inescapable" unless he could give very clear and cogent medical or perhaps other reasons for the refusal. In that case:

A prosperous businessman refused to undergo a test because the mother had been working as a prostitute and there were known to be two other men who might on the facts equally be the father. It would (he said) be unreasonable and unjust to put him alone at risk of having paternity conclusively established against him. But Waite L.J. said (at p. 473) that any man who is unsure of his own paternity and harboured the least doubt as to whether the child he is alleged to have fathered may be that of another man has it within his power to set all doubt at rest by submitting to a test. The accuracy of scientific testing now made it impossible for any man in such circumstances to be forced against his will to accept paternity of a child whom he does not believe to be his.

In most cases, it will of course be necessary to take samples from the child as well as from the adults concerned and it is specifically provided that samples may be taken from a consenting person of sixteen or over; and from a child under that age "if the person who has the care and control of him consents" (section 21(2),(3)). If the person with care and control of the child does *not* consent, the court will not make a blood test direction if it would be against the child's interests to do so. Thus:

> In *Re F (A Minor) (Blood Tests: Parental rights)* [1993] Fam. 314, a man applied for tests to be carried out in an attempt to establish that he was the father of a child born to a woman with whom he had had a brief affair. The mother and her husband were reconciled, and were bringing the child up as the child of their marriage. The Court of Appeal held that the application had been rightly rejected because the stability of the family unit on which the child's security depended might be disturbed by the outcome of tests.

But it seems that today there is a general assumption that it is best for the truth to be discovered and in most cases the court will make a direction for testing:

> In *Re H (Paternity: Blood Test)* [1996] 2 FLR 65, C.A., the child's mother was adamantly opposed to samples being taken because she regretted the association she had had with another man after her husband's vasectomy. It was said that the mother wanted to expunge and treat the relationship almost as if it did not exist. However, the child's fourteen-year-old brother knew of the doubts about the baby's parentage, and the court thought it would be unrealistic to pretend the child himself would not sooner or later have to face those doubts. In the circumstances, it was better that the truth should be determined: this would not undermine his attachment to the husband as his psychological father, and it was better that he should know that he had two "fathers" rather than to leave a timebomb ticking away.

(ii) Human assisted reproduction.   The practice of *artificial insemination* — "manual introduction of sperm into the cervix": *Re B (Parentage)* [1996] 2 FLR 15, 21, *per* Bracewell J. — has long been known as a possible means of human conception, and does not necessarily involve any complex technology or medical skill. Artificial insemination by a donor began to be used on a wide scale after the end of the Second World War ("AID"); and some thousands of children were being conceived in this way by the 1980s. In such cases, the man who provides the sperm is unquestionably the genetic father, but the question whether the law should insist on regarding him as the child's legal father (often in preference to the mother's husband, who might well have suggested artificial insemination as the best way of coping with his infertility) began increasingly to be asked.

Again *surrogacy* (a word which simply means substitution) is not a modern technique; and a surrogate mother (it has been said) "is a woman who bears and carries a child at the behest of another person with a view to that other person subsequently assuming the parental role": *per* Sir J. Arnold P., *Re P (Minors) (Wardship: Surrogacy)* [1987] 2 FLR 421 (and note the similar definition in Surrogacy Arrangements Act 1985, s.1(2)). Nor does surrogacy necessarily involve the use of any of the techniques of human assisted reproduction:

> In *Re an adoption application AA 212/86 (Adoption: Payment)* [1987] 2 FLR 291 the intending father and surrogate mother had (in the judge's words) "physical congress with the sole purpose of procreating a child"

— but it may do so:

> In *Re W (Minors) (Surrogacy)* [1991] 1 FLR 385 a married couple were anxious to have children, but the wife had no womb. She provided eggs which were removed and fertilised *in vitro* with sperm provided by her husband. The resultant embryo was implanted in a woman who was anxious to help the couple; and this "surrogate mother" duly handed over the new born child to the commissioning parents. (Contrast *Re O (Parental Order)* [1996] 1 FLR 369, where the surrogate had entered into the procedure "with the best of intentions but when the time came to relinquish the child that she had carried so devotedly, she was overcome with doubt and at first declined to give her consent", *per* Johnson J. at p. 372).

In any event, it was the development of scientific techniques involving the creation of live human embryos outside the human body (*in vitro fertilisation* or "IVF" — fertilisation in a glass or test tube) which prompted the Government to set up the Committee into Human Fertilisation and Embryology (1984, Cmnd 9314, Chairman Dame Mary Warnock). The Warnock Committee provided the following convenient summary of the human assisted reproduction techniques then available:

(i) *Traditional IVF*

The birth of a baby in 1978 following use of this technique marked the beginning of the new era of Human Assisted Reproduction, and "traditional IVF" is now widely used:

> "A ripe human egg is extracted from the ovary, shortly before it would have been released naturally. Next, the egg is mixed with the semen of the husband or partner, so that fertilisation can occur. The fertilised egg, once it has started to divide, is then transferred back to the mother's uterus." (paragraph 5.2)

(ii) *Egg donation*

"A mature egg is recovered from a fertile woman donor, for example during sterilisation, and is fertilised *in vitro*, using the semen of the husband of the infertile woman. The resulting embryo is then transferred to the patient's uterus. If it implants, she may then carry the pregnancy to term." (paragraph 6.1)

(iii) *Embryo donation*

"The donated egg is fertilised *in vitro* with donated semen and the resulting embryo transferred [surgically] to a woman who is unable to produce an egg herself and whose husband is infertile." (paragraph 7.1)

(iv) *Embryo transfer*

The egg is released naturally from the ovary at the normal time in the donor's menstrual cycle. At the predicted time of ovulation she is artificially inseminated with semen from the husband of the infertile woman (or from a donor if the husband is also infertile). Some three to four days later, before the start of implantation, the donor's uterus is "washed out" and any embryo retrieved is then transferred to the uterus of the infertile woman. If the embryo implants successfully the recipient carries the pregnancy to term." (paragraph 7.1)

The dilemma of human-assisted reproduction

These techniques highlight the dilemma of identifying legal parentage, which might reasonably be attributed to at least three categories of person:

(i) *The genetic parents, i.e.* the persons who have provided the genetic material resulting in the child's conception. On this basis, the sperm donor would be the legal father of an AID child (notwithstanding the fact that he had never had any contact with the child or its mother and that in the great majority of cases he would be wholly ignorant of the fact that a child had been born following his donation).

(ii) *The carrying parent, i.e.* the woman who has born the child to delivery (notwithstanding the fact that she may have provided none of the genetic material from which the child's inherited characteristics will be derived, and that she may have agreed to bear the child for a married couple who may have provided some or all of the material).

(iii) *The social parents, i.e.* those who arranged for the child to be conceived and born and who intend to care for the child in exactly the same way as would the parent of a child conceived and born in the traditional way.

The Warnock Committee's Report convinced the Government of the need to legislate; and the Human Fertilisation and Embryology Act 1990 was enacted. The Act deals with a large number of legal issues arising from developments in human assisted reproduction, and in particular it established the Human Fertilisation and Embryology Authority which has extensive powers to control by licensing and otherwise the provision of treatment. The Agency issues *Codes of Practice* to govern procedures. The interested reader must look elsewhere for a discussion of the many fascinating legal issues dealt with by the Act. So far as parentage is concerned, the position can be summarised as follows:

Maternity.

The woman who bears a child will, at the child's birth, always be regarded as the legal mother: HF & EA 1990, s.27(1).

Paternity.

In principle, the father of a child is the person who provides the sperm which leads to conception: *Re Q (Parental Order)* [1996] 1 FLR 369, 370, Johnson J.; *Re B (Parentage)* [1996] 2 FLR 15, Bracewell J. However, this rule is subject to two exceptions relevant to AID:

(a) *AID and in vitro fertilisation: married women.*

The husband of a woman who is artificially inseminated (or who had been implanted with an embryo not created from the husband's sperm) is treated as the father of the child, unless it is proved that he did not consent to the treatment: HF & EA 1990, s.28(2) and can rebut the presumption that a mother's husband is the father of any child she bears: section 28(5). Thus:

> In *Re CH (Contact: Parentage)* [1996] 1 FLR 569 a married couple tried hard but unsuccessfully to have a child. They received fertility treatment; and were eventually advised that AID would be the most appropriate procedure. The husband gave his written consent to such treatment, and the child was born. The marriage broke down, and the mother established a new relationship. She sought to deny the husband contact, arguing that he was not the child's biological father, and that, just as the law did not recognise any presumption that a step-parent should have contact (see *Re H (A Minor) (Contact)* [1994] 2 FLR 776, C.A.) so it should deny any presumption of contact to her former husband. Judge Callman refused to accept this: Parliament had legislated to place the husband in the same position as the biological father, and to sever that tie would be contrary to the wishes of Parliament.

(b) *AID and in vitro fertilisation: other couples.*

The Act also contains a provision which is evidently intended to equate the position of a couple living together in a stable relationship outside marriage with that of a married couple. It is provided that where sperm has been used "in the course of treatment services" provided for a man and a woman "together" under the licensing procedure established by HF & EA 1990 then the man is treated as the child's father: HF & EA 1990, s.28(3). This statutory deeming provision cannot apply if the treatment was provided by an unlicensed person (*e.g.* in *U v. W (Attorney-General Intervening)*, *The Times*, March 4, 1997, Wilson J., an Italian doctor at a clinic in Rome). There has been some difference of judicial opinion as to the interpretation to be put on the expression "treatment services" in this context. Does this mean that the man concerned must *himself* have received some kind of "treatment" — as Johnson J. suggested in *Re Q (Parental Order)* [1996] 1 FLR 369, 371?

In *Re B (Parentage)* [1996] 2 FLR 15, Bracewell J. doubted whether the provision should be construed so narrowly. She considered that the requirement would be satisfied in a case in which a man gave sperm on the occasion of a visit to a hospital together with the mother, and waited there for a short time to ensure that the sperm was satisfactory. It seems that this latter approach (in effect involving the question whether the couple have embarked on a joint enterprise or not) is more in accordance with the policy of the legislation than Johnson J.'s more restrictive approach, although Johnson J. was certainly correct in saying (see *Re Q (Parental Order)* [1996] 1 FLR 369, 372) that the mere fact that a man is living with a woman does not lead to the conclusion that he was receiving treatment services.

Whether or not doctors should give fertility treatment to unmarried women is of course a controversial matter, but one which is outside the scope of this book: see the discussion in G. Douglas, *Fertility and Reproduction* (1991) Chapter 2.

Sperm donor participating in treatment not the father.

In each of the two cases discussed above where the Act treats the woman's partner as the child's father (irrespective of the fact that he has not himself provided the genetic material from which conception resulted) it is provided that "no other person is to be treated as the father of the child": section 28(3); and in many cases the application of this rule will mean that a sperm donor is not to be treated as the child's legal father. But the Act (in an attempt to protect donors participating in recognised infertility treatment from the legal responsibility which they would otherwise in theory bear as father of a child at common law: see *Re B (Parentage)* [1996] 2 FLR 15, Bracewell J., above) goes further. It provides that a man who donates sperm for the purposes of "treatment services" provided under the HF & EA 1990 — in effect, at an officially licensed centre which is bound to follow certain prescribed procedures in relation to the giving of donors' consents (see HF & EA 1990 Sched. 3) and otherwise — is not to be treated as the child's father: section 28(6) (a). More generally it is provided that if conception results from the use of a man's sperm or an embryo created from it after his death, the deceased donor is not to be treated as the child's father: HF & EA 1990, s.28(6)(b). The much publicised decision in *R v. Human Fertilisation and Embryology Authority, ex p. Blood* [1997] 2 All E.R. 687, C.A., is a vivid reminder of the problems to which the use of human assisted reproduction techniques can give rise.

Presumptions unaffected.

The Human Fertilisation and Embryology Act 1990 does not affect the presumptions created by the common law and by statute. Hence it will be rebuttably presumed that the husband of a married woman is the father of her child; it will be rebuttably presumed that the man whose name is entered as being the child's father in the Register of Births is in fact the father, and the fact that a person has been found to be the father of a child in proceedings under the Children Act 1989 (and certain other statutes) creates a rebuttable presumption that he is indeed the child's father: Civil Evidence Act 1968, as amended by Courts and Legal Services Act 1990, Schedule 16, paragraph 2. Finally, it appears that if the court has exercised the power conferred on it by the Family Law Act 1986 to make a declaration that a named person is, or was, the applicant's parent, then that declaration can be controverted only in the most exceptional circumstances: see Family Law Act 1986, s.58(2); *The Ampthill Peerage* [1977] A.C. 547.

Effect of adoption, etc.

The effect of an adoption order is that the child is treated in law as the child of the adopters, and not of any other person; and such an order — considered in detail in Chapter 15 below will effectively override the rules set out above: Adoption Act 1976, s.39.

Fatherless children?

The rules created by the Human Fertilisation and Embryology Act 1990 have to deal with almost impossibly complex circumstances, and they can no doubt be justified on the basis of a pragmatic assessment of what is expedient in the majority of cases. Unhappily, their effect may be to create the possibility that a child will be legally fatherless. Suppose, for example, that sperm is donated for treatment services in accordance with the provisions of the Act and used on a married woman. If her husband proves that he did not consent to the treatment carried out on his wife, neither he nor the donor (nor anyone else) will be the child's legal father. The same will be true where the mother is a single woman who has received licensed treatment: see, *e.g.* *Re Q (Parental Order)* [1996] 1 FLR 369, 371.

The wrong result?

Another example of the difficulty of establishing a single coherent set of rules to determine parentage was vividly demonstrated while the Bill for the Human Fertilisation and Embryology Act was being debated:

> In *Re W (Minors) (Surrogacy)* [1991] 1 FLR 385 a married woman agreed that she would allow herself to be implanted with an embryo produced *in vitro* by fertilising the commissioning mother's egg with the commissioning father's sperm. The surrogate agreed to hand the child — in fact twins were born — to the commissioning couple; and she did so.
>
> The effect of the rules set out above would have been as follows: first, the surrogate would be treated in law as the mother, notwithstanding the fact that she had not provided any of the genetic material which had resulted in the children's conception, that she had never acted as the children's parent, and did not wish to do so; and secondly, the surrogate's husband would (assuming that he had agreed to the procedure) be treated as the child's father notwithstanding the fact that he had had nothing whatsoever to do with the children's conception or with caring for them. Adoption could of course have been used in this case to make genetic and social parenting congruent with the legal parentage; but, perhaps not surprisingly, the commissioning parents considered that adoption would be inappropriate. As a direct result of publicity about such cases, the legislation was hurriedly amended whilst it was passing through Parliament and now incorporates a provision (section 30) enabling a married couple one or both of whom have provided gametes resulting in a child's conception by AID or *in vitro* fertilisation to apply for a court order — the so-called parental order — which will require the child to be treated in law as their child.

It should also be mentioned that evidence suggests the effect of the complex rules contained in the Human Fertilisation and Embryology Act 1990 is not widely understood, even by consultants working in licensed treatment centres and indeed even by Department of Health officials: *Re Q (Parental Order)* [1996] 1 FLR 369, 372, 374.

The creation of so-called "test-tube babies" seems still, for many people, to be a matter for science fiction; but the reality is that the numbers concerned are substantial: in 1993 the Human Fertilisation and Embryology Authority reported that that there had been more than 2,000 births following AID or *in vitro* fertilisation, and there are no doubt births following AID which do not come to the Authority's notice.

Surrogacy

As already pointed out, surrogacy is not a modern invention; but publicity given to the practice (and in particular to the formation of agencies established to arrange for childless couples to have a child born for them by a surrogate mother) led to the enactment of the Surrogacy Arrangements Act 1985. This Act makes it a criminal offence for any person to initiate or take part in negotiations with a view to the making of a surrogacy arrangement, to offer or agree to negotiate the making of a surrogacy arrangement, or to compile any information with a view to its use in making, or negotiating the making of, surrogacy arrangements; but these prohibitions apply if (and only if) the actions in question were done on a commercial basis. The Act defines "commercial basis" by reference to the making of "payments"; but it is specifically provided that this word does not include payment to or for the benefit of a surrogate mother or prospective surrogate mother: section 2(3). The intention was therefore to make the agency criminally liable, whilst leaving the surrogate mother herself free to accept payments whether or not they were confined to expenses.

Agreements unenforceable.   The 1985 Act left the status of surrogacy agreements unclear; but the Human Fertilisation and Embryology Act (s.36) now provides that no surrogacy arrangement is enforceable by or against any of the persons making it. Hence the surrogate mother could not for example sue for any money agreed to be paid to her, and any provisions dealing with the future care of the child would be unenforceable.

All this may suggest that the law takes a deeply ambivalent attitude towards surrogacy but it is apparently used in cases which are considered appropriate by treatment centres licensed under the Human Fertilisation and Embryology Act: see, *e.g. Re Q (Parental Order)* [1996] 1 FLR 369.

Legal parentage of child born to surrogate.   The legal parentage of a child born to a surrogate mother will be determined under the general rules now laid down in the Human Fertilisation and Embryology Act 1990. The surrogate will therefore be the child's legal mother, and it should be noted that a commissioning husband whose sperm is not used for the creation of the embryo carried by the surrogate is not in law the child's father: the rules relating to AID, etc., only apply where the child is carried by the wife: see *Re Q Parental Order)* [1996] 1 FLR 369.

The child's upbringing.   If there is a dispute about the child's upbringing this could be resolved by the court in proceedings under the Children Act 1989 (see Chapter 11 below). The court would resolve the issue by deciding what course of action would best promote the child's welfare: see *Re P (Minors) (Wardship: Surrogacy)* [1987] 2 FLR 421.

If the commissioning parents wish to be recognised in law as the child's parents they may apply for a "parental order" under section 30 of the Human Fertilisation and Embryology Act.

Parental orders.   As already pointed out, the facts of *Re W (Minors) (Surrogacy)* [1991] 1 FLR 385 illustrated the need for a legal procedure to be available whereby commissioning parents could obtain the legal status of parents of the child whose birth they had arranged; and a clause was inserted into the Human Fertilisation and Embryology Act 1990 giving the court power in certain circumstances to make a "parental order" in respect of a child carried by the surrogate as the result of AID or of an embryo being implanted in her —

(i) *Application by commissioning spouses.*
The order can only be made on the application (made within six months of the child's birth) of an adult married couple, and it can only be made if the gametes of the

husband or the wife or both were used to bring about the creation of an embryo (section 30(1)(a) and (b)). It is fundamental that the child should have a genetic link with either the husband or wife or both: *Re Q (Parental Order)* [1996] 1 FLR 369, 370, *per* Johnson J.

(ii) *Surrogate and legal father to consent.*
    The court must be satisfied that the surrogate and the legal father of the child "have freely, and with full understanding of what is involved, agreed unconditionally to the making of the order": section 30(5); and a consent given by the surrogate within six weeks of the child's birth is ineffective: section 30(6). For these purposes, the question of identifying the child's father is to be resolved by reference to the rules set out above. Thus:

> In *Re Q (Parental Order)* [1996] 1 FLR 369, Johnson J., the child was carried by an unmarried woman who had placed in her an egg of the commissioning wife fertilised with sperm provided by a donor at a treatment centre. Accordingly the donor was not to be treated as the child's father. Since the surrogate was a single woman the provisions deeming a husband to be the father of a child born as a result of AID did not apply. The commissioning husband — although he had had many meetings with the surrogate — was never "treated" with the surrogate. Accordingly the child was legally fatherless, and the only consent required was that of the surrogate.

This provision is clearly modelled on the adoption law (see Chapter 15, below); but adoption law makes provision for dispensing with agreement if it is unreasonably withheld and on a number of other grounds. In contrast the 1990 Act only allows the court to dispense with the agreement of a person who "cannot be found or is incapable of giving agreement": section 30(6). In this context, the facts of *Re Q (Parental Order)* [1996] 1 FLR 369, Johnson J. are again of interest:

> The surrogate "felt emotionally torn in half by the separation from the baby" and said that she had not really been prepared for feeling exactly the same about the baby as she had felt about her own children. Stung by the hospital's refusal to allow her to see the child after birth she decided to take steps to bring the child up herself. In the event, she changed her mind and decided to honour her agreement with the commissioning parents. Had she not done so it would have been impossible for the parental order to be made.

(iii) *No financial inducements.*
    The court must be satisfied that no money or other benefit (other than for expenses reasonably incurred) has been given or received by the commissioning parents for or in consideration of the making of the order, the giving of the consent which is required to the making of an order, the handing over of the child to the commissioning parents, or the making of any arrangements with a view to the making of the order, unless such payments have been authorised by the court. This provision is again clearly influenced by the adoption legislation, but it seems uncertain in scope. However, in *Re Q (Parental Order)* [1996] 1 FLR 369, Johnson J. felt able to authorise retrospectively a payment of £8,250 made to the surrogate by the commissioning parents: £3,280 was a reimbursement of expenses in connection with the pregnancy and the balance was

compensation for her loss of earnings. The judge also expressed the view that the payments were, in the circumstances, "reasonable".

(iv) *Other conditions.*

At the time of the application and of the making of the order the child's home must be with the commissioning parents (so that the Act will have no application where the surrogate refuses to hand over the child). Any agreement by the surrogate to the making of the parental order will be ineffective if given by her less than six weeks after the child's birth.

It is difficult to avoid the conclusion that this legislation is an unsatisfactory and ill thought-out measure. It is true that the Act provides that regulations may extend provisions of the adoption legislation to applications for parental orders (section 30(9)), and this power has been used to deal with the most pressing defects in the law: see Parental Orders (Human Fertilisation and Embryology) Regulations 1994, S.I. 1994 No. 2165; but some will think it unfortunate that matters of such importance — extending even to provisions about the registration of the child's birth and the child's entitlement to property: Adoption Act 1976, ss.30 and 51 — should be left to delegated legislation which receives little detailed Parliamentary or other scrutiny.

The child's right to know about his or her origins

The modern law has thus accepted that the child's legal parents may not be the child's genetic parents; yet genetic parentage may be seen as a matter of great relevance by the child and others. Should the law give a child a right to know the truth about his or her genetic parentage? The question is a difficult one, about which conventional views have changed over the years.

The problem first had to be confronted on the context of legal adoption. Although the principle underlying legal adoption in this country was that there should be a complete severance between the adopted child and the birth parents, and that the child should have no legal right to know anything about the birth parents (or other blood relatives), in 1975 Parliament accepted that an adopted child should have the right to access to the register which might reveal the identity of the child's birth parents; whilst provisions of the Children Act 1989 are intended in appropriate cases to promote contact between the child and his birth relatives. If the adopted child has, in principle at least, the right to know about genetic parentage, can there be any justification for treating the child conceived as a result of human assisted reproduction any differently? After all, it might be argued that such a child has an equal need to discover the truth about his or her genetic inheritance, and that this information may indeed be necessary for medical reasons.

The Warnock Committee considered this issue at some length; but the Committee was evidently impressed by difficulties which it considered stood in the way of giving a right to disclosure. In particular the evidence suggested that parents who had resorted to AID did not in practice disclose this fact to the children. The Committee accordingly rejected suggestions that the child should have an unrestricted right to know the full truth about his or her genetic inheritance; and the Human Fertilisation and Embryology Act adopts something of a compromise in this respect.

The Act (s.31) requires the Human Fertilisation and Embryology Authority to keep a register containing information about the provision of treatment for identifiable individuals or which shows that an identifiable individual was or may have been born in consequence of "treatment services". It also entitles a person who has attained the age of 18 to require the Authority to tell the applicant whether or not the information in its possession shows that a person other than a parent of the applicant would or might (but for the provisions of the Act determining the child's legal parentage) be a parent of the applicant. If the information does suggest that the applicant may have been born (in effect) as a result of human assisted fertilisation, it will give the applicant "so much of that information as relates to the person concerned as the Authority is required by regulations to give (but no other information)": section 31(4) (a).

The matter is therefore to be left to Regulations; but the Act specifically provides that Regulations cannot require the authority actually to *identify the person* whose genetic material has been used: section 31(5). In effect therefore it would seem that the position is that donors are entitled to preserve their anonymity, but there is a possibility that children will be given access to information of a general kind about genetic parentage. (At the date of going to press, no regulations authorising any disclosure have been made).

In an unusual provision, the Act permits Regulations to be made at some future date which will permit *identification* of the gamete donor; but it is stipulated that no such change in the law is to take effect retrospectively: section 31(5). Unlesss and until the statute is amended, therefore, a donor can be told that his (or her) identity will never be disclosed; but donors are also told that non-identifying information may be provided at some future date, and indeed donors are invited "to write something which could be passed on to any child born as a result of your help": see the study by Maclean and Maclean (1996) 8 CFLQ 243.

It seems that in practice those bringing up AID children rarely disclose the circumstances surrounding the conception, so that it is unlikely that they will seek information. It has been said (by Morgan and Lee, *Guide to Human Fertilisation and Embryology Act 1990*, page 160) that these provisions make children the "hostages to the reproduction revolution"; but the issues involved are obviously profoundly difficult.

If a *Parental Order* is made in respect of a surrogate birth, the Registrar General is required to enter the fact in a Parental Orders register, which (like the births register) is open to public inspection. As with adoption, provision has been made for those concerned to trace the records of the original birth entry; and the child may thus identify the surrogate mother: Adoption Act 1976 s.51 as modified by Parental Orders (Human Fertilisation and Embryology) Regulations 1994, S.I. 1994 No. 2156.

Chapter 10

THE LEGAL SIGNIFICANCE OF PARENTAGE

Introduction

Parentage is of importance to the lawyer for two reasons. First, legislation frequently confers rights or imposes duties on a child's "parent" or on his "mother" or "father": for example, a person's mother and father are, in certain circumstances, entitled to share the property of a child who dies without leaving a will while a child's "parents" may claim damages for bereavement against the person whose negligence caused the death: Fatal Accidents Act 1976, s.1(a).

In terms of *duties* the social security legislation provides that men and women are liable to maintain their "children" whilst the Education Act 1944 imposes an obligation on parents to ensure that their children attend school. In terms of daily life, it may well be that it is in this area of the creation of statutory rights and duties that the question "who is the child's parent?" will most often be found to be significant.

The second reason for regarding parentage as important is that the law recognises that a child's parent has certain rights and authority as well as certain duties in relation to that child — for example, to control the child's movements, to take decisions about the child's residence, schooling, religion and so on — and that those rights may continue throughout the child's minority.

A. PARENTAL AUTHORITY AND THE COURTS: THE PRINCIPLE THAT THE CHILD'S WELFARE IS PARAMOUNT

There is sometimes a tendency to minimise the significance of parental authority; and some statutory developments (*e.g.* the provisions of the Child Abduction Act 1984 restricting a parent's right to remove a child from the United Kingdom) and case law provisions (see, *e.g. Re B (A Minor) (Wardship: Sterilisation)* [1988] A.C. 199, 205, *per* Lord Templeman, asserting that the consent of parents was not sufficient authority for the sterilisation of a girl under 18) may be thought to reinforce this trend. But the most important restriction on the unfettered exercise of parental authority is that it is, and for many years has been, the law that when a court determines any question with respect to the upbringing of a child, or the administration of a child's property or the application of any income arising from it, the child's welfare is to be the court's paramount consideration: see now Children Act 1989, s.1(1). Hence, if legal proceedings are brought relating to the child's upbringing, questions of entitlement to parental rights become largely irrelevant, since the child's welfare will override the wishes of natural parents, and even overrides considerations of doing justice to the parents.

The leading case is the decision of the House of Lords in *J v. C* [1970] A.C. 668:

> Should a 10-year-old child be returned to his "unimpeachable" natural parents in Spain, or should he continue to be in the care of the English foster parents who had looked after him for most of his life? It was held that to return a child who had been brought up as an English boy with English ways to a strange environment and to parents who would have had difficulty in coping with his problems of readjustment would be inconsistent with his welfare; and the House of Lords unequivocally accepted that the "welfare" test applied even when the dispute was between unimpeachable parents and someone who had no biological or legal links with the child at all.

Again:

> In *Re B (A Minor) (Wardship: Medical Treatment)* (1981) 3 FLR 117 the parents of a new-born and severely handicapped Down's Syndrome child decided to refuse their consent to the surgical removal of a potentially fatal intestinal blockage. The parents thought that in all the circumstances the kindest thing would be to allow nature to take its course. The Court of Appeal held that it was in the child's interests to be allowed to live. The court was not convinced that the child's life was "demonstrably going to be so awful that the child must be condemned to die" but compare *Re T* [1997] 1 FLR 502, p. 167, below.

— and in fact, it became almost commonplace for courts to overrule parental decisions about medical procedures (see, for example, *Re P (A Minor)* [1986] 1 FLR 272, C.A. — abortion carried out on a 15-year-old girl notwithstanding parental opposition: see further p. 250, below). In every case, the parent's "authority" to act on behalf of a child may be overridden by the court; and this led the Law Commission to say that to talk of "parental rights" was "not only inaccurate as a matter of juristic analysis but also a misleading use of ordinary language" (*Report on Illegitimacy*, Law Com. No. 118 (1982) paragraph 4.18).

But it is quite wrong to suggest that parental authority is unimportant. On the contrary, it remains a concept of vital importance for reasons also stated by the Law Commission in its *Report on Illegitimacy* paragraph 4.19:

> ". . . under our law, unless and until a court order is obtained, a person with parental rights is legally empowered to take action in respect of a child in exercise of those rights. It is true that if appropriate procedures are initiated he or she may be restrained from exercising those rights if it is not in the child's interests that he or she should do so; but unless and until such action is taken the person with parental authority would be legally entitled to act. It is self-evident that the court cannot intervene until its powers have been invoked, and in many cases this intervention might well come too late to be effective."

What is good for the parents is good for the child?

Moreover, in assessing what is best for the child the courts inevitably give great weight to the parents' wishes. This point of view was put very forcefully by Lord Templeman:

> "The best person to bring up a child is the natural parent. It matters not whether the parent is wise or foolish, rich or poor, educated or illiterate, provided the child's moral and physical health are not in danger. Public authorities cannot improve on nature.": *Re KD (A Minor) (Ward: Termination of Access)* [1988] A.C. 806, 812, H.L.).

and this approach seems to have influenced the Court of Appeal in two recent decisions:

> In *Re T (Wardship: Medical Treatment)* [1997] 1 FLR 502, C.A., the court overruled a judge's decision allowing doctors to carry out a life-saving liver transplant, in part because the mother genuinely considered that it would be in the child's interests to let nature take its course rather than again being subjected to the trauma of surgery: see further p. 249, below.

Again:

> In *Re M (Child's Upbringing)* [1996] 2 FLR 441, C.A., the court decided that a Zulu child should be returned by the white woman who had cared for him in England for some years to the child's parents (her former servants) in South Africa.

These cases illustrate the difficulty of distinguishing between the rule of law that the child's welfare is the paramount consideration and the issue of fact as to how welfare may best be served. Thus, there is (as a matter of law) no presumption that an infant child should be in its mother's care, but the House of Lords has asserted that the advantage of maternal care reflected "practical experience and the workings of nature": *Brixey v. Lynas* [1996] 2 FLR 499, H.L. (Scotland).

There are other indications that the courts have come to see that the parents' position should be given special recognition. Thus in recent years it has been accepted that there is at least a *presumption* in favour of recognising a parental right to keep in contact with his or her child — as Lord Oliver put it in *Re KD (A Minor) (Ward: Termination of Access)* [1988] A.C. 806, 827, H.L. there is a "general proposition that a natural parent has a claim to [contact with] his or her child to which the court will pay regard and it would not . . . be inappropriate to describe such a claim as a right".

The importance which may seem to be attached to this presumption can be seen from the unusual facts of *Re CH (Contact: Parentage)* [1996] 1 FLR 569:

> The child had been born as a result of artificial insemination by a donor. The mother wanted to deny the husband contact on the basis that the presumption in favour of contact did not apply since he was not the child's biological father. The court rejected this view: first, as a matter of law, the husband was to be treated as the child's father; and secondly in any event on the merits there were cogent reasons why the husband should have contact.

In contrast there is no such presumption in favour of any other relative such as a grandparent (*Re A*) *(Section 8 Order)* [1995] 2 FLR 153, C.A. or even a stepfather who has been the child's "social" father for some years: *Re H (A Minor) (Contact)* [1994] 2 FLR 776 C.A.

Child's welfare not sufficient to justify state interference.   Moreover, the Children Act 1989, in a provision of great significance, effectively provides that the State cannot remove a child from the parent, however much that might be to the child's advantage, unless it can be proved that the child has been or is at risk of being harmed by a failure in parenting: Children Act 1989, s.31. It may, therefore, be that there has been a shift back towards recognition of the claims of parents to care for their children, but in any event the most important reason why the question of parental authority remains important is, as set out above, that unless and until an application is made to the court the parent may usually act — for example, by giving consent to a surgeon to carry out an operation — and this consent will normally be effective. It will often be too late to undo the act to which the parent has consented.

B. "PARENTAL RESPONSIBILITY" AND THE CHILDREN ACT 1989

Words such as "rights" and "authority" have unfortunate connotations and it had long been accepted that the interests of parents might better be described as "responsibilities" or "duties"; and in accordance with this approach, the Children Act 1989 abandons the precedent of earlier legislation (which was framed in terms of "the parental rights and duties") and adopts the term "parental responsibility" in its place. The legislature's use of these words as a key concept emphasised (said Lord Mackay L.C.) "the reason and sole justification for parental status, namely the duty to raise the child to become a properly developed adult both physically and morally." ((1989) 139 New L.J. 505).

But once again the lawyer has to face the practical world in which legal authority may be important, and in fact the key term "parental responsibility" is defined by the Children Act 1989 as as meaning "all the rights, duties, powers, responsibilities and authority which by law a parent of a child has in relation to the child and his property." The Act thus does nothing directly to define or alter the scope and extent of parental authority, and for the lawyer the expression "parental responsibility" may in this context be thought to be no more than a useful shorthand expression in the drafting of the provisions identifying those who are to be entitled to act on a child's behalf.

"Parental responsibility" conveys a message.   But it is clear that those concerned with the drafting of the Children Act hoped that the use of the expression "parental responsibility" would of itself be beneficial. In this view the perceptions of those who work within the law are vital; and the word "responsibility" was chosen in order to illuminate and reinforce the view of the purpose of parental authority set out above: a perception which is far removed from the concept of parental authority as recognised in this country at least until the end of the last century. The new terminology underlines the policy of moving away from rights and concentrating on responsibilities (see *Re S (Parental Responsibility)* [1995] 2 FLR 648, 657, *per* Ward L.J.) and this approach seems widely held by those dealing with children cases in the courts.

Content of "parental responsibility"

Whatever may be thought about this, the lawyer needs to know the extent of the authority a parent can claim, irrespective of whether he *should* do so, and irrespective of what the court, acting in the child's best interests, would do on the facts of a particular case. What then is the scope and extent of parental authority at common law and thus of parental responsibility in the framework of the Children Act 1989? Curiously enough there is some doubt about the nature and extent of the rights recognised at common law (see *F v. Metropolitan Borough of Wirral DC and Another* [1991] 2 FLR 114, C.A.) and the Children Act does nothing to clarify the position. It may (as the Scottish Law Commission put it) be unsatisfactory and unfair to expect people to work with a definition of parental rights which says in effect that parental rights are what the common law says they are, without providing other assistance: see generally the Scottish Law Commission's *Report on Family Law*, Scot. Law Com. No. 135, 1992, paragraph 2.18; and note that the Children (Scotland) Act 1995, s.2, does provide a short list of the rights which a parent has to enable him or her to perform the parental responsibilities which the Scottish legislation describes.

In the absence of any comparable provision in English law, there is no alternative to reproducing the conventional list of the specific powers enjoyed by a person with parental authority:

   (i)   the right to have the child live with the person concerned or otherwise decide where the child should live;
  (ii)   the right to decide on the child's education and to choose his or her religion;
 (iii)   the right to inflict moderate and reasonable corporal punishment and otherwise to discipline the child;
  (iv)   the right to consent to medical treatment;
   (v)   the right to withhold consent from a proposed marriage;
  (vi)   the right to administer the child's property and to enter into certain contracts on his behalf;
 (vii)   the right to act for the child in legal proceedings;
(viii)   the right to the child's domestic services (and possibly the right to receive payment for work which the child does for others);
  (ix)   various miscellaneous rights such as the right to choose the name by which the child should be known.

C. THE CHILD'S RIGHTS

But where does the child fit into this picture? Is it really true that a parent can legally prohibit a sixteen or seventeen-year-old from leaving home or even from staying with friends or going on a holiday? And what is to happen if parent and child disagree about medical treatment; for example, about whether a fifteen-year-old girl should have a prescription for the contraceptive pill?

The common law was quite clear. It recognised that a wise parent would not seek to enforce his views against the wishes of a mature child; and the law would refuse to lend its aid to a parent who sought to impose his will on a child who had attained the "age of discretion". But as a matter of law the parent retained his authority until the child reached the age of majority (which was 21 until the Family Law Reform Act 1969 reduced it to 18). The fact that a particular child's intellectual or emotional development was advanced was irrelevant in deciding whether or not parental authority continued: see *R v. Howes* [1860] 1 E. & E. 332 and the judgment of Parker L.J. in *Gillick v. West Norfolk and Wisbech Area Health Authority* [1985] FLR 736, C.A.

The *Gillick* decision.   This traditional understanding of the common law position of a parent was overturned by the decision of the House of Lords in *Gillick v. West Norfolk and Wisbech Area Health Authority* [1986] A.C. 112:

> Mrs Victoria Gillick, the mother of four daughters under the age of 16, sought an assurance from the Authority that her daughters would not be given contraceptive treatment without her prior knowledge and evidence of her consent. The authority refused to give such an assurance. Mrs Gillick therefore asked the court to declare that DHSS advice to the effect that young people could in some circumstances be given contraceptive advice and treatment without their parent's knowledge and consent was unlawful and wrong, and that it adversely affected Mrs Gillick's right as the children's parent. The House of Lords, by a 3–2 majority, held that her application should have been dismissed.

The *Gillick* rationale: mature children entitled to take their own decisions?

The basis of the *Gillick* decision seemed to be that in the absence of an express statutory rule (for example, the rules requiring parental consent to the marriage of a minor child), all parental authority "yields to the child's right to make his own decisions when he reaches a sufficient understanding and intelligence to be capable of making up his own mind on the matter requiring decision" (see *per* Lord Scarman at p. 186). The question whether a child had sufficient understanding and intelligence must be an issue of fact in each case, depending on the complexity of the issues involved, and the child's emotional and intellectual maturity. Some decisions (including the decision whether to seek contraceptive advice) were said to require a very high level of maturity and understanding; but less complex issues would require a correspondingly less highly developed intellectual and moral understanding.

The *Gillick* decision did not deal with the question of how the capacity of a child should be assessed if his or her understanding was not stable, but varied from day to day or week to week, perhaps as a result of illness. But this was the issue in *Re R (A Minor) (Wardship: Medical Treatment)* [1992] Fam. 11, C.A.:

> A 15-year-old girl had a history of family problems. Her mental health deteriorated. She threatened to commit suicide and on one occasion attacked her father with a hammer. She was placed in an adolescent psychiatric unit. The question arose whether she had capacity to give a valid consent to the administration of anti-psychotic drugs. Sometimes she was entirely lucid and rational, but sometimes her rationality and capacity to understand recommendations about medical treatment were severely impaired. The Court of Appeal unanimously agreed that *Gillick*-competence was a developmental concept and required a long-term assessment as distinct from a snapshot approach; and the very wide swings in the patient's condition were such that she could not be regarded as *Gillick*-competent.

***Gillick* decision not applicable when statute states rules for capacity.**   This approach permits the courts to apply a broad and realistic test, which seems much more sensible than the strictly chronological tests applicable where capacity is fixed by statute — so that it is for example still the law that at one minute to midnight on the eve of a young person's 18th birthday he or she cannot make a will because the Wills Act 1837 s.7 so provides, and it is still the law that such a person cannot (generally speaking: see the Minors Contracts Act 1987) make an enforceable contract; but at one minute after midnight, he or she can do both these things. The fact that the *Gillick* decision does not affect the many important areas in which the child's legal capacity is governed by statute will be thought a significant weakness by those who favour a flexible approach to the question of young people's legal autonomy.

Right to consent includes right to refuse?   Subsequent decisions have also made clear that there are other important limitations on the *Gillick* doctrine. First, if a child has the right to *consent* to medical treatment (whatever the parents' views) does the child also have a right to *refuse* such treatment? For example:

> In *Re W (a minor) (medical treatment: court's jurisdiction)* [1993] Fam. 64, the judge took the view that a 16-year-old girl suffering from anorexia had sufficient understanding to make informed decisions about her treatment; but he overruled her refusal to accept treatment in a specialist unit. The Court of Appeal upheld the judge's decision; and seemed to accept dicta in the earlier case of *Re R (A Minor) (Wardship: Medical Treatment)* [1992] Fam. 11, C.A. to the effect that although the parents of a *Gillick*-competent child had no right to determine whether or not treatment should be given, yet they still retained the right to give a valid consent (thus overruling their child's own decision).

Many writers find this approach — which has been held to justify the detention of a 16-year-old anorexic in a clinic and the use of "reasonable force" in administering treatment: see *Re C (Detention for Medical Treatment: Court's Jurisdiction)*, *The Times*, March 31, 1997, Wall J. — difficult to accept. In particular, it had seemed that *Gillick* accepted the view that once the child had sufficient maturity the parents' right to take decisions in a particular area yielded to the child's right to decide for him or herself. A young person who had satisfied the demanding tests of comprehension and maturity required to attain *Gillick* capacity to consent ought also to have the capacity to refuse to be subjected to treatment. The concept that a person with the necessary degree of maturity can be compelled against his or her will to undergo treatment which he or she has conscientiously decided to reject seems completely inconsistent with this principle; and the Court of Appeal's approach also seemed quite inconsistent with the policy apparently underlying the Children Act 1989 which, for example (Children Act 1989, s.44(7)) specifically provides that a child "may, if he or she is of sufficient understanding to make an informed decision, refuse to submit" to an examination or other assessment directed to be made by the court in certain circumstances. Of course, it is true that doctors and others will no doubt take the views of the patient very much into account in deciding whether to administer treatment; but that hardly provides an adequate response to those who believe in young people's right to autonomy.

If the law is that a *parent* can authorise something to which the *Gillick*-competent child does not agree it is not surprising that the High Court in the exercise of its inherent jurisdiction over children can authorise medical treatment which the child has declined, see *e.g.*, *Re C (Detention for Medical Treatment: Court's Jurisdiction)* (above). The inherent jurisdiction is derived from the duty of the crown to protect its subjects and particularly children, and it has been said that the judge exercises the court's powers "as national parent" (to quote Staughton L.J., *Re R (A Minor) (Wardship: Medical Treatment)* [1992] Fam. 11, 28, C.A. It may well be that the court's powers to act in what it considers, on the evidence, to be the child's best interests irrespective of the wishes of those (including the parents) concerned is socially valuable; and it is in fact used to exercise control over parents who take controversial and perhaps irreversible decisions (for example to allow their daughter to be sterilised). But the difficulty is that it is only because the person concerned is a child that the court can act "to do what is best", and it has no such general power in respect of an adult:

> In *Home Secretary v. Robb* [1995] 1 FLR 412, Thorpe J. held that the Home Secretary was acting lawfully in not providing treatment for an adult prisoner who went on hunger strike.

— because every *adult* has — so long as he or she retains mental competence: see *Re L (Patient: Non-consensual Treatment)* (1997), *The Times*, Jauncey, Kirkwood JJ. (needle phobia destroyed competence) and *Re MB* [1997] 2 FLR, C.A. — the right to decide whether or not to accept medical treatment even if a refusal may lead to premature death: see *Re T (An Adult) (Consent to Medical Treatment)* [1993] Fam. 95, *per* Lord Donaldson of Lymington M.R. Is it right that youth should be a sufficient basis for exercising compulsion on a person who fully understands the issue, whereas old age is not? The answer to this question may depend on the reader's own preferences about the role of authority in the community; and it should certainly not be assumed that there is universal acceptance of the case for children's rights: see for a powerful statement of the case to the contrary, Melanie Phillips, *All Must Have Prizes* (1996) pp. 260–267; and note the view attributed by *The Daily Telegraph* (January 3, 1997) to the then Secretary of State for Health that too much weight has been given to children's views. But to make the capacity to decide depend on age does give rise to apparent anomalies, as evidenced by the sad facts of *Re E (A Minor) (Wardship: Medical Treatment)* [1993] 1 FLR 386:

> A 15-year-old boy and his parents were Jehovah's Witnesses, and refused to agree to the blood transfusion treatment which doctors considered appropriate to treat his leukaemia. Ward J. held that when viewed objectively the boy's welfare led to only one conclusion, *i.e.* that he should receive treatment; and this was carried out. It is understood that when the boy reached majority he refused further transfusions, and died.

D. RELEVANCE OF LEGITIMACY AND ILLEGITIMACY

So far, the question whether a child's parents are or are not married to one another has only been seen to be directly relevant in so far as the law will *presume* that a married woman's husband is the father of her child unless and until the contrary is proved. Marital status is also *indirectly* relevant in various situations arising from human assisted reproduction; for example, the husband of a married woman will be the legal father of her AID child unless he can show that he did not consent to the treatment, and the provisions relating to parental orders only apply to commissioning parents who are married. But if we look at the broader question of whether a child is to be treated in law as a full member of the family, legal systems have traditionally drawn a sharp distinction between legitimate children (who are regarded as full members of the legal family) on the one hand and illegitimate children (who to a greater or lesser extent are not given full legal recognition) on the other hand; and this distinction usually depends on whether or not the child's parents were married. The general rule was that a child should only be regarded as a full member of the legal family if the parents were lawfully married at the time of the child's birth or conception.

This principle was carried to an extreme by the common law of England, which classified the illegitimate child as *filius nullius* ("the child of no one") and thus for legal purposes a stranger not only to his father but also to his mother and to all other blood relatives. In consequence of this doctrine, the illegitimate child (or "bastard") had, at common law, no legal right to succeed to property, to receive maintenance, or to any of the other benefits derived from the legal relationship of parent and child.

Piecemeal reform: legitimation, etc.

These rules increasingly seemed harsh and unjust, and over the years the legal position of the child born illegitimate was gradually improved. The Legitimacy Act 1926 enabled illegitimate children to be legitimated by the subsequent marriage of the parents; and in 1959 Parliament accepted the civil law doctrine of the putative marriage whereby the child of a void marriage would nevertheless be treated as the legitimate child of the parents if at the time of the act of intercourse resulting in the birth (or at the time of the celebration of the marriage if later) both or either of the parties to the void marriage reasonably believed it to be valid: see now Legitimacy Act 1976, s.1(1). But notwithstanding these developments many children remained illegitimate and the law only gradually adopted the policy that children should not be penalised solely because they were not legitimate.

The Family Law Reform Act 1969 effected a number of improvements, and in particular gave the illegitimate child the right to succeed on the intestacy of either parent (although the child still did not count as a relative for purposes of succession to brothers, sisters, or grandparents); and there remained a number of areas in addition to intestate succession in which the law continued to distinguish between the legal rights of the legitimate and the illegitimate. The clearest example of such discrimination was that an illegitimate child could only obtain a maintenance order against the father in a distinctive form of proceedings (called affiliation proceedings) which had to be brought in the lowest court in the judicial hierarchy (the magistrates' court) and for long there was a (very low) ceiling on the amount of maintenance which could be awarded. Moreover, affiliation proceedings were surrounded by procedural and other rules which caused the illegitimate child to be treated differently from (and usually less favourably than) the legitimate child in pursuing claims for support.

Such discrimination increasingly seemed difficult to justify, and in 1982 the Law Commission published a comprehensive and detailed report (Law Com. No. 118) which concluded that discrimination against those born out of marriage could not be justified as a general policy. This conclusion was reinforced by the fact that to preserve such discrimination would be inconsistent with this country's international obligations under the European Convention on Human Rights and under the European Convention on the Legal Status of Children Born Out of Wedlock.

Reform

The Family Law Reform Act 1987 gave effect to the Law Commission's recommendations, and asserted the general principle that references in legislation "to any relationship between two persons shall, unless the contrary intention appears, be construed without regard to whether or not the father and mother of either of them, or the father and mother of any person through whom the relationship is deduced, have or had been married to each other at any time." Hence, in relation to statutes enacted after April 4, 1988 the common law rule (see *Re M (An Infant)* [1955] 2 Q.B. 479) whereby statutory references to a "parent" did not extend to an illegitimate child: FLRA 1987, s.1(1) has been abolished:

> In *M. v. C and Calderdale Metropolitan Borough Council* [1993] 1 FLR 505 the Court of Appeal held in terms that the word "parent" when used in the Children Act 1989 included the father of an illegitimate child, notwithstanding the fact that the person concerned did not have "parental responsibility" for the child.

It follows that if Parliament now wishes to distinguish between illegitimate and legitimate children it must do so expressly; and factual parentage is accordingly now more important than in the days when status as a legitimate child was often the crucial issue.

But scope of reform limited.   At first sight, the adoption of this general principle would seem to make any further explanation unnecessary: a child was illegitimate if his parents were not married; the question of whether or not his parents are or were married is now to be irrelevant in determining legal relationships, and hence (it might be thought) illegitimacy has been abolished and the concept of legitimacy or illegitimacy thus rendered, in the context of family law, of only historical interest. But unfortunately this is not the case.

First, the principle stated above applies to legislation enacted after the coming into force of the Family Law Reform Act 1987 on April 4, 1988; but not to earlier legislation unless express provision is made for that purpose; and, secondly, the Family Law Reform Act accepted the Law Commission's view that the father of an illegitimate child should not, as such, be entitled as of right to parental authority (or "parental reponsibility" in the terminology subsequently introduced by the Children Act 1989) above over the child:

(a) *Pre-1987 legislation, etc.*
(i) *Citizenship.*

Under the British Nationality Act 1981, the relationship of parent and child exists only between a man and his legitimate child: BNA 1981, s.50(9)(b). An illegitimate child cannot therefore acquire British citizenship through his father; and there are two main factual situations in which a child of unmarried parents will not be entitled to the British citizenship which a child of married parents would take. These are, first, where a child is born in this country to a British father and a foreign mother; and secondly, where a child is born abroad to a British father and a foreign mother or to a mother who is British by descent only. The Government refused to change the law so as to give the illegitimate child who could prove parentage the same rights as a legitimate child, arguing that further consultation was needed. Ten years later, the law remains unchanged.

(ii) Succession to the throne, peerages, rights under pre-1988 dispositions, etc.

Succession to the throne of the United Kingdom is governed by the Act of Settlement 1701, the language of which restricts the right of succession to the legitimate, and the Family Law Reform Act 1987 did not alter the law in this respect. Succession to hereditary peerages is governed by the terms of the relevant letters patent, which limit the succession to heirs "lawfully begotten" (see Law. Com. No. 118, paragraph 8.26) and the right of succession to such peerages (and indeed more generally the right to take property under wills taking effect and settlements made before the implementation of the 1987 Act) will be unaffected.

(b) *The legal position of the father of an illegitimate child.*

The factual relationship of the father of an illegitimate child with the child and the child's mother can (as it has been said: see *Re H (Illegitimate Children: Father: Parental Rights) (No. 2)* [1991] 1 FLR 214, 218, *per* Balcombe L.J.) be infinitely variable:

> "at one end of the spectrum his connection with the child may be only the single act of intercourse (possibly even rape) which led to conception; at the other end of the spectrum he may have played a full part in the child's life, only the formality of marriage to the mother being absent."

It seems that the Law Commission's consultation revealed that influential groups — including those usually recognised as having the interests of illegitimate children and their parents as a primary concern — took the view that automatically to equate the legal position of the father with that of the mother would give rise to considerable social evils; whilst as Ward L.J. has put it:

> — "at its most emotive, but none the less pertinent point of distinction, it would cause offence to right-thinking people that the rapist should claim parental rights . . . over the child which that criminal act produced": *Re S (Parental Responsibility)* [1995] 2 FLR 648, 652.

Even in less dramatic (and more typical) cases there was concern that mothers might be tempted to conceal the father's identity in order to prevent him from being able to exercise the authority which would be conferred on him by law; and, secondly, there was concern that the father's legal right might be exercised in a disruptive way, particularly when the mother had married a third party and established a secure family for herself and the child. The Law Commission reported —

> "a profound division of opinion amongst both legal and non-legal commentators on the parental rights question. We do not think that it would be right for us to ignore such anxieties where we cannot show them to be without foundation, and where the countervailing advantages of the reform are not clearly demonstrable": see Law Com. No. 118, paragraph 4.48.

The Family Law Reform Act 1987 (and the Children Act 1989) accordingly preserve the principle that the father of an illegitimate child has no "parental responsibility" in respect of that child unless, either; (a) the court makes an order in his favour or (b) the child's parents make a Parental Responsibility Agreement in the prescribed form and register it as required by Regulations. The result is that an important distinction between children based solely on their parents' marital status remains embodied in the law, since the father of a child born outside marriage will by virtue of that fact have no parental authority over the child. In this respect, therefore, children are still divided by the law into two categories: those with a "normal" relationship with both parents, and others. But it appears that there is still influential opposition to the notion that parental authority should automatically be vested in the father of an illegitimate child: in 1992 the Scottish Law Commission proposed that all parents should have equal rights and responsibilities, but the Conservative Government did not accept this advice.

The statute book: a victory for political correctness over accuracy?   The Family Law Act 1987 seeks to avoid attaching "labels" such as legitimate or illegitimate (or even "marital" and "non-marital") to children; and it does so by making any distinctions which have to be preserved — such as the question as to who has authority over the child — depend on whether or not the parents were married or not at the time of the child's birth. The reader should be warned that this was only possible by a statutory deeming process so that, for example, children legitimated by their parents' marriage possibly many years after the birth are brought within the definition. The reality is that the expression "child whose parents were married at the time of his birth" means "child who was born legitimate, was subsequently legitimated, or is entitled to be treated as legitimate"; and the attempt to conceal the reality may confuse users of the statute book: see the fuller discussion in the second edition of this book, at paragraph 11–22. The author prefers accuracy to political correctness; and the terms "legitimate" and "illegitimate" are used in this book accordingly, as indeed they continue to be used in the statute book.

Unmarried fathers?   One further point about terminology must be made. This relates to the terms apt to describe the parents of an illegitimate child, who are now often described as the child's "unmarried father" or "unmarried mother" in a further attempt to avoid using the label "illegitimate". The author believes this usage to be unacceptable: the relevant legal issue is never simply whether the parent concerned is "married" or not; it is whether he or she was married to a particular person, *i.e.* the child's other parent. For example, Charles II, King of England, enjoys a certain notoriety as the father of a number of illegitimate children; yet it would be absurd to describe him, in defiance of the facts, as "unmarried". Accordingly, the potentially misleading expression "unmarried parent" is not used in this book to describe the parent of an illegitimate child.

E. WHO IS ENTITLED TO EXERCISE PARENTAL RESPONSIBILITY?

We have already seen how the law responds to the problems of defining parentage and identifying the persons who are to be regarded as a child's "parents" but that does not necessarily conclude the issue of who has "parental responsibility" (which, of course, includes parental authority) for a child. The Children Act 1989 codifes, clarifies, and in some respects reforms, the law on this subject. Under the Act, the following persons have "parental responsibility":

1. Both parents of a legitimate child

The Children Act 1989, s.2(1) provides that where a child's mother and father were "married to each other at the time of his birth" they each have parental responsibility for a child. In fact, (as explained above) the formula "married to each other at the time of his birth" does not mean what it says: the question is in reality whether the child is legitimate or not.

2. The mother of an illegitimate child

The Children Act 1989, s.2(2) provides that the mother of an illegitimate child shall have parental responsibility, but that the father should not have parental responsibility unless he acquires it in accordance with the provisions of the Act.

The Children Act provides two procedures whereby a father may acquire parental responsibility:

(i) *By the making of a parental responsibility order.*

The court may on the father's application order that he "shall have parental responsibility for the child": Children Act 1989, s.4(1)(a). The effect of such an order is virtually to equate the position of the father of a child born out of wedlock with that of the father of a legitimate child: *Re H (Minors) (Local Authority: Parental Rights) (No. 3)* [1991] Fam. 151, 160, *per* Balcombe L.J.

In deciding whether or not to make an order the court will normally ask the question whether to do so would promote the child's welfare (see *Re G (a minor) (parental responsibility order)* [1994] 1 FLR 504, 508, *per* Balcombe L.J.) and it has become clear that in many situations an order will be made. The questions to which the court will attach primary importance are whether the father has shown commitment and attachment to the child and his reasons for seeking the order. What, effectively, a parental responsibility order does is to give a committed father the *status* of parenthood:

> The leading case is now *Re S (Parental Responsibility)* [1995] 2 FLR 648, C.A., where the father had had a good relationship with his child and had supported her financially. However, he was convicted of possessing paedophile literature. The mother was upset and confused, and concerned about the implications of the conviction for the safety of the child; and she resisted the making of a Parental Responsibility Order because of the rights and power which it would give the father. The Court of Appeal unanimously held that a Parental Responsibility order should have been made. It was wrong to place undue and false emphasis on the rights and powers embodied in parental responsibility. If the father abused that authority such abuse could be speedily controlled by the court exercising its powers under the Children Act 1989.

Although "commitment" to the child is an important consideration, it has been held that an order should not be withheld merely because the father has failed to contribute to the child's maintenance:

In *Re H (Parental Responsibility: Maintenance)* [1996] 1 FLR 867, C.A., the father had not provided any financial support for the children at all, alleging that the mother would spend any money on cigarettes and drink. The judge adjourned the father's application for a parental responsibility order to enable the father to demonstrate his commitment by making financial payments. The Court of Appeal held this to be wrong: the weapon of withholding parental responsibility should not be used for the purpose of extracting financial support from the father; and the cases showed that "where a father shows some devotion to his children he should ordinarily be granted a parental responsibility order in the absence of strong countervailing circumstances" (*per* Leggatt L.J. at 872).

Because of the distinctive nature of a parental responsibility order in effectively conferring recognition of the father's *status*, the courts will be prepared to make an order even in cases in which there is no realistic prospect of any immediate factual link between father and child:

In *Re H (A Minor) (Parental Responsibility)* [1993] 1 FLR 484, C.A., the judge found on the facts that the relationship between the mother and the man she had married would be destroyed if the husband were made to tolerate any contact between the father and the child. For that reason, it would (unusually) be wrong to make any order for contact: it would not be in the child's interests for the mother's fragile relationship to be destroyed and the child's stability in their home to be at risk. But the Court of Appeal held that the judge had been plainly wrong to refuse to make a parental responsibility order in the father's favour: in addition to the general advantages to be derived from recognition being given to his status, there could be practical advantages if the mother and stepfather were ever to apply to adopt the child or indeed if their marriage were to break down.

Again —

In *Re L (Contact: Transsexual Applicant)* [1995] 2 FLR 438, Thorpe J., the relationship between a six-year-old child's unmarried parents broke down; and thereafter, on psychiatric advice, the father embarked on treatment which successfully achieved the transition from male to female gender. The court had no doubt that a parental responsibility order should be made (notwithstanding the fact that the father's contact was, for the time being, limited to indirect contact). It was particularly relevant that with the assistance of therapy the relationship would be restored.

Some 4,400 parental responsibility orders are made each year and although generalisations on matters of fact are always dangerous in the context of a highly discretionary jurisdiction, it seems that it is only in rare cases that a parental responsibility order will be denied to a father who genuinely wishes to secure recognition of his legal relationship with the child. But —

In *Re T (A Minor) (Parental Responsibility: Contact)* [1993] 2 FLR 450, C. A. the parents separated during the mother's pregnancy because the father — a man of unbridled hostility, guilty of numerous acts of violence — had assaulted and injured the mother. He had also abducted the child. The Court of Appeal held that the judge had been right to hold that a father guilty of cruel and callous behaviour without a thought for the child's welfare had no worthwhile part whatever to play in the life of the child; and an order had properly been refused.

and —

In *Re P (Minors: Parental Responsibility order)*, *The Times*, April 24, 1997, C.A., a father who was serving a 15-year sentence for an offence of violence committed whilst on home leave was denied a parental responsibility order, in part because imprisonment restricted his ability to exercise parental responsibility and in part because of his failure to recognise the damaging effect of a long sentence on his children.

The court may terminate a parental responsibility order (or agreement: see below) on the application of any person with parental responsibility for the child, or on the application of the child if the court grants leave for such an application to be made. Thus —

In *Re P (Terminating Parental Responsibility)* [1995] 1 FLR 1048, Singer J., the father pleaded guilty to serious physical assaults on his nine-week-old daughter and was sentenced to a term of imprisonment. It was held that the father had forfeited his claim to parental responsibility, and the court would terminate it accordingly.

(ii) *By the parents making a parental responsibility agreement.*

The Children Act 1989 s.4(1)(a) provides that the father and mother of an illegitimate child may by agreement provide for the father to have parental responsibility for the child. It appears that the Law Commission was concerned about the danger of vulnerable mothers being pressured into making such agreements; and in an attempt to provide some protection the Act provides that the agreement must be in a prescribed form. It seems that the Commission's concerns were justified, and also that many agreements were forged. Applicants must now take the form to a court where a J.P. or court official will witness the signatures: see the Parental Responsibility Agreement (Amendment) Regulations 1994 (S.I. 1994 No. 3157). Thereafter the Agreement must be filed in the Principal Registry of the Family Division. In the year following the introduction of more stringent procedures the number of agreements filed (which had been steadily increasing year by year) fell by almost 36 per cent to an estimated 3,455.

Once an agreement has been duly made it can only be brought to an end by court order: Children Act 1989 s.4(1)(a) (as was done in *Re P (Terminating Parental Responsibility)* [1995] 1 FLR 1048, above.)

3. Adoptive parents

The adoptive parents of an adopted child have parental responsibility, and the making of an adoption order operates to extinguish the parental responsibility vested immediately before the making of the order in any other person: Adoption Act 1976, s.12(3), as amended by the Children Act 1989. The effect of this provision is that the birth parent will, once an adoption order has been made, need the leave of the court to make an application for contact; and the courts are most unlikely to grant such leave if there is any risk that the adoptive parents' relationship with the child will be destabilised:

> In *Re C (A Minor) (Adopted Child: Contact)* [1993] 2 FLR 431, Thorpe J., the child's mother had persistently resisted the making of an adoption order and wanted to be kept informed of the development of her child by the receipt of an annual progress report and photograph. The court refused her application for leave to seek a contact order: any benefit in allowing even the limited contact the mother sought would be greatly outweighed by the risk of insecurity and disruption within the newly constituted family. As the law now stands, adoption orders are intended to be permanent and final: see Chapter 15 below.

The making of a parental order under the Human Fertilisation and Embryology Act 1990, s.30, also operates to deprive the surrogate and her husband or partner of parental responsibility and to vest parental responsibility in the commissioning parents.

4. The child's guardians

The Children Act provides procedures whereby parents and guardians may appoint other individuals to be the child's guardian by will or written instrument, whilst in some circumstances the court may appoint a guardian: Children Act 1989, s.5. The Act provides that a guardian should have parental responsibility when his or her appointment takes effect: section 5(6); and broadly speaking, an appointment only takes effect on the death of the last person to have parental responsibility for a child: Children Act 1989, s.5(7). For example:

> H appoints a guardian for his child. He dies, but W survives. The person appointed by H will only be able to exercise parental responsibility on W's death: section 5(8).

However, the position is different if there is a residence order in H's favour alone: the appointment of the guardian would then be effective immediately on H's death: section 8(7) (b). If H and W were divorced after H had made the appointment, the appointment he had made would be revoked: section 6(3A) as amended by Family Law Act 1996, Schedule 8 paragraph 41(2).

The policy underlying these rather complex provisions is that one spouse should not ordinarily be able to dictate from beyond the grave how the other cares for the child during the survivor's lifetime; but that if one person has responsibility for the child under a residence order then it is reasonable that he or she should be able to control the arrangements immediately following his death. The fact that divorce revokes an appointment is based on the supposition that the arrangements for children should be reviewed as part of the divorce process.

5. Other persons who have parental responsibility consequent on the making of a court order

The Children Act adopts the general principle that the person who is actually looking after a child should have the necessary powers and legal authority to do so. In pursuance of that policy the Act provides that in two cases parental responsibility should automatically be given to the person in whose favour an order under the Act has been made:

(a) Residence order.   Where the court makes a residence order (*i.e.* an order settling the arrangements about the person with whom the child is to live) in favour of a person who is not a parent or guardian of the child, that person will thereby have parental responsibility for the child for so long as the order remains in force: Children Act 1989, s.12(2).

In a few unusual cases the court has made a residence order specifically to deal with parental responsibility:

> In *Re AB (Adoption: Joint Residence)* [1996] 1 FLR 27, Cazalet J., the foster-parents of a five-year-old child had lived together for twenty years, had a wholly committed relationship, and intended to spend the rest of their lives together. They wanted to adopt the child, but the adoption legislation does not allow a joint adoption order to be made unless the prospective adopters are married. They decided therefore that the foster-father should apply for an adoption order, and the judge granted the application. But that would mean the foster-mother would not have parental responsibility (and the procedure described above for making a parental responsibility order is only available to the child's father). The judge decided to make a joint residence order in favour of the two foster-parents. The position in law would thereafter be that the foster-father would be treated in law as the child's father; but that the foster-mother would, so long as the residence order was in force, also have parental responsibility for the child.

No doubt the orders made were appropriate in the very special circumstances of that case; but as the judge pointed out the legal position of the child's "mother" would be very different from that of a legal parent. In particular, it would carry no inheritance or other rights derived from status; and the residence order would only be effective during the child's minority whereas adoption (like birth parentage) is for life.

It should also be noted that the Children Act provides (section 12(3)) that the parental authority flowing from the making of a residence order is limited in two specific respects: first, it does not include the right to withhold consent to the making of adoption orders; and secondly it does not confer any right to appoint a guardian for the child.

(b) Care orders and emergency protection orders.   While a care order is in force with respect to a child, the local authority designated by the order has parental responsibility for the child: Children Act 1989, s.33(3)(a), and generally Chapter 13 below; and this fact has been of importance in cases in which the court has had to decide whether it is in the child's interests to make such an order. The (happily unusual) facts of *Re M (Care Order: Parental Responsibility)* [1996] 2 FLR 84, Cazalet J. provide a dramatic illustration of what may be involved:

> A new born baby boy, apparently of Afro-Caribbean origin, was found abandoned on the steps of a health centre, and it proved impossible to trace his relatives. Medical investigation gave rise to anxiety; and in particular there were suggestions that HIV testing might be appropriate in due course. The local

authority at first cared for the boy under their general duties relating to children in need; but the authority became increasingly concerned about their lack of specific legal powers to authorise intrusive medical testing. The judge was satisfied that he had jurisdiction to make a care order, and that the child's welfare required that the local authority have parental responsibility to implement decisions of major importance which would need to be taken about the child's future, if need be at short notice.

In contrast, the mere fact that children are orphaned does not necessarily lead to the conclusion that their welfare would be served by the making of a care order: see *Birmingham City Council v. D* [1994] 2 FLR 502, Thorpe J. where the children were well settled, well cared for and presented no problems (and contrast *Re SH (Care Order: Orphan)* [1995] 1 FLR 746, Hollis J. where there were risks arising from the possibility that the child would run away).

Once again, the scope of the parental responsibility flowing from the making of a care order is limited in so far as it does not extend to giving agreement to adoption or to the appointment of a guardian, nor does it give the local authority the right to cause the child to be brought up in a different religious persuasion from that in which he would have been brought up had the order not been made: Children Act 1989, s.33(6).

Shared parental responsibility.   It is a fundamental principle of the Children Act that parental responsibility is not easily lost: in particular, a person with parental responsibility does not lose it solely because another person also acquires parental responsibility: Children Act 1989, s.2(6). An example may help to make this clear: suppose that the court makes a residence order in favour of the two grandparents of a legitimate child. In consequence of that order they will (as we have seen) both have parental responsibility: C.A. 1989, s.12(2). But the child's parents had parental responsibility for the child at birth, and they do not lose it merely because of the making of the residence order in favour of the grandparents. In the result, there are four people with parental responsibility for the child, and the Act specifically provides that where more than one person has parental responsibility for a child, each of those persons may act alone and without the other in "meeting that responsibility": C.A. 1989, s.2(7). In effect, parental responsibility is enjoyed jointly and severally.

This principle is often convenient in practical terms: it will be sufficient to find one person with parental responsibility in order to give agreement to emergency surgery, for example. But the convenience is purchased at the cost of creating potential difficulties where those who share parental responsibility are not on good terms.

The Act provides a partial remedy for this problem by a provision (section 2(8)) that parental responsibility does not entitle a person to act inconsistently with any order made with respect to the child under the Act. Hence, if for example the court makes a residence order in favour of one of the parents on divorce, the other — although still possessing parental responsibility — would not be entitled to do anything incompatible with the residence order (such as removing the child from home). For example:

In *Re P (A Minor) (Parental Responsibility)* [1994] 1 FLR 578, Wilson J. there was bad feeling between the unmarried parents; and a residence order was made that the five-year-old girl should live with her mother. The magistrates refused to make a parental responsibility order in favour of the father because they were concerned he would question aspects of the child's upbringing. But (as Wilson J.

in allowing the father's appeal pointed out) the residence order gave the mother the right to determine all matters arising in the day to day management of the child's life, and the father could not properly act inconsistently with it. It is also true that if there were a dispute about a particular matter the court would be able to resolve it, if appropriate by making a specific issue order.

But the position is not always wholly satisfactory:

In *Re G (Parental Responsibility: Education)* [1994] 2 FLR 964 the father, who had the day to day care of the nine-year-old boy decided, without consulting the mother, to send him to a local authority boarding school. The Court of Appeal held that, although the father was not acting incompatibly with any court order, there was "no doubt" that the mother, having parental responsibility, was "entitled to and indeed ought to have been" consulted about the important step of taking her child away from the day school that he had been attending and sending him to a boarding school.

The reality is that each person with parental responsibility does have the power effectively to authorise action which others would strongly oppose; and the only effective safeguard in such circumstances is to obtain orders from the court defining the areas of responsibility.

The most dramatic example of a potential clash arises in cases in which the court makes a care order. In many cases, the parents will be opposed to the making of the order, and it is not easy to see why a local authority should wish to obtain a care order unless it envisages a real prospect of having to exercise or to threaten to exercise compulsion against the parents. But the Act adheres to the philosophy that the fact that a local authority has acquired parental responsibility should not deprive the parents of their responsibility; and it seeks to deal with — the often very real — potential conflict by providing that the local authority should have power "to determine the extent to which a parent or guardian of the child may meet his parental responsibility for the child": Children Act 1989, s.33(3)(b). In effect, therefore, this provision gives the local authority power to restrict the parents' exercise of parental authority but it is also provided that the authority may only exercise that power if satisfied that it is "necessary" to do so in order to safeguard or promote the child's welfare: C.A. 1989, s.33(4); see further p. 236, below.

Responsibility not transferable.   The Children Act (s.2(a)) prohibits the surrender or transfer of parental responsibility. The provision prohibiting transfer of parental responsibility prevents parents from allowing children to be privately adopted or even 'sold'; and reflects the common law rule that children are not a marketable commodity. The prohibition on surrendering parental responsibility underlines the policy adopted by the Act that the sanction of a court order is required before a person can be rid of parental responsibility, and in one respect this represents a significant change in policy. Before the enactment of the Children Act 1989 local authorities could in certain circumstances acquire parental authority by administrative action (the so-called "parental rights resolution"); and this procedure could be used in many cases in which the parents agreed that they were not capable of providing proper care for their children. The Children Act abolished that procedure, and the result may occasionally seem rather strange:

In *Re M (a minor) (care order: threshold conditions)* [1994] A.C. 424, H.L., the child's father killed the mother with a meat cleaver in the presence of the child and the mother's three other children. The father was duly sentenced to life imprisonment and a recommendation that he be deported at the end of his sentence was also made. The Court of Appeal held that the trial judge had had no power to make a care order, and the Court of Appeal made a residence order in favour of the mother's sister. The father evidently preferred that the child should be in the care of the local authority with a view to adoption, and he therefore appealed to the House of Lords. Before the passing of the Children Act he would have been able to achieve the result he wanted by agreeing to the local authority assuming parental rights by resolution.

How does the fact that parental responsibility is not transferable affect such routine situations as a child being left in the care of a nanny or au pair whilst the parents are away on a business trip or foreign holiday, or a child being sent to boarding school or on an adventure training course? The Act (s. 2(9)) expressly permits a person with parental responsibility to arrange for "some or all of it to be met" by one or more persons acting on behalf of the person with parental responsibility. It also expressly provides that the "person with whom any such arrangement is made may himself be a person who already has parental responsibility for the child"; and it seems that this provision is intended to encourage parents to make their own arrangements for what they consider to be best if their relationship breaks down. But no such agreement can exclude the power of the court to impose a different solution; whilst the Act also provides that the making of such an arrangement does not affect any liability — perhaps prosecution for child neglect — arising from a failure to meet the responsibility: C.A. 1989, s.2(11).

Action by a person without parental responsibility. It is not necessary to have parental responsibility to be entitled to take, perhaps (but not necessarily) in an emergency, action in a child's interests. The Children Act (s.3(5)) provides that a person who "has care" of a child without having parental responsibility may do "what is reasonable in all the circumstances of the case for the purpose of safeguarding or promoting the child's welfare". This provision makes it clear that someone caring for a child in the parent's absence may, for example, arrange emergency medical treatment; and it has been suggested that a foster-parent might, for example, rely on this provision to justify a refusal to hand over the child to the parents in the middle of the night: see White, Carr and Lowe, *The Children Act in Practice* (2nd ed. 1995, paragraph 3.71). It is quite clear that some provision to legitimise short term and emergency measures is necessary to protect the position of people such as school-teachers, doctors and paramedics. But the scope of the present provision is not clear, and it seems that relatives or others caring for an orphaned child would be best advised to apply to the court for an order appointing them as guardians (and in that capacity people with full parental responsibility for the child).

Responsibility without parental responsibility? Although the use of the expression "parental responsibility" can be justified because of the message it conveys it remains true that the expression is in some respects rather misleading. In particular, the fact that the father of an illegitimate child does not have parental responsibility in the absence of a court order or parental responsibility agreement does not mean that he has no responsibility to support the child: the Child Support and Social Security legislation impose an obligation on the father, and he may also be subject to orders under the Children Act to make financial provision for the child. It would perhaps surprise a layman, told in one breath that he had no parental responsibility for a child, to be told in the next breath that he nonetheless did have an obligation to support the child. Again, a step-parent does not (as such) have parental responsibility; and accordingly a step-parent, in the absence of a court order, has no legal authority over the child. Yet the child will almost certainly be a "child of the (step-parent's) family" with the result that the court will have jurisdiction to make financial orders against the step-parent under the Children Act or the divorce legislation.

Authority without responsibility?   Conversely, in some cases the Children Act confers authority, but does not provide any machinery whereby the person with such authority can be made to discharge any duty of support. For example, although a guardian has "parental responsibility" for a child, the Act provides no procedure whereby a guardian can, as such, be required to provide financial support for the child. Again, a person who has parental responsibility as a consequence of having a residence order made in his favour does not thereby come under any obligation to provide financial support for the child.

Chapter 11

COURT ORDERS DEALING WITH CHILDREN'S UPBRINGING: THE ISSUES

When can the court adjudicate?

Chapters 9 and 10 of this book tried to show how the law identifies a child's parents and summarised the legal incidents of parentage — which include the right to take many decisions affecting the child unless and until a court orders otherwise. We now have to consider the circumstances in which the courts can interfere in the autonomy of the family unit by making orders regulating the way in which parents bring up a child; or even by making orders which give the state the right to take over the child's upbringing.

The courts as coercive agencies of the state

The law is almost inevitably complex, but the student should not allow the mass of detail to conceal the fact that there are major issues of principle involved. In particular it is necessary to remember that the courts, in this as in other respects, exercise the coercive judicial power of the state, and ultimately court orders are enforceable by sanctions which include imprisonment. It is easy enough to say — as the Family Law Act 1996, s.1(c) does say — that as a general principle there should be a continuing relationship between a divorced couple and any children affected and it is often quite easy to say on the facts of a particular case that it is in a child's interests to have regular contact with his father. But what is to happen if the mother adamantly refuses to allow such contact?

> In *Z v. Z (Refusal of Contact: Committal)* [1996] 1 FCR 538 the mother claimed that her ex-husband's drinking would have a bad effect on the child. She stated on oath that she would not comply with the court's contact order even on pain of imprisonment. As a last resort, the judge imposed a sentence of imprisonment for contempt. (After two nights in prison the mother changed her mind and agreed to comply with the order). Was the judge right?

It seems that the Court of Appeal would agree with him:

> In *A v. N (Commital: Refusal of Contact)* [1997] 1 FLR 533, C.A., Ward L.J., upholding a sentence of six week's imprisonment on a mother who had flagrantly and persistently flouted an order, said it was appropriate that the message go out in "loud and clear terms that there does come a limit to the tolerance of the court to see its orders flouted"; whilst Beldam L.J. said that if "the court were to yield to such persistent intransigence, respect for its orders and for the administration of justice would be at an end". Since the child's upbringing was not the central issue in deciding the appropriate sanction for breach it was questionable whether the welfare of the child was the paramount consideration.

Two major issues: (i) who can bring cases to the court?

There are serious issues about the role which the courts are to play in dealing with disputes about children. First, there is what lawyers call the issue of *standing*: who is to have the right to initiate court proceedings relating to a child? For example, can a neighbour who thinks that parents have an unsatisfactory lifestyle ask the court to make an order about how the parents should bring up their child? Should a pressure group be able to apply for an order overriding parental agreement to some form of medical procedure — perhaps the termination of a daughter's pregnancy? Should a grandparent be able to seek an order that a parent send a child to a particular school? Should a local authority be able to apply for an order that a child be removed to a children's home because the authority considers that the parents' attitude to the child's upbringing is unsatisfactory? What about the child himself? Can a rebellious teenager apply to the court for an order overruling the parents' refusal to allow him to live with or even go on a foreign holiday with a friend? Is it to be possible for a child to seek what the newspapers often call a divorce from his parents — presumably an order debarring the parents from having anything further to do with him?

(ii) On what principles should the court act?

Secondly, there is the question of the basis upon which this judicial power is to be exercised. Again, it is easy enough to say that the child's welfare should be the paramount concern. But views as to what is best for a child differ between individuals and from time to time: there are still people who believe that the biblical text, "He that spareth the rod hateth his son" justifies recourse to severe corporal punishment, but there are also those who believe that parents should not be allowed to administer what the Scottish Law Commission described as "ordinary safe smacks": see *Report on Family Law* (Scot. Law Com. No. 135) paragraph 2.95 and compare *Sutton London Borough Council v. Davis* [1994] Fam. 241:

> A local authority justified its refusal to register a childminder who would not accept its no smacking policy by expert evidence. The childminder in turn called a professor of psychology to justify her own views.

Again:

In *Re Thain* [1926] Ch. 676 a judge refused to attach weight to the suggestion that a child would be harmed if she were removed from the couple who had cared for her for five years since infancy. The judge said that "at her tender age, one knows from experience how mercifully transient are the effects of partings and other sorrows, and how soon the novelty of fresh surroundings and new associations effaces the recollection of former days and kind friends". This view is completely inconsistent with the theories of modern child psychiatrists, who give great importance to the attachment which a child forms in early infancy.

Relationship between standing and governing principles

Perhaps it must be accepted that opinions change over the years and differ between individuals, and it may be that once an issue is before the court it must simply do its best on the evidence before it. But this makes it clear that there is a relationship between the two issues of, on the one hand, determining the circumstances in which people are to be allowed to bring cases about the child's future to the court, and on the other hand the issue of what test is to be applied in the cases which do come before it. Thus, if it is the state which wants to interfere, the court cannot act merely on the basis of its perception of the child's welfare, for this would (as Lord Mackay of Clashfern put it) be to permit children to be removed from their families simply on the basis that a court considered that the state could do better for the child than his or her family. On the other hand, if the parents themselves disagree about the child's upbringing it is difficult to deny them the right to bring the matter to the court, and it is difficult to think of any more satisfactory principle than to require the court to take whatever course the evidence suggests will be best for the child. But does it follow that we should allow a neighbour or a pressure group the same unqualified right which a parent has to put parental decisions into question by a court — with all the attendant tension and uncertainty — even if the court would be guided solely by its perception of the child's interests in deciding the matter? As we shall see, the legislation answers this question by allowing certain people an unfettered right to bring issues to the court, allowing others to do so if the applicant can obtain the leave of the court, whilst prohibiting others from making applications altogether.

The legislative framework

The enactment of the Children Act 1989 makes it less difficult for the student to address these issues, since the Act strips away much of the procedural and structural complexity of the law previously governing these matters, and creates (for the first time in English law) a single and consistent scheme of orders in any family proceedings. But, as already noted one element of structural complexity remains. Since 1926 English law has allowed courts in certain circumstances to make adoption orders, the effect of which can now be summarised as the irrevocable transfer of a child from one family group to another for virtually all legal purposes: the child will be treated in law as if he had been born as a child of the adoptive parents and not as the child of his birth parents or anyone else: Adoption Act 1976, s.39. Perhaps largely for historical reasons, adoption has always been regarded as a legal institution to be dealt with on different principles than other legal procedures relating to children; and, notwithstanding the fact that in reality adoption is nowadays often the final step in the legal procedures instituted by a local authority which believes the child to be the victim of inadequate parenting, the Children Act 1989 did not make major changes in adoption law, much less assimilate it. At the time of going to press reform of adoption law is under discussion.

Arrangement of text

These matters have influenced the layout of the remaining chapters of this book:

Chapter 12 deals with the court's powers to make what are called private law orders relating to children's upbringing.

Chapter 13 deals with the court's powers to make care, supervision, and other orders in what are called public law proceedings, *i.e.* when the state seeks to intervene in the child's upbringing.

Chapter 14 deals with the principles on which the court should decide whether or not to make orders, and the extent to which the child's welfare is the determining factor.

Chapter 15 deals with the legal institution of adoption.

Chapter 12

THE COURTS' POWERS TO MAKE ORDERS DEALING WITH CHILDREN'S UPBRINGING: THE PRIVATE LAW.

Introduction

The essence of the scheme established by the Children Act is elegant and simple. In its barest essentials it can be seen by asking three questions.

First, are there "family proceedings" before the court? If so, the question of standing is answered positively, and the court will have power to make orders for which application has been made (or even to make orders of its own motion if it considers it right to do so).

This then takes us to the second question: *what* orders are available to the court in the proceedings? This highlights the distinction already drawn between so-called private law and so-called public law proceedings: the court can make any of a range of orders relating to such matters as where the child is to live in favour of individuals; but it cannot make a care order save on the application of a local authority (or other recognised child protection agency) which must first have established what is called the "threshold criterion", *i.e.* that the child has suffered or is likely to suffer significant harm as a result of a failure in parenting. Nor can the court make a residence order in favour of a local authority, because to do so would enable the local authority to bring a child in its care without meeting the threshold criterion.

The answers to these questions take us to the third. In the light of the guidelines which are laid down in the Act, should the court in fact make an order, and if so, what should be the terms of the order?

The text adapts this approach: this Chapter first explains the expression "family proceedings" and explains who is entitled to institute such proceedings so as to give the court power to make orders under the Children Act 1989. The text then summarises the orders which can be made in any family proceedings under section 8 of the Children Act; and it examines certain ancillary powers, for example to order welfare reports. Finally it discusses the distinctive characteristics of certain family proceedings.

A. ARE THERE FAMILY PROCEEDINGS BEFORE THE COURT?

The Act answers the question of standing — should the court even consider the child's upbringing — by giving it power to make orders (described by the Act as "section 8

191

orders") relating to such matters as where the child should live, "in any family proceedings in which a question arises with respect to a child".

The Act gives a comprehensive definition of "family proceedings" (section 8(3)). For present purposes, they fall into two groups: those which are perhaps most easily described as "spin-offs" from other family litigation; and secondly what are often described as "free-standing applications".

"Family proceedings": the "spin-off" jurisdiction.   If, for example, there are divorce proceedings or an application for an adoption order, or if one parent has applied for an order against molestation or relating to the occupation of the family home, those proceedings are within the definition of family proceedings and the court has power to exercise its powers under the Children Act 1989. In effect, the fact that there is family litigation is a sufficient justification for the court to exercise its powers over the children.

The only pre-condition to the exercise of these powers is that the "family proceedings" themselves should have been properly constituted: for example, only a married person can bring divorce proceedings, and (as explained in Chapter 3 above) divorce proceedings cannot be started within three months of the spouse having attended an "information meeting". It follows that it will only be possible for the court to make Children Act orders in respect of a child within that three month period if some other "family proceedings" — perhaps an application for an order relating to the occupation of the family home — are started, *or* if a parent or other qualified person makes a "free-standing" application for an order under the Children Act. The question of who may make such applications is dealt with below.

The fact that there are "family proceedings" before the court gives the court power to make Children Act orders, but it does not mean that the court can disregard any distinctive provisions contained in the legislation governing the "family proceedings" in question. To take the example of divorce again, the divorce legislation, contained in the Matrimonial Causes Act 1973 as amended by the Family Law Act 1996 also gives the court certain powers, and imposes on it certain duties in respect of children: see in particular Family Law Act 1996, s.11. Those provisions continue to apply; and for this reason the Children Act cannot be seen as an entirely comprehensive codification of the law relating to the upbringing of children. It will often still be necessary to refer to the legislation under which the particular proceedings started; and the relationship between the Children Act and the legislation governing particular "family proceedings" (such as divorce, adoption, etc.) is therefore explained somewhat more fully towards the end of this Chapter.

"Free-standing" applications under the Children Act 1989.   This brings us to the second main category of "family proceedings", the so-called "free-standing" applications. The Act deals with the difficult question of identifying the people who should be allowed to start legal proceedings by providing what the Law Commission (Law Com. No. 173, paragraph 4.41) described as a "filter" protecting the child and the family against unwarranted interference whilst ensuring that the child's interests are properly protected.

The scheme of the Act is effectively to create four categories.

First, certain people are to be *entitled* to apply for any of the residence and other orders under section 8 of the Act dealing with matters relating to the exercise of "parental responsibility" in respect of a child.

Secondly, certain people are entitled to apply for orders relating to the person with whom the child is to live (a "residence order") and orders requiring the person with whom the child is to live to allow contact by the applicant with the child (a "contact order").

Thirdly, subject to restrictions imposed by the Act — in particular those imposed in an attempt to prevent local authorities from unwarranted intervention in the family — anyone else may apply to the court for leave to make an application, and the Act lays down guidelines for the court in deciding such applications for leave. In particular, it will be noted that the child can only apply for an order with leave of the court and there are special factors to be considered in relation to such applications.

Fourthly certain people are in effect debarred from seeking orders. We consider these in turn.

(i) *Persons entitled to apply for any section 8 order.*

The Act provides (section 10(4) (a)) that any parent or guardian and any person in whose favour a residence order is in force is entitled to apply for any order. This provision, in effect, defines those who are deemed to have a legitimate interest in seeking the court's intervention, irrespective of the particular circumstances of the case. Thus, for example one spouse should be able to apply for a residence order even if he or she does not want to bring divorce proceedings. Again, although as we have seen, the father of an illegitimate child does not (in the absence of a court order or parental responsibility agreement) have parental responsibility for the child it was thought reasonable to give him the right to apply to the court for a residence order, a contact order, an order giving directions about any question relating to the exercise of parental responsibility for the child (a "specific issue order") or an order prohibiting the taking of certain steps in relation to the child (a "prohibited steps" order).

The reason why the Act includes anyone in whose favour a residence order has been made in the class of those entitled to apply for orders is less self-evident but in fact follows logically from the scheme of the Act. As we have seen, a person who has a residence order has thereby parental responsibility. Accordingly, such a person may need to seek a specific issue order or a prohibited steps order to enable that responsibility to be properly met.

Of course, the fact that a person is entitled to apply for an order does not mean that it will be appropriate to grant it; nor does it mean that the entitlement is absolute. The legislature was conscious that vexatious or harassing applications might be made, even by a parent. For that reason the court is given power (section 91(14)) on disposing of any application to make an order that any named person be debarred from making any application for an order under the Act without leave of the court. For example:

In *Re N (Section 91(14) Order)* [1996] 1 FLR 356, C.A. there had been a multiplicity of proceedings about a child. There was no dispute that the father should have contact with the child, but the father continued to make applications about matters such as medication, karate lessons, walking to school and the like. The Court of Appeal held that the judge, having made a contact order, had been right to order that the father make no further applications without leave of the court. The provisions of section 91(14) were (said Hale J.) to prevent "unnecessary and disruptive applications"; and in the present case the judge had rightly been concerned that there had been too much in the way of litigation and that the child needed to know exactly where he stood.

Such an order has rightly been described (by Sir Stephen Brown P. in *F v. Kent County Council and Others* [1993] 1 FLR 432) as "draconian", and it is to be noted that a person debarred from making an application may still apply for leave to do so. On such an application the court will grant leave if it thinks the applicant has an arguable case: *Re G (Child Cases: Parental Involvement)* [1996] 1 FLR 857, 866, *per* Butler-Sloss L.J.

(ii) *Persons entitled to apply for residence or contact orders.*

Some people may have or have had a sufficiently close link with the child to justify their being entitled to apply for contact, or to justify their seeking to have care of the child in their home, without it being appropriate for them to have the right to make applications which would interfere with the specific decision taking powers of those who have "parental responsibility" for the child. The detailed provisions (contained in section 10(5)) are complex; but the scheme may be summarised by saying that any of three groups of person is entitled to apply for a residence or for a contact order:

(i)   Anyone to whom the child has ever been a "child of the family", for example anyone who has at any time been the child's step-parent. It should be noted that for this purpose the applicant must have been married: a party to an extra-marital relationship which has broken down cannot qualify under this head because of the way in which "child of the family" is defined: see *J v. J (Property Transfer)* [1993] 2 FLR 56, Eastham J.

(ii) Anyone with whom the child has lived for three or more years. The period need not necessarily be continuous, but must not have ended more than three months before the application: section 10(10). Again, the principle seems to be that such a person has established a case to have a claim for contact or even residence considered on the evidence by a court even though he or she should not be entitled as of right to get the court to decide on other specific aspects of parental responsibility (such as where the child should go to school or whether the child should undergo medical treatment).

(iii) Anyone who has the consent of either,

(a) all those who have a residence order (the principle presumably being that if those people see no reason why the court should not hear a contact or residence application, others — perhaps at a greater distance in terms of factual relationship with the child — should not be allowed to stand in the way); or

(b) if the child is in care under a care order anyone who has the consent of the local authority (the principle being presumably that in such a case the local authority is effectively "in the driving seat" and will have to act in accordance with the guidelines governing the exercise of its statutory discretions: see Children Act 1989, s.22(5));

(c) in other cases, the consent of everyone with parental responsibility for the child: section 10(5).

These provisions are alternative: a foster-parent can apply for a residence order — which as we shall see effectively supplants a care order — if the foster parent has had the child living with him or her for three years — notwithstanding the fact that the local authority in fact wants to remove the child from the foster-parent's care.

(iii) *Persons who require leave to apply.*

The Act adopts what is sometimes described as the "open door" policy; and it provides that the court may make a section 8 order if an application for the order has been made by any person who has obtained the leave of the court to make the application: section 10(1)(a)(ii). The Rules (Family Proceedings Rules 1991, r.4.3) stipulate that an applicant must make the request for leave in writing setting out the reasons for the request and providing a draft of the application in respect of which leave is sought. In effect, therefore, anyone (unless debarred under the rules summarised at p. 198 may bring an issue to the court's notice; and the decision whether to allow the application to proceed is dependent on the exercise of a judicial discretion.

Principles to be applied in determining applications for leave to apply for an order: (a) applications by persons other than the child concerned

The Act (s.10(9)) provides that in deciding whether to grant leave or not the court is to have "particular regard" to:

(a) the nature of the proposed application for the section 8 order;
(b) the applicant's connection with the child;
(c) any risk there might be of that proposed application disrupting the child's life to such an extent that he would be harmed by it; and
(d) where the child is being looked after by a local authority,
   (i) the authority's plans for the child's future; and
   (ii) the wishes and feelings of the child's parents.

The Court of Appeal has held that these specific guidelines mean that a court hearing an application for leave is *not* bound to apply the general principle that the child's welfare is the paramount consideration:

In *Re A (minors) (residence orders: leave to apply)* [1992] Fam. 182, C.A., an unmarried middle-aged lady who had devoted her life to the care of children — sometimes more than thirty at one time — from very difficult and disturbed backgrounds had looked after the children (who were in local authority care). She objected to the fact that the local authority thought the children should be placed elsewhere, and sought leave to apply for a residence order. At first instance, the judge considered that the children's welfare was the paramount consideration and that accordingly the question was whether it might reasonably be held on the evidence that making the residence order would be in the child's interests. It was held that this approach was incorrect: in particular, it might have led the judge to think that the children's welfare overrode the mother's wishes and feelings; whilst the statutory guidelines specifically require the court to consider the authority's plans for the child's future. In all the circumstances, the application for leave should be refused.

The court must therefore direct itself by reference to the statutory guidelines set out in section 10(9); and the question seems ultimately to be whether the matter is one which the court thinks appropriate for judicial decision:

In *C v. Salford City Council* [1994] 2 FLR 926, Hale J., the parents of a three-year-old Down's Syndrome child were unable to care for her; but they were concerned that she should be properly cared for in the manner required by orthodox Judaism as to diet, dress, exposure to television, and religious observance. The child was placed with foster-parents; but the parents eventually decided they wanted their daughter to be adopted by orthodox Jews. The foster-parents sought leave to apply for a residence order, and their application for leave was granted. The judge considered all the matters set out in the statutory guidelines — such as the fact that the child had a close attachment to the foster-parents who were seeking to cement and provide security for that attachment (section 10(9)(b)) as against the risk of disrupting plans for the child's adoption in accordance with the parents' wishes (section 10(9)(c)). The judge concluded that an application by the foster-parents was certainly not hopeless but that it was not bound to succeed; and that was precisely why it was right to grant leave so that the matter could be decided by the court on all the evidence.

Of course, the great majority of cases in which applications for leave are made do not present great difficulties, and in particular it will be rare that grandparents or other close relatives are denied leave to seek contact. As Lord Mackay L.C. put it, in many such cases the application will be a formality; but the law nonetheless provides some protection to children against wholly unwarranted applications by grandparents or other relatives whose interest was not necessarily benign even if well-intentioned.

It is important to remember that the fact that leave is given does not alter the court's approach to resolving the substantive application. In particular:

In *Re A (Section 8 Order: Grandparent Application)* [1995] 2 FLR 153, C.A., it was held that the fact that grandparents had obtained leave to pursue a contact application did not mean that there would be a presumption in favour of granting the substantive application. Applications for leave were often granted simply on the papers (as provided for by Family Proceedings Rules 1991, r. 4.3(2) (a)) and it would be rare for there to be a court welfare officer's report at that time. At the hearing of a contested substantive application there would, in contrast, almost always be oral evidence and a report.

Principles to be applied in determining applications for leave to apply for an order: (b) applications by the child concerned

The Children Act provides (section 10(8)) that where the application is made by the child concerned the court must be satisfied that he or she has sufficient understanding to make the proposed application; and it seems that the court is not required to apply the further guidelines governing applications by others discussed above. The question of whether the child has "sufficient understanding" is determined by reference to the gravity and complexity of the issues involved[1], but there are particular — and potentially damaging — aspects of the legal process that the child should understand. In particular:

---

[1] As already explained at p. 170, above, in the context of the *Gillick* decision.

In *Re C (Residence: Child's Application for Leave)* [1995] 1 FLR 927, Stuart-White J., there had been much litigation between parents about the upbringing of a 14-year-old girl. Eventually, the girl (who had been living with her father) sought leave to apply for a residence order in favour of her mother. The judge pointed out that "once a child is a party to proceedings between warring parents, that leads the child to be in a position in which the child is likely to be present hearing the evidence of those parents, hearing the parent cross-examined, hearing perhaps of many matters which at the tender age of the child, it would be better for her not to hear", and the child herself might be subjected to cross-examination.

For this reason, the level of understanding required is high: as Sir Thomas Bingham M.R. put it in *Re S (A Minor) (Independent Representation)* [1993] Fam. 263, 276:

"Where any sound judgment on the issues calls for insight and imagination which only maturity and experience can bring, . . . the court . . . will be slow to conclude that the child's understanding is sufficient."

Even if the court concludes that the child is competent, there is a discretion — in the exercise of which the child's prospects of success in the substantive application are relevant — whether or not to grant leave:

In *Re C (Residence: Child's Application for Leave)* [1995] 1 FLR 927 (above) Stuart-White J, decided that the 14-year-old should be given leave; as did Booth J, in *Re SC (A Minor) (Leave to seek residence order)* [1994] 1 FLR 96 (where the application was by a 14-year-old girl living in a children's home who sought leave to seek a residence order in favour of a friend). In contrast —

in *Re C (A Minor) (Leave to seek section 8 order)* [1994] 1 FLR 26, Johnson J. decided not to give a 15-year-old girl leave to seek a specific issue order authorising her to go on holiday to Bulgaria with a family other than her own, in part because of the triviality of the issue which the judge did not feel was the sort of issue Parliament had envisaged bring brought to the courts by children, and in part because it would be wrong to give the girl the impression that she had won some kind of victory against her parents.

To quote again the words of Sir Thomas Bingham M.R. in *Re S (A Minor) (Independent Representation)* [1993] Fam 263, 276:

"The 1989 Act enables and requires a judicious balance to be struck between two considerations. First is the principle . . . that children are human beings with individual minds and wills, views and emotions, which should command serious attention. A child's wishes are not to be discounted or dismissed simply because he is a child. He should be free to express them and decision makers should listen. Secondly is the fact that a child is, after all, a child. The reason why the law is particularly solicitous in protecting the interests of children is because they are likely to be vulnerable and impressionable, lacking the maturity to weigh the longer term against the shorter, lacking the insight to know how they will react and the imagination to know how others will react in certain situations, lacking the experience to measure the probable against the possible . . ."

(iv) *Persons who are debarred from applying for residence and other orders.*

One of the cardinal principles adopted by the Children Act is that local authorities and other state agencies should not be entitled to interfere in family life without good cause. But once a court had decided that the authority entitled to seek the court's intervention, and that it would be in the child's best interests to make a care order in its favour then the local authority should have control over the discharge of its responsibilities to children in care. For this reason, the Act provides that a person who has been the child's local authority foster-parent within the last six months may not seek leave to apply for a residence or other section 8 order: section 9(3). There are exceptions to this general principle: a foster-parent who is a relative of the child is not subject to the bar nor is a foster-parent with whom the child has lived for three years: section 9(3). In this way, the Act allows the local authority to plan for the child's future — which may, for example, involve removing the child from foster-parents and placing the child for adoption — without the fear that those plans will be upset by a comparatively short term foster-parent applying for a residence order.

The same principle of defining the limits of state intervention accounts for the rules barring a local authority from applying, for a residence or contact order and prohibiting the court from making such orders in favour of a local authority: section 9(2).

B. PRIVATE LAW ORDERS UNDER THE CHILDREN ACT 1989

Introduction

The orders which the court has power to make under the Children Act 1989 can conveniently be divided into four main groups. First of all, there are the so-called "section 8 orders" as defined in section 8 of the Act which is entitled "Residence contact and other orders with respect to children". As already noted, these orders can be made in any "family proceedings" in which a question arises with respect to the welfare of a child; and they are conveniently described as "private law" orders because they are the orders usually made in proceedings brought by private individuals on or after the breakdown of their relationship. It is however important to note that these orders *can* be made in *any* family proceedings, so that the court has power to make a residence order in favour of a relative (for example) in a case in which a local authority has applied for a care order and it equally has power to make a contact order in proceedings brought by an applicant for an adoption order.

The second main group of orders are often called "public law" orders because they can only be made on the application of local authorities or other specially qualified agencies who can establish the so-called "threshold criteria". The public law proceedings, and the orders which may be made in them, are dealt with in Chapter 13.

The third group of orders are the orders for financial relief with respect to children which can be made in proceedings started for that purpose under Children Act 1989 s.15 and Schedule 1. These orders have been dealt with in the part of this book concerned with property and financial aspects of family law: see Chapter 8.

The fourth (and last) group of orders can loosely be described as "ancillary orders". They include orders requiring probation officers or others to make a welfare report (Children Act 1989, s.7), orders directing a local authority to investigate a case with a view to bringing care proceedings (Children Act 1989, s.37), and other miscellaneous orders, such as the family assistance order made under Children Act 1989 s.16 which requires a probation officer or social worker to "advise, assist and (where appropriate) befriend" the person named in the order. These orders are, in consequence of their miscellaneous nature, dealt with at the most appropriate places in the text.

This Chapter deals with the section 8 "menu" of orders which, as already stated, are usually made in private law proceedings but which may be made in care and other public law proceedings.

The section 8 "menu" of orders.   "Section 8 orders" are defined as follows:

(i) *A contact order* is defined by Children Act 1989 s.8(1) as "an order requiring the person with whom a child lives, or is to live, to allow the child to visit or stay with the person named in the order, or for that person and the child otherwise to have contact with each other." Such an order enables the court to give effect to the general principle that it is desirable for a child to preserve links with both parents; and many orders (some 27,000 each year) are made.

In cases in which there is difficulty about the details, the order may be very specific and detailed — sometimes for example providing that contact should be supervised, or take place at a particular place (perhaps a family centre of the kind now found in many towns). Contact may be ordered with any named person. A grandparent may well seek contact, and sometimes teenagers seek orders for contact with a named friend.

"Contact" is not limited to face-to-face visits: an order may be made for contact by letter or greetings card:

> In *Re O (Contact: Imposition of Conditions)* [1995] 2 FLR 124, C.A., the mother of a two-year-old boy was implacably opposed to having anything to do with the father, and the judge eventually made an order that there should be "indirect" contact, the mother sending the father photographs of the child and reporting significant developments to him, and requiring her to accept delivery by post of cards and presents for the child. The Court of Appeal rejected an argument that the judge had no jurisdiction to order the mother to send photographs and so on and that he had no jurisdiction to require an unwilling mother to read cards and other communications to the child. The powers conferred by Children Act 1989 s.11(7) to impose conditions on a section 8 order were a sufficient basis for making an order of this kind; and it was wrong to suggest that the court could not impose positive obligations on a parent with whom the child was living.

Conversely, there are situations in which the court concludes that there should be no contact between a named individual and a child; and in *Nottingham County Council v. P* [1994] Fam. 18, 38–39, C.A., it was held that such an order came within the definition of a "contact order". (The significance of this order was that a local authority is debarred from seeking a contact order, a residence order or an order having the like effect. The policy[2] is that local authorities should make use of the "public law" orders if they wish to prevent people having contact with children.)

The enforcement of contact orders is often difficult; and — although the Children Act Advisory Committee has stated that penal enforcement of contact order is unlikely

---

[2] As explained more fully at p. 255, below.

to be in the interests of the child and should not be encouraged: see *Annual Report 1994/1995* at 36 and Annex B — the courts as we have seen sometimes consider there to be no alternative to using the sanction of imprisonment.

(ii) *A Prohibited Steps Order* is "an order that no step which could be taken by a parent in meeting his parental responsibility for a child, and which is of a kind specified in the order, shall be taken by any person without consent of the court". Such orders — which may, for example, prohibit the removal of a child from his home, direct that a child should not be brought into contact with a named person or taken to a particular place, or forbid the carrying out of medical treatment on the child — are extremely useful in situations of family breakdown; and there seem to be some 4,000 applications (and 3,000 orders made) each year: see *Children Act Advisory Committee Annual Report 1994/1995*, Table 3C. A prohibited steps order can be made against anyone (whether or not that person has parental responsibility and whether or not he is a party to the proceedings). For example:

> In *Re H (Prohibited Steps Order)* [1995] 1 FLR 638, C.A., a man with whom the mother was living sexually abused her daughter. The Court of Appeal held that the court had power to make a prohibited steps order against the man forbidding him from seeking contact with any of the children, notwithstanding the fact that he was not a party to the proceedings and had not been heard. If, having been served with the order, he wished to contest it he would be enabled to do so.

The action prohibited must be of a kind which could be "taken by a parent in meeting his parental responsibility" (as defined by C.A. 1989, s.3); and occasionally it is necessary to decide what this means:

> In *Re Z (A Minor) (Freedom of Publication)* [1996] 1 FLR 191, C.A., a child and her parents were in the glare of publicity. The child had special educational needs, and had made great progress at a specialised institution which wanted to publicise its work by making a television programme to which public attention would be drawn by naming the child and her parents. The mother — who sincerely believed that the benefits of the work should be more widely available and that her daughter's confidence would be enhanced by the appearance — was prepared to agree; but the father did not agree. The Court of Appeal held that giving consent to medical treatment and arranging for education were aspects of parental responsibility; that the child herself had a right of confidentiality in respect of these matters; and that it would be an incident of the mother's parental responsibility to decide whether to preserve that confidentiality or not. Accordingly, there was power to make a prohibited steps order, and since the question involved a decision about the child's upbringing her welfare was the paramount consideration: Children Act 1989, s.1. In the circumstances, a prohibited steps order protecting her against publicity should be made.

In contrast:

> In *Croydon London Borough Council v. A* [1992] Fam. 169, Hollings J., the father was a man of violent disposition who had been convicted of assaulting the child. The mother lied about whether she was still seeing the father; but eventually the

children were placed with the mother in a charitable institution in an attempt to ensure the bonding of the mother and children for their long-term benefit. The court, believing that the children were at risk from the father, made an order prohibiting the mother from having any verbal or personal contact or even contact by correspondence with the father. On appeal, it was held that there was no jurisdiction to make such an order since one adult having contact with another for their own purposes was not a "step which could be taken by a parent in meeting his parental responsibility for a child."

(iii) *A Residence Order* is "an order settling the arrangements to be made as to the person with whom a child is to live"; and this was often the matter to which parties to a relationship have traditionally attached the greatest importance. According to the *Children Act Advisory Committee Annual Report 1994/1995*, Table 3A there are some 16,000 applications and 12,000 residence orders made each year.

In accordance with the "plain words" approach adopted by the Children Act, the legislation no longer refers to obscure concepts such as "custody". Rather, a residence order simply says in plain English what arrangements are to be made about the child's care; and — again consistently with the philosophy of the Act — the making of a residence order does not operate to deprive any other person of his or her parental responsibility. Thus, the making of a residence order in favour of the child's mother does not deprive the father of his right to take decisions about education or any other matter (although as already noted he must not act inconsistently with the terms of any court order, and thus could not, for example, remove the child from the mother's home).

Shared residence? The Children Act 1989 provides that where a residence order is made in favour of two or more persons who do not themselves all live together, the order may specify the periods during which the child is to live in the different households concerned (section 11(4)); and it thus clearly envisages the there may be occasions on which the court will wish to make what is sometimes called a "shared residence order" perhaps providing for the child to spend a week with one parent and then a week with the other but (probably more commonly) providing that the child spend weekdays with one parent and weekends with the other. The question whether it is appropriate to make such an order is governed by the principle that the child's welfare is the paramount consideration. Thus:

In *A v. A (Minors) (Shared Residence Order)* [1994] 1 FLR 669, C.A., two young girls were — in part because the mother had had to undergo hospital treatment — spending a significant part of their lives being looked after by the father; and he applied for a residence order providing for the children to live with him for about one-third of the year. The Court of Appeal agreed that the judge had been right to regard such an order as appropriate in the particular circumstances of that case; but — although the court declined to give any general guidance as to when shared residence orders should be made — it did indicate that shared orders would not be appropriate in normal conventional cases where parents separated. Rather, they would only be made where there was something unusual about the case which made such an order positively beneficial to the children. The importance of the child having a settled home rather than passing to and fro between the parents (particularly if they were at odds) would normally point against the making of a shared residence order.

Incidental consequences of a residence order. Although the general policy of the Act is to favour the principle that orders should mean what they say and mean no more than they say, the making of a residence order has certain important incidental consequences. First, the making of a residence order automatically prohibits change of the child's surname without the written consent of all those who have parental responsibility or the approval of the court: section 13(1) (a). Secondly, it prohibits the child's removal from the United Kingdom (except, for a period of less than a month — perhaps for a holiday — by the person in whose favour the order is made). Thirdly, the making of a residence order terminates any care order. Hence an application for a residence order may be a technique for seeking to remove a child from local authority care. Finally — and perhaps most important — the making of a residence order confers "parental responsibility" on the person in whose favour it is made (if that person is not a parent or guardian); and this has given rise to the question whether a shared residence order should be used as a means of giving parental responsibility to someone, for example, a stepfather, who would not otherwise have it:

> In *Re H (Shared Residence: Parental Responsibility)* [1995] 2 FLR 883, C.A., a 14-year-old boy had been brought up to believe (wrongly) that the husband was his father. In divorce proceedings, the judge made a joint residence order, in part because conferring parental responsibility on the husband would formally recognise that the relationship between the boy and the husband was effectively that of father and son. Otherwise the boy might be confused by a feeling that the husband had done something wrong and that as a result something had to be taken away from him. The Court of Appeal held the judge had been plainly right: given the boy's shock at the discovery of his true parentage, everything should be done to lead him to believe that life had not changed.

(iv) *A Specific Issue Order* is an "order giving directions for the purpose of determining a specific question which has arisen, or which may arise, in connection with any aspect of parental responsibility for a child." A specific issue order enables the court to make rulings about particular matters (rather than giving a parent or other person a general right to take decisions about the child's upbringing — as is the effect of a residence order or a parental responsibility order, for example.

It is not necessary that there be any dispute about the exercise of parental responsibility for the court to resolve; and indeed in some cases — notably contraceptive sterilisation and the donation of bone marrow — the courts have indicated that leave should be sought even though all concerned are agreed: see *Re HG (Specific Issue Order: Sterilisation)* [1993] 1 FLR 587, Peter Singer Q.C. Often of course there will be a dispute:

> In *Re R (A Minor) (Blood Transfusion)* [1993] 2 FLR 757, Booth J., medical experts were unequivocally of the view that blood transfusions were necessary to maximise the prospects of success in treating a 10-month-old baby suffering from leukaemia. The parents were opposed to such treatment, in part because they were Jehovah's Witnesses and such treatment was contrary to their scriptural conscience; but they were also anxious about the known hazards of blood transfusions and made the point that advances in medicine might provide alternative treatment. The judge held on the evidence that the parents' objections should be overridden.

Applications for specific issue orders are commonly made to seek leave to take a child to live abroad, and the question is determined by reference to the child's welfare (although it is accepted that the parent with primary care is entitled to select the place and country of residence unless that choice is shown to be plainly incompatible with the child's welfare or otherwise objectionable: see *Re T (Removal from Jurisdiction)* [1996] 2 FLR 352, 355, *per* Thorpe L.J.). A more unusual example which demonstrates the extent of "parental responsibility" and the flexibility of the legislation is —

> *Re F (Specific Issue: Child Interview)* [1995] 1 FLR 819 where the father of 11-year-old twins was charged with assault on their mother. The father's solicitor wanted to interview the boys (who had been on the scene at the time of the incident) to see if they had relevant evidence, but the mother refused to allow him to do so. The father applied for, and was granted, a specific issue order permitting the interview to take place. Amongst the considerations which influenced the evaluation of the children's welfare was that it was vital the boys should know their father (who was an important figure in their lives and minds) should have a fair trial.

As in the case of prohibited steps orders, the issue on which a decision is sought must relate to the exercise of "parental responsibility"; and there is no other formal restriction on the courts' powers. But the Court of Appeal has held that a specific issue order cannot be used to order the ejection of a man from the home of which he is a joint tenant: see *Pearson v. Franklin (Parental Home: Ouster)* [1994] 1 FLR 246, C.A.; and the court apparently considered that Parliament could not have intended to give the courts power to override property rights without using specific words to do so.

The question of how far a direction about the exercise of parental responsibility can directly or indirectly restrict the freedom of the individual is a difficult one. There can be no doubt that the court could, for example, direct a parent not to have any contact with a child, but suppose parent and child were living under the same roof? In fact such issues would now be dealt with under the provisions of Part IV of the Family Law Act 1996 which specifically deal with occupation of the family home; but the general question — of considerable importance — remains unresolved.

Conditions and directions

The Children Act 1989 contains a useful power allowing the court to give directions about how a section 8 order is to be carried into effect, and to impose conditions which must be complied with by any person with whom the child is living, any person in whose favour the order is made, and any parent or other person with parental responsibility: section 8(7). Residence orders may thus contain directions about how the child is to be prepared for a change of home or they may contain a condition that the child reside with one parent provided that parent hands over all passports and travel documents, or that the child reside with a parent provided that the parent continues to live at a certain house, or that the child is not allowed to come into contact with a named third party. Contact orders may (and very often do) contain detailed provisions about the arrangements to be made.

The power to make contact orders is wide: as we have seen, it was used in *Re O (Contact: Imposition of Conditions)* [1995] 2 FLR 124, C.A., to require a mother to take positive acts (sending photographs and the like) in order to achieve meaningful indirect contact. But the power is not limitless:

> In *D v. D (county court: jurisdiction)* [1993] 2 FLR 802, C.A., the judge hearing a mother's application for a residence order was strongly critical of action taken by the police and social services in investigating complaints made by the father about the child's treatment, and made a "direction" that they should take no further action without prior leave of the court. It was held that the power to make "such incidental, supplemental or consequential provision as the court thinks fit" could not extend to prohibit public authorities from discharging their statutory and common law powers.

In particular, the power to impose conditions should not be used effectively to negate the terms of the main order:

> In *Birmingham City Council v. H* [1992] 2 FLR 323, Ward J., a 15-year-old mother was desperately anxious to fulfil her role as a mother and had entered a residential home where she received a great deal of help and support. Although the mother accepted that she needed such help, the situation deteriorated and there was concern about her ability to provide adequate care for the baby. The mother asked the court, rather than making a care order in favour of the local authority, to make a residence order in her favour subject to conditions requiring her to reside at a particular institution, that she would comply with all reasonable instructions from the staff and would indeed hand over the child to the care of the staff if so required. The judge held that such conditions (effectively allowing someone else, without any judgment of the court, to assume the parental responsibility which goes with a care order) would be inconsistent with the existence of a residence order. An interim care order was made, under the provisions discussed in Chapter 13.

Restrictions on the court's power to make orders

The Children Act 1989 contains a number of provisions restricting the power which the court would otherwise have to make orders:

(i) *Age.*
   The Act provides that no court shall make a section 8 order with respect to a child who has attained the age of 16 unless the circumstances of the case are exceptional (section 8(7)) and that (with the same proviso) no court is to make an order to have effect after the child is 16.

(ii) *Local authorities debarred from applying for residence and contact, etc., orders.*
   The Act provides (section 9(2)) that no application may be made by a local authority for a residence or contact order; and the court is debarred from making such orders. This gives effect to the policy[3] that the state is not to be allowed to interfere in the upbringing of children merely because its intervention would be of benefit, and that it may only do so if it can satisfy the more demanding requirements laid down in the "public law" Part IV of the Act. The same policy is presumably what underlies the provision (section 9(5)) prohibiting the court from exercising its powers to make a

---

[3] Explained at p. 225, below.

specific issue order or prohibited steps order "with a view to achieving a result which could be achieved by making a residence or contact order": local authorities should not be debarred from seeking such orders — for example, like anyone else with responsibility they may need a direction about medical treatment for the child, and they may need an order prohibiting some named person from doing acts injurious to the child (such as abducting him). But local authorities are not to be allowed to use these two orders so as to circumvent the prohibition on their seeking residence orders:

> In *Nottingham CC v. P* [1994] Fam. 18, C.A., a father had persistently abused his daughter by having sexual intercourse with her and committing buggery upon her; and the judge found that — the mother being weak and lacking the capacity to protect her other four children — the children were seriously at risk. The local authority however "persistently and obstinately refused" to seek a care order, and the court has no power to make such an order except on application. The reason for this refusal was presumably financial; and the local authority did apply for a prohibited steps order excluding the father from the home and prohibiting him from having any contact with the children. The Court of Appeal held that the result of such an order could have been achieved by a residence order; and that accordingly the court had had no power to grant it. The children remained at risk.

(iii) *Prohibition on using prohibited steps and specific issue orders applies to all applicants.*
   It is perhaps easy to see why the draftsman thought it necessary to include a provision preventing local authorities from evading the prohibition on their seeking residence orders; but the rule debarring the court from making specific issue or prohibited steps orders having a result which could be obtained by a residence order (section 9(5)(a)) is general in scope and not confined to local authorities. It may be that this is because the draughtsman was concerned that a person might in effect have a child in his or her care without having parental responsibility; but the result of the rule is to create difficulties in what should be straightforward cases:

> In *Re B (minors) (residence orders)* [1992] Fam. 162, C.A., the father wanted orders to deal with a child snatched by the children's mother; but the judge held that he could not make a prohibited steps order against the children being removed because the same result could have been achieved by a residence order. Although the Court of Appeal, by a powerful exercise of purposive judicial interpretation, overruled that decision on the basis that Parliament could not have intended to stop the courts exercising their long established powers to deal with child snatching the precise scope of the troublesome restriction is not clear.

C. ANCILLARY ORDERS WHICH THE COURT MAY MAKE IN FAMILY PROCEEDINGS

(i) *The Family Assistance Order.*
   Courts are as already pointed out bodies which deploy the coercive power of the state to enforce orders which they make having adjudicated on a particular issue. They

are thus not well-equipped to act directly as welfare agencies; but there is no reason why they should not ensure that help from such agencies is available to those who appear before them, and there is a long tradition whereby the probation service is available to assist in this respect.

The Children Act 1989, s.16, provides that a court which has power to make a section 8 order (or other order under Part II of the Act — in effect "private law" orders) may make an order requiring a probation officer or local authority social worker to be made available to "advise assist and (where appropriate) befriend" the child, the child's parent or guardian, or any other person with whom the child is living or who has a contact order. Such an order cannot last for more than six months, and the distinctive nature of the procedure is evidenced by the fact that the court can only make the order in "exceptional circumstances" and cannot make the order without the consent of the person to whom it is addressed.

The objective is to enable short term independent help to be provided: *Re C (Family Assistance Order)* [1996] 1 FLR 424, 425, Johnson J. The facts of that case illustrate the circumstances in which the court may think it appropriate to make such an order:

> A 10-year-old boy was living with his aunt and uncle following the break-up of his parents' marriage; and some publicity was given to the case when the press claimed that his application for a residence order was the first English case in which a child had sought to "divorce his parents". The judge thought that, in the light of the hurtful publicity and the need for some independent assistance to re-establish contact between the boy and his mother (whom the boy blamed for the break-up of his parents' marriage), a family assistance order directed to the boy, his mother, and his aunt and uncle would be "tailor-made for the task".

Unhappily, the local authority declined to implement the order:

> "Our resources are finite and, as a local authority, we have to allocate our social service budget and personnel to meet the demands of many children and others. The allocation of resources is a matter for us, as a local authority, and our decision is that we do not have the resources to help this boy".

The judge held that in the circumstances there was nothing appropriate or sensible that he could do; and, as will appear in a number of places in this book, it is clear that the Children Act deliberately allocates many decisions involving the expenditure of money to the local authority whose decision is only open to review (if at all) in proceedings for judicial review.

(ii) *Ordering a welfare report.*

Civil litigation in England is usually conducted on the basis of the so-called adversarial system in which the court listens to such evidence as the parties choose to put before it; but it is self-evident that such a procedure would be quite unsuitable for ascertaining what is truly in a child's interests, not least because in many cases the voice of the child would not be heard at all. For many years the courts have had power in family cases to commission welfare reports from independent persons so that the court can be put in possession of the material which it needs to decide on the action it should take, and to this extent it is quite inaccurate to describe family proceedings as being adversarial.

The Children Act (s. 7(1)) now provides that a court considering any question with respect to a child under the Act may ask a probation officer or local authority to arrange for a report to be made to the court "on such matters relating to the welfare of that child as are required to be dealt with in the report"; and extensive use is made of this power. In 1994, the probation service provided no less than 34,697 written reports; and there are welfare reports in some 40 per cent of hearings for section 8 orders.

The probation officer directed to make a report is likely to be a member of the Court Welfare Service, but the court may invite the assistance of other qualified persons:

> In *Re W (Welfare Reports)* [1995] 2 FLR 142, C.A., Waite L.J. pointed out that court welfare officers are, in the nature of their duty, "accustomed to the court process, to interviewing the child and the adults concerned in the child's life, to attending court, to making recommendations orally or in writing and to submitting to be questioned by the parties. Social workers, on the other hand, are familiar with the reporting routine in the much wider context of preparing reports for use at case conferences and for placing on file for the assistance of other social workers, and so on. Their knowledge of the court process may be much more limited, and frequently their role will be confined to fact-finding reports, and will not involve the making of any recommendations at all."

The primary function of a reporter, whether a court welfare officer or local authority social worker, is to assist the court by providing the court with the factual information on which it can make a decision: *Scott v. Scott* [1986] 2 FLR 320. The welfare officer has power to inspect the court file; and he or she will then usually interview all the parties and visit the parents' home, see the parents' children and others involved, see the children with their parents in their homes, and see doctors and teachers if that would be appropriate in the circumstances.

A full welfare report should contain a statement of the different proposals made by the parties for the future care of the children concerned: *Re H (Conciliation: Welfare Reports)* [1986] 1 FLR 476. It should also contain: a statement of the conditions, both material and otherwise, in which the children are living or in which it is proposed that they should live; a reference to, or summary of, any relevant reports on the family and the children by independent persons such as doctors, school teachers, social workers, probation officers and police records; a statement of the relations of the children with each of their parents, including, when the children are old enough, a summary of their own views about their respective parents and their homes, and their own wishes as to the future.

Preparing a welfare report is a time consuming occupation, and cannot be done solely on the basis of an interview with the parties in the reporter's office. Inevitably an order to prepare a report entails delay. The court must decide, applying the criterion of what would.best promote the child's welfare, whether the benefits of having a report outweigh the delay: see *Re H (Minors) (Welfare Report)* [1990] 2 FLR 172, C.A. Various techniques — for example, restricting the scope of the enquiry which the court directs — are used in attempts to avoid wastage of scarce resources: see the *Best Practice Note, January (Children Act Advisory Committee Annual Report 1993/1994,* p. 59).

Welfare officers are concerned to promote the welfare of families; and many individual welfare officers have a strong commitment to the ideals of mediation and conciliation. But the courts have emphasised the important differences between the functions of a conciliator and a welfare officer.

The welfare officer's report can be inspected by the parties, but it is to be treated as confidential and must not be shown to anyone other than the parties and their legal advisers. The court may, if it thinks it appropriate, order the officer to attend the hearing and submit to cross-examination.

The welfare officer's report may (and usually will) contain a recommendation; and this may be of great significance because it is well-established that (although the decision is for the court, not for the welfare officer) a court which does not follow those recommendations must explain its reasons for not doing so:

> In *Re CB (Access: Attendance of Court Welfare Officer)* [1995] 1 FLR 622, C.A., the grandfather of a 14-year-old girl sought contact with her. But he had been convicted of sexually abusing her and (although he had consistently denied having done so) the welfare officer's report concluded that the child would be at risk from contact with the grandfather and recommended that any contact should be supervised. The judge made an order for unsupervised contact. The Court of Appeal held that he had been wrong to do so, and wrong to form conclusions directly contrary to the welfare officer's recommendations without at least hearing oral evidence from the welfare officer.

Welfare reports almost by definition contain "hearsay" — that is to say they give an account of what the reporter has been told by other persons such as the child's school teacher. The Children Act contains a general provision that the court may, regardless of the normal rules of evidence, take account of statements contained in the report, and evidence given in respect of the matters referred to in the report so far as they are considered to be relevant: section 7(4). But this does not mean that the court should be uncritical; and it should obviously exercise caution in accepting the truth of untested statements made by someone not before the court: *Thompson v. Thompson* [1986] 1 FLR 212.

(iii) *Power to direct local authority investigation.*

Before the enactment of the Children Act 1989 it was possible, in exceptional circumstances, for a court hearing divorce and certain other "private law" cases to make an order committing a child to local authority care; but such a power was inconsistent with the doctrine underlying the Children Act that the state should only be entitled to seek to interfere with the parents' role if certain threshold criteria were first established. But it was accepted that matters might emerge in "private law" proceedings which would suggest the need for state intervention; and accordingly the Children Act 1989, s.37, provides that if a question arises in family proceedings with respect to the welfare of a child such as to cause the court to think it might be appropriate for a care or supervision order to be made, the court may direct the local authority to undertake an investigation of the child's circumstances, and to consider whether they should apply for a care or supervision order (or provide services or assistance for the child or his family or take other action with respect to the child). For example:

> In *Re H (A Minor) (Section 37 Direction)* [1993] 2 FLR 541, Scott Baker J., a lesbian couple wanted to bring up as their own a baby born in circumstances akin to a surrogacy agreement; but the authorities forbade adoption or fostering. The

couple therefore applied for a residence order. The judge was concerned about the longer term future of the child, and he considered on the evidence before him that a care or supervision order would be appropriate. However, he had no power to make such orders, and he accordingly ordered a section 37 investigation which would require the local authority to consider whether a care or supervision order should be sought.

What if the local authority, having made their investigation, decide not to seek an order? The Act provides (section 37(3)) that the authority must inform the court of their reasons (and also state what other steps it proposes to take in relation to assisting the child, etc.); but their decision is, perhaps subject to the possibility of judicial review, final:

> In *Nottingham CC v. P* [1994] Fam. 18, C.A. both the trial judge and the Court of Appeal considered that a care order would be appropriate; but the local authority refused to make an application. As the President of the Family Division put it: "if a local authority doggedly resists taking the steps which are appropriate to the case of children at risk of suffering significant harm it appears that the court is powerless": see further p. 226, below.

The relationship between the court and local authorities is considered further at pp. 235–238, below.

D. DISTINCTIVE CHARACTERISTICS OF CERTAIN FAMILY PROCEEDINGS

1. Proceedings under statutes

The Children Act defines "family proceedings" as, first, proceedings under certain enactments, and, secondly proceedings under the inherent jurisdiction of the High Court in relation to children. Of the "enactments" the Family Law Act 1996 is particularly important: some 160,000 divorce suits are started each year, and some 150,000 "children of the family" are involved in them. Moreover, the protection of the welfare of children whose parents divorce has long been a major concern of the legislature; and the Family Law Act 1996 follows a well-established pattern by introducing further refinements into the law. These factors justify giving further prominence to the interaction of the Children Act and the divorce legislation originally embodied in the Divorce Reform Act 1969 and now substantially amended by the Family Law Act 1996.

"Children of the family".   The court's powers and duties in divorce proceedings arise in respect of any "children of the family"; and this expression is widely defined by the Matrimonial Causes Act 1973, s.52(1):

> "child of the family" in relation to the parties to a marriage, means:
> (a) a child of both of those parties; and
> (b) any other child, not being a child who is placed with those parties as foster-parents by a local authority or voluntary organisation, who has been treated by both of those parties as a child of their family."

Hence all children — whether legitimate, legitimated, illegitimate, or adopted — of the two parties to the marriage are included within the definition and the inclusion of children "treated" as a child of the family by both parties makes the existence of a biological (or even a formal legal relationship, such as adoption) between the child and the parties irrelevant. The most obvious example of a child of the family who is not the child of both spouses is a step-child living with the spouses; but the definition is wide enough to cover a child looked after by married relatives on a long term basis and a child privately fostered by them. However the definition is not all-embracing. In particular, it has been held to be impossible to treat an unborn child as a child of the family: if a man marries a woman who is pregnant by someone else the baby will be a child of their family if the husband treats it as such after birth even if the wife has deceived him into thinking that he is the father; but if the relationship breaks down before the birth the child will be outside the definition whatever the husband may have said about his intentions to treat the baby as his own: see *A v. A (Family: Unborn Child)* [1974] Fam. 6.

There are other provisions designed to protect children whose parents divorce:

(i) *Longer period for "reflection and consideration".*

If there are any children of the family under the age of 16 when application is made for a divorce order, the nine month period for "reflection and consideration" is (as we have seen) extended by six months unless the court is satisfied that delaying the making of a divorce order would be significantly detrimental to the welfare of the child: FLA 1996, s.7(11) and 7(12)(b).

(ii) *Separate representation for children.*

In the course of debates on the 1996 divorce reforms, concern was expressed about the extent to which the voice of the child (as distinct from the voice of those purporting to speak for him or her) was heard in divorce proceedings. The Government's response was to accept a provision empowering the Lord Chancellor by regulation to provide for the separate representation of children in proceedings which relate to any matter in respect of which a question has arisen, or may arise, under the legislation governing divorce and separation orders. There is some anxiety that separate representation could in fact exacerbate the disputes between the parents and thus further damage the child; and it was clear that the Conservative Government intended to take a cautious approach. Pilot projects are likely to be set up as a preliminary to decisions on wider implementation.

(iii) *Children's welfare as fundamental general principle of divorce legislation.*

As noted at p. 44, above, the Family Law Act directs the court and others to "have regard to" certain "general principles". These include two matters of particular relevance to children affected by marital breakdown. First, the principle that a marriage which has irretrievably broken down and is being brought to an end should be brought to an end with minimum distress to the parties and to the children affected (section 1(c)(i)), and with questions dealt with in a manner designed to promote as good a continuing relationship between the parties and any children affected as is possible in the circumstances (section 1(c)(ii)). Secondly, the Act embodies the principle that "any risk to one of the parties to a marriage, and to any children, of violence from the other party should, so far as reasonably practicable, be removed or diminished" (section 1(d)). These matters must be taken into consideration not only by courts in adjudicating on matters which call for the exercise of a discretion, but by those exercising functions in respect of the grant of legal aid, and by others involved (including, for example, those providing information at information meetings).

(iv) *Court's investigative role.*

Long before these general principles were enunciated there was widespread concern about the welfare of children involved in parental divorce; and this led Parliament, as long ago as 1958, to give the divorce court a special inquisitorial and protective role in an attempt to ensure that satisfactory arrangements were made for the upbringing of children to be affected by a parental divorce. The provisions introduced by the Family Law Act 1996 to this end are discussed at p. 51, above. It is not easy to predict how these provisions will operate in practice. Presumably the court's inquiry into the arrangements for the children will still be based initially on a scrutiny of written documents completed by the parties; and these will have to be drafted in such a way as to elicit relevant information about the conduct of the parties and potential risk to the child. It seems questionable whether such enquiries will foster the conciliatory approach supposedly lying at the heart of the new divorce legislation.

2. Proceedings under the "inherent jurisdiction"

The Children Act 1989 provides that "family proceedings" include any proceedings under the "inherent jurisdiction" of the High Court in relation to children.

What is the inherent jurisdiction? The origins of the court's "inherent jurisdiction" over children lies in the doctrine that it was the Crown's prerogative as *parens patriae* (father of the nation) to have the care of those who could not look after themselves: the crown has a duty to protect its subjects and "particularly children who are the generations of the future" (*per* Lord Donaldson of Lymington M.R., *Re C (A Minor) (Wardship: Medical Treatment) (No. 2)* [1990] Fam. 39, 46. This jurisdiction was delegated to the Court of Chancery; and for many years was normally invoked by making the child a "ward of court". Thereafter, no important step in the life of the ward could be taken without leave of the court. However, in recent years it has come to be appreciated that wardship was the result of an exercise of the inherent jurisdiction and not the ground for the exercise of that jurisdiction. In effect, the court may be asked to take action which is necessary for the protection and well-being of the child (for example, by authorising medical treatment) whether or not the child has been made a ward of court. But for many years the exercise of the inherent jurisdiction was synonymous with wardship.

Increasing recourse to wardship. Although wardship was for long used almost exclusively by the wealthy, the Law Reform (Miscellaneous Provisions) Act 1949 abolished any requirement that the ward be entitled to property and allowed a child to be made a ward simply by the issue of a summons to that effect. Wardship became even more accessible when legal aid became available in 1949, and (as the Law Commission put it in Working Paper No. 101, paragraph 3.2) over the years wardship "came to be regarded not so much as a refuge for orphaned heiresses and a bulwark against predatory adventurers but rather as a means of resolving all kinds of disputes over children . . .". The increased popularity of wardship can be seen from the statistics: in 1951, there were only 74 originating summonses issued to make a child a ward. By 1971, the figure had risen to 622; by 1981 to 1,903, and in 1991 there were 4,791 applications to make a child a ward: see *per* Ward L.J., *Re Z (A Minor) (Freedom of Publication)* [1996] 1 FLR 191, 197. (This judgment gives a full account of the evolution of the jurisdiction and its contemporary significance.)

The reason for this increased recourse to wardship was, in part at least, its great flexibility. There was no need to establish any "ground" before a child could be made a ward: the issue of a summons had the immediate effect that the child became a ward, and thereafter (so long as the wardship continued) no important step in the child's life could be taken without the court's consent. Moreover, in deciding questions relating to the child's upbringing the court would apply the principle that the child's welfare was paramount and the flexibility and wide range of powers at the courts' disposal made wardship a remarkable example of the successful adaptation of a long standing institution to modern circumstances.

Children Act imposes restrictions.   However, for a number of reasons — including the considerable burden which the use of wardship placed on scarce judicial resources — wardship became unpopular with those responsible for the administration of the courts; and the Children Act 1989 accordingly imposed significant restrictions on the use of wardship by local authorities: these restrictions (some of which were also made necessary to give effect to the legislative policy that the mere fact that local authority action would be in the child's best interests was not a sufficient justification for state intervention) are considered in Chapter 13 below.

Effect of Children Act on use of inherent jurisdiction by private individuals.   The Children Act 1989 did not impose any restriction on the use of wardship by private individuals; but the courts discouraged unnecessary recourse to it:

> In *Re T (a minor) (child: representation)* [1994] Fam. 49, C.A., Waite L.J. said the "courts' undoubted discretion to allow wardship to go forward in a suitable case is subject to their clear duty, in loyalty to the scheme and purpose of the Children Act legislation, to permit recourse to wardship only when it becomes apparent to the judge in any particular case that the question which the court is determining . . . cannot be resolved under the statutory procedures in Part II of the Act which deals with the 'private law' procedures (set out at p. 192, above), in a way that secures the best interests of the child; or where the minor's person is in a state of jeopardy from which he can only be protected by giving him the status of a ward of court, or where the court's functions need to be secured from the effects, potentially injurious to the child, of external influences (intrusive publicity for example) and it is decided that conferring on the child the status of a ward will prove a more efficient deterrent" than the use of proceedings for contempt of court.

It appears that this judicial discouragement has been effective. In 1993 there were only 269 wardship applications (see White, Carr and Lowe, *The Children Act in Practice* (2nd ed. 1995, paragraph 12.12); and anecdotal evidence suggests that few private individuals now seek recourse to the jurisdiction, whilst the statutory provisions restricting the availability of the inherent jurisdiction in local authority cases have obviously had a major impact. But the inherent jurisdiction of the High Court over children still has a significant role.

The residual role of the inherent jurisdiction

The inherent jurisdiction of the court over children may still be invoked for the following reasons:

(i) *Immediacy.*

It is still the law (see Supreme Court Act 1981, s.41(2) as amended by C.A. 1989, Schedule 13, paragraph 45(2)) that a child (unless he or she is already subject to a care order) becomes a ward on the issue of a summons making the application; and that thereafter no important step may be taken in the ward's life without leave of the court. It is not easy to achieve this result so speedily and effectively in any of the statutory procedures established by the Children Act 1989. If there is a danger that potentially irreversible damage might be done to a child's welfare (perhaps by withdrawing medical treatment) the wardship jurisdiction may well be favoured.

(ii) *Flexible procedures.*

The High Court exercising the inherent jurisdiction can remain formally seised of his case without it being necessary to make a fresh application for a particular specific issue or prohibited steps order as and when this is thought desirable. Presumably this is one of the reasons for the Official Solicitor's view that the "procedural and administrative difficulties" attaching to applications under section 8 of the Children Act 1989 "are such that the preferred course" in applications for leave to sterilise a child is to invoke the inherent jurisdiction: see *Practice Note — Official Solicitor: Sterilisation* [1996] 2 FLR 111.

(iii) *Extensive powers.*

No precise limit has ever been placed on the inherent jurisdiction; and it has been said that the judge has limitless power to protect the child from any interference with his or her welfare, direct or indirect: *Re K (Wards: Leave to Call as Witnesses)* [1988] 1 FLR 435, 442. For this reason, the inherent jurisdiction has been invoked in cases in which media publicity would damage the child's welfare:

> In *Re AB (Wardship: Jurisdiction)* [1985] FLR 470, Balcombe J., the court held that it had power to grant such an injunction prohibiting publication of facts which would have revealed that the ward's mother was Mary Bell (a person convicted when 11 years old, after a particularly sensational trial, of killing two small boys). The court considered that if the mother's true identity were disclosed, it would "damage the fragile stability she had achieved and thereby endanger the well-being of her own infant child".

But such cases involve an obvious conflict with the public interest in freedom of expression; and more recently the courts have been concerned to restrict the use of the inherent jurisdiction to situations in which either the publicity was directed at the child or those caring for the child, or to protect the proper functioning of the court's own jurisdiction (for example, by preserving the anonymity of witnesses) —
On the one hand:

> In *Re C (A Minor) (Wardship: Medical Treatment) (No. 2)* [1990] Fam. 39, C.A., 5 FLR 263, 271, the court gave leave for medical treatment to a severely brain

damaged terminally ill baby to be restricted to whatever was necessary to relieve the baby's suffering. An injunction was granted in wide terms preventing any publication identifying the baby, the hospital, and its medical and nursing staff. This was justified, first on the basis that the quality of care given to the child could be adversely affected by harassment of those concerned, and secondly on the basis that the hospital and its staff protected those who had invoked the jurisdiction of the court who might otherwise be deterred from doing so.

In contrast:

In *R (Mrs) v. Central Independent Television plc* [1994] Fam. 192, C.A., a father was convicted of offences of indecency against small boys, and the television company made a documentary which might enable him to be identified as the father of a five-year-old girl. The Court of Appeal held that it would be wrong to prohibit the broadcast merely because the child might suffer as a result of her father's criminal record becoming known: the programme was not a programme about her nor did it suggest that her upbringing had been affected by his criminal activities.

It seems that the court will not seek to achieve for the child any more than wise parents or guardians could themselves achieve for the child: *Re Z (A Minor) (Freedom of Publication)* [1996] 1 FLR 191, 206, *per* Ward L.J.; and there are indeed other important albeit self-imposed restrictions on the availability of the inherent jurisdiction. For example —

(i) *There is no jurisdiction in respect of an unborn child:*

In *Re F (in utero) (Wardship)* [1988] 2 FLR 307, C.A. a pregnant woman who had a history of severe mental disturbance disappeared shortly before the expected date of her child's birth. An application was made to ward the unborn child; and it was intended to ask the court to make orders to help trace the mother and to ensure that she lived in a suitable place until the birth. The Court of Appeal held that, for three reasons, the wardship jurisdiction was not available. First, a foetus has no right of action, and is incapable of being a party to an action. Secondly, the only practical consequence of warding the foetus would be to control the mother, and in such a sensitive field which affected the liberty of the subject, it was for Parliament rather than the courts to take any necessary action. Finally, conflicts of interest could arise between the foetus and the mother (for example, if a mother wanted her pregnancy to be terminated) and the wardship jurisdiction was not appropriate for the resolution of such conflicts since it is concerned to promote only one of those interests, the welfare of the child.

(ii) *No interference with exercise of statutory discretion vested in local authorities, etc.*
Another important qualification stems from the well settled principle of administrative law that the inherent jurisdiction of the courts is not to be allowed to interfere with action properly taken under a comprehensive legislative code. The most important example of this doctrine dates from before the Children Act:

In *A v. Liverpool City Council* (1981) 2 FLR 222, H.L., a mother made her child, who was the subject of a care order, a ward of court in an attempt to challenge the local authority's decision to reduce her access to him from once weekly to once monthly. The House of Lords — influenced to some extent by the cost and delay caused by excessive use of the wardship jurisdiction — held that the courts could not exercise that jurisdiction in order to review the merits of the authority's decision. This was because Parliament had, in the child care code, marked out an area in which, subject to the enacted limitations and safeguards, decisions for the child's welfare were removed from the parents and from supervision by the courts.

The effect of the *Liverpool* decision in preventing the courts from exercising any control over parents' contact with children in care has been greatly reduced by the availability of care contact orders under Children Act 1989, s.34 dealt with at p. 236 below. But the general principle remains unaffected by this change. The following cases would still be decided in the same way:

In *Re JS (A Minor) (Wardship: Boy Soldier)* [1991] FLR 7 a boy soldier, who was unhappy in the army, went absent without leave in order to live with his parents. The boy's mother made him a ward of court, and sought an order restraining the Secretary of State for Defence from arresting her son. The court refused: even if a soldier could be warded, questions of military control would be left to the military authorities.

Again:

In *Re Mohammed Arif (an infant)* [1968] Ch. 643 two men started wardship proceedings to stop children being deported as illegal immigrants. The court struck out the applications: the court (said Denning L.J. at p. 662) will not exercise its jurisdiction so as to interfere with the statutory machinery set up by Parliament. The wardship process is not to be used so as to put a clog on the decisions of the immigration officers or as a means of reviewing them.

The inherent jurisdiction and local authorities.   The Children Act prohibits local authorities from using the inherent jurisdiction to require a child to be placed in its care, etc: Children Act 1989, s.100(2). Local authorities who wish to take control of a child are required to use the statutory procedures dealt with in Chapter 13, below. Local authorities may invoke the inherent jurisdiction for other purposes (for example, to protect a child from an undesirable relationship or in some cases in which medical issues arise) but they must first seek the court's leave which can only be granted in closely defined circumstances: section 100(4) and see generally White, Carr and Lowe, *The Children Act in Practice* (2nd ed. 1995) Chapter 12 where this complex subject is fully explored.

Chapter 13

COURT ORDERS DEALING WITH CHILDREN'S UPBRINGING: THE STATE'S ROLE

Introduction: The scope and purposes of state intervention

The community has always assumed some limited duties to orphans and other deprived children. For many years this was done primarily through the medium of the poor law; but in the twentieth century it gradually came to be appreciated that more far-reaching measures were required. Eventually in 1948, as part of the creation of the modern Welfare State after the Second World War, the Children Act 1948 imposed a general duty on local authorities to provide care for all children deprived of a normal home life.

The Children Act 1948 created the concept of "voluntary care": local authorities had a duty to receive into their care orphans, the abandoned, and children whose parents were prevented from providing accommodation, maintenance and upbringing for them. The main purpose of the 1948 Act was to provide a comprehensive nationwide service for children to replace the hotchpotch of provision of varying quality made by voluntary and other agencies; and it is important to understand that the duty to *receive* was not a power to *take* into care. On the contrary, the local authority was under a positive duty to seek to rehabilitate the family unit, so far as this was consistent with the child's welfare.

The emphasis of the 1948 Act was thus clearly on preventing the need for children to be kept away from their families; and this policy was reinforced by the enactment of the Children and Young Persons Act 1963. The 1963 Act imposed a duty on local authorities to make available guidance and assistance (including "in exceptional circumstances" cash assistance) in order to diminish the need to receive children into care or keep them in care.

Compulsion may sometimes be necessary to protect child

The fact that the emphasis of the 1948 Children Act was so clearly on collaboration between state and parent, and on the provision of services for children rather than on imposing sanctions on parents, does not mean that the legislature ignored the fact that there are and always have been circumstances in which a family is unwilling or unable to accept help. There have long been provisions allowing the community to take over the parents' authority and to impose its own standards — for example, the Poor Law

Act 1899, s.1 gave power to the poor law guardians to take over the parents' rights in respect of children for whom the parents were unable to care by reason of their "vicious habits or mode of life"; and the poor law guardians would often then — more than a quarter of a century before the Adoption Act 1926 gave general recognition to adoption — arrange for the child to be "adopted" by some fit person.

Sometimes the assumption of parental authority was effected by administrative process — latterly by the so-called parental rights resolution under the Child Care Act 1980, s.3; sometimes it was done by means of a court order latterly by the making of a care order under the provisions of the Children and Young Persons Act 1969 on the basis that the child's health was being avoidably impaired and that the child was in need of care and control which he or she was unlikely to receive unless the court made an order.

The relevance of the Criminal Law

Sometimes the child's problems resulted from parental abuse; and in the nineteenth century Parliament began to enact the large body of legislation creating criminal offences — ranging from the general offence of child cruelty (Children and Young Persons Act 1933, s.1) through a wide range of sexual offences (such as incest) to the very specific (such as allowing a child to be in a room containing an unguarded heating appliance: Children and Young Persons Act 1933, s.11) — in respect of mistreatment of children.

The fact that a parent's behaviour might be the basis for social services action whilst at the same time being the basis on which the parent could be prosecuted gives rise to many difficulties, relating, for example, to the right of a person accused of a criminal offence to remain silent and to the differing standards of proof in criminal cases (where the case must be proved beyond reasonable doubt) and civil litigation (in which the criterion is normally simply whether the court considers on the evidence it to be more probable than not that the matters in issue occurred). For example:

> In *Re H and R (Child Sexual Abuse: Standard of proof)* [1996] 1 FLR 80, H.L., a 15-year-old girl alleged that her stepfather had sexually abused her over a period of seven years, and that on four occasions he had raped her. The father was prosecuted for rape but acquitted. Subsequently, the judge hearing an application made by the local authority for care orders under the Children Act 1989 said that he was "more than a little suspicious" that the stepfather had done what was alleged and that the girl's account of what had happened was true. Was this suspicion sufficient to establish that the child's brothers and sisters were likely to suffer significant harm, so that the court could make a care order?

Much media comment on the law relating to children confuses the two issues of whether compulsory measures should be taken to safeguard the child's welfare on the one hand and whether a parent should be prosecuted and (if convicted) punished on the other; but it is important for the reader to avoid this confusion. This text is concerned solely with civil proceedings designed to protect the child, and refers to the criminal law only when it has a direct bearing on the work of the family courts.

Background to the Children Act 1989

There are thus two main strands (in addition to the role of the state in prosecuting and punishing those who are guilty of offences against children) in the involvement of the state in children's upbringing. First, the state provides services for children — most obviously in relation to education and health, but also in respect of many social service activities such as the protection of children against abuse and the provision of help for children whose parents cannot provide the care they need. Secondly, the state provides machinery whereby children can if necessary be removed from their parents and placed in care, possibly in a children's home, but more often with foster-parents (and, increasingly, with a view to the child ultimately being adopted outside the family).

Between 1948 (when, as already explained, the modern child care system came into being) and the enactment of the Children Act 1989 there were many shifts of opinion in relation to the proper balance between these two aspects of state provision and in particular about the relationship between protecting the child on the one hand and preserving the right of parents to bring up children in accordance with their own philosophy without interference from social workers or other agents of the state on the other hand. There were also many developments in social work philosophy and in the administration of local authority social services departments.

The result was that the legislation governing the relationship between the child, the family and the state became complex, confused and sometimes inconsistent. For example, the Children Act 1975 was heavily influenced by the belief that children were being allowed to "drift" in voluntary care, and the Act therefore provided that a local authority could assume parental rights not only on grounds of a culpable failure to provide adequate parenting but simply on the ground that a child had been in the local authority's care for three years. The 1975 Act was also concerned to protect children against the risk of precipitate removal from voluntary care, and the Act therefore required a parent to give 28 days' notice of intention to remove a child who had been in care for six months. The underlying philosophy clearly seemed to be that the child's welfare was the dominant concern, even if this involved interfering with what some regarded as the parents' legitimate rights. But it remained true that the mere fact a child was at risk (however well-founded that concern might be) was not sufficient to justify a local authority removing a child from its parents' home: the courts had held that a care order under section 1(2)(a) of the Children and Young Persons Act 1969 could only be made on the basis of something which had already occurred, and that mere apprehension of risk was not sufficient.

In this respect, therefore, the law seemed over-careful of parents' rights, and insufficiently mindful of the need to protect children. But the local authority could overcome the shortcomings of the Children and Young Persons Act 1969, by making the child a ward of court, and claiming that "exceptional circumstances" justified the court's committing the child to care on the basis that to do so would best serve the child's interests. The fact that the local authority would fail if it sought a care order in the magistrates' court under the 1969 Act was irrelevant. The remedies available in cases of suspected child abuse thus differed sharply depending on the court in which the proceedings were started, and this increasingly seemed difficult to justify.

In 1983, the Law Commission began a comprehensive review of the private law relating to the upbringing of children; and at much the same time the House of Commons Social Services Select Committee began the process which led to a comprehensive Inter-Departmental Review of Child Care Law (1985). But it required a widely publicised disaster to create the climate of opinion in which legislative reform can be carried through; and the massive publicity given to events in Cleveland in 1987 — when a large number of children were removed from their homes by the local authority because of suspicions of sexual abuse, and the legal and administrative systems came close to collapse — led directly to the establishment of a wide-ranging enquiry under the chairmanship of Mrs Justice Butler-Sloss (*Report of the Enquiry into Child Abuse in Cleveland* 1987, 1988, Cm. 412) and created pressure for legislation. The Children Act 1989 was the outcome.

Impact of the Children Act 1989

The earlier Chapters of this book have shown how the Children Act 1989 has rationalised and codified the private law relating to children, but the Act has also had a revolutionary impact on the public law. First, it codifies and reforms the legal rules governing the powers and duties of local authorities in relation to the provision of support for children and families. Secondly, the Act makes sweeping changes affecting the legal position of children who are being looked after by local authorities. Thirdly, the Act makes radical changes in the law governing the circumstances in which a local authority may intervene compulsorily in the upbringing of a child — perhaps by removing the child from its parents. Moreover, the new legislative code governing the circumstances in which compulsion may be exercised is skilfully integrated with the provisions of the Children Act 1989 governing private law disputes between a child's parents and other members of the family circle; so that — to take the most obvious example — it is now possible for a court which considers the welfare of a child at risk to be best served by the child being in the care of a relative (rather than becoming the responsibility of a local authority under a care order) to make a residence order in the relative's favour.

The rules defining the circumstances in which the state may exercise compulsion traditionally (and rightly) receive most attention from lawyers and in student text books. But it would be wrong to ignore the other aspects of child care legislation (in particular, the duty of local authorities to provide support) since the legislation quite clearly espouses the doctrine that the development of a working partnership with parents is usually the most effective route to providing supplementary or substitute care for their children, that there are unique advantages for children in experiencing normal family life in their own birth family, that every effort should be made to preserve the child's home and family links, and that family links with the wider family as well as with parents should be actively fostered even if a child has to be cared for by others.

Arrangement of text

The text therefore considers in turn: (i) the powers and duties of local authorities in relation to children; (ii) the legal position of children who are being looked after by a local authority; (iii) the circumstances in which a local authority can exercise compulsion — for example to remove a child from the parents, and place the child with foster parents with a view to adoption by them; (iv) the emergency procedures available to protect children from harm. Finally, it will be apparent that care proceedings have many unusual and distinctive characteristics, and the concluding part of the Chapter seeks to highlight some of these.

A. LOCAL AUTHORITIES' POWERS AND DUTIES

The Children Act draws together local authority functions in respect of children, and creates a significant range of new duties. Part III of the Act imposes a general duty on local authorities to safeguard and promote the welfare of children in the authority's area who are "in need"; and that term is widely defined (section 17(10). Every local authority has a general duty to provide a range and level of services appropriate to the needs of children in their area so as to safeguard and promote the welfare of such children; and, so far as is consistent with that duty, to promote their upbringing by their families.

The requirement that local authorities should promote children's upbringing by their families (C.A. 1989, s.17(1)) is significant, and is supported by a duty to make appropriate provision for services (ranging from advice, through home help, to travel and holiday facilities or assistance) to be available for children in need while they are living with their families: Schedule 2, paragraph 8.

The Act imposes a general duty on local authorities to take reasonable steps to reduce the need to bring care or other family proceedings in respect of children in their area; and a similar duty to "take reasonable steps through the provision of services to prevent children in the area suffering neglect or ill-treatment": C.A. 1989, Schedule 2, paragraph 4(1).

The Children Act 1989 also contains specific provisions dealing with family centres and day care services such as day nurseries, play-groups, child-minding, and out-of-school clubs and holiday schemes. It is impossible in a short student's textbook to elaborate all the extensive powers and duties of local authorities under these provisions. But they are significant not least because an authority which seeks a care order is likely to find that it is asked questions about whether the child's welfare could not better be promoted by support furnished under the Act.

This may suggest that local authorities are anxious to take children into care; but in fact "care" is an expensive option and case law increasingly suggests that some local authorities are heavily influenced by financial considerations in deciding whether to bring care proceedings: see for example *Nottingham County Council v. P* [1994] 18, C.A.; and *Re K (Care Order or Residence Order)* [1995] 1 FLR 674, Stuart-White J. Considerations of finance also seem to have a strong influence on the scale of provision in fact made by local authorities in the performance of the duties imposed on them by Part III of the Children Act. It might be thought that the Act is clear enough but individuals are given little effective redress against a local authority which does not provide the range or scale of services he or she considers appropriate:

(i) *Court has no jurisdiction to make specific issue order that child "in need".*
The hands-off attitude of the court to seeking to interfere with local authority decisions is well exemplified by *Re J (Specific Issue Order: Leave to Apply)* [1995] 1 FLR 669, Wall J.:

> A 17-year-old child sought leave to apply for a specific issue order declaring him to be a child in need and requiring the local authority to make appropriate provision for him. The court refused. It was clear that the exercise of the local authority's powers and duties under Part III of the Children Act was not to be the subject of judicial scrutiny or control save to the extent provided by judicial review, and statute has empowered the local authority alone to make the decision as to whether a child is in need.

(ii) *No action for damages for breach of statutory duty.*

In *X and others (minors) v. Bedfordshire County Council* [1995] 2 A.C. 633, H.L., the House of Lords discouraged the use of tort actions to enforce the performance of the duties laid on local authorities by legislation. The purpose of the child care legislation is to establish an essentially administrative system designed to promote the social welfare of the community; and to allow tort actions to be brought against those concerned would be inconsistent with the whole statutory system set up for the protection of children at risk:

> The complaint was that the local authority had, over a five year period, failed to take appropriate action to protect the five child plaintiffs against parental neglect and the risk of abuse. Another complaint was that social workers and a consultant psychiatrist had failed to exercise proper care and thoroughness in investigating suspicions of sexual abuse, and that this failure had led to mother and child being separated by court order and to their suffering anxiety neurosis in consequence. The House of Lords held that these claims had properly been struck out as disclosing no reasonable cause of action.

Again —

> In *Barrett v. Enfield London Borough Council, The Times*, April 22, 1997, C.A., a young man who had been in the local authority's care throughout his childhood claimed damages for the authority's failure to obtain the psychiatric treatment he had needed, its failure to provide proper placements and its failure to arrange his adoption. The Court of Appeal, whilst acknowledging that social workers could be liable for failing to carry out the authority's instructions properly, held that the claim had been properly struck out as disclosing no reasonable cause of action. It would be wrong in principle to expose parents to liability in damages for mistaken decisions about their child's upbringing; and decisions taken by local authorities in place of parents should be treated in the same way. To hold otherwise would lead to local authorities taking an excessively cautious and defensive approach to their duties; and the right redress for someone who thought errors had been made was to invoke the powers of the Ombudsman.

(iii) *But judicial review may be available in some cases.*

The apparently increased readiness of the courts to review administrative action has become a matter of much public attention in recent years, but it is important to remember that the procedure is one whereby the *legality* of the decision taking process (as distinct from the *merits* of the decision arrived at) is considered; and that even then the court will only interfere if there has been a mistake in interpreting the limits of the power in question, procedural irregularity, or so-called *Wednesbury* unreasonableness (said by Lord Brightman to mean "unreasonableness verging on absurdity": *R v. Hillingdon LB, ex parte Puhlhofer* [1986] A.C. 484, H.L.). But on occasion a judicial review application is successful in questioning the exercise of child support functions:

> In *Re T (Accommodation by Local Authority)* [1995] 1 FLR 159, Johnson J. a 17-year-old girl had had a tragic background, but had managed to escape from it and was given a steady, loving and committed home by foster-parents. She applied to the local authority for the Authority formally to accommodate her,

which would mean that the foster-parents would receive a boarding-out allowance and that she would become eligible for ongoing support from the local authority until she was 21. The court quashed the local authority's refusal to accommodate her: the local authority had not taken into account the relevant considerations.

(iv) *Complaints procedures available.*

The Children Act 1989, s.26, requires local authorities to establish procedures for considering representations (including complaints) made to them by a wide range of people likely to be affected by decisions about the exercise of local authority powers and the discharge of their duties. At least one person independent of the Authority must participate. The Department of Health and the Social Services Inspectorate have given guidance on the conduct of reviews, and the local authority is required by law to have "due regard" to the findings of the panel. However, the decision as to whether panel recommendations should be followed remains one for the local authority — and, as in *Re T (Accommodation by Local Authority)* [1995] 1 FLR 159, Johnson J. (above) where the review panel, after a "searching and vigorous enquiry" had upheld the complaint — the local authority may not follow the recommendations. In that event, a complaint may in some circumstances be taken to the Ombudsman (Local Commissioner for Administration) — a course (as we have seen) favoured by the Court of Appeal in *Barrett v. Enfield London Borough Council, The Times,* April 22, 1997.

The attitude of the courts (led by the House of Lords in the *Bedfordshire County Council* case, above) is that these procedures provide appropriate means to have grievances investigated; see *e.g. R v. Birmingham City Council, ex parte A (A Minor), The Times,* February 19, 1997, Sir S. Brown P (complaints procedure appropriate in cases of alleged delay); but it is questionable whether those whose lives have been so profoundly affected as were the families in that case would regard such procedures as adequate; whilst research conducted by C. Williams and H. Jordan has revealed the need for considerable improvements in the procedures. Certainly, complaints procedures cannot meet the need for the openness and publicity provided by the traditional remedy of legal action in the ordinary courts.

B. CHILDREN LOOKED AFTER BY A LOCAL AUTHORITY

Looking after (i) children in care, and (ii) other children.   Local authorities "look after" children who are committed to their care by a care order, and they also have parental responsibility for such children. One aspect of that responsibility is the duty to provide accommodation — whether in a residential institution, with foster-parents, or even (subject to elaborate safeguards) with the parents — for the child in care; but the Act also gives effect to the policy that local authorities may (and in some circumstances must) "provide accommodation" for other children as part of the services available to families.

Types of accommodation provided.   There are various ways in which a local authority may provide accommodation, of which the most important for present purposes is perhaps the so called "family placement" which means placement with a local authority foster-parent, *i.e.* a family, relative or other suitable person: section 23(2). Regulations lay down detailed provisions requiring the approval of foster-parents, and for the decision-taking procedures leading up to a placement of a child: see the Arrangements for Placement of Children (General) Regulations 1991, and the Foster Placement (Children) Regulations 1991. There are also detailed provisions governing placement in children's homes.

Duty to provide accommodation; power to provide accommodation.   The detailed rules are complex, but in essence local authorities are placed under a *duty* to provide accommodation for children who require accommodation as a result of their being abandoned or there being no person who has parental responsibility or as a result of the person who has been caring for the child being prevented from providing the child with suitable accommodation or care (section 20(1)); and the local authority *may* provide accommodation for any child in their area if to do so would safeguard or promote the child's welfare.

Matters to be considered in local authorities' decision taking.   The general policy of the Act is to emphasise the need to promote the welfare of children whom the local authority is looking after, if at all possible by a partnership between the authority and the others concerned. In addition to the general duty (s.17(1)(b)) to promote the welfare of children in need, and "so far as is consistent with that duty, to promote their upbringing by their families", the Act imposes on local authorities a specific statutory duty to safeguard and promote the welfare of children they are looking after (section 22(3)). The local authority must also "so far as is reasonably practicable" ascertain the wishes and feeling of (a) any child they are looking after (or proposing to look after); (b) his parents; (c) any other person who has parental responsibility for him; and (d) any other person whose wishes and feelings the authority considers to be relevant. In making any decision with respect to such a child the local authority is obliged to give due consideration to the wishes and feelings of such persons as well as to the wishes and feelings of the child ("having regard to his age and understanding") and to the child's "religious persuasion, racial origin and cultural and linguistic background": section 22(5).

But parents may prevent children being accommodated.   Partnership is a key concept in the policy to which the legislation gives effect; and the Act gives substantial recognition to the rights and authority of parents. In particular, the local authority is prohibited from providing accommodation for a child if a person who has parental responsibility and is able and willing to provide (or arrange for the provision of) accommodation objects: section 20(7). This power of parental veto does not apply if the child is 16 or over (so the rebellious teenager can refuse to return to the parental home); nor does it apply if there is a residence order in force in favour of someone who agrees to the child being accommodated.

Parental right to remove child from local authority accommodation.   The most dramatic illustration of the Act's recognition of parental authority is to be found in the provision (section 20(8)) that "any person who has parental responsibility for a child may at any time remove the child from accommodation provided" under the legislation. Thus:

In *Nottinghamshire County Council v. J* (1993) 26 November, (unreported) (Ward J.) it was held that a local authority was powerless to stop a mother removing her children from local authority accommodation unless there was a court order in force preventing her from doing so. Neither the statutory provision empowering a person to take reasonable action to promote a child's welfare nor the specific duty imposed on local authorities to safeguard and promote children's welfare could be sufficient justification.

These provisions of the Children Act 1989 mark a significant shift of policy from the regime of "voluntary care" introduced by the Children Act 1948 and redefined in the Children Act 1975. Under that legislation a parent had to give prior notice of the intention to remove a child from local authority accommodation; and the local authority would thus be in a position to apply to the court for the appropriate order (an Emergency Protection Order, or a Care Order) if it considered removal of the child to be inconsistent with the child's welfare. The power given to parents suddenly to remove a child from what may have been his home for several years seems to give little weight to the child's own feelings, and in this respect the "partnership" which the Act seeks to foster between local authorities and families seems distinctly unequal.

C. COMPULSION — ACQUISITION OF PARENTAL RESPONSIBILITY BY LOCAL AUTHORITY

Court order essential for compulsory intervention

A court order is necessary to vest parental responsibility and with it parental authority in a local authority. The days when a local authority could assume parental authority by passing a resolution have gone. It follows that there must be a court hearing in every case in which parental responsibility is to be vested in the state, however willing the parents may be to accept the local authority's plans for the child. As Lord Mackay (then the Lord Chancellor) put it in explaining the policy to which the Children Act 1989 seeks to give effect:

> Unless there is evidence that a child is being, or is likely to be, positively harmed because of a failure in the family, the State, whether in the guise of a local authority or a court, should not interfere.

The Conservative Government took a deliberate decision to reject the notion that state intervention could be justified merely because there was evidence that the child's welfare so required. In this view, there is a crucial distinction between the criteria upon which the court could resolve disputes between members of a family (where a broad discretion guided by the principle of the child's best interests would be appropriate and defensible) and cases in which State intervention could be justified. In the latter situation, certain minimum circumstances,

> "should always be found to exist before it can ever be justified for a court even to begin to contemplate whether the State should be enabled to intervene compulsorily in family life . . . The integrity and independence of the family is the basic building block of a free and democratic society and the need to defend it should be clearly perceivable in the law . . . to provide otherwise would make it

lawful for children to be removed from their families simply on the basis that a court considered that the state could do better for the child than his family. The threat to the poor and to minority groups, whose views of what is good for a child may not coincide closely with that of the majority, is all too apparent . . ." (1989) 139 New L.J. 505, 507.

The text therefore first considers the conditions which have to be satisfied before the court has power to authorise such intervention. It then discusses the powers which are available to the court, and the effect of the various orders which it can make.[1]

1. Preconditions for intervention

The court can only make a care order or supervision order if:

(a) there is an application by a local authority (or "authorised person", in practice the NSPCC);
(b) the court is satisfied that the "threshold criteria" set out in section 31 of the Children Act are met;
(c) the court considers:
   (i) having directed itself by reference to the matters to which section 1(3) of the Act requires it to have "particular regard" that the making of an order would promote the child's welfare (that being at this stage — in contrast to what is relevant at stage (b) — the paramount consideration); and
   (ii) the court is satisfied that making an order would be better for the child than making no order at all: Children Act 1989, s.1(5).

These matters are considered in turn.

(a) Application by local authority or authorised person

The Act adopts the principle that care or supervision orders are not to be made unless those who have the responsibility for dealing with the welfare of children consider that such an outcome would be desirable. It is impossible for the court to make an order however clear it may be that the necessary conditions are satisfied and that the making of a care order is required to protect the child:

In Nottingham County Council v. P [1994] Fam. 18, C.A., a man had persistently sexually abused his daughter; and the judge considered that her two younger sisters were at serious risk of abuse. All the individuals concerned were prepared to accept a supervision order; but the local authority refused to make the necessary application. The President of the Family Division expressed "deep concern" at the court's inability to direct the local authority to take the steps necessary to protect the children, but pointed out that "if a local authority

---

[1] In practice, compulsory local authority intervention often begins by the taking of so-called emergency measures (notably by an application for an Emergency Protection Order) but it is convenient to deal with those procedures separately after the key concepts in the legislative code have been explained: see p. 240, below.

doggedly resists taking the steps which are appropriate to the case of children at risk of suffering significant harm . . . the court is powerless . . .''

The decision taking process. The decision whether or not to seek compulsory intervention can be a difficult one; and the Department of Health's *Guidance* (1991) stated that "applications for a care or supervision order should be part of a carefully planned process": Volume 1, paragraph 3.2. In fact an elaborate decision-taking structure has been established — with Area Child Protection Committees, Child Protection Registers, Case Conferences and so on — in an attempt to ensure that there is the necessary "close working relationship between social services departments, the police service, medical practitioners, community health workers, schools, voluntary agencies and others (*Working Together* (HMSO 1991, paragraph 1.9)). The aim is to establish a partnership not only between the different agencies involved in child protection work but also so far as possible with the family:

"A multi-disciplinary, multi-agency case conference should always be held, . . . and it should seek to recommend an agreed course of action. Parents, the child (if of sufficient age and understanding) and others with a legitimate interest in the child's future should be involved wherever possible. Involvement will mean much more than attendance; families should be able to participate in the decision-making process and they will need to be kept informed of decisions as they are made, the reasoning behind those decisions and their likely cons-quences." (Department of Health's *Guidance* (1991) Volume 1 paragraph 3.10).

Not surprisingly some legal difficulties have arisen about this decision-taking process. Can the police (who will routinely be present at case conferences) require statements — perhaps incriminating statements — by parents to be handed over to them and used in subsequent prosecutions? Do the parents have a right to representa-tion at case conferences? Can decisions taken at case conferences be reviewed by the courts: see, e.g. *R v. Norfolk County Council, ex parte M* [1989] Q.B. 619, Waite J.?

Before instituting care proceedings, local authorities are exhorted to consider all alternatives (including encouraging a relative to apply for a residence order) and to satisfy themselves that the child's needs can only be properly met by compulsory measures.

Finally it should be mentioned that an authority may seek a care order notwithstand-ing the fact that it did not itself initiate the family proceedings in question: a court may — provided that the relevant conditions (including the requirement that the local authority apply for the order) are satisfied — make a care or supervision order in any family proceedings: see section 31(4). For example, a local authority could intervene in a "freestanding" application by the father of an illegitimate child, and seek a care order, and as already noted the Children Act 1989, s.37, empowers a court hearing family proceedings to direct the local authority to make an investigation of the child's circumstances and to consider whether to apply for a care or supervision order (or to take other action). However, consistently with the general philosophy of the Act the decision is one for the local authority: if the Authority concludes that it does not wish to seek such an order it must make a report giving reasons for its decision to the court; but the court cannot require the Authority to seek an order.

(b) The threshold stage

Condition precedent to making of care or supervision order.   The court only has jurisdiction to make a care or supervision order if it is satisfied that the conditions set out in section 31(2) of the Act are satisfied. To adapt the words of the Lord Chancellor[2] unless and until the court is so satisfied it cannot "even begin to consider" committing the child to the care or supervision of the local authority. If, but only if, the threshold criterion is satisfied the court goes on to the next stage and considers whether it should in fact exercise the discretion which it will then have to make a care or supervision order. These two distinct stages in the decision-taking process are conveniently described as "the threshold stage" and "the welfare stage": *Re M and R (Child Abuse: Evidence)* [1996] 2 FLR 195, 202, *per* Butler-Sloss L.J.

But court can make section 8 order even if threshold criterion not satisfied.   At the risk of confusing the reader it must be pointed out that even an unsuccessful application for a care order does give the court a right to intervene in the family's life. This is because the court can make any of the section 8 orders[3] if it considers that to do so would best serve the child's welfare:

> In *Re M (A Minor) (Care Order: Threshold Conditions)* [1994] Fam. 95, C.A., the Court of Appeal held — wrongly, as the House of Lords subsequently decided[4] — that the threshold criterion was not satisfied in a case in which a four-month-old baby's mother had been killed with a meat cleaver by the father. The court held that it would be appropriate to make a residence order in favour of a relative of the mother who had been caring for the mother's other children.

The statutory test.   The statutory rules are complex, and the drafting caused considerable problems. It seems best, therefore, to set out the rules exactly as they appear in the statute: The court must be satisfied:

> (a) that the child concerned is suffering, or is likely to suffer, significant harm; and
> (b) that the harm, or likelihood of harm, is attributable to:
>> (i) the care given to the child, or likely to be given to him if the order were not made, not being what it would be reasonable to expect a parent to give to him; or
>> (ii) the child's being beyond parental control.

The court cannot make a care or supervision order if the child has reached the age of 17 (or 16 in the case of a married child); and the Act (s. 31(9)) further defines certain elements in the "threshold" test:

> "harm" means "ill-treatment or the impairment of health or development"; "development" means "physical, intellectual, emotional, social or behavioural

---

[2] Set out at p. 225, above
[3] Discussed at p. 199, above
[4] See at p. 231, below

development"; "health" means "physical or mental health"; and "ill-treatment" includes "sexual abuse and forms of treatment which are not physical".

Notwithstanding the Lord Chancellor's statement that the Children Act 1989 was so clearly drafted that ordinary people would be able to understand it without needing to consult lawyers of other experts, and the statement by the President of the Family Division that the courts should not be "invited to perform in every case a strict legalistic analysis of the statutory meaning" of the threshold test, there has been a mass of reported case law on the construction of the public law provisions of the Act. As Professor M. D. A. Freeman prophesied (in *Children and the Law*, ed. by D. Freestone (1990) at 135) almost every word has required judicial interpretation and analysis.

In a book of this kind it is neither necessary nor desirable to seek to give a comprehensive account of the case law. Rather a number of key issues will be identified:

(i) *Proof required.*

The courts administering the care jurisdiction — like other courts — can only act on the basis of proof; and the onus of proving the case rests on the applicant. Having heard the admissible evidence, the court must be satisfied on the balance of probabilities, that the events in question occurred. Unresolved judicial doubts and suspicions are insufficient. Thus:

> In *Re H and R (Child Sexual Abuse: Standard of Proof)* [1996] 1 FLR 80, H.L.[5] the court had no power to make a care order. The allegation that the stepfather had sexually abused a child had not been proved, and there were no other facts upon which a finding of significant harm could be based.

The difficulty with this approach is that (as Rose L.J. put it in *Re G and R (Child Sexual Abuse: Standard of Proof)* [1995] 2 FLR 867, 881) a finding that sexual abuse has not been proved "does not equate with a finding that . . . abuse did not occur, any more than a finding of not guilty equates with a finding of innocence"; and there is accordingly a risk that the family justice system will fail adequately to protect the vulnerable. However, it is very rare for the factual substratum on the basis of which the court is invited to make a finding of significant harm to be limited to a single matter; and (as Lord Nicholls of Birkenhead put it in *Re H and R (Child Sexual Abuse: Standard of Proof)* (above):

> ". . . there will be cases where, although the alleged maltreatment itself is not proved, the evidence does establish a combination of profoundly worrying features affecting the care of the child within the family. In such cases, it would be open to a court to find . . . on the basis of such facts as are proved that the threshold criterion is satisfied."

For example:

---

[5] The facts of which have been given at p. 218, above. The decision is powerfully criticised by M. Hayes (1997) 17 L.S. 1.

In *Re G and R (Child Sexual Abuse: Standard of Proof)* [1995] 2 FLR 867, C.A. the children had severe behavioural problems. The judge held that allegations of sexual abuse against the father had not been made out; but the Court of Appeal held that the evidence — which included much evidence of poor parenting and of the children being severely disturbed — "overwhelmingly established" that a two-year-old was likely to suffer significant harm if she were returned to the care of her parents.

Many cases involve an assessment of whether or not a child has been or is likely to have been physically or psychologically damaged; and in such cases the court will almost invariably have available to it evidence from paediatricians, child psychiatrists or child psychologists, and the opinion of such persons on any relevant matter about which they are qualified to give expert evidence is, contrary to the general rule that witnesses must only speak to the facts, admissible: Civil Evidence Act 1972, s.3. But in some cases the court will have to decide whether or not to believe a child or other witness about what has happened in the family; and there has been some doubt as to the court's power to admit "experts" opinions about whether a witness — perhaps a person with a propensity to fantasise — is or is not likely to be telling the truth on the matter in question. The Court of Appeal has declared that such evidence is admissible; but the assessment of its value is a matter for the court: see *Re M and R (Child Abuse: Evidence)* [1996] 2 FLR 195, C.A.

(ii) *What is significant harm?*

In many cases (for example, where a child has been severely injured or neglected) the question of whether he or she has suffered or is at risk of suffering "significant" harm may not be controversial, and judges will often simply refer to dictionary definitions. (The Oxford English Dictionary defines "significant" as meaning "considerable, noteworthy or important"): see *Humberside County Council v. B* [1993] 1 FLR 257, 263. The question must depend on an assessment of all the circumstances: in one sense, the fact that a child has broken an arm is clearly significant, but the fact that he or she has a single cigarette burn may be of much greater relevance in the context of the decision-taking process envisaged by the Act.

The Act provides that "where the question of whether harm suffered by a child is significant turns on the child's health or development, his health or development shall be compared with that which could reasonably be expected of a similar child" (section 31(10)); and this would seem to be an invitation for the local authority to lead expert evidence comparing the child's development with that which would be expected on the basis of statistical data about such matters as weight, size, and so on. And it seems clear that the reference to a "similar" child is intended to compare like children with like children: a blind child with a blind child, a Down's Syndrome child with a Down's Syndrome child, for example. But although there will be many cases in which the "significance" of the harm cannot really be questioned, anyone who has heard expressions such as "just a few cuts and bruises", or "a nasty shock but she'll soon forget about it, won't she?" will realise that the decision whether harm is of "significance" involves answering the questions, "What can a child be expected to tolerate? What do adults believe to be tolerable?"; and these are necessarily highly subjective issues. But in practice the problem is not as great as could be feared, since any court left in doubt about whether the harm suffered might truly be described as "significant" would be unlikely to be satisfied about the benefits of making an order.

(iii) *Harm, past, present or future?*

(a) *"is suffering"*.

The Law Commission's draft legislation provided that it was sufficient to satisfy the threshold criterion if the child *had* suffered significant harm; and this formulation could have been justified on the basis that to "cross the threshold" did not mean that a care order would necessarily be made but would merely give the court power to make an order if at the time of the hearing the child's welfare so required. But the Government was concerned about the possibility of children being removed from their parents by over-zealous social workers on the basis of some long past failure; and accordingly the Bill was amended. It must be shown that the child *is* (or is likely to be) suffering harm: see section 31(2)(a) (above).

That wording soon gave rise to difficulty. For example, it would surely be absurd to deny the court the power to make orders in cases in which the child had been removed from an appalling situation of violence and risk under the Act's emergency provisions merely because at the time of the substantive hearing the child was being well cared for in hospital or by foster-parents. The difficulties came to a head in *Re M (A Minor) (Care Order: Threshold Conditions)*:

> A husband brutally murdered his wife in the presence of their four-month-old son and their three other children. The local authority applied for a care order with a view to the child being placed for adoption outside the family. But at the time of the hearing before the judge the child was living happily with a short term foster-mother; and Mrs W. (the deceased mother's cousin, "a lady who" as Lord Templeman put it "would undoubtedly be kind to" the child) had applied for a residence order so that she could bring him up together with his older siblings for whom she was already caring.
>
> The Court of Appeal held that the threshold criteria were not satisfied: the first (*is* suffering) limb of the statutory formulation could not be satisfied unless the child was shown to be suffering such harm *at the date of the hearing* (and there was no evidence that the child was *likely* to suffer such harm in the future, see (b) below): [1994] Fam. 95, C.A.
>
> The House of Lords [1994] 2 A.C. 424 disagreed. The Court of Appeal's approach would deprive the "is suffering" test of any effect: Parliament could not have intended to make it impossible for a local authority removing a child under emergency powers subsequently to seek a care order. The House of Lords ruled that, if interim local authority arrangements had been continuously in place from the date at which protective measures were first taken down to the time of the hearing, the court could properly look back to the earlier date.

It must be admitted that this interpretation does not solve all possible difficulties — when, for example, do "arrangements for the protection of the child" begin — but it seems to provide a reasonable pragmatic solution in the great majority of cases.

(b) *"is likely to suffer"*.

It was the clearly articulated policy that compulsory measures should be available in cases in which a child was seriously at risk, notwithstanding the fact that no harm had actually yet been suffered. An obvious example of the kind of case contemplated would be that of a child born in hospital to a heroin addicted mother who would be manifestly incapable of providing any adequate standard of care once the child left hospital: see *Re D (A Minor)* [1987] A.C. 317, H.L. But the word "likely" is susceptible to many interpretations:

> In *Re H and R (Child Sexual Abuse: Standard of Proof)* (above) the House of Lords by a 3:2 majority ruled that the question was whether, on the basis of the facts as admitted or found, there was a "real possibility" — a possibility that could not sensibly be ignored having regard to the feared harm in the particular case — that the child would suffer significant harm.

These refinements may seem almost metaphysical; and it is not always easy to see how some of the reported cases would now be decided. As already pointed out, *Re H and R (Child Sexual Abuse: Standard of Proof)* (above) was an unusual case in which the only fact alleged as being the basis for a determination that the child was at risk was an allegation (held not to have been substantiated) that the father had sexually abused his daughter. In *Re M (A Minor) (Care Order: Threshold Conditions)* (above) the Court of Appeal held that the local authority's view that Mrs W. might have been unable to provide the special quality of care the child required was "a thousand miles away" from satisfying the relevant requirement; but the House of Lords did not find it necessary to comment on this view, or on the decision of the Court of Appeal in *Oldham Metropolitan Borough Council v. E* [1994] 1 FLR 568, 572 to the effect that if there were some suitable relative "willing and able to give the child care to a reasonable (*sic*) parental standard" the "likely to suffer" criterion could not be satisfied.

It seems probable, that the question is one for the court in each case evaluating the risk of significant harm befalling the child. This will often be a matter on which different tribunals will reach different views (see *Re C (A Minor) (Adoption: Parental Agreement)* [1993] 2 FLR 260, C.A., *per* Steyn and Hoffmann L.JJ.); and it is chastening to remember that the expert evidence which convinced the experienced High Court judge in *Re M (A Minor) (Care Order: Threshold Conditions)* of the need for a complete severance of all the ties between M and his birth family was completely falsified by the events. As a result of the Court of Appeal's view of the law he had been in the care of Mrs W. and, in part because of her sensitive nurture, had become a boisterous, healthy and happy child notwithstanding the social worker's doubts about her ability to satisfy his needs. This merely illustrates the humility becoming even the most experienced and knowledgeable child development expert and the caution appropriate to a judge adjudicating on the extent of the risks involved.

(iv) *Harm is attributable to failure of parenting.*

A child might be suffering or at risk of suffering significant harm by reason of illness, accident or other misfortune; and it would obviously be absurd to give the court power to remove the child from caring parents in such cases. The Children Act 1989 therefore stipulates that the harm must be "attributable" to one of two specified matters, each (as Lord Browne-Wilkinson put it in *Re C Interim Care Order* [1997] 1 FLR 1, 6, likely to involve an assessment of the relationship between the child and the parents):

(a) *Lack of reasonable parental care.*

The Act refers to the care given by "a" parent (rather than by "the" parent); and it seems therefore that the test to be applied in deciding whether the harm is attributable to the care "not being what it would be reasonable to expect a parent to give" is to be answered by reference to what a hypothetical reasonable parent would provide. The fact that the child's parent is in fact disadvantaged and perhaps not able to do what a better educated, more intelligent, or more affluent parent would do is not material.

It also appears to be irrelevant in determining whether the threshold criterion is satisfied that adequate care might be given to the child by someone else (for example a relative) if an order were not made:

> In *Northamptonshire County Council v. S and Others* [1993] 1 FLR 554, Ewbank J., the court held that significant harm had been caused to the child by the mother's neglect. However, the grandmother was prepared to care for the child. It was held: (i) that the threshold test related only to the parent or other carer whose lack of care had caused the harm referred to; but (ii) the fact that someone else was prepared to care for the child would be highly material at the subsequent stage of deciding whether to make a care order or not. At that stage the court would have to decide what would better serve the child's interests.

(b) *Child beyond parental control.*

The question is again one of objective fact. The relationship between child and parents is critical (*per* Lord Browne-Wilkinson, *Re C (Interim Care Order)* [1997] 1 FLR 1, 6) and it appears to be immaterial that the parents are in no way culpable:

> In *M v. Birmingham City Council* [1994] 2 FLR 141, Stuart-White J., a 13-year-old girl had developed a wayward, uncontrollable and disturbed pattern of behaviour, sometimes involving violence and the making of serious unfounded allegations against those with whom she came into contact. She absconded from the unit in which attempts were made to treat her and she took drug overdoses. The judge held that she had presented and continued to present a serious problem to anyone who had the duty of caring for her. The fact that her mother was a caring person who had tried to get appropriate help to deal with the child's problems did not affect the fact that the harm she was likely to suffer was attributable to her being beyond parental (or indeed any other) control. The threshold criterion was thus satisfied.

Again:

> In *Re O (A Minor) (Care Order: Education: Procedure)* [1992] 2 FLR 7, Ewbank J., a 15-year-old girl had been persistently truanting for several years. The court held that her failure to attend school would cause her significant harm; and if a child was not attending school without proper excuse the child must either be beyond parental control or suffering from a parental failure to provide proper care. In the event, a care order was made: the girl would be placed in a children's home and taken to school each day until a pattern of regular attendance had been established.

(c) The welfare stage: exercise of the discretion to make a care or supervision order.
The court cannot make a care or supervision order unless the threshold criteria are satisfied but it does not follow from the fact that the threshold criteria have been satisfied that the court will make a care or supervision (or indeed any) order. If the criteria are met, the court has a discretion whether to make a care or supervision order or not; and if it decides not to do so it may either make a section 8 "menu" order, or it may decide to make no order at all.

In deciding on the exercise of the discretion, the court must apply both the principle that the child's welfare is paramount, and the "no order" presumption. In cases in which the court is considering whether to make, vary or discharge a care or supervision order, the court is required to have regard "in particular" to the matters listed in the statutory checklist (see section 1(3)). These are discussed in detail in Chapter 14; but it is appropriate to highlight some issues particularly relevant to care and supervision orders in this Chapter.

Proof required
In approaching the exercise of its discretion, the court must act on the basis of proven fact rather than mere suspicion or mere doubts:

> In *Re M and R (Child Abuse: Evidence)* [1996] 2 FLR 195, C.A., children had been subjected to emotional abuse and the judge accordingly held that the threshold criteria were satisfied. He found that, although there was a real possibility that they had been sexually abused by their mother and two men, the evidence was insufficient to make a finding that such abuse had occurred. Accordingly, he made interim orders and adjourned the case for three months. The local authority unsuccessfully appealed on the basis that the judge should have taken the "real possibility" that sexual abuse had occurred into account. The court's order must be based on the finding that the harm which the child was at risk of suffering did not include sexual abuse.

Matters to be considered.
Amongst the matters to which the checklist specifically directs the court's attention is (section 1(3)(g)) the range of powers available to the court under the Children Act. Accordingly, it will need to consider whether there is any other order (such as a residence order in favour of a relative) which might be more likely to promote the child's welfare. Having considered the specified matters, and any other considerations relevant to the child's welfare, the court must ask whether making the care or supervision order (or indeed any other order) would "be better for the child than making no order at all": section 1(5). The court will therefore need to ask precisely what benefit the making of a care order will give the child, and this inevitably means that the court will need to have details of the local authority's plans for the child on the assumption that the care or supervision order for which the local authority is asking is made.

In order to understand the courts' approach to these matters it is necessary to outline the effect of care and supervision orders.[6]

---

[6] The effect of the section 8 "menu" orders which the court has power to make is considered at p. 199, above.

Effect and duration of care and supervision orders

A. Care orders.

(a) *Local authority acquires parental responsibility.*

A care order requires the local authority to "receive the child into their care and to keep him in their care while the order remains in force": section 33(1). The local authority will have "parental responsibility" for the child — although the authority cannot give the parental consent necessary in adoption or freeing for adoption, cannot appoint a guardian, and must not cause the child to be brought up in any religious persuasion "other than that in which he would have been brought up if the order had not been made": section 33(6)(a). As a result of the making of a care order the child will be "looked after" by the local authority, and the local authority will in consequence be under a duty to provide accommodation and maintenance for the child (section 23(1)) and will have the powers to provide other services as set out above. But the Children Act 1989 strikes a delicate balance between the local authority's need to have the powers to make effective plans for the long-term welfare of children and the notion that there should be a partnership between the local authority and the parents.

(b) *Parents retain "parental responsibility".*

The fact that the local authority acquires parental responsibility does not mean that the parents lose their parental responsibility: Children Act 1989, section 2(6). But the Act provides that while a care order is in force the local authority has the power "to determine the extent to which a parent or guardian may meet their parental responsibility for" the child (section 33(3)(b)) — albeit only if the authority is "satisfied that it is necessary to do so in order to safeguard or promote the child's welfare": section 33(4). The broad effect of these provisions is inevitably that the local authority, having (as section 22(4) of the Act requires them to do) ascertained the wishes of the parents the child and others, has effective power. The methods whereby parents can question a local authority decision to deny them the right to exercise their parental responsibility (for example, by stipulating that the child receive a certain kind of medical treatment) are dealt with below.

(c) *Local authority may allow child to reside with parents.*

In many cases, the making of a care order will mean that the child is placed with foster-parents or in residential care. But, in an appropriate case — and subject to the provisions of the Placement of Children with Parents, etc. Regulations 1991 which are designed to ensure that a child is not returned to a situation of danger — the court may make a care order in cases in which the local authority intend to place the child in the parents' home:

> In *Re T (A Minor) (Care or Supervision Order)* [1994] 1 FLR 103, C.A., all the professionals concerned were agreed that a six-month-old baby was at risk because of a gradual and unremitting decline in the parents' ability to cope. A care order was appropriate because it would give the local authority time to plan an alternative placement without the delay which would be involved in court proceedings if the standard of parenting in fact declined. But the child was not at risk of sudden injury at the hands of the parents; and the local authority planned to leave the baby girl in the day-to-day care of the parents for the time being.

(d) *Parental contact with a child subject to a care order.*

Cases in which children in care continue to live in the parental home are infrequent, and one of the most important issues which has to be decided in planning the child's future is the extent to which the parents are to be allowed to have contact with their child.

The legal position of parents before the Children Act 1989 was profoundly unsatisfactory:

> In *A v. Liverpool City Council* [1982] A.C. 363, H.L., the local authority decided to restrict the mother's access to her two-year-old child to one monthly supervised visit at a day nursery. The House of Lords held that the court had no power in the exercise of its inherent jurisdiction to question that decision.

In effect, therefore, once a care order had been made, it seemed that a local authority could restrict access and then, when the bond between parent and child was adjudged to have become sufficiently tenuous, place the child for adoption. The court hearing the application for an adoption order in such a case might well hold that the links between parent and child had become so tenuous as to justify it holding that the parent was unreasonable in withholding agreement to the adoption order[7] with the result that all links between parent and child would be irrevocably severed.

The Children Act 1989 has (as Hale J. pointed out in *Berkshire County Council v. B* [1997] 1 FLR 139, 174) made a "fundamental change" in the law and seeks to provide a better balanced system, as follows:

Local Authority's care plan to be considered before making care order.   In deciding whether it is in the child's interests that a care order be made or not the court must consider the authority's arrangements for contact (section 34(11)) and the other matters included in the care plan which the courts require: see *Manchester City Council v. F* [1993] 1 FLR 419. The care plan is accordingly an "extremely important document" (*per* Wall J., *Re J (Minors) (Care: Care Plan)* [1994] 1 FLR 253, 258; and if the court disagreed with the local authority's proposals it would have power to refuse to make a care order: *Re T (A Minor) (Care Order: Conditions)* [1994] 2 FLR 223, C.A.

Presumption of parental contact.   What is the position about continuing contact if the court makes a care order? The Act requires the Authority to allow a child in care "reasonable contact" with the parents (and some others): section 34(1). The Authority may only deny such contact on its own initiative if satisfied that is "necessary" to do so to safeguard or promote the child's welfare, the refusal is decided on as a matter of urgency, and does not last for more than seven days: section 34(6).

Court has final decision.   The question of whether continuing contact is to be allowed is often crucial in deciding the child's long-term future. On the one hand, there is (as shown above) a presumption of contact; but on the other hand (as Butler-Sloss L.J. put it in *Re B (Minors) (Termination of Contact: Paramount Consideration)* [1993] Fam. 301:

---

[7] See at p. 281 below.

"The presumption of contact . . . has always to be balanced against the long-term welfare of the child and particularly where he will live in the future. Contact must not be allowed to destabilise or endanger the arrangements for the child and in many cases the plans for the child will be decisive . . .

Parliament (as Butler-Sloss L.J. went on to say) has given the court the duty to decide on contact. First, the Children Act 1989, s.34(3), provides that the parent, certain other persons and anyone who obtains leave may apply to the court, which may make such order as — applying the welfare principle — it considers appropriate with respect to the contact to be allowed between the child and the applicant. Section 34(2) gives a similar right to make applications to the child and the local authority. Secondly, the Act (s.34(4)) provides that the court may, on an application of the child or the local authority, make an order authorising the Authority to *refuse* to allow contact between the child and the parents, etc., and such orders denying contact may also be made when the care order is first made or in any family proceedings relating to a child in care: see , e.g. *Re David H (Care: Termination of Contract)* [1997] 1 FLR 841, C.A.

The result is that so long as there are prospects of links between the child and the parents being maintained, the court will adjudicate on the reasonableness of the contact which is to be allowed, considering the circumstances of the particular child before it. Although (as Hale J. recognised in *Berkshire County Council v. B* [1997] 1 FLR 171, 176) there are cases at one end of the spectrum in which the child clearly needs a new family for life and contact with the birth family would bring little or not benefit, there are many others in which contact will be of singular importance to the child —

"first, in giving the child the security of knowing that his parents love him and are interested in his welfare; secondly, by avoiding any damaging sense of loss to the child in seeing himself abandoned by his parents; thirdly, by enabling the child to commit himself to the substitute fmaily with the seal of approval of the natural parents; and, fourthly, by giving the child the necessary sense of family and personal identity. Contact, if maintained, is capable of reinforcing and increasing the chances of success of a permanent placement, whether on a long-term fostering basis or by adoption": *Re E (A Minor) (Care Order: Contact)* [1994] 1 FLR 146, 154–155, *per* Simon Brown L.J.

Of course, the court equally has the power to decide that contact should be denied but the issue is one for the court:

In *Re L (Sexual Abuse: Standard of Proof)* [1996] 1 FLR 116, C.A. the court found that, although the children had been sexually abused, there was a "fair chance" that the children could be rehabilitated with their mother; but it was accepted that they would have to remain in care for some time. The judge however, accepted·a submission from the guardian *ad litem* that he should make an order authorising the local authority to refuse to allow contact between the children and the family. This (he thought) could do no harm if the authority did not wish to deny contact, but would be useful in avoiding a further court hearing — the original hearing had taken 17 days — if for whatever reason the professionals concerned thought contact ought to be refused. The Court of Appeal held the judge had been wrong: an order under section 34(4) would be appropriate if there were no likelihood of rehabilitation and the child was to be placed for adoption; but it was not right to do so simply to avoid the need for a further hearing. It was wrong for the court to hand over its residual responsibility to the local authority.

But if care order made, court cannot control exercise of other local authority powers.   Under the law in force before the Children Act 1989 the High Court through the medium of the wardship jurisdiction retained in certain circumstances a degree of control over some children in care at least if there were gaps in the statutory regime or the court's intervention was necessary to support the local authority: *A v. Liverpool City Council* [1982] A.C. 363, H.L. But, on issues other than contact, the Children Act 1989 shifted the balance further in favour of the local authority. There are now statutory restrictions on the exercise of the court's wardship and inherent jurisdiction in local authority cases; and it is clear that the court cannot (see *per* Hale J. *Berkshire County Council v. B* [1997] 1 FLR 171, 174) direct a local authority how it should look after a child in care (for example, by directing a particular kind of placement, "whether it be at home or in foster care or in a residential home or anywhere else"), the court cannot direct that particular services be provided for a child, nor does it have power to direct the child's guardian *ad litem* to continue his or her involvement in the case: see *Kent County Council v. C* [1993] Fam. 57. Once a care order has been made, the local authority has the right to take decisions about such vital matters as whether the child should be placed with short-term or long-term foster parents and even whether the child should be placed for adoption: as Butler-Sloss L.J. has put it: when a care order is made "the local authority is thereafter in the driving seat . . .": *Re C (Interim Care Order: Assessment)* [1996] 2 FLR 708, 711, C.A.

In some cases, the lack of any power to exercise ongoing supervision of the child's upbringing may confront the Court with a cruel dilemma:

> In *Re S and D (Children: Powers of Court)* [1995] 2 FLR 456, C.A., the local authority's plan was to rehabilitate the children with an unreliable and inade-quate mother; but the judge was convinced that the children would be exposed to serious risk of harm if they were returned to her care. The Court of Appeal held that a judge faced with the dilemma that a care order would empower the local authority to implement a care plan exposing the children to risk but refusing to make such an offer would leave the children in the care of an inappropriate and irresponsible parent simply had to choose what, on the evidence, the judge believed to be the lesser of two evils. (In the event, further events since the first instance hearing gave convincing evidence that the judge's fears had been well founded, and the local authority changed its care plan accordingly.)

Duration of care order.   A care order lasts until the child is 18 unless it is brought to an end earlier. The child, the local authority, and any person with parental authority may apply to the court for the discharge of a care order (section 39(1)). There are a number of provisions designed to inhibit repeated fruitless applications: see Children Act 1989 s.91.

Applications for discharge must be decided by reference to the child's welfare:

> In *Re S (Discharge of Care Order)* [1995] 2 FLR 639, C.A., the care order had been made on the basis of allegations that the mother was aware the children had

been sexually abused. The mother adamantly denied this and the local authority, applying a principle now widely accepted in social work practice, considered that this made her unamenable to therapeutic assistance and thus for rehabilitation. Accordingly they gradually reduced the mother's contact.

Three years later in other proceedings a High Court judge criticised some of the investigative techniques used by those involved in the original hearing. The Court of Appeal held that the court hearing a discharge application would be bound to have regard to any harm which the child had suffered or was, at the time of the hearing of the discharge application, likely to suffer, and this requirement could in some cases involve the court reassessing, in the light of subsequent events, the soundness of the findings in the original hearing.

A care order will also be brought to an end if the court makes a residence order, and an application for such an order constitutes an alternative method of questioning its continued existence.

B. Supervision orders.

A supervision order places the child under the supervision of a designated local authority or of a probation officer (section 31(1)) whose duty it is to "advise, assist and befriend" the child — not, be it noted, the parents –- and to take such steps as are reasonably necessary to give effect to the order: section 35(1). The supervisor may give directions to the child as to where he or she should live, or to participate in activities. Directions (for example, that all reasonable steps be taken to ensure that the supervised child complies) may also be given by the supervisor (but not by the court) to the person with whom the child is living or those who have parental responsibility if, but only if, that person consents. The order may require the child to undergo psychiatric or medical examinations or procedures subject to a number of conditions, notably that a child who has the understanding to make an informed decision must consent: see generally Children Act 1989, Schedule 3, paragraphs 3 and 4.

Making a supervision order may indirectly provide a substantial measure of protection for the child:

> "You can have a supervision order which guarantees access into the home by a social worker when asked for . . . You can have a care plan with which [the parents may be willing to co-operate] . . . You have the availability of an emergency protection order which can be obtained at about 2 hours' notice in the event of [a] . . . reason emerging for immediate removal of the child. The child is on the 'at risk register' which means that the local authority is required to conduct periodic reviews . . . That is . . . a fairly strong package." (*Re S (J) (A Minor) (Care or Supervision Order)* [1993] 2 FLR 919, 947, *per* Judge Coningsby Q.C.).

— but the protection is in fact limited precisely because the order is based on supervision. A supervision order does not give the local authority parental responsibility for the child, and the parent rather than the local authority is primarily responsible for the child's safety. A supervision order does not place the local authority under the duty imposed by section 22 of the Children Act 1989 to safeguard the individual child's welfare, and the only sanction available to the supervisor is to return to the court and ask it to make a care order. Moreover, the court cannot directly enforce any requirements which the supervisor may impose.

The danger seems to be that a supervision order may be attractive to the court in so far as it may lack the stigma attaching to a care order, but that the limited effect of such an order may not be given appropriate weight:

> In *Re V (care or supervision order)* [1996] 1 FLR 776, C.A., a 17-year-old boy suffering from cerebral palsy was cared for by his parents to standards which were "beyond criticism on the grounds of devotion and affection." But the boy's mother felt that he was being subjected to too much pressure at the special school he attended, and kept him away from the school on the slightest pretext. The judge had no doubt the threshold criteria were satisfied, but was reluctant to make a care order because he thought that to do so might precipitate a breakdown of the parents' marriage. Accordingly, he made a supervision order to which he purported to attach directions relating to the child's attendance at the school. The Court of Appeal held there was no jurisdiction to attach such directions; and that there was no way in which such an order could ensure he received the desired result of his continued attendance at the school. A care order should have been made.

In reality care and supervision orders are different in scope and effect; but — notwithstanding what has been said above — there must (as Hale J. pointed out in *Re O (Care or Supervision Order)* [1996] 2 FLR 755. 759) be *some* cases in which the supervision order is appropriate. Courts should accordingly analyse the likely impact of the two orders and make an informed choice between them. A care order is "the most Draconian order" which is permitted under the 1989 Act (see *Re O (Care or Supervision Order)* [1996] 2 FLR 755, 763, *per* Hale J.) and, where the need is solely for close monitoring rather than removal of children from their home it may be that courts should carefully consider whether a supervision order (which could be supplanted by a care order if events indicted the stronger order to be necessary) would not be the appropriate solution: see *e.g. Re B (Care or Supervision Order)* [1996] 2 FLR 693.

Duration of supervision orders.   A supervision order is a short term measure and will normally come to an end after one year: Schedule 3, paragraph 6(1). The supervisor may apply to extend the order, but it cannot be extended beyond three years from the date when it was made. A care order, in contrast, will last until the child attains 18, if not brought to an end earlier: section 91(12). There are provisions whereby the child, any person with parental responsibility for the child, and the supervisor may apply to the court for the discharge or variation of a supervision order: section 39(2).

D. EMERGENCY PROCEDURES: INTERIM ORDERS

However streamlined the procedure for dealing with applications for care orders, it is self-evident that there will be cases in which emergency action needs to be taken before the requisite full judicial hearing. A child cannot, for example, be left with parents who are starving him or her, and care must be given for a child whose parent has been arrested and detained in respect of a criminal offence. Moreover, there may be cases in which the parents refuse to allow the child to be examined, even though there is ground for concern about the child's welfare.

Under the law in force before the Children Act 1989 application could be made for a "place of safety order" in such circumstances; but the *Report of the (Butler-Sloss) Inquiry into Child Abuse in Cleveland* 1987 (Cm. 412) revealed many disturbing features of the use to which that procedure had been put. In particular, applications were made *ex parte* without any notification to the parents; applications were made to a single magistrate sometimes sitting in his or her home (notwithstanding the fact that the hearing took place during court hours); record keeping was defective; and there was little understanding of the legal rights of those concerned. The result was that access by the parents was often improperly denied, medical examinations were (perhaps improperly) carried out, and, generally, the procedure seemed to be used in an attempt to obtain control over the situation for the local authority.

The Children Act 1989 seeks to balance the conflicting interests involved by providing that courts may make Emergency Protection Orders and Child Assessment Orders. (The police also have limited powers to remove and protect a child: section 46.) Anyone who has reasonable cause to believe that the child is likely to suffer significant harm if he or she is not moved (or if the child does not remain where he or she is) may apply for an *emergency protection order*; and application may be made by local authorities or authorised persons on somewhat broader grounds: section 44(1). Any application must be made to a court (although *ex parte* applications may in certain circumstances be made to a single justice); and the court will apply the welfare principle and the "no order" presumption.

An emergency protection order requires any person who is in a position to do so to produce the child, and authorises the applicant to remove the child or prevent the child's removal from a hospital or other place — for example, a foster home — in which the child was being accommodated: section 44(4)(c).

Whilst an emergency protection order is in force, the applicant has parental responsibility for the child: section 44(4)(c), but the Act imposes severe limits on the exercise of that responsibility. In particular, the applicant may only take action reasonably required to safeguard or promote the welfare of the child: section 44(5). Moreover, the court may give directions about the parental and other contact to be allowed with the child, and about medical examination or other assessment procedures: section 44(6), although a child of sufficient understanding may refuse to undergo such procedures.

An emergency protection order is not to continue beyond eight days (although the court may order one extension of no more than seven days: section 45). Application may be made to discharge the order after 72 hours.

There is no appeal against a decision to grant or refuse an emergency protection order: section 45(10):

> In *Re P (emergency protection order)* [1996] 1 FLR 482, Johnson J., a new born baby came very near to death, and the suspicion was that the mother had tried to suffocate the child. The Family Proceedings Court refused to extend the order to allow the further medical investigations which were thought necessary; and the judge, drawing attention to the fact that the local authority had no procedure available to it whereby it could effectively challenge that decision, suggested that a mechanism for speedy review of such cases should be introduced.

The Child Assessment Order.   These orders are intended to provide for cases in which there is reasonable concern about the child, the people caring for him or her are unco-operative, yet there are insufficient grounds to obtain an emergency protection order or care order: see *an Introduction to the Children Act 1989*, (HMSO, paragraph 6.41).

The applicant for a Child Assessment Order must be a local authority (or authorised person); and the applicant must satisfy the court that there is reasonable cause to suspect that the child is suffering or is likely to suffer significant harm. The applicant must also satisfy the court that an assessment of the child's health or development is necessary to enable the applicant to determine whether or not the child is in fact suffering or likely to suffer significant harm. A Child Assessment Order permits the making of an assessment; but the child may only be kept away from home in specified circumstances, and may (if of sufficient understanding) refuse to submit to any assessment.

It is not clear whether the Child Assessment Order is effective in serving the purposes for which those who campaigned for its introduction hoped.

Interim Orders.   Notwithstanding many improvements in court structures and pro-cedures introduced in the wake of the Children Act there may well be circumstances; (for example, the need to obtain and consider expert medical evidence), in which an application for a care or supervision order cannot be dealt with at once. In many of these cases, the child might be at risk in the period pending final determination of the application for a care order; and the Act accordingly (section 38) permits a court adjourning proceedings for a care or supervision order, or directing an investigation under Children Act 1989 s.37, to make an interim care order (or an interim supervision order) if it is satisfied that there are *reasonable grounds for believing* that the threshold criteria set out in section 31(2) of the Act are met. This is a lower threshold than is required for the making of a final care order (*Re C (Interim Care Order: Residential Assessment*) [1997] 1 FLR 1, 6, *per* Lord Browne-Wilkinson); and, in finding that "reasonable grounds" exist, the court is not prejudging the question of whether the threshold criterion for the making of a full care or supervision order will be satisfied: the interim care order is a neutral way of preserving the status quo which in no way prejudges the final outcome: *Re G (Minors) (Interim Care Order)* [1993] 2 FLR 839, C.A.

The effect of an interim care order is, so long as it is in force, broadly comparable to that of a final order; and in particular the local authority is required to receive and keep the child in its care, is given parental responsibility, and has the power to determine the extent to which parents and others having parental responsibility are allowed to meet such responsibilities: see Children Act 1989 s.31(11). It follows that the court making an interim care order cannot in principle impose conditions as to where the child is to live:

> In *Re L (Interim Care Order: Power of Court)* [1996] 2 FLR 742, C.A. there were serious concerns about a two-year-old boy whose mother was associating with a man thought to be involved in criminal activity and drug abuse; and it was conceded that the criteria for making an interim care order were satisfied. The mother urged that the judge direct that the child should live with her whilst assessments were made; but the Court of Appeal held that the court had no power to do so. The manner in which the child was to be cared for passed to the local authority, although the judge could indicate that he would hope any assessment would be carried out at home.

However, it is for the court (rather than the local authority) to decide what evidence is needed to reach a decision and accordingly the Act gives the court an overriding power to give such directions as it considers appropriate for the medical, psychiatric or other assessment of the child: section 38(6). The Act also provides (section 38(7)) that the court may prohibit an examination or assessment which the local authority would otherwise be able to commission under the parental responsibility vested in it by an interim care order; and it has been said that this power is "manifestly directed to the type of conduct by social services revealed by the Cleveland Inquiry, *i.e.* repeated interviews and assessments of the child and his parents which are detrimental to the child": *Re C (Interim Care Order: Residential Assessment)* [1997] 1 FLR 1, 8, *per* Lord Browne-Wilkinson.

The power to direct an assessment is not limited to medical investigations, and extends to an assessment of the capabilities of a parent properly to care for the child at home. But certain types of assessment may be extremely expensive, and local authorities may feel that expenditure on the scale required is not a sensible allocation of its recources. As we have seen[8] the Children Act seemed to accept that decisions about the allocation of resources are to be left to the local authority; but,

> In *Re C (Interim Care Order: Residential Assessment)* [1997] 1 FLR 1, H.L. teenage parents were suspected of physically abusing their baby causing him perhaps permanent brain damage. The local authority obtained an emergency protection order and the baby was living with foster-parents. A lengthy investigation by social workers concluded that there might be a possibility of the baby being rehabilitated with the parents but this could only be determined after a residential assessment of the parents and their baby directed to the parents' ability to cope with the baby over long periods of time and in stressful situations. Such an assessment would cost the local authority as much as £24,000; and in any event the local authority believed, in the light of all the evidence, that any consideration of rehabilitation would expose the baby to an unacceptable level of risk. Accordingly, the authority refused to agree to, or pay for, the residential assessment proposed. The Court of Appeal held that the court could only direct that an assessment of the child be made, and it had no power to direct a local authority to place parents with their child in a residential unit. But the House of Lords allowed the parents' appeal. Lord Browne-Wilkinson (delivering a speech in which the other Law Lords concurred) favoured a broad construction of the relevant provisions. The power to direct an assessment was not (as had been argued) limited to assessments of the child but extended to an assessment of the capabilities of a parent properly to care for the child at home. Moreover, the decision on what material was requisite to enable the court to reach a proper decision at the final hearing of the application for a full care order was for the court, not for the local authority. Of course, the court, in exercising its discretion whether to order any particular examination or assessment, must take the costs "and the fact that local authorities' resources are notoriously limited" into account (although the question whether it is appropriate for the court to enter into a detailed consideration of the resources of the local authority and the allocation of such resources was left open).

[8] See at p. 221, above.

The child, if of sufficient understanding to make an informed decision may decline to undergo an assessment directed to be made under this provision; but it has been held that the High Court, in the exercise of its inherent jurisdiction, can override such a refusal: *South Glamorgan County Council v. W and B* [1993] 1 FLR 574, Douglas Brown J.

Interim orders may be made for up to eight weeks, but may be extended for further periods of up to four weeks. There is in principle no limit to the number of interim orders which can be made: *Gateshead MBC v. N* [1993] 1 FLR 811, Connell J.

Statute (Children Act 1989, s.32) requires the court dealing with care and other orders under Part IV of the Act to draw up a timetable and give directions to ensure so far as practicable that it is adhered to; and these provisions have been reinforced by judicial guidance emphasising the need to ensure that the substantial issue is tried and determined at the earliest possible date: *Hampshire County Council v. S* [1993] 1 FLR 559, Cazalet J. But it appears that there are wide differences in practice, and that delay sometimes occurs: *Avoiding Delay in Children Act Cases*, by Dame M. Booth (1996), paragraphs 2.11.1 and 3.8.18. It is also disturbing to note suggestions that some courts make use of repeated interim orders because of lack of confidence in the local authority's ability to carry out the care plan, and a desire to keep — contrary to the clear policy of the Children Act — some ongoing control over the case: *Children Act Advisory Committee, Annual Report 1992/1993*, p. 35.

E. THE NATURE OF CARE PROCEEDINGS

Adversarial or Inquisitorial?   We have seen that the court can only make a care or supervision order if certain matters are proved and so far little or nothing has been said to suggest that the courts dealing with care and other family cases are in any essential respect different from any other court. But for many years the High Court administering the wardship jurisdiction took the view that its role was crucially different from that of other courts. Whereas ordinary English litigation is conducted in accordance with the "adversarial" system with the court simply listening to the evidence which the parties choose to put before it and then reaches its decision on the basis of that evidence, wardship was (so it was claimed) different: the wardship jurisdiction was not based on the rights of parents but was primarily concerned to protect the interests of children and it would accordingly sometimes be the court's duty to look beyond the material which the parties chose to produce and to do whatever it judged necessary to promote the children's welfare.

The House of Lords has now held that the same principle applies to cases brought under the Children Act: they are not adversarial but fall into a special category "where the court is bound to undertake all necessary steps to arrive at" a result which will best serve the interests of the child: see *per* Sir Stephen Brown P., *Oxfordshire County Council v. M* [1994] Fam. 151, 161, approved in *Re L (Police Investigation: Privilege)* [1996] 1 FLR 731, H.L. In that case:

> A mother claimed in care proceedings that her child had taken methadone accidentally. An expert instructed on the mother's behalf concluded that her explanation was not at all likely, and the mother's solicitor (as he was required to do by the Family Proceedings Rules) filed the report with the court. The police asked the court to order that they be given copies of the report for the purpose

of investigating criminal offences. The House of Lords by a 3:2 majority held that the police were entitled to the order. What was in issue was litigation privilege (*i.e.* the right of a party to litigation not to produce privileged documents if it is not in that party's interest to produce them); and the majority took the view that such privilege was an incident of adversarial litigation which accordingly did not exist in care proceedings.

That particular case raises more questions than it answers. Does it follow, for example, that a solicitor who comes into possession of evidence damaging to the client's case is obliged to disclose it against the client's will? How far can a parent refuse to incriminate himself? It is impossible in a book of this character to explore its implications any further than to say that there are many difficult and as yet unresolved problems awaiting solution.

Listening to the child.   The need for the child's interests to be properly represented was dramatically illustrated in the case of Maria Colwell:

> Maria's mother applied, under the legislation then in force, for her to be returned to her care. Although the local authority was aware that the mother's partner was a source of considerable risk to Maria it also believed that the policy of the local magistrates' court was to favour return of children in care to their parents unless there was clear evidence that this would be contrary to the child's interests. The local authority concluded that it would probably not be able to satisfy the court, and therefore it decided not to oppose the revocation of the care order. Maria was returned home and was killed by her stepfather.

In one respect such cases demonstrate the need for a non-adversarial procedure: the court must be able to ensure it has all the information needed to make a decision on the child's future; but in another way they also demonstrate the need for the child's case to be put forward by someone who is wholly committed to the child and does not simply put forward what seems a reasonable compromise taking account of all the various competing considerations.

The legal system deals with these differing needs in two ways. First, as we have seen, the court can (and often will) order that a welfare officer interview the children and others concerned, and make a report to the court; and in this way it is to be hoped that the court will be provided with the evidence which is felt to be needed. Secondly, in care and other "specified" proceedings the legislation goes further. Building on experience gained under provisions introduced by the Children Act 1975 and intended to ensure that the child's voice was properly heard in cases such as Maria Colwell's, the Children Act 1989 provides that in care and some other proceedings the court must appoint a guardian *ad litem* "unless satisfied that it is not necessary to do so in order to safeguard" the child's interests: section 41(1). The guardian *ad litem* is intended to be an independent voice speaking for the child; but the guardian's role combines elements of the social worker making enquiries, the advocate protecting the child's interests, and also the independent expert presenting an informed view to the court.

Meaning of "guardian ad litem".   The expression guardian *ad litem* means, literally, a guardian "appointed for the purpose of litigation". Such guardians were traditionally appointed to defend actions brought against infants and other persons under disability.

Social workers began to be involved as guardians *ad litem* in adoption cases (where the guardian was given special duties) and the concept thus became a familiar one in the family courts. But the role of a guardian in care and other specified proceedings is highly distinctive.

When will a guardian ad litem be appointed?   A guardian will, as already mentioned, be appointed in almost all care and other "specified proceedings" which for present purposes means in "public law" proceedings; and nearly 8,000 appointments, involving more than 18,000 children, are requested annually: *Children Act Advisory Committee, Annual Report 1994/1995*, at p. 69.

The guardian's independence.   It is intended that the guardian should be wholly independent of any local authority involved, and the guardian will be appointed by the court from a panel established in accordance with Regulations. The Rules establish a procedure for appointing people to be panel members; but it does not stipulate any particular qualifications. In practice, most guardians appear to have a social work background, and it has been said that guardians tend to have more experience than the average social worker: White, Carr and Lowe, *The Children Act in Practice* (2nd ed. 1995, paragraph 10.46). National Standards for guardians have now been published.

Rules of Court prohibit the appointment of employees of local authorities involved in the case; and the courts have been careful to emphasise the need for the independence of guardians to be safeguarded:

> In *R v. Cornwall County Council, ex parte G* [1992] 1 FLR 270, Sir Stephen Brown P., the county council's Director of Social Services informed the members of the guardians' panel that no more than a specified amount of time should be spent on cases; and stated that "absolutely no payment" would be made for hours worked in excess of the number authorised. The Divisional Court, in judicial review proceedings, quashed the county council's decision and accepted the guardians' case that the decision impugned their independence. The President of the Family Division emphasised that it was vital that the guardian's independence should not be compromised by any restriction placed directly or indirectly on him or her in carrying out his or her duties. Guardians should not only be seen to be independent, but should also be able to be assured themselves of their independence in the carrying out of their duties.

The guardian's powers and duties.   The Act requires the guardian to safeguard the interests of the child in the manner prescribed by Rules. The guardian accordingly plays a central role in care proceedings, and has wide-ranging and important powers and duties. He must for example, ascertain the child's wishes, and carry out investigations and commission expert reports. To facilitate the guardian's investigatory role, the Act gives the guardian specific rights to examine and copy local authority records: section 42 —

> In *Re T (A Minor) (Guardian ad litem: Case Record)* [1994] 1 FLR 632, C.A., the local authority's plan was to place a child for adoption, and in the exercise of their functions as an adoption agency it had prepared a detailed form relating to the prospective adopters and other matters. Notwithstanding the confidentiality of adoption reports, the Court of Appeal held that the guardian *ad litem* was

entitled to see the materials. The guardian *ad litem* could not fulfil the statutory obligation to inquire into the arrangements which were to be made under the care order unless the documents were disclosed.

The guardian will attend all directions appointments and all hearings, and advise the court on a wide range of matters including the wishes of the child, the appropriate forum for the hearing (Family Proceedings Court or county court Care Centre, for example), the appropriate timing for the proceedings, the options available to the court, and any other matter concerning which the court seeks the guardian's advice or concerning which the guardian considers the court should be informed: the Family Proceedings Courts (Children Act 1989) Rules 1991, r.11. Guardians often co-ordinate and chair meetings of expert witnesses: *Children Act Advisory Committee, Annual Report 1994/1995* at p. 70.

The guardian is required to appoint a solicitor for the child (unless one has been already appointed). However the solicitor's duty is to represent the child (rather than the guardian): Children Act 1989, s.41(5). The Law Society has established a panel of solicitors with appropriate knowledge and experience in children's cases and the Children Act Advisory Committee has stated that representation of any party in proceedings under the Children Act is "a specialised type of advocacy which should only be exercised by barristers and solicitors who have undergone specific training and satisfied an independent body as to their competence and suitability: *Annual Report 1994/1995*, at p. 31.

In most cases, the guardian will instruct the solicitor on the child's behalf, but the solicitor will conduct the case in accordance with the child's instructions if those instructions conflict with the guardian *ad litem*'s (provided that the solicitor considers the child is capable of understanding the matter). Conflicts of interest can arise if more than one child is involved:

> In *Re P (Representation)* [1996] 1 FLR 486, C.A., the local authority proposed that six children should be taken into care with a view to adoptive placements. The eldest child "rejected the . . . proposals fervently and wished to have her own lawyer to put her case to the judge." The Court of Appeal held that the judge had been wrong to deny (on the ground that delay would be caused) this application since it would be impossible for a single advocate to support the local authority's care plan "and at the same time to mount an all-out attack on that care plan on behalf of the one dissenting child."

In cases in which the child is separately represented by a solicitor, the guardian may wish to be himself represented by a solicitor; but difficulties have been caused by the fact that there is no provision for legal aid in respect of such representation.

The guardian's report.   The guardian is required to file a report not less than seven days before the final hearing (Family Proceedings Courts (Children Act 1989) Rules 1991, r.11(7)) and that report will be served on all the parties. It is to be expected that the guardian will be asked to justify the recommendation made in the report by any party who is dissatisfied with it. The recommendation will obviously be of great importance, not least because it has been held that the court must give clear reasons if it decides not to adopt the guardian's recommendation: *Devon County Council v. G* [1985] FLR 1159, C.A. It has been suggested that courts often prefer the advice of the guardian to the plans of the local authority; and questions have been asked as to whether any such preference is justified: White, Carr and Lowe, *The Children Act in Practice* (2nd ed. 1995, at 246–247, paragraph 10.46).

Role of welfare officer and guardian compared.   The respective roles of welfare officer and guardian are very different; and the functions of the two have been well summarised by Butler-Sloss L.J.:

> ". . . each has a duty to report to the court; each has a duty to consider the welfare of the interests of the child; each may be cross-examined on any report which they give. However, a court welfare officer is not a party to the proceedings, whereas the guardian *ad litem*, through his representation on behalf of the child, is. Nonetheless, each has a similar duty to the court, which is to advise the court as to what is best for the child independently of the other parties to the proceedings . . . the distinction between the two is that the guardian has the added duty of representing the child in court and if necessary instructing legal representation for the child." (*Re S (A Minor) (Guardian ad Litem: Welfare Officer*) [1993] 1 FLR 110, C.A.).

Chapter 14

SHOULD THE COURT MAKE AN ORDER? THE WELFARE PRINCIPLE

The overriding consideration in deciding whether to make an order in private law proceedings about the child's upbringing, and if so what terms the order should contain, is whether the child's welfare would thereby be promoted; and the same considerations apply to the exercise of the court's discretion in care proceedings once the court passes from the threshold stage to the welfare stage.

A. CHILD'S WELFARE PARAMOUNT

Section 1 of the Children Act 1989 reasserts the principle that when a court determines any question with respect to the upbringing of a child or the administration of a child's property or the application of any income arising from it, the child's welfare shall be the court's paramount consideration.

Principle applied to all issues about children's upbringing

The courts sometimes have to decide dramatic cases of life and death:

> In *Re B (A Minor) (Wardship: Medical Treatment)* (1981) 3 FLR 117, C.A. the court had to decide whether a severely handicapped baby should be allowed to live or die. The court decided in favour of life.

In contrast,

> In *Re T (Wardship: Medical Treatment)* [1997] 1 FLR 502, C.A. a child born with a life-threatening liver defect had been given unsuccessful and painful surgery, but two consultant paediatricians recommended that a liver transplant be carried out. The mother refused her consent because she was not willing to permit her child to undergo once again the pain and discomfort of invasive surgery. The Court of Appeal overruled the judge's decision giving the doctors leave to carry out the transplant. The welfare of the child was indeed the first and paramount consideration; and although the parents' refusal to consent was an important

249

consideration to weigh in the balance the decision became one for the court. To prolong life was not the sole objective of the court, and on the evidence the court considered that it would not be in the child's interests to direct the mother to take on the total commitment when she did not agree with what was proposed; and the best interests of the child required that his future treatment be left in the hands of his devoted parents.

The fact that the court will form its own view on the evidence of what is in the child's interests is again exemplified in —

> *Re P (A Minor)* [1986] 1 FLR 272 where the court had to decide whether an abortion should be carried out on a 15-year-old, Shirley. Shirley was already caring for a baby born when she was 13. Shirley's parents objected to abortion on religious grounds and because they thought Shirley would live to regret having her child aborted; and they offered to care for Shirley's existing baby so that she could herself care for the new-born child. The court decided that Shirley's pregnancy be terminated to avoid risk of injury to her mental health and to avoid her own growing-up being endangered.

But often the issues are much less dramatic. For example:

> In *Re A (A Minor) (Wardship: Criminal Proceedings)* [1989] Fam. 103 a 16-year-old boy admitted a number of sexual offences; and the prosecution service proposed that a verbal caution be given. This would involve the boy admitting his guilt, and the caution would be recorded in police files for reference in any subsequent proceedings, and the boy's fingerprints would also be retained. The court concluded that it was in the child's interests to agree.

The routine business of the courts is to decide issues about where the child should live, whether there should be continued contact between a divorced parent and a child of the family (and if so, the frequency of that contact) and so on; and the general principle that such issues are decided by reference to the child's welfare as the decisive consideration is clearly established. But that does not mean that the child's welfare will determine the outcome of every matter which comes before the courts.

Limitations on application of the welfare principle

Although the wording of the Children Act 1989 is broad it is not all embracing: the principle that the child's welfare is the paramount consideration only applies where the child's *upbringing* is *directly* in issue. This means that there are three important qualifications on the applicability of the welfare principle:

(i) *Issue must relate to child's upbringing, etc.*
   Questions of where the child should live or be educated clearly do relate to the child's upbringing; but in *Re A and W (Residence Order: Leave to Apply)* [1992] Fam. 182, C.A. it was held that in granting or refusing an application for leave to apply for a section 8 order, the court was not determining such a question. The Court of Appeal held that such a question only arose when the court, having granted leave, heard the application. It seems therefore that the child's welfare will not be the paramount

consideration in many of the procedural issues which have to be resolved in the conduct of litigation.

Again, although the child's welfare *is* the paramount consideration in deciding questions about the *administration* of the child's property (and would therefore govern a decision about whether the child's money should be invested in buying a house where he could live or whether it would be better to invest the money and use the income to pay rent and so on) it is not the paramount consideration in deciding whether or not to make an order requiring a parent to maintain the child:

> In *K v. K (Minors: Property Transfer)* [1992] 2 FLR 220 the judge ordered a father to transfer to the mother for the benefit of the children the local authority flat in which the family had been living. But the effect of the order would be to deprive the father of the "right to buy" which was worth perhaps £50,000 to him and was his sole capital asset. The Court of Appeal held that the judge had been wrong in basing his order on the principle that the children's welfare was the paramount consideration.

The question of precisely what questions do relate to the child's upbringing can be a difficult one.

> In *A v. N (Committal: Refusal of Contact)* [1997] 1 FLR 533, C.A., a mother had been given endless opportunities to comply with sympathetic attempts made by the judge to meet her flimsy objections to the child having contact with the father, but had spurned them and flagrantly set herself upon a course of collision with the court's order. Eventually she was sentenced to imprisonment for contempt, but it was argued on her behalf that the judge in passing sentence should have regarded the child's welfare as paramount and not had recourse to a remedy once described (*per* Ormrod L.J., *Churchard v. Churchard* [1984] FLR 635, 638, C.A.) as "legalistic" and "futile". The Court of Appeal disagreed: in fact the judge had been fully mindful of the distressing consequences her mother's imprisonment would have for the child, but that had to be balanced against the importance to her of knowing her father as she grew up and the long term damage which she would otherwise suffer. But in any event Ward L.J. doubted (at p. 540) whether the child's welfare was the paramount consideration in deciding whether there should be a committal for breach of a court order.

Again —

> In *Re Z (A Minor) (Freedom of Publication)* [1996] 1 FLR 191, C.A.[1] the court accepted that the decision whether to prevent publication of material about a child and how the child was being brought up did not (although the exercise by

---

[1] The facts of which have been given at p. 200, above. The courts have not provided wholly satisfactory answers to the question of how to apply the paramountcy principle to cases where the welfare of more than one child is in issue, and the children's interests are not identical (for example, there may be a conflict between a fifteen-year-old mother and her baby or between two brothers: see *Birmingham City Council v. H (a minor)* [1994] 2 A.C. 212, H.L.; *F v. Leeds City Council* [1994] 2 FLR 60, C.A.; *Re T and E (proceedings: conflicting interests)* [1995] 1 FLR 851, Wall J.

the mother of her right to allow the disclosure of confidential matter relating to her child's medical treatment and education did) fall within the definition.

(ii) *The question of upbringing must be the central issue for decision.*

The House of Lords has decisively held that the child's welfare is not the governing factor where the question of upbringing arises only incidentally, for example in an application relating to the occupation of the family home:

> In *Richards v. Richards* [1984] A.C. 174, H.L. the question was whether the court had power to make an order excluding a husband from the matrimonial home on the basis that the wife (with whom, it was accepted, the child had to live) could no longer bear to be under the same roof. The trial judge made an order excluding the husband, since the child's welfare would better be promoted by living with her mother in the house than by living with her in unsatisfactory accommodation. The House of Lords held that the judge had been wrong: the child's upbringing was not the central issue before the court.

(iii) *Matter within court's jurisdiction.*

To say that the court can only make orders if the matter is properly before it and within its jurisdiction may seem a statement of the obvious; but there are two reasons why in the present context this general principle needs to be kept in mind. First — as already pointed out — there is no jurisdiction to make care or supervision orders unless certain specific criteria are satisfied. Secondly, the court has no power to make an adoption order (even if to do so would be manifestly in the child's best interests) unless the parents have consented or the court has dispensed with that agreement on one of the grounds set out in the Adoption Act 1976.

The welfare checklist

How is the court to determine what is in the child's interest? The Children Act 1989 contains a checklist of matters, and it was hoped in this way to achieve greater consistency and clarity in the application of the law. The "check-list" will be a useful *aide-memoire* in almost all cases; but the court is only *obliged* "to have regard in particular" to the matters specified in the checklist in two cases. First, where the application is opposed; and, secondly, where the application relates to a care or supervision order. For some years it seemed that the court's order — particularly if the court was a magistrates' Family Proceedings court composed of lay justices: see *R v. Oxfordshire County Council (Secure Accommodation Order)* [1992] Fam. 150 — might be liable to be set aside if the court had not made sufficient findings of fact about the specified matters, and directed itself about the weight to be attached to each of them and it is certainly the case that the checklist is an extremely useful and important discipline the use of which ensures proper consideration of all appropriate matters: *B v. B (Minor: Residence Order) The Times*, June 6, 1997. However, a Lord Justice of Appeal has stated:

> "Perhaps one should remember, that when one calls it a checklist, that it is not like the list of checks which an airline pilot has to make with his co-pilot, aloud one to the other before he takes off. The statute does not say that the judge has to read out the seven items in section 1(3) and pronounce his conclusion on each.

Sometimes judges will do that, maybe more often than not; but it is not mandatory": *H v. H (Residence Order: Leave to Remove from Jurisdiction* [1995] 1 FLR 529, 532 *per* Staughton L.J.

Matters referred to in the check-list. The matters to which the checklist specifically draws attention are as follows:

(a) *The ascertainable wishes and feelings of the child concerned (considered in the light of his age and understanding).*

The relevance of a child's own wishes has been reinforced by the *Gillick* decision[2]; and the weight which may be given to the views of a teenager is well demonstrated by the Court of Appeal decision in *Re P (A Minor) (Education)* [1992] 1 FLR 316, C.A.:

> Divorced parents disagreed about whether their 14-year-old son should go as a boarder to a public school or as a day pupil to an independent day school. The boy himself decided, after the first instance hearing, that he would prefer the day school; and the Court of Appeal held that this view should be respected. The courts (said Butler-Sloss L.J.) have "become increasingly aware of the import-ance of listening to the view of older children and taking into account what children say, not necessarily agreeing with what they want nor indeed doing what they want, but paying proper respect to older children who are at an age and have the maturity to make their minds up as to what they think is best for them, bearing in mind that older children very often have an appreciation of their own situation which is worthy of consideration by, and the respect of, the adults, and particularly including the courts. . . ." If the boy had been 11 the court would not have hesitated "to pack him off to boarding school" but the views of a 14-year-old carried more weight.

But the courts have emphasised that decisions in these cases are for the court, and not for the child; and in particular the court has been aware of the dangers of putting the burden of making a choice on the child:

> In *Adams v. Adams* [1984] 5 FLR 768, C.A., for example, Dunn L.J. remarked that the pressures on children were "quite sufficient when the marriage has broken down and one of the parents has left home without putting on the additional burden of being made to feel that they have to decide their own future".

It is true that the court must consider how realistic it would be to make the order:

> In *Re B (Change of Surname)* [1996] 1 FLR 791, C.A. — a case in which a mother appealed against a judge's refusal to give her leave to cause her children's surname to be changed to that of her present husband — Wilson J. said: "I agree . . . that orders nowadays which run flatly counter to the wishes of normal children aged 16, 14 and 12 are virtually unknown to family law. But in my view there is a big distinction between, for example, a residence or contact order made

---

[2] See at p. 170, above.

in the teeth of such opposition and the order made by the judge here . . . There is no point . . . in the court ordering children of that age to reside in a home where they will refuse to reside or to have contact with a parent with whom they will refuse to have contact". In effect, the court could not constrain the children (who would be known by whatever names they chose) but it could and would prevent the mother from formalising any change in name not least to avoid conveying the message that the children's father was of the past and not the present.

The fact that children's *wishes* can never be the paramount consideration is demonstrated by the cases in which the court has overruled the child's sincerely held views about medical treatment[3]; and the Court of Appeal has made it quite clear that there is no absolute prohibition even on making a child change his religion:

> In *Re R (A Minor) (Residence: Religion)* [1993] 2 FLR 163, C.A., a boy of nine had been living wholly within what the judge described as the "stifling" religious conditions of the Exclusive Brethren. In accordance with the beliefs of the Brethren the boy believed he should neither live with nor even see his father because the father had in the Brethren's view done wrong; and the boy believed that if he lived with his father (his only surviving parent) he would no longer be able to have anything to do with the Brethren whose beliefs he shared "with extraordinary depth of feeling for a boy of his age". The Court held that to be bound by the child's religious beliefs would amount to an abandonment of its duty to decide what the child's welfare, viewed objectively, required. A residence order in favour of the father was made accordingly.

How is the court to ascertain the wishes of the child? There are occasions when judges have themselves interviewed children in private, but this practice may give rise to difficulties, and in private law proceedings the court will rely on the investigation made by a welfare officer. In public law proceedings the child will often be represented by a guardian *ad litem*; and there are exceptional cases in which the court will allow a child to appear as a party without any adult intermediary: see *Re S (A Minor) (Independent Representation)* [1993] Fam. 263, C.A.

(b) *The child's physical, emotional and educational needs.*
The need to provide for a child's *physical* care is self-evident: the court would not, for example, make a residence order in favour of a parent who was homeless and had no prospect of obtaining housing. It is true that it has been said that in most cases "disadvantages of a material sort must be of little weight" (*Stephenson v. Stephenson* [1985] FLR 1140, 1148); but a basic minimum of physical provision is required.
In recent years the courts have attached very great weight to the children's *emotional* needs: see, for example, the facts of *J v. C* [1970] A.C. 668, H.L.[4], and contrast the attitude taken by the court 45 years earlier in *Re Thain*. Judges have been receptive to the findings of child psychiatrists; but it is important for law students to remember that courts should act on evidence and neither courts nor lawyers should profess an

---

[3] Discussed at p. 171, above.
[4] Set out at p. 166, above.

expertise in child development, etc., which they do not possess: *cf. C v. C (A Minor) (Custody: Appeal)* [1991] 1 FLR 223, C.A. and *B v. B (Minors) (Custody, Care and Control)* [1991] 1 FLR 202[5] both dealing with the impact of the sexual orientation of those caring for a child, but in only one of which was expert evidence available. Although specific evidence is desirable, it is clear that views conventionally accepted by psychiatrists on such matters as the need for continuity of care (see below) have been persuasive.

There was a time when the courts tended to apply presumptions — for example that young children should be with their mother, that girls approaching puberty should be with their mother, and that boys over a certain age should be with their father. Although the more modern approach (*Re S (A Minor) (Custody)*) [1991] 2 FLR 388, 392, C.A.) is not to make any such presumption, it seems that there is still a likelihood that the courts will think it natural that young children should be with their mothers notwithstanding the fact but there has been a change in the social order as a result of which more men care for children. As the House of Lords pointed out in the Scottish case of *Brixey v. Lynas* [1996] 2 FLR 499, 505:

"... the advantage to a very young child of being with its mother is a consideration which must be taken into account in deciding where lie its best interests ... It is neither a presumption nor a principle but rather recognition of a widely held belief based on practical experience and the workings of nature ... where a very young child has been with its mother since birth and there is no criticism of her ability to care for the child only the strongest competing advantages are likely to prevail."

It now seems to be accepted that a home with natural parents is in principle the best outcome, and there is accordingly a strong supposition that other things being equal it is in the child's best interests that it remain with the parents. But that "has to give way to particular needs in particular circumstances": *Re H (A Minor) (Custody: Interim Care and Control)* [1991] 2 FLR 109.

In considering questions of *education*, the court will often be primarily concerned with the dangers of uprooting a child from a school where satisfactory progress is being made (and see the facts of *Re P (A Minor) (Education)*, above). But there may be cases in which there is a clash of values to be resolved:

In *May v. May* [1986] 1 FLR 325, C.A. the question was whether two boys, aged six and eight, should live with their father or their mother. There was no conflict about the competence of either parent, but there was a conflict of values between them. The father attached importance to academic achievement, punctuality, tidiness, and giving assistance in the household. The mother and her cohabitant had, in contrast, a much more free and easy approach to life and to such issues as the amount of time that the children should spend working, the time they should spend watching television and so on. The Court of Appeal refused to upset the trial judge's decision that the children should live with the father.

---

[5] Both discussed at p. 257, below.

(c) *The likely effect on the child of any change in his circumstances.*

As mentioned above, one of the matters on which the views of child development specialists has been pervasive:

> In *Re Thain* [1926] Ch. 676 the question was whether a six-year-old girl who had been brought up from infancy by an uncle and aunt should be returned to the care of her father. The judge admitted that "the little girl will be greatly distressed and upset . . . but, at her tender age, one knows from experience how mercifully transient are the effects of partings of other sorrows . . . and I cannot attach much weight to this aspect of the case." But it is inconceivable that a judge should today express himself in these terms: the danger of psychological harm arising from a change in care is now widely recognised and forms part of the general knowledge and experience of the judges.

The fundamental rule for child care is now that stability is all important, and the courts will accordingly (as already mentioned) be extremely cautious in disturbing an arrangement which is well-established. Courts are accordingly reluctant to interfere with the status quo (*i.e.* the existing arrangements) unless there is clear justification for doing so.

(d) *The child's age, sex, background and any characteristics of his which the court considers relevant.*

It has already been mentioned that the courts no longer follow presumptions to the effect that very young children should be in the care of their mother, for example. Nevertheless — as the House of Lords decision in *Brixey v. Lynas* [1996] 2 FLR 506 has again emphasised — the children's age and sex obviously affects their needs; while the statutory reference to "background" may involve the court in a consideration of the child's cultural and religious background:

> In *Re P (A Minor) (Adoption)* [1990] 1 FLR 96, C.A., the mixed-race child had been cared for from infancy by a white European. The Court of Appeal held that the judge had been entitled, on the evidence presented to him, to conclude that the advantages to a child of mixed race of being brought up in a black family outweighed the importance of preserving the existing well-settled arrangements.

For many years custody disputes were often concerned with religious issues — with the soul, rather than the body, of the child: see *Re J M Carroll* [1931] 1 K.B. 317, 331, *per* Scrutton L.J. But in recent years the courts have become reluctant to pass judgment on the parents' belief; and religion only becomes relevant where, for example, adherence to a particular religious sect could cause the child emotional disturbance or physical harm: see, *e.g. Re R (A Minor) (Residence: Religion)* [1993] 2 FLR 163, C.A. (above).

(e) *Any harm which the child has suffered or is at risk of suffering.*

"Harm" is defined by the Children Act 1989 (ss.31(9), 105(1)) as "ill-treatment or the impairment of health or development"; and accordingly has a broad meaning:

> In *Re D (A Minor) (Contact)* [1993] 2 FLR 1, C.A. the mother was in fear of the father (who had caused disturbances at her home late at night and intimidated

her by bringing twelve associates to a court hearing and following her to work). Although it was said that the father was a reformed character, the mother was extremely anxious about the impact of visits to a two-year-old child by the father; and the court considered on the evidence that the mother's attitude to contact would put the child at serious risk of major emotional harm if she were compelled to accept it. The Court of Appeal refused to interfere with the judge's dismissal of the father's application for contact.

In recent years, allegations that one parent has been guilty of sexual abuse have increasingly been made; and it seems that Family Division judges may even be "sated with circuit sex abuse" cases: see, *per* Ward J., *Ravenscroft v. Rederiaktiebølaget Transatlantic* [1991] 3 All E.R. 73, 76. The court will have to weigh up the evidence as to whether such behaviour has occurred or not, and then determine the risk of harm on the basis of the facts which have been proved:

> In *Re M and R (minors) (child abuse: evidence)* [1996] 2 FLR 195, C.A. there were allegations of sexual abuse, but the court found that they had not been proved. Accordingly its order had to be based on the assumption that the child had not suffered sexual abuse, and in the absence of any other evidence, that he was not at risk of suffering such abuse in the future. Court decisions about children's upbringing are to be based on fact, not suspicion.

The fact that there is a proven risk of sexual abuse is only one element in the decision taking process. It has been said that in seeking to protect children from sexual abuse, society may cause other, and possibly greater, harm to the children it seeks to protect, *per* Balcombe L.J., *Re H (Minors) (Wardship: Sexual Abuse)* [1991] 2 FLR 416, C.A. Hence, the court must exercise its discretion, weighing in the balance all the relevant factors in order to assess the relative weight of advantages and risks to the child of the possible courses of action. For example:

> In *Re B (A Minor) (Child Abuse: Custody)* [1990] 2 FLR 317, Ward J., the Judge found that it was "overwhelmingly likely" that a four-year-old boy had seen sexual behaviour between his parents which he ought not to have seen, that he had seen indecent videos and that there was a serious lack of awareness on the part of the child's parents as to "quite where boundaries are to be drawn". However, notwithstanding the fact that the judge held that there was an unacceptable risk that the child had been subjected to sexual abuse and that on balance there was a risk of further abuse, that risk did not outweigh the advantage of preserving links with a "warm playful father" who had a good relationship with his son.

In several recent cases the courts have had to consider whether the fact that a parent has an homosexual orientation and relationship should affect his or her right to care for the child:

> In *C v. C (A Minor) (Custody: Appeal)* [1991] 1 FLR 223 the Court of Appeal held, on the facts, that a judge had been wrong to allow a mother (a prison officer who had formed a lesbian relationship with a prisoner) to have the care of a young girl rather than entrusting care of the girl to the father (who had re-

married and was living in a "classic husband and wife relationship"). However, the court emphasised that the decision depended on evidence, and that a court might well decide that a "sensitive, loving lesbian relationship is a more satisfactory environment for a child than a less sensitive or loving alternative".

In contrast:

> In *B v. B (Minors) (Custody, Care and Control)* [1991] 1 FLR 402, H.H.J. Callman, expert evidence about the impact of the parental relationship was available, and that evidence enabled the judge to deal with the concerns expressed by the welfare officer and in some of the earlier cases about the likely outcome. The mother, who was living in a lesbian relationship, was given the care of a two-and-a-half year-old child.

(f) *How capable each of his parents, and any other person in relation to whom the court considers the question to be relevant, is of meeting the child's needs.*
   For example;

> In *Dicocco v. Milne* (1983) 4 FLR 247 the court had given custody of a one-year-old boy to his father. The welfare report indicated that the mother had low standards of hygiene and mixed with what the health visitor believed to be the "wrong sort" of people; and that the child was often left unwashed and unprovided with clean or adequate nappies by an immature and, by implication, lazy mother. However, the Court of Appeal considered that there was no lack of love and affection on her part, no finding that she had neglected or ill-treated the child, and that the father's proposals would involve the child's care being divided between at least three and possibly four adults. Taking into account the fact that the child had been in the care of the mother and that accordingly should not be removed unless there were strong reasons for doing so, it was ordered that the child remain with the mother.

Sometimes, financial matters may be relevant:

> In *Re R (Residence Order: Finance)* [1995] 2 FLR 612 the child was with the father in the former matrimonial home and the paternal grandmother looked after her during the working week. The mother was also in full-time work, and had the child to stay most weekends and part of the holidays. The judge hearing the mother's application for a residence order was influenced by the probable consequences of the mother giving up her work and drawing state benefits; and made orders preserving the existing arrangements. The Court of Appeal refused to interfere.

(g) *The range of powers available to the court under the Children Act in the proceedings in question.*
   This provision requires the court to consider what it can achieve by exercising the powers which it has under the legislation. In particular, the court may want to consider imposing conditions on the making of a residence order, it may want to consider the desirability of making contact orders with other relatives — particularly bearing in mind the fact that the Act expressly permits the court to make an order if it considers

that it should do so "even though no . . . application has been made" for the order (section 10(1)(b)). The court may think it appropriate to make a Family Assistance Order.[6] The court may also consider making financial orders (although this power can only be exercised on application).

The flexibility of the Act in the private law sphere can be illustrated by a hypothetical case:

> H and W start divorce proceedings. They cannot agree on the arrangements to be made for the upbringing of their child, Caroline; and W's mother is concerned that she will lose touch with her granddaughter. The court might order that Caroline reside with W (residence order) but that she be allowed to stay with H at Christmas and Easter, and on alternate weekends, and with her grandmother for a week once a year (contact order). It could also order that Caroline be educated at a named convent (specific issue order), that H should not take her outside England and Wales for even a short period (prohibited steps order). The court could make these orders whether or not any application had been made: section 10(1)(b). It could also on application by W order H to pay Caroline's school fees (financial order).

In public law proceedings, the crucial question for the court will often be whether the child's welfare requires the making of a court order or supervision order, or whether to make a private law order (often a residence order) would better serve the child's interests.

B. THE WELFARE PRINCIPLE: SPECIFIC PROVISIONS

The Children Act contains two important provisions designed to safeguard the welfare of children in family proceedings: the first is concerned with the effect of delay on children, and the second — the so-called no-order presumption — requires the court to ask precisely how the making of an order could promote the child's welfare.

1. Delay harmful.   The Act provides (section 1(2)) that in any proceedings in which any question with respect to the upbringing of a child arises the court shall have regard to the "general principle" that any delay in determining the question "is likely to prejudice the welfare of the child". This general statement of principle is fleshed out by rules (section 11(1), (2)) requiring the court to draw up a timetable for determining the question and to give appropriate directions to ensure that the timetable is followed; and the Family Proceedings Rules 1991 (S.I. 1991 No. 1247) contain provisions enabling the court to discharge these duties (for example, where the rules lay down a time within which things should be done such as filing expert evidence that time cannot be extended by consent of the parties but only by court order; and the court is, in principle, to fix dates for resuming hearings which have been adjourned rather than leaving this to the parties: see Rules 4.14–16). As the official *Guide to the Children Act* puts it, the Act recognises that "the child's sense of time may be more

---

[6] See at p. 205, above.

acute than an adult's and that delay in determining the proceedings may in itself be harmful to the child" (paragraph 3.23), and that delay in court proceedings may put stress on all those involved which may rub off generally in damage to the child.

However, it is important to note that the legislation merely states a principle. It certainly does not seek to prescribe that a case should never be adjourned, or to prevent the court from a deliberate decision that delay might be beneficial: see *C v. Solihull Metropolitan Borough Council* [1994] 2 FLR 290, 304, *per* Ward J. Not only would any such attempt be futile, it would in fact be harmful to children's welfare. In particular, where the situation is still volatile after the breakdown of the parents' relationship, there may well be a strong case for moving slowly and carefully:

> In *S v. S (Minors: custody)*, *The Times*, June 7, 1991, C.A., the stability of a new relationship formed by the mother was not yet established; and the Court of Appeal considered that she had still to demonstrate that she was a stable parent, in the sense of being a mother willing to remain in one place and not move at a whim from one part of the country to another "according to the ups and downs of any relationship she happens to be maintaining". It had therefore been wrong to make a custody order in her favour; and the Court substituted what was in effect a temporary order with a view to review in three months' time.

There may also be cases in which taking time in exploring the possibility of a settlement may be well spent, particularly if contested court proceedings can thereby be avoided. The Act is aimed at minimising mere "drift" and the welfare of the child — which may well be served by purposive delay — is the paramount consideration. For example:

> In *Re G (A Minor)*, *The Times*, February 6, 1991, the parties had asked that a custody case be adjourned because they wanted more time. The judge however held that there was ample evidence, no indication that the hearing at a later date would produce a different decision, and that the need to decide children's cases within the shortest possible time would outweigh the importance of obtaining parental consent.

Apart from the question of what is desirable, there are often serious practical problems in avoiding delay. For example, what is to happen if the police are considering prosecuting a parent for abuse? What is to happen if decisions about the treatment appropriate for a child depend on findings as to whether suspicions that a child has been abused are well founded? Practical solutions to deal with such issues have been made (see in particular the judgment of Wall J. in *Re A and B (Minors) (No. 2)* [1995] 1 FLR 351); and a wide ranging enquiry into *Delay in Children Cases* has been carried out by Dame Margaret Booth.

2. The no order presumption. The Law Commission in its Report on Guardianship and Custody (Law Com. No. 172, 1988, paragraph 3.2) expressed concern over what it believed to be a common tendency to assume that some order about children should always be made in divorce and other matrimonial proceedings in effect, as "part of the package" provided by the legal system for litigants and clients. The Commission thought that there was a risk that orders allocating "custody" and "access" might polarise the parents' roles, and perhaps alienate the child. As Waite J. put it in *S v. S (Minors: custody)*, *The Times*, June 7, 1991, C.A. "once a father or a mother is given custody, they regard themselves as clothed with parental authority and a new chapter begins" notwithstanding the fact that in principle orders relating to the care of children are never "final" in any technical sense.

In an attempt to meet this concern, the Children Act provides (section 1(5)) that "where a court is considering whether or not to make one or more orders under this Act with respect to a child, it shall not make the order or any of the orders unless it considers that doing so would be better for the child than making no order at all." — (section 1(5)). In effect, the court therefore, needs to justify a decision to make an order, rather than making no order and leaving matters to be resolved from time to time if and when a court decision is required. The court must ask itself what, precisely, would be the effect of making an order, and whether this would or would not be positively in the child's interests; and the court should only make an order if it reaches a decision that an order would be better for the child than making no order.

There will obviously be many cases in which the court will find no difficulty in satisfying itself that the making of an order would be better for the child than not to do so. For example:

(a) *If there has been a dispute* which the court has had to resolve, the case for making an order would seem to be almost unanswerable. The dispute might be between divorcing parents about who should have the daily care of the child; or it might be between unmarried parents about whether or not the father should have any contact with his child, and —

In *Re S (Contact: Grandparents)* [1996] 1 FLR 158, C.A., the mother alleged that the father had sexually abused the child, but investigations into these allegations were protracted and eventually inconclusive. The mother resisted an application by the paternal grandparents for contact because she was fearful that the grandparents would bring the child into contact with the father. Notwithstanding a finding by the judge that the grandparents' application had overwhelming merit (and indeed that the child would suffer significant harm if contact were denied) the judge decided to make no order because he considered it likely that the mother would, with the passage of time, become reconciled to the grandparents having contact without the need for an order. The Court of Appeal held this to be wrong: the child's welfare clearly required that an order be made.

The court should also make an order if the child's welfare requires a parent to do what the court considers to be in the child's interest, notwithstanding that parent's opposition. For example:

In *Re S (Minors: Access)* [1990] 2 FLR 166, C.A. a Sikh mother was terrified of her husband who (she alleged) had beaten and attacked her. One child was living with the father, and the other with the mother, and the mother was "implacably opposed to any access which might lead her into contact with the father". The judge made no order for access. The Court of Appeal held that it was wrong in principle for a court to abrogate responsibility and not even try to ensure the continued contact with the child's welfare required merely because of the mother's implacable attitude.[7]

---

[7] See also *A v. N (Commital: Refusal of Contact)* [1997] 1 FLR 533, C.A., p. 251, above.

(b) *Giving formality to an agreement.*

Even when there is no dispute, an order may be desirable so as — in the Law Commission's words (paragraph 3.2) — "to confirm and give stability to the existing arrangements, to clarify the respective roles of the parents, to reassure the parent with whom the child will be living, and even to reassure the public authorities responsible for housing and income support that such arrangements have in fact been made." For example:

> In *B v. B (A Minor) (Residence Order)* [1992] 2 FLR 327, C.A., a teenage mother's child was being cared for by its grandmother. The court made a residence order in the grandmother's favour in part to confer parental responsibility on her — there had been problems with the local education authority, who questioned whether the grandmother could authorise school trips and so on — and in part to make it plain that the mother was not to remove the child merely because she found that her having a dependent child would improve her housing entitlement.

There may also be cases in which the fact that the making of a residence order will confer parental responsibility on (for example) a step-parent will be thought to justify doing so: see *Re H (Shared Residence: Parental Responsibility)* [1995] 2 FLR 883, C.A.

(c) There are *other more technical factors* which might incline the court towards making an order. For example, court orders may be useful if a child is removed to a foreign country, and indeed may be essential if recovery of the child is sought under the provisions of the European Convention on Recognition and Enforcement of Custody Decisions (as embodied in the Child Abduction and Custody Act 1985).

Finally, it should be noted that the "no order presumption" relates to the making of any order under the Act, including for example not only orders from the "menu" set out in section 8, but the making of a care or supervision order under Part III of the Act, and indeed the making of emergency orders.

Chapter 15

ADOPTION

Introduction

Adoption as a legal transplant? The legal theory of adoption as it now exists in English law is simple and dramatic. An adoption order transfers a child from one family to another, and once made the order is irrevocable:

> In *Re B (Adoption: Jurisdiction to Set Aside)* [1995] Fam. 239, C.A. a child was born in a nursing home in 1959 to a Kuwaiti Arab father and a Roman Catholic mother. The matron arranged for him to be adopted by an orthodox Jewish couple, who believed that the child was Jewish. When they discovered this to be untrue they arranged for him to be received into the Jewish faith and continued to bring him up in the Jewish tradition. When he grew up, the boy decided to emigrate to Israel but (apparently because of his appearance) was suspected of being a spy and was declared *persona non grata*. He made enquiries into his origins (see p. 267 below) and traced his birth father in Kuwait, but he could not find work in Kuwait or in any other Arab state. He felt that he did not belong to either the Jewish or Arab communities, and he applied to the court to set aside the adoption order. The President of the Family Division (whose decision was upheld by the Court of Appeal) refused to do so: to allow a mistake such as had occurred in this case to invalidate an adoption order would undermine the whole basis on which legal adoption in the country was founded, *i.e.* that the child became the child of the adopters for all legal purposes and save in certain prescribed and restricted circumstances an order once made was irrevocable.

The legal machinery whereby the transfer is effected is to vest parental responsibility for a child in the adopters and to extinguish the parental responsibility of the birth parent: Adoption Act 1976, s.12(1). The same Act provides (s.39) that the effect of an adoption order is that the child is thenceforth treated as if he or she had been born as a child of the adopters' marriage and not as the child of anyone else; and it declares that the legislation prevents an adopted child from being illegitimate: AA 1976, s.39. In principle, therefore, the adopted child is treated for succession purposes as a member of his adoptive family and not of his birth family, and a foreign child adopted by a British citizen becomes a British citizen: British Nationality Act 1981, s.1(5).

There are certain statutory modifications of the general principle. For example, the prohibited degrees of marriage between the adopted child and the birth family are unaffected by the adoption; and although the child is brought within the prohibited degrees in relation to his or her adoptive parents the legislation does not create any prohibitions on marriage with other members of the adoptive family (so that, surprisingly, an adopted child may legally marry his adoptive sister, for example, not to say his adoptive grandmother). But notwithstanding this exception the general principle remains clear — albeit, as we shall see, increasingly controversial in the light of social, demographic and other changes which have dramatically affected the use made of adoption.

Changing concepts of adoption.   Although adoption (in the sense of enabling people who cared for children to have some legal security for their relationship) has only formed part of English law since 1926, the policy of the law has changed over the years more than is often realised. The 1926 Act was limited in scope (amounting to little more than a process whereby, with minimal safeguards, the courts registered and ratified a private contract giving the adopters some but by no means all of the legal attributes of parentage). The decisive shift towards the legal transplant model did not come until 1949, when the Adoption Act introduced a procedure under which the court could make an adoption order without the mother knowing the adopters' identity; and the law came to accept the desirability of complete secrecy so that the child and the birth parents could never subsequently re-establish contact.

Adoption as a means of acquiring a substitute family.   The law certainly seemed to meet a need: the number of adoption orders made each year increased steadily to a peak of 25,000 in 1968. It seems that adoption was at that time seen primarily as a method whereby a healthy, white (and usually illegitimate) baby — half the children adopted in 1968 were babies less than a year old — was placed with a childless couple who would bring him or her up as their own child. Specialist agencies (traditionally voluntary agencies often with a religious inspiration) were active in supplying the need to ensure that pregnant women gave birth in secrecy to children who were then placed for adoption, usually with infertile couples who would often conceal the child's origins from the outside world and indeed from the child.

Changing patterns of adoption.   In the past thirty years, however, a number of factors have significantly influenced the use to which adoption is put and the extent to which it is used. The number of babies available for adoption in the typical pattern described above has been greatly reduced, in part by the practice of terminating unwanted pregnancies, and in part by the greater readiness of society (at least until very recently) to accept the lone parent and to support her and her child by welfare and housing benefits. It is not surprising that there should have been a sharp decline in the total number of orders made each year: in 1995 only 5,317 of adoption orders were made (see *Judicial Statistics Annual Report* 1995, Cm. 3290, Table 5.4); whilst the number of "traditional" adoptions has declined even more sharply: in 1991 the number of children adopted soon after birth had fallen to under 900 (only 12 per cent of the total) and there were even fewer adoptions of illegitimate children by people neither of whom was a parent.

Eligibility to adopt and be adopted.   The basic rules about who may adopt and be adopted under English law are laid down by statue:

(i) *The person to be adopted.*

The Act (AA 1976, s.12(5)) provides that the person to be adopted must be under 18 years of age and must never have been married. In this way, English law makes it clear that it is concerned with providing for a child "the social and psychological benefits of truly belonging to a family" *(Re R (Adoption)* [1967] 1 W.L.R. 34, 41, Buckley J.). In contrast, adoption is used in many civil law countries to establish inheritance rights.

But there is nothing to stop the adoption of a "child" who is nearly 18 if in all the circumstances that will be for his benefit and the other relevant conditions are satisfied:

> In *Re D (A Minor) (Adoption Order: Validity)* [1991] 2 FLR 66, C.A., an order was made in respect of a child just six days before his 18th birthday. The child, who was severely handicapped and had a comprehension age of four, had been in the care of foster-parents throughout his childhood, but latterly his mother had conducted a campaign of harassment against them and had had to be restrained by injunction. The foster-parents applied for an adoption order, apparently because the injunction would terminate when the child reached majority and they would then be again exposed to harassment. The Court of Appeal held that it was not necessary to show that the making of an adoption order would benefit the child during the six days before he became an adult; the fact that adoption would confer substantial benefits on him was sufficient.

(ii) *Who may adopt?*

An adoptive parent must be at least 21 years of age (although a parent adopting his or her own child need only be 18 years of age).

An adoption order may be made in favour of a married couple, but with that important exception an adoption order may not be made on the application of more than one person. The result is that it is not possible for a brother and sister or an unmarried couple jointly to adopt a child. However, in appropriate cases, the court may make an adoption order in favour of one cohabiting partner and a joint residence order in favour of the two partners:

> In *Re AB (Adoption: Joint Residence)* [1996] 1 FLR 27, Cazalet J., a five-year-old child in local authority care had been placed with a couple who (although unmarried) had lived together in a wholly committed relationship for more than twenty years and had a happy, united and responsible family life.
>
> In *Re W (a minor) (Adoption: Homosexual Adopter)*, *The Times*, May 21, 1997, Singer J., it was held that an adoption order could, in principle, be made in favour of a single applicant, cohabiting in a homosexual relationship.

The Act provides that if a sole applicant is married an adoption order can only be made if the court is satisfied that the applicant's spouse cannot be found, or is incapable by reason of ill health of applying, or that the spouses have separated and are living apart and that the separation is likely to be permanent. Rather oddly, perhaps, these rules do not prevent an adoption order being made in favour of a married couple who are separated:

> In *Re M (Adoption: Non-Patrial)* [1997] 1 FLR 132, Johnson J., a married couple had adopted a child in El Salvador and brought him to their home in this country. Since the El Salvador order was not recognised by English law, the couple applied for an adoption order here but by the time of the hearing they had separated. The judge made an adoption order, to do so was not prohibited; and on the unusual facts there would be real advantage to the child (not least in that the arrangements for his future would have to be reviewed by the court hearing a divorce application). Indeed on the facts, there was no other option available which would not involve subjecting the child to the risk of considerable harm.

It must be emphasised that these are the minimum requirements laid down by law about the personal attributes of the parties to an adoption: no adoption order can be made in other cases. But in practice, adoption agencies, in the exercise of their discretion in arranging placements, are likely to apply very much more demanding tests. The law does not, for example, set an upper age limit for adopters, but in practice few agencies will place a young and healthy child for adoption with a couple unless the husband is aged well under forty and the wife is under 35. (The situation may be different if the child has "special needs").

Adoption increasingly an aspect of local authority care work.   The role of adoption agencies and the nature of the work they carry out has also changed. In one sense, the Children Act 1975 reinforced the trend towards specialism by outlawing the making of arrangements for adoption by private individuals (typically doctors or maternity home proprietors); but the 1975 Act also gave effect to the policy that adoption should be integrated with other child care services and imposed on every local authority a duty to establish and maintain a comprehensive adoption service. The result has been that although voluntary agencies still play a significant part in arranging adoptions, adoption services have increasingly become regarded as merely one facet of local authorities' child care work; and, in this context, the concern to achieve permanency and security for children who have come into local authority care because their relationship with their birth parents has broken down (or never existed) has had an important impact. Adoption has increasingly come to be seen as the appropriate solution for many children taken into care by local authorities under care orders (see *per* Hale J., *Berkshire County Council v. B* [1997] 1 FLR 171, 176, F); and this has been equally true for children who have traditionally been regarded as difficult to place, for example because they were of mixed race, handicapped or had emotional or behavioural problems. As part of the same trend, adoption is now often used for older children: in 1992, 12 per cent of adoption orders were in respect of children aged 10 or over; and 88 per cent of all adoptions were of children in the higher age groups (*i.e.* over one year old).

Relative adoptions.   Another factor has much affected the traditional image of adoption. This was that in the 1960s and 1970s adoption became widely used by relatives and in particular, a very large proportion of all adoptions (nearly 70 per cent in 1975) were in favour of a parent and step-parent. The popularity of such adoptions was founded to a substantial extent on the wish of those who had re-married to integrate the child — usually the mother's child — for all legal purposes into the new family created by her re-marriage. The factual situation in such cases was far removed from that on which the traditional notion of adoption had been based; and in 1972 a Government Committee (the Houghton Committee) expressed concern about the dangers of adoption by relatives. In particular, the Committee was concerned that adoption might be used to conceal the truth about the child's parentage (so that the child adopted by her grandparents might be led to think that her mother was her sister). Another important concern was that adoption by a step-parent might be used to sever the child's relationship — in law and in fact — with the birth parent after divorce. These concerns were influential and the Children Act 1975 introduced specific provisions designed to discourage adoptions by step-parents and relatives unless there were special circumstances making adoption desirable in the interest of the child's welfare. But these provisions were, in practice, found to be unsatisfactory and not easy to apply; and they have been repealed by the Children Act 1989. Step-parent adoptions now account for more than half of all adoptions.

Adoption: secrets and lies?   The changing use to which adoption is put has created a tension between the so-called "total transplant" concept of adoption, still firmly embedded in the statutory framework, and practical reality. In particular, it has come to be questioned whether the law should not permit, or even in some cases facilitate, the retention by an adopted person of legal links with the birth family. Since 1949 the legislation has been formulated on the assumption that there would be no contact at all. Such contact would (it was thought) be undesirable not only in the child's interest, but in the interests both of the adopting parents (who might find themselves harassed by the birth parents) and of the birth mother (who might have agreed to place her child for adoption only on the basis that she could conceal from everyone — including perhaps her husband — the fact that she had ever given birth to a child).

To meet this demand, procedures enabling adoptive parents to conceal their identity from the birth parents were developed and became widely used. But it has for long been regarded as good practice for a child to be brought up with knowledge that he had been adopted and about the circumstances leading up to the adoption; and adoptive parents are given written background information about the child and the birth family in an attempt to help them bring up the child in the knowledge of the adoption from an early age. Regulations now provide that adopters should be advised to make the information available to the child "at a time when they consider appropriate but not later than the child's eighteenth birthday": Adoption Agencies and Children (Arrangements for Placement and Reviews) (Miscellaneous Amendments) Regulations S.I. 1997 No. 649, reg. 2(13). But it has increasingly been recognised that many adopted people wish to go further and to trace their genetic origins; and it has also come to be realised that, sometimes, the birth parents wish to know what has become of the child.

The Children Act 1975 began the process of removing some of the secrecy from the adoption process, and introduced measures whereby adopted children might be able to trace their birth parents: on attaining the age of 18, an adopted child is now entitled to access to the original birth records which will reveal his or her original name and parentage in so far as that is recorded: AA 1976, s.51.

The philosophy that birth parents might also wish to know what had become of their children was recognised by provisions in the Children Act 1989 which established the legislative framework for an adoption contact register. Relatives of an adopted person who wish to contact him or her can have their details recorded in the register, and the information will be passed on if the adopted person has given notice indicating a wish to contact relatives: AA 1976, s.51A (as inserted by Children Act 1989, Schedule 10, paragraph 21). But the courts have strongly resisted any suggestion that the Registrar-General's records (which could reveal the child's birth parentage) should be opened in any other circumstances than are either provided by the 1989 Act or can properly be described as "truly exceptional" (for example, to warn of the need for genetic screening): see *D v. Registrar-General* [1997] 1 FLR 713.

These provisions have little relevance to the increasing number of cases where an adoption order is made in respect of an older child. In these cases, the child will often continue to have links with the birth family: the adoption order cuts the legal tie between the child and his birth family, but it does not and could not necessarily cut the factual tie. All that it can do is to confer on the adoptive parents the same right as any other parent would have to exercise parental authority by restraining (or permitting) contact between the child and others. In some cases the birth parents (and others, such as the child's grandparents) have evidently been concerned that the adopters might prevent contact, and have asked the court to make legally binding provision for continuing contact: see p. 287, below.

The benefits and disadvantages of destroying the secrecy once attached to parentage has been the subject of public discussion in part prompted by the announcement that a leading Labour MP, Mrs Clare Short, had established contact with the son she had placed for adoption some thirty years before, and by the successful film, *Secrets and Lies*. No doubt in many cases it will be beneficial to all concerned to facilitate contact between the adopted person and the birth family; but it appears that some birth parents have suffered grave distress when traced and approached by an adopted person, and the disturbing facts of *R v. Registrar General, ex parte Smith* [1991] 1 FLR 255, C.A. show all too clearly the dangers which disclosure and openness may create:

> The applicant was a patient in Broadmoor Hospital who had brutally and sadistically murdered a fellow prisoner (apparently under the delusion that the victim was his adoptive mother). Disturbed and unstable, he continued to express hatred for his adoptive parents. He exercised his statutory right to seek the information which would enable him to trace his birth certificate, and thereby to be in a position to trace his birth parents. There were real fears that he would seek to harm the birth parents whom he blamed for his problems; and the Court of Appeal accepted that, in the circumstances, it had been right to deny him the statutory right of access to his birth certificate.

Adoption: a matter for social workers or the courts?

One of the most remarkable features of the adoption process in England is the way in which it has been transformed into a matter in which most of the effective decisions are taken by social workers. In 1926 and for some years afterwards the activities of adoption agencies in arranging adoption were viewed with some suspicion; and in 1939 the Adoption of Children (Regulation) Act imposed restrictions on those who arranged adoptions. But, as we have already seen, by the mid-seventies it was the private placement which was viewed with suspicion; and it is now a criminal offence for anyone other than an adoption agency to make arrangements for the adoption of a child or to place a child for adoption: AA 1976, s.11. For these purposes an adoption agency is either a local authority or an adoption society (such societies being usually described as "voluntary agencies"); and a great deal of adoption work is in fact done by local authority social services departments. It is the adoption agency which does most of the investigation and counselling now required by legislation; and as a result the role of the court is in most cases symbolic rather than in any real sense judicial.

Although it remains the case that only the court can make an adoption order, the court cannot itself carry out any adequate investigation of the issues which arise in deciding whether the making of an adoption order would be for the benefit of the child. Accordingly, it is necessary for these investigations to be made by skilled experts whose assessment will be available to the court; and adoption agencies — whether local authorities or voluntary agencies — have a vital part to play in these matters. Their duties are now prescribed in detail by rules (the Adoption Agencies Regulations 1983 as amended by S.I. 1997 No. 649) while other rules, notably the Adoption Rules 1984, prescribe in detail the content of the reports which must be provided to the court. It is important to have some understanding of these procedures, not only because a great deal of adoption practice is governed by them, but also to enable the reader to make a comparison with the (generally much less elaborate) procedures applicable to other cases concerned with the upbringing of children. Before examining the procedures, however, something must be said about another aspect of the adoption legislation — the concern that legal adoption might be used as a cloak to conceal trafficking in children by establishing a market in which they could be bought and sold. The legislation has two provisions designed to minimise this risk: first, the prohibition on making payments in connection with adoption; and secondly the rule, already referred to, prohibiting placements of children other than those arranged by adoption agencies.

(i) *Illegal payments, etc.*

Ever since 1926, the law has prohibited the making of payments or the giving of rewards in connection with adoption; and section 57 of the Adoption Act 1976 now provides in very broad language that it is not lawful to make or give to any person any "payment or reward for or in consideration of" the handing over of a child with a view to the child's adoption and a number of other steps in the adoption process. The courts have however been prepared to adopt a purposive approach to the interpretation of this provision. In some cases they have held that the payment is not illegal unless the motive was commercial or profit directed:

> In *Re Adoption Application: Surrogacy AA 212/86* [1987] Fam. 81, Latey J. a woman, who wanted to help childless couples, agreed to bear a child under a surrogacy agreement. The commissioning parents undertook to pay her £10,000 (representing her loss of earnings and her expenses in connection with the pregnancy). The judge held that this was not a payment or reward for the purposes of the Adoption Act provisions since the parties only began to think of adoption after the payment had been made.

Not all courts have accepted that construction (see *Re AW (Adoption Application)* [1993] 1 FLR 62, Bracewell J.); but the legislation empowers the court to authorise the making of payments (AA 1976, s.57(3)) and it seems to be accepted that this power can be exercised after the event:

In *Re MW (Adoption: Surrogacy)* [1995] 2 FLR 759, Judge Callman, a married couple agreed to pay a woman £7,500 to bear a child for them. The court held that if these payments were (contrary to the decision in *Re Adoption Application: Surrogacy AA 212/86* above) within the statutory prohibition, the welfare of the child pointed so strongly in favour of adoption that the making of the payments should be retrospectively authorised.

But the court will be not be prepared to authorise a payment which would in effect ratify the sale of a child:

In *Re C (A Minor) (Adoption Application)* [1993] 1 FLR 87, Booth J., a long-distance lorry driver and his wife wished to have an adopted child, but knew they would face difficulties in having a child placed with them by an agency. They were introduced to a pregnant woman and devised a complex and wholly deceitful plan whereby the lorry driver pretended to be the child's father so that (they believed) the placement (which actually took place in the car-park of the maternity hospital) would not be illegal. The couple paid sums of £2,000 or more to the mother for her to hand over the child and with a view to ensuring that the mother kept to the false story. The judge held that to authorise such a payment would sweep away the protection given by the Act to children. Accordingly, the court could not make an adoption order even if it would otherwise have been prepared to do so: Adoption Act 1976 s.24(2).

There are some exemptions from this bar on making payments (Adoption Act 1976, s.57(3A) and in some cases adoption agencies may pay allowances to those adopting children — particularly if their doing so results in the loss of local authority payments they had received as foster parents: Adoption Act 1976, s.57A.

The legislation also contains prohibitions against the publication of advertisements by parents and prospective adopters: Adoption Act 1976, s.58.

(ii) *Independent placements prohibited.*

As we have already seen, independent placements by persons such as nursing home matrons are now unlawful; and the reader who has been reminded of the facts of *Re B (Adoption: Jurisdiction to Set Aside)* [1995] Fam. 239, C.A.[1] will readily understand the view that adoption placement is a matter for the specialist. But the bar does not extend to a private placement made with a "relative" of the child, a term which includes the father of an illegitimate child but not (Adoption Act 1976, s.11(1), s.72; *Re S (Arrangements for Adoption)* [1985] FLR 579), a great-uncle. But once again (although in this case there is no express statutory basis for this practice) it has been held that the fact that a placement is illegal does not prevent the court from making an adoption order if it considers that the child's welfare would be best promoted by doing so:

In *Re MW (Adoption: Surrogacy)* [1995] 2 FLR 759, Judge Callman, a married couple entered into a surrogacy agreement and the husband successfully impregnated the mother. The child was handed over to the husband and wife and flourished in their care. But the mother wanted to remain in contact with the

[1] See at p. 263, above.

child, and opposed the husband's and wife's application for an adoption order. It was held that the wife was (as in effect a stepmother) not within the statutory definition of "relative"; but in all the circumstances the arguments in favour of adoption were so strong that the court made the order.

The adoption process: The Adoption Agency's duties.

Statute (AA 1976, s.6) provides that in reaching any decision relating to an adoption of a child the Agency must have regard to all the circumstances, first consideration being given to the need to safeguard and promote the welfare of the child throughout childhood. Agencies are specifically required "so far as practicable" to ascertain the wishes and feelings of the child regarding the decision and give due consideration to them, having regard to the child's age and understanding: AA 1976, s.6. This general duty is elaborated in the specific procedures laid down by the Adoption Agencies Regulations 1983 (as amended in a number of significant respects by the Adoption Agencies and Children (Arrangements for Placement and Reviews) (Miscellaneous Amendments) Regulations, S.I. 1997 No. 649):

(a) **Investigation, reports and counselling.**   The Agency has extensive duties to obtain reports about the child, his birth parents, and the prospective adopters. For example, it must obtain a health history covering the birth parents and their family, giving details of serious or inherited or congenital disease and the Agency must find out the birth parents' wishes and feelings about adoption. The Agency must make a full investigation into the circumstances of the prospective adopters (including such matters as their financial position, and their previous experience of caring for children), and it must assess their ability to bring up an adopted child throughout childhood. There must be a medical report, which will include details of any daily consumption of alcohol, tobacco and habit-forming drugs. The child must be medically examined, and a detailed account produced dealing with such matters as personality and social development, educational attainment, the extent of the relationship with the birth family, and the child's wishes and feelings in relation to adoption. The Agency must also provide a counselling service for the birth parents, the child, and prospective adopters. (For an example of what this may mean in practice see *Re T (A Minor) (Adoption: Validity of Order)* [1986] 1 FLR 31).

(b) **Reference to the adoption panel.**   In an attempt to introduce a further check on unsuitable placements the Regulations require the Agency to establish a panel including social workers, a medical adviser, and at least three independent members. Wherever reasonably practicable the "independent persons" must include an adoptive parent and an adopted adult.

The Agency must include in the written report placed before the Adoption Panel its assessment of the prospective adopter's suitability to be an adoptive parent, but — presumably in an attempt to meet criticisms that suitable applicants were being rejected by social workers on trivial grounds — that assessment must first have been copied to the prospective adopter, who is given an opportunity to make observations about it.

The panel must consider all the information and reports referred to above, and may seek other relevant information, and it must obtain legal advice about each case. It is then for the panel to consider whether adoption is in the best interests of the child, whether a prospective adopter is suitable to be the adoptive parent, and whether he or she is suitable to be the adoptive parent of the particular child.

The Agency must not take a decision on these matters until it has taken account of the panel's recommendations. But it the Agency decides that the prospective adopter is unsuitable, the agency must notify him or her, provide reasons, and invite representations (which will be passed on to the Adoption Panel, which will once again consider the case and make a recommendation to the Agency). Throughout this complex decision taking process it is for the panel to recommend, but it is for the Agency to decide.

(c) **Placement.** If, but only if, an Agency has decided in accordance with these procedures, and after considering the recommendations of the adoption panel, that a prospective adopter would be a suitable adopter for a particular child, it may make written proposals to the prospective adopter for a placement. This proposal will be accompanied by written information about the child, his or her personal history and background, including religion and cultural background, and the child's current state of health.

If the prospective adopter accepts the proposal, the child may be "placed for adoption" — but it will be appreciated that this will often be simply a change of legal status in that the child will already often be living with the prospective adopters. Written notice of the placement must be given to the child's parents. Where the child is already in the care of the prospective adopters (for example because he has been fostered with them), they too must be given written notice. The Agency also has duties to supervise the placement, to carry out periodic reviews of such matters as the child's needs and the working of any arrangements for contact and to give advice and assistance.

Perhaps fortunately, it has been held (*Re T*, above) that the complex provisions regulating placement are directory rather than mandatory, and that accordingly failure to comply with them will not invalidate the adoption application.

Once the child has been placed, it is for the prospective adopter to apply to the court for an adoption order; and the Agency is obliged to review the case at least every six months until an application is made. The Agency may remove a child at any time after placement; and the court has no power to intervene unless and until the applicant has filed an adoption application (in which event leave of the court is required): see *Re C and F (Adoption: Removal Notice)* [1997] 1 FLR 190, C.A.

Cases where no agency involved. Notwithstanding the policy that all adoption cases be channelled through Adoption Agencies, there are still many adoption applications in which no Agency has previously been involved — particularly in the case of adoption by step-parents and relatives, and in the increasing number of cases in which a child is "placed" for adoption in a foreign country but is then brought to this country to complete the legal procedures. In these cases, the applicant must give notice of intention to apply for adoption to the local authority in whose area they have their home; and the local authority will perform investigatory and reporting functions along the lines described above. There has been a sharp increase in the number of cases in which children are brought to this country with a view to adoption, and it seems that the demands on local authorities are, in some areas, imposing considerable strains on the resources available: *R v. Secretary of State for Health, ex parte Luff* [1992] 1 FLR 59.

THE ADOPTION PROCESS: THE COURT'S ROLE

Although it is clear that most of the effective steps in relation to adoption are taken by social workers and others, it remains a fundamental principle that an adoption order can only be made by a court. Any private agreement purporting to transfer parental responsibility in respect of a child would have been void at common law, and would now be invalid because of the prohibition imposed by the Children Act 1989 s.2(1) against a person with parental responsibility surrendering or transferring it.

Adoption orders can only be made by an "authorised court" as defined by section 62 of the Adoption Act 1976. In cases not involving a foreign element, the magistrates' Family Proceedings Court, the county court and the High Court, all fall within the definition and have jurisdiction to deal with adoption applications. In practice, in recent years the great majority of applications have been to the county court. The Children (Allocation of Proceedings) Order 1991 (S.I. 1991 No. 1677) provides for transfers between the different courts, and contested applications in the county court will normally be heard at a specialist Family Hearing Centre.

Adoption applications as "family proceedings". Adoption proceedings must be started by the proposed adopter issuing an application in the form prescribed by the relevant rules. Such proceedings constitute "family proceedings" within the definition in Children Act 1989, see section 8(4)(d). This has the consequence that the court may, whether it makes an adoption order or not, make a contact residence or other "section 8 order" (and, indeed, it may do so whether or not any application for a section 8 order has been made: C.A. 1989 s.10(1)(b)). The converse is not true: the court cannot make an adoption order except in proceedings started with that end in view, although it can in Children Act proceedings authorise the *placement* of the child for adoption.

Deciding whether adoption in child's interests. The Adoption Act 1976 provides that:

> "In reaching any decision relating to the adoption of a child a court or adoption agency shall have regard to all the circumstances, first consideration being given to the need to safeguard and promote the welfare of the child throughout his childhood; and shall so far as practicable ascertain the wishes and feelings of the child regarding the decision and give due consideration to them, having regard to his age and understanding".

How is the court to be in a position to decide whether adoption would promote the child's welfare? The court will be supplied with a detailed report (commonly called a Home Study Report) prepared by the Adoption Agency (or, in non-agency cases, such as adoption by relatives, by the local authority). The report will deal with the child, his natural parents, and the prospective adopters: for example, it must comment on the stability of the prospective adopters' marriage, give particulars of their home and living conditions and details of income and living standards, the prospective adopters' reasons for wishing to adopt the child, and their "hopes and expectations for the child's future": Adoption Rules 1984, Schedule 2. Medical reports will also be before the court.

If it appears that a parent is unwilling to agree to the application (or there are special circumstances) the court may also appoint a guardian *ad litem* (whose duties are laid down in the Rules: Adoption Rules 1984 r.6) to investigate and report.

In order that the child should have had time to settle in the home, for the applicants to adjust to their new role as parents, and in an attempt to ensure that the Home Study Reports are based on a full opportunity to make an assessment of the relationship between the child and the prospective adopters, the Adoption Act 1976 provides that an order must not be made unless the child is at least 19 weeks old, and has at all times during the preceding 13 weeks had his home with the applicants or one of them. If the child has not been placed with the applicants by an adoption agency (for example, a fosterchild or a child brought to this country from overseas) a longer period of 12 months is required unless the applicant or one of the applicants is a parent, step-parent or relative. There is an overriding rule that no order may be made unless the court is satisfied that the adoption agency or local authority has had sufficient opportunities to see the child with the applicants together in the home environment: AA 1976, s.13(3). Of course, sometimes the Home Study Report's findings are falsified by events:

> In *Re W (Foreign Child: Adopters Separated)* [1996] 2 FLR, Johnson J., the local authority's social worker had reported that the applicants' marriage was stable. Shortly thereafter the applicants separated.

Again:

> In *D v. D (Nullity)* [1979] Fam. 70, Dunn J., the Church of England Children's Society suggested that a priest and his wife should adopt children they had previously fostered. Unknown to the guardian *ad litem* or the judge, the marriage was in difficulties (the wife having refused to consummate it, and the husband suffering from frustration) and the couple disagreed about the children's upbringing. An adoption order was made. The marriage broke down and the husband petitioned for and obtained a decree of nullity.

Preventing removal of the child. The requirement that the child live with the prospective adopters for some time before the court considers the application might allow a birth parent to exercise parental authority, remove the child, and thereby prevent the prospective adopters satisfying the condition that the child should have his home with the applicants. The Adoption Act 1976 contains three provisions intended to minimise this risk. First, a parent or guardian who has once agreed (even informally: *Re T (A Minor) (Adoption: Validity of Order)* [1986] 2 FLR 31, C.A.) to the making of an adoption order is not entitled, so long as an adoption application is pending, to remove the child from the home of the person with whom the child is living without leave of the court: AA 1976, s.27(1). Secondly, if an application to free a child for adoption is pending, no parent or guardian of the child may remove the child from his or her home without the leave of the court: section 27(2). This provision applies even where there has never been any parental agreement to the freeing. It will be noted that, curiously, there is no prohibition against people with parental responsibility other than the parent or guardian (such as a relative in whose favour a residence order has been made) exercising that responsibility so as to remove the child. Thirdly, if a child has had his home with a person for five years, and that person starts adoption proceedings or gives written notice of his intention to do so, the child must not be removed without leave of the court: AA 1976, s.28. This last provision is particularly widely drawn: for example, it would prevent the local authority which has placed a child with foster parents removing him or her if the foster-parents having cared for the child for five years apply against the authority's wishes for adoption.

Adoption must promote child's welfare; and parental agreement necessary

When a court determines questions relating to the upbringing of a child, the child's welfare is, in principle, the court's paramount consideration: Children Act 1989, s.1. Adoption is different; and the difference of legal concept between adoption on the one hand and other methods of providing long-term substitute care for children has been summarised as follows (see *J v. C* [1970] A.C. 668, H.L. *per* Lord Upjohn at p. 930)):

(i) An adoption order is permanent and irrevocable; other orders dealing with the child's upbringing can be varied at any time.

(ii) Adoption affects legal status and thus such matters as the child's succession rights and citizenship. Other court orders dealing with upbringing do not have such consequences.

(iii) Adoption severs the legal family ties between the child and the birth parents and their relatives. Once an adoption order has been made, the parents lose the *right* even to apply for contact (see *Re R (A Minor) (Adoption: Access)* [1991] 2 FLR 78, C.A.) although, like anyone else, the birth parents could seek leave to apply to the court for contact with the child.

For these reasons, although as stated above the Act (s.6) provides that the court is to give first consideration to the need to safeguard and promote the welfare of the child throughout his or her childhood, that provision does not override the fundamental principle that an adoption order is not to be made unless each parent or guardian of the child "freely, and with full understanding of what is involved, agrees unconditionally to the making of an adoption order" (AA 1976, s.16(1)(b)). It is true that the court does have power to dispense with parental agreement, but the grounds upon which it may do so are restricted.

The result is that the court's decision on whether to make an adoption order involves a two stage process. First, the court must consider whether it would promote the child's welfare to make an adoption order; secondly if, but only if, the court decides that adoption would be in the child's interest, it will consider whether it should dispense with the parent's agreement. These are separate issues which (it has been held) should be dealt with in that order: *Re D (A Minor) (Adoption Order: Validity)* [1991] 1 FLR 48, C.A.:

In *Re B (Adoption: Child's Welfare)* [1995] 1 FLR 895, Wall J. the parents of a two-year-old Gambian girl brought her to stay with friends in England. There was a misunderstanding between the adults involved about the basis on which the child was left in the care of the applicants; and when the parents were made aware of the nature of an English adoption order they opposed it. Wall J. held that the enactment of the Children Act 1989 had made no difference to the principle that adoption was different, although he did point out that if the court refused to make an adoption order it would now go on to consider whether it should make a residence order. On the facts he held that (notwithstanding the harm which breaking the attachment the child had formed to the applicants would cause her) it would not be in the child's interests to be adopted; and accordingly the question of the parents' refusal to agree to the making of an adoption order did not arise.

(i) The first question: would the making of an adoption order safeguard and promote the child's welfare?

In determining the first question, it is clear that the welfare of the child is *not* the paramount consideration (*i.e.* outweighing *all* other considerations); but the fact that it is the *first* consideration means (so it has been held) that it outweighs *any* other consideration: *Re D (An Infant: Parent's Consent)* [1977] A.C. 602, 638, *per* Lord Simon of Glaisdale.

This is a difficult distinction to apply; and it has been said that the complexities of adoption law would test the ingenuity of an examiner and that a judge might not feel confident that he would pass the test: *Re V (A Minor) (Adoption: Consent)* [1987] Fam. 57, 80. Certainly it would seem that the courts' attitudes to the benefits conferred by adoption vary from time to time and from judge to judge. As Hoffmann and Steyn L.JJ. put it in *Re C (A Minor) (Adoption: Parental Agreement: Contact)* [1993] 2 FLR 260, 273:

> "Judges who are all conscientiously trying to make a decision which reflects generally accepted values may in fact be employing somewhat different scales. It is natural, for example, that one judge may give less weight than another to parental interests when they stand in the way of his firmly held views about what the interests of the child require".

But in many cases the advantages of adoption are readily apparent. For example:

> In *Re S (Adoption or Custodianship)* [1987] 2 FLR 331, C.A. the Court had (under statutory provisions subsequently repealed) to weigh up the advantages of adoption against some other form of order which would also give the child's grandparents long term care. The court considered that adoption would give greater legal security for the child's relationship with those caring for him and would minimise the risk of disruption.

Again:

> In *Re R (Adoption)* [1967] 1 W.L.R. 34, an adoption order was made in respect of a refugee from a totalitarian country. It would be for the adopted child's benefit to have the social and psychological benefits of truly belonging to a family as well as the benefit of acquiring British nationality.

And —

> In *Re D (A Minor) (Adoption Order: Validity)* [1991] 2 FLR 66, C.A. the court heard an application by foster-parents to adopt a severely handicapped child six days before he attained his majority. The court held that adoption would be beneficial in integrating him legally into the family of those who had cared for him in his infancy, and in minimising the risk that his birth parents would be able to continue to harass the applicants.

Racial and ethnic factors.   The question of what would be beneficial to a child may involve difficult considerations of racial or ethnic identity; and the courts have attached considerable weight to this factor:

> In *Re B (Adoption: Child's Welfare)* [1995] 1 FLR 895, Wall J. the child had two loving and competent parents who wished to care for her in their home in the Gambia. It would not be in the child's interests for the parents' parental responsibility for her to be extinguished; whilst there was a danger that she would lose the advantages of her cultural heritage and her sense of identity as the child of African parents.

Again,

> In *Re N (A Minor) (Adoption)* [1990] 1 FLR 58, Bush J., a black illegitimate child was placed with white foster parents under a private fostering agreement. The child remained in their care for more than three years, and they applied for an adoption order. The judge considered that adoption would not be in the child's interest because the child's father would have a useful and important part to play in her life when she wanted to seek out her cultural roots. The child should remain in the foster parent's care, but remain legally her birth parents' child.

Where adoption not in child's interests.   There are other cases which fall quite clearly on the wrong side of the line:

> In *Re K (A Minor) (Wardship: Adoption)* [1991] 1 FLR 57 the mother became unexpectedly pregnant at a time of particular difficulty and stress in a stormy and unstable marriage. She went to a Greek restaurant, where she met a middle-aged childless couple who wanted to care for a child on a long-term basis. The baby was handed over by the mother six weeks after the birth, but the mother soon decided that she wanted the child back. The Court of Appeal unanimously held that the adoption by the couple would not be in the child's best interest. In particular, their age counted against them: they would be 65 and 57 when the child was 10; and their background — in terms of origins, language and religion — was in every way different from the child's. A factor of crucial importance was that the mother genuinely wanted her child back and that she had cared properly for her other children; and accordingly it would not be in the child's interest to deprive her of any chance of her own family: *per* Butler-Sloss L.J., at 62.

Prospects of rehabilitation with birth family often crucial.   In many cases the crucial factor will be whether there is any realistic prospect of the child being re-integrated into its birth family; and this should be fully explored before a decision is taken to sever all legal links between the child and the birth family.

> In *Re C (A Minor) (Adoption: Parental Agreement: Contact)* [1993] 2 FLR 260, C.A., the question was (*per* Hoffmann and Steyn L.JJ. at 270) whether a couple in their late forties should be permanently deprived of all future contact with their 4-year-old daughter. Everyone agreed that they loved her and desperately wanted to keep her. They, for their part, could not understand what they had done to deserve having to lose their child. The judge found on the facts that there were no realistic prospects of such re-integration occurring; and that accordingly adoption would be in the child's interests.

Can judges be objective?   The question of whether the making of an adoption order would benefit the child is primarily one of evidence, but as pointed out above, different judges will have different predispositions. Indeed a circuit judge has expressed strong views against seeing adoption as a generally acceptable solution:

> In *Re L (A Minor) (Care Proceedings: Wardship) (No. 2)* [1991] 1 FLR 29 the local authority considered that a child should be adopted notwithstanding the fact that the child's grandparents wished to care for her. Judge Willis said that adoption was a trial and error situation about which too little was known. "Many adopted people start looking for their roots, particularly in adolescence . . . adoption should only be the last resort when no-one in the wider family is available and suitable to look after a child. Parentage is not always perfect, but parentage in the family is preferable to the unknown risks of adoption". The Judge stated that every child had a right, whenever possible, to be brought up by its own genetic family, and that there must be "strong, cogent and positive reasons" for denying that right.

It may be questioned whether the parental preference is in fact correctly to be given as much weight as Judge Willis suggested and the Court of Appeal has subsequently held that the question is simply what the evidence establishes would be best for the child; but that there is a strong supposition, other things being equal, that it is in the interests of the child to be brought up by his natural parents: see *Re W (A Minor) (Residence Order)* [1993] 2 FLR 625, 633, *per* Balcombe L.J.

Relevance of public policy and other factors.   The fact that the child's welfare is only the "first" consideration means that the court can properly consider other matters. In particular, the fact that adoption may be used to confer British nationality on a foreign child led the courts to stipulate that if the true motive for the adoption application was to obtain British nationality (rather than to serve the child's general welfare) the application should be dismissed:

> In *Re B (Adoption: Child's Welfare)* [1995] 2 FCR 749, 782, Wall J., the judge found that the motive for the adoption application was to secure the child's immigration status and the application should fail on that ground.

In contrast:

In *Re H (Adoption: Non-Patrial)* [1996] 2 FLR 187, C.A., a couple of Pakistani origin who were unable to conceive applied to adopt a relative who had come to this country initially on a short visit. The judge had found that the applicants' motive was not primarily to secure the child's immigration status and that the adoption would promote his welfare. This decision was upheld by the Court of Appeal (although doubts were expressed as to whether the traditional two stage approach set out above was consistent with the wording of Adoption Act 1976, s.6; and Peter Gibson L.J. in terms dissented from the view that a genuine adoption application could be rejected merely on the ground that it was not primarily motivated by the welfare consideration).

Child's wishes.   The Adoption Act 1976, s.6, requires the court "so far as practicable [to] ascertain the wishes and feelings of the child regarding the decision and give due consideration to them, having regard to his age and understanding." In practice, if the child's wishes are ascertained it will require clear evidence to justify the court in not giving effect to them:

In *Re D (Minors) (Adoption by Step-Parent)* (1981) FLR 102, C.A., the question was whether an adoption order should be made in favour of the stepfather of girls aged 10 and 12, both of whom were in favour of the adoption order being made. It was held that this was a weighty factor.

But there is, as the law now stands, no formal requirement that the agreement of the child to the making of an adoption order be obtained. To some this seems anomalous.

(ii) The second question: does each parent or guardian of the child agree to the making of the adoption order?

In principle, as already mentioned, the court may not make an adoption order, however beneficial such an order would be for the child, unless every parent (and guardian) has given a free and informed agreement to the making of the order: Adoption Act 1976, s.16(1). This second stage of the two stage process is intended to protect the rights of the parent: see *Re C (A Minor) (Adoption: Parental Agreement: Contact)* [1993] 2 FLR 260, 269, *per* Balcombe L.J.; and this fact evidences the distinction embodied in the law between adoption as a legal process transferring a child irrevocably from one family group to another on the one hand and the making of a residence of other order (where the decision is to be made in accordance with the principle that the child's welfare is the paramount consideration on the other hand).

The procedure for giving agreement.   An agreement given by the mother within six weeks of the child's birth is ineffective: AA 1976 ss.16(4), The policy underlying this provision is that the mother should have time to get over the physical and emotional effects of giving birth.

More generally, the agreement must be an informed one, and the court must appoint a reporting officer to ensure (amongst other things) that the parent understands fully what adoption involves and is willing to agree without condition. The reporting officer is to witness the parents' written agreement: Adoption Rules 1984, r.5. However, although forms are prescribed it appears that their use is not mandatory.

The agreement must be to a specific adoption with a particular adopter or adopters, but in practice the applicant can preserve anonymity and thus minimise the risk that the mother will seek to interfere with the child's upbringing by asking the court to allocate a serial number; and the proceedings must then be conducted with a view to ensuring that the applicant is neither seen by, nor made known, to the parents: Adoption Rules 1984, r.14, 23(3).

If it appears that a parent or guardian is unwilling to agree to the making of the adoption order, the court must appoint a guardian *ad litem* to safeguard the child's welfare, and carry out prescribed duties: Adoption Rules, r.18(1).

A parent may withdraw the agreement at any time before the making of the order. It seems that some parents are reluctant to "sign away" their children, even though in fact they realise that adoption is inevitable and in the child's interests. It also appears that in recent years there has been a greater readiness for agencies to pursue adoption applications notwithstanding the lack of parental agreement.

Who is the child's parent? The agreement required is that of "each parent or guardian of the child". The father of an illegitimate child is not for these purposes regarded as the child's "parent" unless the father has parental responsibility for the child: AA 1976, s.72(1) as amended; and see *Re C (A Minor) (Adoption: Parental Agreement: Contact)* [1993] 2 FLR 260, C.A. Such parental responsibility may flow from the fact that the parents have made a parental responsibility agreement, or that the court has made a parental responsibility order or a residence order in favour of the father. The fact that the making of a parental responsibility order will give the father standing as a party in any adoption application has been seen to be a factor influencing the court in favour of making such an order in the child's interests: *D v. Hereford and Worcester CC* [1991] 1 FLR 205; *Re H (Local Authority: Parental Rights) (No. 3)* [1991] Fam. 151, C.A.

Dispensing with parental agreement. The Act (s.16(2), (5)) provides six grounds on which the court may dispense with the parent's (or guardian's) agreement to adoption, *viz.* that the parent or guardian:

"(a) cannot be found or is incapable of giving agreement;
(b) is withholding his agreement unreasonably;
(c) has persistently failed without reasonable cause to discharge his parental responsibility for the child;
(d) has abandoned or neglected the child;
(e) has persistently ill-treated the child;
(f) has seriously ill-treated the child" and the circumstances are such that the rehabilitation of the child within the household of the parent or guardian is unlikely.

There is a considerable amount of case law on the subject of dispensing with parental agreement, but to some extent the lengthy analysis necessary in even an introductory text book may give a misleading impression of the practical significance of this issue. This is in part because (as we shall see) the grounds upon which a court will hold that a parent is unreasonably withholding agreement are now so heavily influenced by the decision that adoption would be for the child's benefit that (as the Inter-Departmental Working Group's *Report to Ministers*, paragraph 12.1 put it in

1992) "there is in practice very little room left for the court to give any weight to parental views"; and in part because of the — no doubt related — fact emerging from research studies that the great majority of adoption applications, whether opposed or not, eventually result in the order being granted: Lowe and Murch: *Pathways to Adoption* (1991) at 210 and note Table 2.13(a).

Nevertheless, the grounds must be examined in order to assess the extent to which the courts take a different approach to adoption cases than to procedures (*e.g.* applications for residence orders) in which the welfare of the child is avowedly the paramount consideration.

(a) Cannot be found or is incapable of giving agreement.   This provision will normally apply to cases in which the whereabouts of the person whose consent is required are unknown and cannot be discovered, or where he or she lacks the mental capacity to give consent. But it has been held that a person "cannot be found" for the purposes of this section if there are no practical means of communication, even if the physical whereabouts are in fact known:

> In *Re R (Adoption)* [1967] 1 W.L.R. 34 the parents lived in a totalitarian country and any attempt to communicate with them would involve embarrassment and danger. The court dispensed with their agreement.

(b) Is withholding his agreement unreasonably.   The leading case on the interpretation of this provision (which is much the most frequently invoked ground for dispensing with agreement) is *Re W (An Infant)* [1971] A.C. 682 in which the House of Lords laid down a number of principles:

(i) Child's welfare not only factor.

There is a clear distinction between adoption and cases merely concerned with the child's upbringing. The legal relationship of parent and child is not to be sundered lightly and without good reason; and the fact that the court is required by statute (AA 1976, s.6 to give "first consideration" to the child's welfare has not altered that principle: *Re P (An Infant) (Adoption: Parental Consent)* [1977] Fam. 25.

It follows that a parent may in deciding whether or not to agree to adoption, reasonably take into account not only the welfare of the child, but also the parent's own wishes and welfare and the welfare of other persons (such as siblings and grandparents) who would be affected. For example:

> In *Re V (A Minor) (Adoption: Dispensing with Agreement)* [1987] 2 FLR 89, the mother had left her 21-month-old daughter with foster-parents. At one time the mother agreed that the foster-parents should adopt the child, but she changed her mind; and by the time of the hearing (when the child had been with the foster-parents for nearly three years) she had decided that in the long term she wanted the child back to live with her and her two younger children. The Court of Appeal held that the court should not have dispensed with the mother's agreement. It was not unreasonable for the mother to hope to reunite her family. The foster-parents should continue to have the care of the child, but the mother should have contact with her.

(ii) *Child's welfare relevant to extent that reasonable parent would so regard it.*
In the words of Lord Hailsham in *Re W* (above):

> "... the fact that a reasonable parent does pay regard to the welfare of his child must enter into the question of reasonableness as a relevant factor. It is relevant in all cases if and to the extent that a reasonable parent would take it into account. It is decisive in those cases where a reasonable parent must so regard it."

(iii) *Test is reasonableness not culpability.*
Since the test to be applied is the reasonableness of the parent's decision, the court may dispense with agreement even though the parent has been wholly innocent of any breach of parental responsibility and is in no way responsible for the state of affairs which has led to the adoption application:

> In *Re El-G (Minors) (Wardship and Adoption)* (1982) 4 FLR 589, C.A., the mother had been struck down by what Slade L.J. aptly described as "a series of terrible blows which destroyed her health and prevented her from fulfilling her maternal role in spite of her desire to do so." Her inability to care for her children had been entirely the result of misfortune, but the court nonetheless dispensed with her agreement.

There was a similar outcome in *Re C (A Minor) (Adoption: Parental Agreement: Contact)* [1993] 2 FLR 260, C.A.:

> The two-year-old child was taken into care because of an erroneous diagnosis of sexual abuse. But the mother's limited intelligence, and the father's inability to comprehend its effect or to provide acceptable care in her place, meant that the child suffered emotional deprivation in their home. It was held that the parents' agreement was being unreasonably withheld.

(iv) *Court must not substitute its own view as to what is reasonable for that of parent.*
It has been stressed that the court should not substitute its own view for that of the parent. This is because (to quote Lord Hailsham, in *Re W* at p. 700, again):

> "Two reasonable parents can perfectly reasonably come to opposite conclusions on the same set of facts without forfeiting their title to be regarded as reasonable. The question in any given case is whether a parental veto comes within the band of possible reasonable decisions and not whether it is right or mistaken. Not every reasonable exercise of judgment is right, and not every mistaken exercise of judgment is unreasonable. There is a band of decisions within which no court should seek to replace the individual's judgment with its own."

In effect, therefore, a decision should only be held to be unreasonable if no reasonable parent could have taken it: a parent may be wrong or mistaken without being unreasonable (*per* Balcombe L.J., *Re E (A Minor) (Adoption)* [1989] 1 FLR 126).

Difficulties of applying the "unreasonableness" test. The principles laid down by the House of Lords provide an intellectually satisfying criterion for distinguishing between the test applicable in adoption (where it is not sufficient to show that adoption would promote the child's welfare) and in applications for residence and other private law Children Act orders (where the child's welfare is paramount). But the *application* of these principles demonstrates that it is not wholly satisfactory in striking a balance between the welfare of the child and the rights of parents to retain some link with their child. In particular, the concept of the reasonable parent is one of considerable difficulty. The court is to ask how a parent —

"in the circumstances of the actual [parent], but (hypothetically) endowed with a mind and temperament capable of making reasonable decisions, would approach a complex question involving a judgment as to the present and as to the future and the probable impact of these on a child" (*per* Lord Wilberforce, *Re D (An Infant) (Adoption: Parent's Consent)* [1977] A.C. 602, 625 H.L.).

The effect of this approach has been demonstrated by Steyn and Hoffmann L.JJ. in a subsequent decision of the Court of Appeal, *Re C (A Minor) (Adoption: Parental Agreement: Contact)* [1993] 2 FLR 260, 272, C.A. (the facts of which are summarised at p. 284 below):

The court is required "to assume that the mother was not, as she in fact was, a person of limited intelligence and inadequate grasp of the emotional and other needs of a lively little girl of four. Instead she had to be assumed to be a woman with a full perception of her own deficiencies and an ability to evaluate dispassionately the evidence and opinions of the experts. She was also to be endowed with the intelligence and altruism needed to appreciate, if such were the case, that her child's welfare would be so much better served by adoption and that her own maternal feelings should take second place.

Such a paragon does not of course exist: she shares with the 'reasonable man' the quality of being, as Lord Radcliffe once said, an 'anthropomorphic conception of justice'. The law conjures the imaginary parent into existence to give expression to what it considers that justice requires . . .

[F]or those who feel some embarrassment at having to consult the views of so improbable a legal fiction, we venture to observe that precisely the same question may be raised in a demythologised form by the judge asking himself whether, having regard to the evidence and applying the current values of our society, the advantages of adoption for the welfare of the child appear sufficiently strong to justify overriding the views and interests of the objecting parent or parents . . ."

Notwithstanding the clear injunction laid down against the court substituting its own judgment for that of the parent one judge's views may well differ from another's:

"It is natural . . . that one judge may give less weight than another to parental interests when they stand in the way of his firmly held view about what the interests of the child require. His 'reasonable mother' will be more altruistic, more impressed by expert opinion than her sister in the court of a different judge" (*Re C (A Minor) (Adoption: Parental Agreement: Contact)* [1993] 2 FLR 260, 273, C.A., *per* Steyn and Hoffmann L.JJ.).

Reported cases indicate how far the courts are able to regard the matter as determined by their own assessment of the child's welfare; and in particular the extent to which it has now become accepted that a reasonable parent who cannot bring up the child should accept adoption notwithstanding the fact that an adoption order severs the family link for all time:

> In *Re F (Adoption: Parental Agreement)* [1982] 3 FLR 101, C.A., a two-year-old child who had been ill-treated and neglected by his mother was placed with foster-parents in whose care he remained at the hearing of their adoption application three years later. The mother accepted that the child should remain in the care of the foster parents, but nevertheless genuinely thought that it would be beneficial to the child that she should continue to have some contact with him in the future. On this basis the President of the Family Division held that a reasonable mother could reasonably conclude that she should withhold her agreement to adoption, and refused to dispense with the mother's agreement. On appeal, however, it was held that there were in fact no reasonable prospects of the mother re-establishing contact with the child, and that a reasonable parent would have accepted that it was wrong to deny the child the advantage of eliminating the uncertainty implicit in fostering arrangements.

Again:

> In *Re B (A Minor) (Adoption: Parental Agreement)* [1990] 2 FLR 383, C.A., foster-parents applied to adopt an 11-year-old boy who had been in their care for seven years. It was not in dispute that his future lay with the applicants; and the boy himself strongly favoured adoption. However, the mother refused to agree to the making of an adoption order because she wanted to preserve her legal right to a degree of contact with the child. The Court of Appeal held that a reasonable parent would regard the advantages to the child of the legal security conferred by adoption (coupled with the fact that the child would be "devastated by the result if the adoption did not take place" and that adoption would in all probability not have any impact on continuing contact) as outweighing any disadvantages. Accordingly, a reasonable parent would have come to the conclusion that adoption was in the best long-term interests of the child, and an order should be made.

Adoption favoured if no realistic prospect of re-establishing family link.   The view that the lack of any reasonable likelihood of re-establishing a functioning familial link has come to be seen as the crucial step in determining that a parental refusal to agree to adoption is unreasonable was carried to a logical conclusion in *Re C (A Minor) (Adoption: Parental Agreement: Contact)* [1993] 2 FLR 260, C.A.:

> The mother of a two-year-old girl was of limited intellectual ability and she experienced difficulty in caring for the child. The father worked long hours and was not able to give very much time to the child. The local authority were concerned about the child's emotional and social development, but they did not take compulsory measures until a consultant made a diagnosis (eventually found to be wrong) that she had been sexually abused. There was a dramatic change in the girl's development whilst she was in the care of foster-parents; and eventually the local authority, accepting the view that the parents would not be able to cope,

abandoned their plan to rehabilitate the child with the parents. The parents were shocked, sought to discharge the care order, and applied for residence and contact. The judge held that it would not be in the child's interests to return her to the parents, and, on that basis, he held that adoption would promote her welfare. He then held that the parents' inability to accept that the child would not return to them would be likely to upset the stability of any fostering. In the circumstances, any reasonable parent would regard the case for adoption as so overwhelming that he or she would agree to adoption. Accordingly, the court would dispense with parental agreement.

The Court of Appeal unanimously dismissed the parents' appeal; but there was some difference of emphasis. Hoffmann and Steyn L.JJ. considered that the question was essentially whether the advantages of adoption for the welfare of the child appeared sufficiently strong to justify overriding the views and interests of the objecting parent or parents. Balcombe L.J. on the other hand expressed concern that parents who were wholly blameless were to be deprived of all links with their child, and that in effect once it had been decided that adoption would be in the child's interests there was in practice little room left for the court to give any weight to parental views. This would be to make the child's welfare paramount; and he doubted whether the balance between the welfare of the child and the rights of the parent had been correctly struck in such cases.

Notwithstanding the emphasis placed in earlier judgments on the need to distinguish clearly between adoption and other forms of long term child care, it is difficult to avoid the conclusion that this approach erodes (or perhaps demonstrates the artificiality) of the "unreasonable" withholding criterion. As Balcombe L.J. put it (at 269):

"the only failure on the part of the parents was their inability to give [the child] the standard of parental care necessary for her social and emotional development, which was primarily attributable to the mother's limited intellectual capacity and the father's inability to comprehend the effect of this or himself to provide an acceptable alternative. If normal social work intervention should prove ineffective, this could well justify [the child] being taken into care and placed during the remainder of her childhood with long-term foster-parents, but I doubt whether Parliament intended that it should be a ground for irrevocably terminating the parents' . . . legal relationship with the child. It has the flavour of social engineering . . ."

The rather different approach favoured by Steyn and Hoffmann L.JJ. may best promote the interests of the children concerned; but as Slade L.J. put it, a parent who loves her children and is not a lawyer may well find it difficult to understand how she can ever be said to be acting unreasonably if she refuses to consent to an adoption which would deprive her of any right to maintain contact with them: *Re El-G (Minors) (Wardship and Adoption)* (1982) 4 FLR 589, 601. It may also be thought paradoxical to deny any value to preserving the *legal* bond between parent and child in the context of adoption applications whilst at the same time asserting the value of such recognition in applications for parental responsibility orders.[2] Does it make sense to tell the

---

[2] See at p. 177, above.

uncomprehending mother in *Re C (A Minor) (Adoption: Parental Agreement: Contact)* (above) that she is not only to lose any contact with the child she had born, loved, and cared for to the best of her ability but also to have the formal legal link deliberately destroyed so that legally it is to be as if she had never borne the child, whilst being prepared to accept that a father who has displayed some kind of commitment to a child born outside marriage is to have his legal parentage recognised even though he cannot have any contact or other involvement with the child?

It is necessary to keep a sense of proportion in these matters. There are few cases in which a parent's refusal to agree to an adoption demonstrably for the child's benefit is vigorously maintained; and it seems that parental withholding of agreement is sometimes only a token resistance to "signing away" their own child: Lowe and Murch: *Pathways to Adoption* (1991) 135. On the other hand, the decision is almost always an extremely painful one for the birth parent: *op. cit.* paragraph 8.5.2.

(c) Has persistently failed without reasonable cause to discharge his parental responsibility for the child.   In order to satisfy this ground two conditions must be fulfilled.

First, there must have been a persistent failure. This apparently connotes a permanent abrogation of responsibility: has the parent "washed his hands" of the child? (see *M v. Wigan MBC* [1980] Fam. 36).

Secondly, the failure must be "without reasonable cause". Two cases may be contrasted. On the one hand:

> In *Re M (An Infant)* (1965) 109 S.J. 574 it was held that an unmarried mother's wish to conceal the birth from her parents was a sufficiently reasonable cause.

But in contrast —

> In *Re P (Infants)* [1962] 1 W.L.R. 1296 the mother had simply given up the children soon after birth and had no excuse for not having them with her or at least visiting them in their foster home. She had also continued to collect welfare benefits in respect of the children but had not supported them to any significant extent. It was held that parental responsibility includes both the natural and moral duty of a parent to show affection, care and interest towards the child and the parent's legal duty of maintenance; and the court dispensed with the mother's agreement.

(d) Has abandoned or neglected the child.   The word "abandoned" has been held to mean such conduct as would expose a parent to the sanctions of the criminal law. It seems that there are few acts which will satisfy the restrictively interpreted ground:

> In *Watson v. Nikolaisen* [1955] 2 Q.B. 286 a mother had given her illegitimate daughter over to foster-parents who wanted to adopt her, and in whom she had confidence. The child was in the foster-parents' care for some two years, and during that time the mother made no contribution to her support — she kept the welfare benefit paid for the child — and saw her only once. The court held that she had not abandoned the child since she genuinely wanted the child to remain hers and not be adopted.

A similarly restricted interpretation has been given to the word "neglected."

(e) Has persistently ill-treated the child.   The requirement that the ill-treatment be persistent means that a single incident (however grave) cannot suffice. There must be a continuous state of affairs; but the period need not be lengthy:

> For example, in *Re A (A Minor) (Adoption: Dispensing with Consent)* (1979) 2 FLR 173 there had been severe and repeated assaults on an 11-month-old child over a period of three weeks. The court dispensed with parental agreement.

Moreover, it is the child in question who must have been ill-treated:

> This requirement was not satisfied in *Re F(T) (An Infant)* [1970] 1 W.L.R. 192 where the father had killed the child's mother and been convicted of manslaughter.

It would seem to follow that the court could not dispense with the parents' agreement to the adoption of one child on this ground merely because the parent had ill-treated another child in the same family.

(f) Has seriously ill-treated the child, and (whether because of the ill-treatment or for other reasons) the rehabilitation of the child in the parent's household is unlikely.   In contrast to the ground of persistent ill-treatment discussed above, there is no need to show a course of conduct: a single act of ill-treatment could suffice provided that it was sufficiently serious. However, the proviso (that agreement cannot be dispensed with on this ground unless, whether because of the ill-treatment or for other reasons, the rehabilitation of the child within the household of the parent or guardian is unlikely) is important, not least because it is independent of the first condition. Hence, it would apparently suffice if the parents' deteriorating mental or physical condition (or even the lack of proper housing) was the factor making rehabilitation unlikely.

CONTACT AFTER ADOPTION: "OPEN ADOPTION"

We have seen that the traditional pattern for adoption in this country is to create a complete severance between the birth parent and the adopted child. Adoptions were surrounded by secrecy, and it was thought to be generally undesirable to make an order which was in any way inconsistent with the adopters' full legal parenthood:

> In *Re S (A Minor) (Blood Transfusion: Adoption Order Condition)* [1994] 2 FLR 416, C.A., the adopters were committed Jehovah's Witnesses. The judge was concerned by the possibility that the child would need a blood transfusion to which the adopters would refuse consent, and a term was included in the order that the adopters would not withhold the necessary consent. The Court of Appeal held this was wrong. In the words of Waite L.J. (at 421) the "imposition of a condition resented or objected to by the adopters may threaten the very peace and security for the child which it is the aim of adoption to achieve. It is liable, moreover, to be difficult not only to supervise such a condition, because of the confidentiality which the adoption process requires, but also to enforce it, because it can seldom be desirable to place adopters at risk of punishment for contempt of court".

The question of how far the parental responsibility of adoptive parents should be controlled by terms imposed in the adoption order has usually arisen in the context of an application that the order include a provision giving birth relatives some right to continued contact. But the courts have consistently taken the view that, even if the adoption had been arranged on the basis that some degree of contact would be preserved, in the ultimate analysis the decision on whether to permit it was a matter for the adopters to decide in the exercise of their parental responsibility: *Re V (A Minor) (Adoption: Consent)* [1987] Fam. 57, *per* Oliver L.J. at 78.

It is not surprising, therefore, to find the courts declining to impose conditions about continued contact with which the adopters did not agree. This (it could be said) would:

> "be to create a potentially frictional situation which would be hardly likely to safeguard or promote the welfare of the child": *per* Lord Ackner, *Re C (A Minor) (Adoption Order: Conditions)* [1989] A.C. 1, 17.

The Children Act 1989, as we have already seen, created a machinery whereby the court may in adoption and freeing for adoption applications make orders for contact, whether direct or indirect (for example, by an annual progress report with photographs: see *Re T (Adopted Children: Contact)* [1995] 2 FLR 792); but the policy set out above seems still to survive:

> In *Re T (Adoption: Contact)* [1995] 2 FLR 251, C.A., the adopters had agreed that the mother should continue to see the child once a year, and the judge attached an order to that effect to the adoption order. The Court of Appeal held he had been wrong to do so, since the finality of adoption and the importance of letting the adoptive family find its feet ought not to be threatened by an order (all the more so since if they wished to stop the birth mother's visits they would have to incur the expense of an application to the court). The principle (see Children Act 1989, s.1(5)) that the court should not make orders unless the welfare of the child will be better served by doing so than by making no order was to be applied, and the onus should be on the birth mother to seek leave to apply for a contact order if she considered the adopters were behaving unreasonably in denying her contact.

This is not to say that an adoption order containing a provision for contact will never be made:

> In *Re O (Transracial Adoption: Contact)* [1995] 2 FLR 597, Thorpe J. held that the security of a 10-year-old Nigerian girl could only be obtained by an adoption order; and that a reasonable Nigerian parent would see that this was the case. Accordingly he dispensed with the mother's agreement, and made an adoption order; but he considered that the order should require contact with the mother, in part because the child was being brought up in a family and in a locality where it was very difficult to buttress her Nigerian heritage. (The cases cited above are not referred to in the judgment).

In some parts of the world a much more "open" approach to adoption has evolved and in New Zealand (for example) some form of on-going contact between birth and adoptive families is the norm. In this country it is increasingly being said (consistently with the approach taken by Thorpe J. in *Re O*, above) that there is a conflict between the legal concept of adoption and a reality in which adopted persons are often older children with a knowledge of their own families and background. The Conservative Government's White Paper noted "an increasing tendency in recent years to favour maintaining some contact between an adopted child and his birth family" (*Adoption: The Future* (1993) Cm. 228, paragraph 4.14). Yet there are very few reported cases in which contact has been ordered, and it seems that there is some considerable resistance on the part of prospective adopters to any requirement of continued contact. As Butler-Sloss L.J. said in *Re A (A Minor) (Adoption: Contact Order)* [1993] 2 FLR 645, 649–650:

> "We are moving perceptibly into a new and broader perception of adoption . . . The view, however, of open adoption embraced by the experts does not seem to be shared by many prospective adopters . . ."

Finally, it should be noted that although the Children Act provides a structure within which a contact order to an adopted child can be made, the birth parent is no longer a "parent" within the definition in the Children Act; and the birth parent thus loses the entitlement to bring an application for contact (or other section 8 order). The birth parent may, however, seek leave to make such an application. Various procedural measures have been devised in an attempt to minimise the risk of the adopters being unnecessarily disturbed by applications for leave which have little chance of success: *Re T (Adopted Children: Contact)* [1995] 2 FLR 792.

FREEING FOR ADOPTION: THE REFORM THAT FAILED

Until 1984 a parent could only consent to a specific adoption and that consent could be withdrawn after the child had been placed with the prospective adopters and at any time up to the making of the final order. As a result, local authorities who feared that there would have to be a traumatic contest about dispensing with the birth parent's agreement may have been reluctant to place children for adoption. Moreover, the fact that an agreement once given could nevertheless be withdrawn may have encouraged indecisiveness on the part of the birth parents; and it certainly seems likely to have made the waiting period very tense for almost all prospective adopters. The procedure for "freeing" a child for adoption was introduced in the Children Act 1975, following the recommendations of the Houghton Report. The intention was to provide a means whereby any doubts about parental agreement could be resolved at an early stage, and usually before the child had been placed for adoption.

The legislation (now contained in Adoption Act 1976, s.18) provides that the court may, on the application of an adoption agency, make an order declaring a child "free for adoption" and thereafter an adoption order may be made without further evidence of parental consent. The court will of course only make a freeing order if it considers it to be in the interests of the child (AA 1976, s.6; paragraph 12–13 above); and the Act requires that the court must be satisfied in the case of each parent or guardian of the child *either* that "he freely and with full understanding of what is involved, agrees generally and unconditionally to the making of an adoption order," *or* alternatively that agreement should be dispensed with on one of the grounds considered at pp. 280–287, above.

The expectation was that the "freeing procedure" would facilitate adoptions, particularly in cases where there was doubt about the birth parents' attitude and in cases in which it was known that the parent would oppose the making of an adoption order considered by the local authority or other agency to be the best way of promoting the child's welfare.

However, in practice there have been serious difficulties with the "freeing" procedure. In part, this is because of the grounds upon which the court may dispense with agreement. Where a child has actually been placed for adoption, it is not too difficult for the parents to weigh up the advantages and disadvantages of adoption by the particular prospective adopters concerned; and it follows that it will not be difficult for the court to decide whether a withholding of agreement to that particular adoption is or is not unreasonable. However, where there has been no placement, the question whether a parent is unreasonable in withholding agreement is much more difficult:

> In *Re E (Minors) (Adoption: Parental Agreement)* [1990] 2 FLR 397, C.A.,[3] a local authority started freeing procedures at a time when the children had been with prospective adopters for only one month. There was no evidence as to how the placement had worked during that month, nor was there any evidence that the mother knew then how the placement had worked. At the time of the hearing, the court considered that the evidence did point to the conclusion that the children's welfare required their long-term future to be with the prospective adopters, and preferably without any access by the natural mother. But the Court of Appeal held that the mother was not unreasonable in withholding her agreement: she was entitled to say that she should have a proper opportunity to demonstrate that continued contact by her with the children would be of benefit. Her action in refusing consent came within the broad band of decisions which could be regarded as reasonable, notwithstanding the fact that its effect might be to prevent the adoption of her children. It was relevant also to note that the prospective adopters were apparently prepared to continue to care for the children even if they were not able to adopt them.

There are also problems about the effect of a freeing order. The Act provides that the making of an order extinguishes the parental responsibility of the parents and others and vests parental responsibility in the adoption agency: AA 1976, s.18(5); and these provisions work satisfactorily if an adoption order is ultimately made. But difficulties can arise if it proves impossible to arrange an adoption. The Act provides that, unless the birth parent makes a declaration that he or she does not want to be further involved with the adoption, the parent must be informed after 12 months whether the child has been adopted or is placed for adoption. If the child has not been adopted or "placed" the parent may apply for revocation of the freeing order; but if the court simply grants that application the parents will immediately resume their parental responsibility, unfettered by any care order which may have been in force before the freeing order:

---

[3] Under the provisions of the Children Act 1989, the court can make a contact order in "freeing" proceedings; and the decision in this case that it had been premature to start freeing proceedings at a time when contact was still taking place would not now be followed: see *Re A (A Minor) (Adoption: Contact Order)* [1993] 2 FLR 645, C.A. But the statement in the text remains true.

In *Re G (a minor) (Adoption: Freeing Order)* [1997] 2 All E.R. 534, H.L., a young and immature mother had been unable to care for her son. A freeing order was made, and the child was placed for adoption. However, the adoption placement broke down, the mother was notified of the fact that the child remained unadopted and not placed for adoption; and she applied to revoke the freeing order. The Court of Appeal said there was a stark choice between granting that application (which would have the effect of reviving the mother's parental responsibility) and refusing (which would mean the child remaining in a legal limbo, a "statutory orphan" "freed for adoption" but without prospects of a successful placement.) The House of Lords disagreed with the Court of Appeal's decision that the mother's application should have been rejected. Making a freeing order was a draconian step, justifiable only because it would enable an adoption to take place. The child's welfare could be adequately protected by making the revocation of the freeing order conditional on the making of a care order or other appropriate action under the Children Act 1989.

But there remain difficulties. What, for example, is the position if a child "freed for adoption" reaches the age of 18 without an adoption order having been made, while the legislation contains no provision removing the child from his birth family for such purposes as succession rights or the prohibited degrees of marriage.

In the circumstances, it is not surprising that research has confirmed that local authority policies in relation to freeing differ, and the procedure has not been used as extensively as was envisaged: see generally [1990] JSWL 220 (N.V. Lowe). It seems likely that the procedure of freeing for adoption will be abolished in any future reform of adoption law, and replaced by an alternative procedure.

REFORM OF ADOPTION LAW

The quarter of a century since the 1972 Houghton Report's adoption reform recommendations (now the basis of the Adoption Act 1976) have seen many social and demographic changes. The Children Act 1989 did make a number of minor changes to adapt the technicalities of adoption law to the major restructuring of child law but it did not deal with the many issues of policy — whether a degree of openness should be introduced into the adoption procedure, whether the "total transplant" concept of adoption was still appropriate, whether the secrecy which "engulfs the adoption process" is still necessary — about which anxiety had been voiced. At the same time, the practices of local authorities and other adoption agencies began to be the focus of comment in some parts of the media: it was claimed that political correctness had come to dominate the assessment process, and in particular that the concern shown by adoption agencies for placing ethnic minority children in homes where their cultural heritage would be safeguarded led to suitable prospective adopters being rejected.

As part of the Conservative Government's programme of Family Law reform, the Department of Health carried out an impressively thorough Review of Adoption Law and practice, and in 1993 the Government issued a White Paper (*Adoption: The Future*) which set out decisions on a number of matters. Further consultation on some particularly difficult areas followed, and in 1996 the Conservative Government circulated a 104 clause draft Adoption Bill to a wide range of interested parties. Although Ministers stated that the Bill would be introduced into Parliament "at the earliest opportunity" it soon became clear that the proposals were not uncontroversial. It appears that reservations were voiced by bodies such as The Law Society's Family Law Committee and the Solicitors' Family Law Association; but it may be that ministerial fears of the Bill becoming a "battleground for MPs with strong views on morality and the family" (and the potential for excited debate on such matters as adoption by homosexuals) weighed all the more heavily with a Government which had recent experience of the embarrassment which family law legislation can cause. The Bill did not appear in the Conservative Government's legislative programme for 1996/1997 and there was no mention of adoption law reform in the Queen's Speech on the Opening of Parliament in May 1997.

The Conservative Government did introduce some modest reforms in adoption practice which were introduced by delegated legislation (the Adoption Agencies and Children (Arrangements for Placement and Reviews) (Miscellaneous Amendments) Regulations, S.I. 1997 No. 649) but the future prospects for reform remain uncertain. In the circumstances, it seems appropriate to give only a brief account of the more important proposals in the 1996 draft legislation:

(i) *Child's welfare to be paramount consideration.*

The Conservative Government's Bill provided that the paramount consideration in any adoption agency or court decision relating to the adoption of a child was to be "the child's welfare, in childhood and later. Consistently with the pattern established by the Children Act 1989 a checklist of matters to be considered was provided.

(ii) *Parental consent.*

The Bill proposed that a child should not be *placed* for adoption unless the parents consented, or the court made a placement order. The court would only be able to make such an order against the opposition of a parent if the parent could not be found or was incapable of giving a consent, or if the "court is satisfied that the welfare of the child requires the consent to be dispensed with": clause 46. This may be a less demanding test than the present "unreasonable withholding" ground; and it is not surprising that some apparently believed the change "would make the courts more likely to force a child to be adopted, against the wishes of its natural parents, if social workers convinced a judge that it was best for the child" (*The Times*, August 26, 1996). On the other hand, the Bill would also require a placement order to be obtained in respect of children in local authority care; and, arguably, that would provide greater protection than is available under the present law.

(iii) *Consent of the child.*

The Bill would require courts and agencies to have regard to the child's "ascertainable wishes and feelings regarding any decision about adoption (considered in the light of the child's age and understanding)"; but it would go further than the present law in debarring the court from making an adoption order in respect of a child aged 12 or more unless the child "freely, and with full understanding of what is involved, consents unconditionally to the making of the adoption order": clause 41(7). Rather curiously, there seems to be no such requirement in relation to a placement order.

(iv) *No joint adoptions by unmarried couples.*

The Conservative Government believed that there should be a strong presumption in favour of adoption by married couples; although it is accepted that there may be a "small number of exceptional circumstances where adoption by a single person may be sensible". It appears that the Government had in mind adoption by unmarried women, women no longer married or women widowed early, or widowed stepfathers: *Adoption: The Future* (Cm. 2288, 1993, paragraphs 4.35–4.40). The draft Bill would accordingly not allow adoption by an unmarried couple. Whether this decision is in line with court decisions making an adoption order in favour of one party to a cohabiting partnership and a joint residence order or with the court's decision that there is no objection of principle to child adoption order in favour of a homosexual intending to bring up the child jointly with his partner is a matter on which opinions may differ.

(v) *Step-parents.*

As the law now stands, a "step-parent adoption" is effected by a joint order in favour of the child's birth parent and his or her spouse, thus perhaps suggesting that the parent ceases to be the birth parent. In order to remedy this, the Bill proposed that a married step-parent shall be able to adopt his or her spouse's child (clause 45(1)(a)); and in such a case the adopted child would be treated as a child of the step-parents' marriage: clause 51(2)(a).

In a further attempt to provide a less unsatisfactory legal regime for the large number of step-families the Bill proposed that a step-parent be able to obtain parental responsibility by parental responsibility agreement or parental responsibility order made under the Children Act 1989, s.4: clause 85. The Conservative Government considered this an alternative to adoption which many parents would be likely to see as meeting their objectives more simply: *Adoption: The Future* (Cm. 2288, 1993, paragraph 5.21).

The draft Bill did not contain provision for the so-called guardianship order at one time favoured to allow relatives or others caring for a child (including long-term foster-parents) to obtain legal recognition of their role: *Adoption: The Future* (Cm. 2288, 1993, paragraph 5.24). However, it was proposed to amend the Children Act 1989 so that residence orders could be made to cover the child up to the age of 18; and to impose a special requirement that leave be obtained for any application for variation.

(vi) *Children in care and adoption.*

A local authority would be obliged by statute (as distinct from mere judicial statements of good practice) to provide a care plan in respect of every application for a care or supervision order. If the care plan included a proposal for adoption, notice would have to be given to relatives and others specified by delegated legislation, and the Authority would have to combine the application with an application for a placement order: clause 87.

(vii) *Common sense to replace ideology.*

A constant theme of the Conservative Government's White Paper, *Adoption: The Future* (Cm. 2288, 1993) was the need for decisions to "avoid reliance on ideology" and rather be based on "common sense and objective professional assessment" paragraph 4.28 and in particular the Conservative Government (responding in this respect to criticism voiced in the media) considered that questions of "ethnicity and culture" may have been given an "unjustifiably decisive influence" in some cases (paragraph 4.32). It appears that these "common sense human judgments" were to reflect "the value placed on traditional parenting and the need for stable and secure relationships between parents and between them and their children" (paragraph 2.6);

and it was apparently intended that these approaches be reinforced by official "guidance" (which could, of course, be changed without parliamentary scrutiny). Some may feel that the Conservative Government failed to appreciate that to deny ideology in favour of an undefined "common sense" is itself an ideology.

INDEX